AT THE CROSSROADS

OF EMPIRES

At the Crossroads of Empires

Middlemen, Social Networks, and State-Building in Republican Shanghai

Edited by NARA DILLON *and* JEAN C. OI

STANFORD UNIVERSITY PRESS
STANFORD, CALIFORNIA
2008

Stanford University Press
Stanford, California
www.sup.org

Printed in the United States of America on acid-free, archival-quality paper

Library of Congress Cataloging-in-Publication Data

At the crossroads of empires : middlemen, social networks, and state-building in republican Shanghai / edited by Nara Dillon and Jean C. Oi.
p. cm.
Includes bibliographical references and index.
ISBN 978-0-8047-5619-8 (cloth : alk. paper)
1. Social networks—China—Shanghai—History—20th century. 2. Pluralism (Social sciences)—China—Shanghai—History—20th century. 3. Shanghai (China)—History—20th century. 4. Shanghai (China)—Politics and government—20th century. I. Dillon, Nara. II. Oi, Jean Chun.

HN740.S484A8 2008
302.40951'13209041—dc22

2007008887

Typeset by Newgen in 10/12.5 Palatino

To the memory of Frederic Wakeman, Jr., 1937–2006

Contents

Acknowledgments

This volume was made possible by the generous support of Stanford's Center for Chinese Studies (CEAS). Nara Dillon and Kuiyi Shen were CEAS's first recipients of its newly established Chinese Studies Postdoctoral Fellowships in 2001. The idea for the conference and the volume that followed were conceived in conversations between Nara, Kuiyi, and Jean Oi, who was CEAS director at the time. The idea was to have Shanghai scholars revisit their previous research with our questions about Shanghai's changing social networks in mind. We thank Kuiyi for his invaluable help in organizing the conference.

Stanford's Asian Pacific Research Center in the Freeman Spogli Institute for International Studies provided staff support and excellent conference facilities. In addition to our volume contributors, we also want to thank Julia Andrews, who was among our original conference paper writers. We want to give special thanks to our invited discussants—Mark Granovetter, Richard Vinograd, and Andrew Walder—for their comparative and China-specific insights and questions that kept our discussion in perspective and sharpened our thinking. We feel especially fortunate also to have had Frederic Wakeman as an invited discussant. We are greatly saddened to learn of his passing as this volume goes to press. It is with respect and admiration that we dedicate this volume to him.

Contributors

Sei Jeong Chin is a Ph.D. candidate in History and East Asian Languages at Harvard University. She is currently writing a dissertation entitled "Negotiating Public Opinion: Law, Politics, and the News Media, 1931–1957." Her research interests concern political history, legal history, and the history of political communication and the news media in Nationalist China and the early PRC. Beginning fall 2007, she will be teaching at the University of Wisconsin, Madison.

Parks M. Coble is Professor of East Asian History at the University of Nebraska. His most recent book is *Chinese Capitalists in Japan's New Order: The Occupied Lower Yangzi, 1937–1945* (University of California Press, 2003). He is currently working on a research project, "China at War, 1937–1945: Remembering and Re-remembering China's War of Resistance."

Nara Dillon is Assistant Professor of Political Studies and Asian Studies at Bard College. She received her Ph.D. from the University of California, Berkeley, and is now completing a book manuscript entitled, "The Paradox of the Welfare State: The Politics of Privilege in Revolutionary Shanghai."

Bryna Goodman is Professor of History, University of Oregon. She is author of *Native Place, City, and Nation: Regional Networks and Identities in Shanghai, 1853–1937* (University of California Press, 1995); editor of *Transnationalism and the Chinese Press* (special issue, *China Review, 2004)*;

and coeditor of *Gender in Motion: Divisions of Labor and Cultural Change in Late Imperial and Modern China* (Rowman and Littlefield, 2005).

Brian G. Martin is Visiting Fellow of the Research School of Pacific and Asian Studies, Australian National University. He is the author of *The Shanghai Green Gang: Politics and Organized Crime, 1919–1937* (University of California Press, 1996). He is currently working on a research project on Zhou Fohai and the politics of collaboration in the Wang Jingwei regime (1940–1945).

Jean C. Oi is William Haas Professor of Chinese Politics, Professor of Political Science, and Director of the China Program at Stanford University. Her most recent books are *Rural China Takes Off: Institutional Foundations of Economic Reform* (University of California Press, 1999) and, as coeditor with Andrew Walder, *Property Rights and Economic Reform in China* (Stanford University Press, 1999). She is currently working on corporate restructuring in China's state-owned firms.

Elizabeth J. Perry is Henry Rosovsky Professor of Government at Harvard University. Her most recent books are *Patrolling the Revolution: Worker Militias, Citizenship and the Modern Chinese State* (Rowman and Littlefield, 2006) and, as coeditor with Merle Goldman, *Grassroots Political Reform in Contemporary China* (Harvard University Press, 2007). She is currently working on a study of the labor movement at the Anyuan coal mine.

Kuiyi Shen is Associate Professor of Art History at University of California, San Diego. Among previous publications he has authored or coauthored are *A Century in Crisis: Tradition and Modernity in the Art of Twentieth Century China* (Guggenheim Museum/Abrams, 1998); *Between the Thunder and the Rain: Chinese Paintings from the Opium War to the Cultural Revolution* (Asian Art Museum of San Francisco, 2000); *Word and Meaning* (University at Buffalo Art Gallery, 2000); *Zhou Brothers* (Hatje Cantz, 2004); *Shanghai Modern* (Hatje Cantz, 2005); and *Elegant Gathering* (Asian Art Museum of San Francisco, 2006).

Jeffrey N. Wasserstrom is Professor of History at the University of California, Irvine. His books include *Student Protests in Twentieth-Century China: The View from Shanghai* (Stanford University Press, 1991) and *China's Brave New World—And Other Tales for Global Times* (Indiana University Press, 2007). He is currently completing work on *Global Shanghai, 1850–2010*, a study of the city's past and present encounters with international forces to be published by Routledge.

Wen-hsin Yeh is Richard H. and Laurie C. Morrison Professor in History and Director, Institute of East Asian Studies, at the University of California, Berkeley. She is the author, most recently, of *Shanghai Splendor: Economic Sentiments and the Making of Modern China, 1843–1945* (University of California Press, 2007) and the editor of several volumes, including *Becoming Chinese: Passages to Modernity and Beyond, 1900–1950* (University of California Press, 2000).

PART ONE

Introduction

CHAPTER 1

Middlemen, Social Networks, and State-Building in Republican Shanghai

NARA DILLON AND JEAN C. OI

SHANGHAI IS ARGUABLY CHINA'S most famous city and certainly its most infamous. It was the Shanghai of the Republican period (1911–1949) that gained this notoriety. As the financial and trading entrepôt of East Asia, industrial and commercial center of China, publishing and artistic mecca for China's new intelligentsia, and hiding ground for radicals and revolutionaries from all over the world, Shanghai quickly earned its reputation as a city of extremes. Obscene wealth could be found next to degrading poverty. Radical anarchists vied with conservative Confucians for public attention, while both bible-thumping missionaries and criminal bosses recruited followers among the newcomers flocking to the city. Shanghai attracted these extremes because of its position at the juncture of several empires. Indeed, for almost a century, the boundaries of the Chinese, British, American, and French empires came together physically in the three cities that comprised Shanghai: the Chinese City, the International Settlement, and the French Concession. As a crossroads, Shanghai attracted great wealth and inherited an even greater struggle for a share of it.

What held Shanghai together during this volatile period? In particular, how did Shanghai function as a city without a unified state to bind it together and establish common ground? To a degree uncommon in other Chinese cities, indeed uncommon in most cities in the world, Republican Shanghai had no center. Shanghai's territory was divided among three (sometimes more) municipal governments integrated into just as many separate national states and empires. Furthermore, no government building, no religious institution, not even a public plaza gave Shanghai a "center" where its residents could gather. In addition to this political and physical fragmentation, Shanghai's people were divided among dozens of languages, races, classes, religions, and political loyalties.

Yet in the midst of these deep cleavages, the city managed to function as a coherent whole. In everyday terms, businessmen traded goods and services, creating markets and entire industries, without a state to define and enforce the "rules of the game." Artists and intellectuals created a vibrant new culture without political stability to provide them with the freedom and leisure to pursue their calling. Teachers educated children, doctors treated patients, and chefs fed diners without a common set of government regulations to guide them. Even more surprising than these everyday acts of cooperation was the fact that in moments of crisis, the city did not descend into anarchy. The Republican period was replete with crises: stock markets crashed; typhoons destroyed lives and property; foreign invasions leveled entire districts of the city. Still Shanghai functioned and managed to recover time and time again.

While Republican Shanghai is in some ways unique in the degree of its divisions and statelessness, it nevertheless provides a kind of natural experiment for conditions that are more common than anyone would wish. With the spread of urbanization to every continent around the globe in the twentieth century, enormous cities have developed in countries with extremely weak states, and even failed states. Contemporary São Paulo or Lagos may not harbor colonial enclaves, but state authority fails to penetrate all the neighborhoods in their vast urban landscapes. Rebellions, civil wars, and regional conflicts have left other cities, such as Baghdad and Kinshasa, more overtly divided. For these cities, Shanghai has as much, if not more, to teach us than Paris or London.

The cities of western Europe have provided us with many of our key concepts for understanding the development of cities and their relationship to the state, such as the bourgeoisie, the public sphere, and civil society, to name a few of the most influential. All of these concepts emerge from a pattern of historical development in which strong national states and wealthy urban centers developed gradually over centuries, both in tandem and in competition with one another. Differences in the sources and nature of their power gave the relationship between kings and burghers a vibrancy that proved to be creative and productive for both sides—and an important element of Europe's subsequent rise to world dominance. Because this dynamic relationship proved to be so critical in Europe, scholars have looked for its counterpart in the rest of the world. In the China field alone, the search for a modern bourgeoisie and anything approximating a civil society have consumed decades of research and debate.

While this search has helped explain why other regions did not follow the path blazed by the Europeans, it has been less helpful in understanding the development of different kinds of relationships between cities and states. The focus on what has been missing has to some extent distracted us from seeing and comprehending what actually existed in cities such as Shanghai. Given the enormity of the differences between state-building and urbanization in early modern Europe and twentieth-century China, we should not be surprised that very different relationships may have developed between cities and states. By avoiding any presumptions about the autonomy and interests of either city or state—presumptions inherent in concepts such as the bourgeoisie and civil society—this volume tries to look at Shanghai with fresh eyes.

With this goal in mind, we seek to answer one simple question: What held Shanghai together? While the question is simple, finding an answer is less straightforward because it resides in the interstices of Shanghai's many worlds. It is the efflorescence of Shanghai studies in China, Japan, North America, Europe, and Australia over the last 25 years that makes the attempt possible. This flood of research into Republican Shanghai's merchants, gangsters, policemen, workers, prostitutes, writers, painters, revolutionaries, professionals, colonists, and many others means that we are now approaching a depth of knowledge about a Chinese city (albeit in a very short historical period) that is somewhat comparable to the historiography of Europe's famous cities.[1] Taking advantage of this accumulation of knowledge, the authors of this volume were asked to seek an answer to the simple question just posed, within the context of their own research into Republican Shanghai. We then came together to put our findings side by side and search for the connections across them, to look for the critical common ground that could help us answer our central question.[2]

In case after case, we found that the connections lay in particular individuals—men like Wang Yiting—who used their wealth, extensive relationships, and seemingly boundless interests and energy to play a prominent role in a bewildering variety of occupations, organizations, and social circles. Although many of them were professional middlemen, such as the compradors who served as intermediaries for foreign-owned companies, they did much more than facilitate economic exchange; they also crossed national, cultural, social, and political boundaries to create a new hybrid urban culture. These middlemen were members of Shanghai's elite, and wealth was an important source of their power and ubiquity.

Our central conclusion is that these elite middlemen and the broader social networks in which they were embedded provided the glue that held Republican Shanghai together on a day-to-day basis. In moments both of everyday cooperation and of extraordinary crisis, these elite networks served as a mechanism for communication and coordination across the city's many divisions. But the role of these middlemen and the resilience of their social networks were by no means a constant in the life of the city and, in fact, both proved to be fragile at key turning points in Shanghai's history.

Peace, prosperity, and political movements based on inclusive identities were conditions that strengthened and broadened Shanghai's social networks. Economic hardship and polarizing politics undermined them. While these tendencies seem straightforward, perhaps even obvious, the relationship between state-building and the strength of social networks proved to be more surprising. Contrary to the common assumption that state power tends to undermine the domination and strength of local society, periods of state-building at the local level, such as the New Policies period in the late Qing dynasty and the mid-1930s under the Nationalist regime, were actually periods in which Shanghai's elite networks strengthened and grew more resilient.

Retracing the well-worn history of Republican Shanghai with these social networks in focus provides a new perspective on state–society relations and the dynamics of the Chinese revolution. Furthermore, even with all of Shanghai's peculiarities, this perspective can shed light on the struggle of other cities to prosper under the rule of weak or failed states in the modern world. As in western Europe, state builders and elites in Shanghai relied on very different sources and kinds of power. But unlike their European counterparts, theirs was a far from level playing field, especially by the twentieth century. Not just because Shanghai's elite was less capitalist, less cohesive, or less independent than its European predecessors but because modern military power changed the nature of the competition entirely. Japan's invasions of Shanghai in the 1930s were the most vivid illustration of how much the rules of the game shifted in the intervening centuries. The other key difference in Shanghai's historical experience was the rise of mass politics, which provided new kinds of power to urban elites but also posed new threats to their long-term dominance.

These differences in the nature of military power and the role of the masses in politics resulted in a distinctly different pattern of development in Shanghai that reveals both the vulnerabilities and the interdependence of city and state in the modern world. This volume focuses on personal networks to show their heretofore underappreciated role in state-building. We try to delineate the kinds of individual networks and the contexts in which they worked to undergird a weak state.

Elites and the State in the Republican Period

The inconclusive civil society debate in the China field has been one skirmish in a much longer battle over whether and how to apply models drawn from Western experience in order to understand the contours of social and political change in China.[3] Before the state–society paradigm became so popular, social classes were seen as the primary forces of social and political change.[4] The gradual rise of China's bourgeoisie and proletariat was considered the fundamental transformation of the late nineteenth and early twentieth centuries, and the role and nature of the state was interpreted in that light. The Qing dynasty was viewed as rooted in agrarian society and hostile toward China's new urban classes. Similarly, the warlords who followed were characterized as hostile to both of these "modern" social forces. In contrast, the Nationalists were viewed in a somewhat more positive light because the bourgeoisie was seen as one key element of the regime's social base. In keeping with this focus on socioeconomic change, class analysis highlighted revolutions as historical turning points and placed Shanghai center stage, since China's industry was so heavily concentrated there. Nevertheless, Shanghai's bourgeoisie remained of secondary importance compared to understanding the development of the working class and its role in the Communist revolution.

While class analysis conformed to the broad contours of the Republican period, anomalies called for elaboration. Why did the urban revolution fail in 1927 if the "modern" social classes were behind it? Why was the relationship between the bourgeoisie and the Nationalist regime so conflictual during the Nanjing decade? In 1949, when social revolution finally did succeed, why did some elements of the bourgeoisie forsake "their" regime and welcome their class enemies? Most of these anomalies were explained in terms of deformations in the development of these social classes in China, whether they were divided internally or contaminated by their connections to imperial powers, or both.[5]

The state–society paradigm has in many ways provided a more flexible analytical framework for the study of Republican China.[6] Separating out the interests of state and society, as well as taking a more comprehensive, less stringent view of what constituted either state or society, has opened up a much richer perspective into the period, especially the Nanjing decade of 1927–1937, which has received the lion's share of attention. By taking a broader, less prescriptive view of society, the state–society paradigm expands our view of urban elites beyond the bourgeoisie to include merchants, compradors, party cadres, professionals, and even organized crime bosses.

The state is no longer reduced to the expression of class interests but is considered an institutional force that to some extent structures and defines the interests of this complex elite. The key historical turning points from the state–society perspective were marked by the rise and fall of new states (1911, 1927, and 1937). While Shanghai's status as a partially colonized city made it less central to the story of state-building in Nanjing, it still has received more attention than any other Chinese city (including Nanjing) because it was the economic linchpin of the fledgling state.

One reason behind the intense focus on the Nanjing decade is because it represents the only decade during the Republican period when a central Chinese state functioned effectively. It therefore raises questions of state–society relations in a way that the rest of the Republican era does not. For example, Nationalist state-building imposed new constraints on Shanghai's elite, leveraging its resources, seizing the initiative in addressing local problems, and even nationalizing key private companies, such as the modern banking sector. Considerable debate has ensued over whether this new relationship amounted to complete state domination of Shanghai's elite or to a more subtle incorporation and interpenetration of state and society.[7]

All sides in this debate over the relationship between state and society during the Republican period agree that these concepts need to be tailored to the very different circumstances of the Chinese case if they are to be useful. They stress the nuances of the relationship between state and society: that their competition is not a zero-sum game, that they need to be disaggregated into their constituent parts, that the borders between them are not clear-cut.[8] Even with these caveats, however, it is difficult to escape the Eurocentric assumptions built into the state–society paradigm, and the overall message of this literature is that the collapse of the Qing state ushered in a period of autonomy for

Shanghai's elite that was interrupted by the state-building efforts of the Nationalist regime from 1927 to 1937. The implicit assumption is that the strength of Shanghai's elite and the task of state-building were mutually exclusive; that is, the interests of state and society were in direct conflict with one another.

Yet it is difficult to square this analysis with the behavior of Shanghai's elite during this period. If the central story of the Nanjing decade was a struggle for dominance between local elites and a centralizing state, why did local elites fail to resist and indeed sometimes cooperate with their state-building rivals? Was it because they feared the mobilization of the working class, as earlier scholars employing the class analysis paradigm claimed? Was it the result of the internal divisions among this elite, combined with the misguided opportunism on the part of a few key leaders?[9] Or was it the exchange of local autonomy for access to power in a wider arena?[10]

Another puzzle is the long-term impact of state-building in the Nanjing decade. Although few studies of state–society relations address the impact of war and occupation directly, the implicit or explicit claim is that the state-building achievements of the 1920s and 1930s shaped the state-building project of the Communists more than 20 years later. However, the way in which this legacy survived the disruptions of the Second World War is often left unclear.

Social Networks and Shanghai's Elites

Simpler analytical building blocks may take us much further in explaining these puzzles than the state–society paradigm. While conceptually simpler than class analysis and the Marxist theory of social change underlying it, the state–society paradigm still incorporates problematic assumptions, such as the premise that the interests of states and elites (especially urban elites) are fundamentally opposed. Many of these premises do not travel as far as the concepts they underpin. Perhaps simpler analytical concepts might reorient our comparative reference point away from the West toward other parts of the world that may have more in common with China.

Social networks offer just such an analytical building block. Social networks have long been recognized as an important element of Chinese society, shaping its culture, economy, and politics.[11] As a consequence, we do not need to begin our analysis with a debate over whether social networks ever existed in Republican China. Instead, we commence immediately with questions of how social networks affected the city and how and why they changed over time. Furthermore, with the extensive research conducted on social networks around the world, they provide a much more ready comparison to other places and times than more complex concepts such as civil society, the bourgeoisie, and the public sphere.[12]

In addition to simplifying the conceptual framework, pulling back from the intense focus on the Nanjing decade to look at the entire Republican period helps put some of the puzzles of the class and state–society paradigms in perspective. Rather than focus exclusively on the high point of Republican-era state-building efforts under the Nationalist regime, it is also important to examine the low points of the warlord period and the Civil War to see the effect on both state and society. For the purposes of this volume, we focus on the activity of the elites, whom we argue were the glue holding the city together as the state showed itself unable or unwilling to perform that function.

To try to understand the dynamics of Shanghai's elite networks and how they evolved, we sought to gain a bottom-up perspective on their development, independent from the major political events that have defined the Republican period. Of course, this kind of bottom-up analysis is difficult to carry out without demarcating a discrete period to limit what could be an endless research effort. The Shanghai case, however, is especially appropriate for this type of inquiry because its Republican-era elite had a short life span. This distinctive social group emerged, reached its peak of wealth and power, and then was eliminated in just over 100 years—a long century, if you will, that began with the opening of Shanghai as a treaty port in 1843 and came to a close with the socialization of industry in 1956. These two major turning points marking the rise and fall of Shanghai's Republican-era elite frame our joint inquiry, allowing us to range across the late Imperial, Republican, and early Communist periods to trace the nodes of this elite's overlapping networks and activities.

From the perspective of this long century, the fragility of the local elite's domination is in many ways quite striking, especially considering the spectacular wealth, power, and cultural creativity that it managed to achieve in that short period. Yet both the strength and the vulnerability of Shanghai's Republican elite stemmed from the same source: Shanghai's position as a crossroads of Euro-American and Asian empires. Initially marginal to all of these empires, this crossroads gained strategic importance as the city and its economy grew. As Shanghai developed into a new center of power, Shanghai's elite gained unique influence and at the same time became uniquely vulnerable to rival contenders, whether Chinese warlords or Japanese imperialists.

Too heterogeneous to be usefully considered a social class, this elite was composed of local gentry, government officials, compradors, bankers, merchants, industrialists, gangsters, intellectuals, artists, professionals, and partisan cadres, to name a few of its constituent groups. Just as the rest of Shanghai's population was remarkably diverse, the elite was divided by national, ethnic, religious, and political affiliations. To get a handle on this diverse group, we have concentrated our attention on the personal networks of three men who emerged as key middlemen in our research: activist Huang Yanpei, comprador Wang Yiting, and gangster Du Yuesheng.

Chapters 2 through 4 of this volume examine the backgrounds of these three individuals and their participation in various organizations and networks. Later chapters show how these different organizations and networks interacted and developed over time. While Du Yuesheng has achieved considerable prominence in the literature on Shanghai, Wang Yiting and Huang Yanpei are not as well known. Nevertheless, all three played prominent roles in Shanghai's political and social circles, emerging again and again as key players at critical points in the city's history. While these three men are by no means representative of Shanghai's elite, they do feature some of the diversity of that broader social group.

Such individuals shared little in terms of common background or experience. Self-made millionaires such as comprador Wang Yiting came from poor families and received limited formal education, in contrast to the much more privileged and cultured background of those like educator and activist Huang Yanpei. Gangster Du Yuesheng may have shared Wang's humble origins, but his meteoric rise to wealth and power came through the rough world of opium smuggling and protection rackets rather than apprenticeships in native banks and Japanese trading companies.

The medium, or link, that these men shared was their wealth, which in turn contributed to their social prestige (albeit of very different kinds). These economic and social resources put each of these middlemen in central positions in a dense web of relationships within Shanghai's elite and beyond. Wealth, social prestige, and central positions in social networks were also the source of their considerable power. While the leverage that wealth and prestige can provide are well understood, the power that may be gained from positions in a complex and ever-changing pattern of relationships is perhaps more ambiguous.

Serving as the intersection of multiple elite networks turned these men into brokers between different worlds. For example, Du Yuesheng was a key broker between the French authorities in Shanghai and Chinese state authorities (see Chapter 4). Wang Yiting bridged the religious and the business worlds and in both guises helped find common ground between Shanghai's Japanese and Chinese residents (see Chapter 3). Huang Yanpei not only crossed the boundaries between culture and business, his political activism helped create a whole new conception of education, as well as the institutional infrastructure to make it happen (see Chapter 2).

In addition to the coordination these middlemen could engineer by virtue of their position at the intersection of multiple elite networks, their networks also reached beyond this narrow strata—up to state officials and revolutionary statemakers, down to workers and the lower classes within the city, out to neighboring regions, and even to the empires that lay far beyond China's borders. For example, Huang Yanpei served as a government official in the early years of the Republic and maintained long-lasting relationships with both Nationalist officials and Communist cadres. A distinctive source of Du Yuesheng's power was his web of relationships with labor racketeers and the city's large underclass of petty criminals and beggars. Similarly, Wang Yiting and other philanthropists could draw on native place networks to tackle social problems that extended far beyond Shanghai's borders, as in the work of the Anti-Kidnapping Society (see Chapter 8).

The power that individuals gained from this multidimensional brokerage system could be considerable. As Elizabeth Perry argues in Chapter 5 of this volume, social networks were the building blocks of collective action in Shanghai. Parks Coble similarly argues in Chapter 6 that the National Salvation Movement achieved rapid influence primarily because it was able to plug into an "existing set of social networks" and a "coalition of constituent organizations, each based on profession and status." These networks could also help provide some protection for activists confronted with efforts to undermine their political mobilization. Sei Jeong Chin's Chapter 7 on the media shows that the links to Huang Yanpei as well as Du Yuesheng allowed certain publications such as *New Life Weekly* to escape the censor's ax when speaking out against the Japanese during the National Salvation Movement. At crucial points, the media was able to sidestep political repression and censorship by the fledgling Nationalist government. Just as important, if not more so, these networks were vital to the Chinese state, which lacked the capacity to enforce its censorship policies without the active cooperation of publishers and editors. Both state and society derived power from the networks that linked them together.

But brokers in these overlapping networks used their power for demobilization as well. The comprador Yu Xiaqing managed to exert leverage over hundreds of thousands of protesters, strikers, and boycotters during the May 30th movement against imperialism in 1925, providing a vivid illustration of this kind of power. Taking advantage of his pivotal position between merchant, student, and working-class networks and the Nationalist and Communist revolutionaries who were mobilizing them, Yu was able to exert personal control over the strike fund financing the movement (see Chapter 5 on popular protest).

Although this kind of brokerage power could be decisive, it was in fact fatally dependent on the strength and the structure of the networks that produced it. Because such power stemmed from the ability of these middlemen to cross social, cultural, and political boundaries in ways no others could, ironically, it depended on the continuation of these cleavages. After Shanghai was unified in the wake of the Second World War and the elimination of the colonial concessions, brokers were never able to achieve the same centrality and power they had enjoyed beforehand. Middlemen like Du Yuesheng could no longer counter state power as effectively as they had before the unification of the city, since state agents could now develop autonomous sources of power and influence. Du responded to these new circumstances with considerable creativity, seeking to expand his social networks in new directions by reaching out to the new middle classes in the Perseverance Society (see Chapter 4). Even with these new efforts, however, Du Yuesheng was never able to regain the kind of power he enjoyed before the Second World War.

These networks did more than place middlemen like Wang, Du, and Huang in positions of power. They also helped foster a distinctive hybrid urban elite culture that created commonality where none existed before. A clear illustration of this common ground was the fact that all three of these men ended up working closely together in founding new organizations, confronting the problems of the city, and advancing a shared vision for the nation. Chapter 2 of this volume examines the emergence of a new mercantile elite and culture that began in the second half of the nineteenth century. Wealth obviously was a common denominator bringing together different elites. An essential prior development that made such interactions possible was the legitimization of wealth and business in China. The transformed representation of those who engaged in business and industrial undertakings as solely concerned with profit-seeking pursuits that enriched the wily and unprincipled to that of being "patriotic deeds that brought benefits to the Chinese nation and its people" was central in the formation of Shanghai's distinctive elite as well as in the development of Shanghai's identity as a city. As Wen-hsin Yeh argues in Chapter 2, "Capitalist enterprises, thus legitimized, won the sponsorship of the state as well as the patronage of the liberal-minded gentry-elite." As Chin shows in Chapter 7, journalism also bridged the long-standing divide in Chinese thought between commerce and culture, helping to foster a new national identity in a semicolonial city.

Philanthropy was another prominent aspect of this newly forming common ground. Chapter 9 examines philanthropy as a marker of power and a vehicle for enhancing social prestige—a route accessible through wealth, regardless of how it was acquired. Legitimate businessmen like Wang Yiting were key members of major relief efforts, but so was Du Yuesheng, best known for his Green Gang activities. Understanding the networks that formed in such forums provides new insights into how an illiterate gangster like Du Yuesheng could operate in the same social/cultural circles and in prominent public positions with men like Wang Yiting and Huang Yanpei. This phenomenon reflects a transformation that goes deeper than the "corruption" of Shanghai society. The development of a common cultural milieu within such a fragmented society has to be considered a contribution to the life of the city, even if it did incorporate the city's underworld denizens as well as its more legitimate residents.

In Chapter 3, Kuiyi Shen also shows how philanthropy helped bridge the worlds of commerce and art in Shanghai, funneling critically needed resources to artists and fostering the creation of a distinct style of painting. The Shanghai school of painting experimented with European impressionism and Chinese ink brush painting techniques, helping to bridge the East/West divide. In Chapter 10, Jeffrey Wasserstrom points to the role of key individuals in crossing these kinds of national and cultural divisions in Shanghai society. These "border-crossers" had the linguistic and cultural skills to live, work, and socialize with both the foreign colonial elite and their Chinese counterparts. While there remained segregated Chinese and foreign communities in

Shanghai, Wasserstrom suggests that one of the reasons Shanghai was able to thrive economically and survive crisis was that "many individual members of the local Chinese and foreign elites were either part of the same social circles or part of overlapping ones."

Social networks and the bridges they provided were also an impetus to collective action. Particularistic identities such as native place were not necessarily obstacles to collective action in Shanghai but helped shape innovative, hybrid local/national identities. Perry shows in Chapter 5 that particularistic identities not only existed side by side with broader conceptions of class and nation but that these narrow identities could serve as the basis for large-scale collective action. In Chapter 8, Bryna Goodman examines how a sense of the public evolved out of native place associations and their philanthropic efforts. Hybrid identities were not necessarily an obstacle to social cohesion in Republican Shanghai—in many cases they provided the basis for it. Yeh underscores in Chapter 2 how new and old styles of networking were not mutually exclusive.

Elites and the State: Historical Implications of a Network Approach

While social networks provide a simple starting point for analysis, they can open up a rich perspective on complex phenomena such as state-building and revolution. For example, this analytical approach puts the "problem" of Shanghai's many political and socioeconomic divisions in another light. The political divisions between the French, Anglo-American, and Chinese cities created enormous profits and power for the middlemen who bridged them, as did the social divisions between different classes and native places. But the strength and the fragility of Shanghai's elite networks also depended on maintaining a delicate balance of power. When the expanding Japanese empire threatened this balance of power in the Shanghai of the 1930s, these middlemen became some of the strongest supporters of the Nationalist regime's state-building project, providing both resources and leadership.

Comparably, the development of hybrid identities and cultures helps explain how and why many members of Shanghai's elite embraced the Chinese Communist Party in the late 1940s. As the corruption and the incompetence of the Nationalist regime undermined the day-to-day functioning of the city even as the state sought to crowd out Shanghai's elites from the public arena, the Communists' competence seemed to offer a new foundation for political order. In addition to sharing this common goal, the policies and rhetoric of New Democracy seemed to promise a new hybrid identity and hybrid political culture with a central place for cities like Shanghai and elite middlemen like Huang Yanpei.

This bottom-up perspective on the rise and fall of Shanghai's distinctive elite suggests a historiography different from either the social forces or the state–society paradigms. Rather than being defined by revolutions or the establishment of new states, from this perspective the key historical turning points were defined by war. The Opium War turned Shanghai into a semicolonial, divided city and created the conditions for the emergence of a new hybrid elite. The Taiping Rebellion pushed local gentry from throughout the Jiangnan region to seek the safety of the foreign concessions, further fueling the formation of this elite. The First World War laid the foundations for Chinese industry to flourish and expand.

If these wars shaped the formation of Shanghai's elite, clearly the Second World War contributed to its demise by undermining its wealth and cohesion. Furthermore, unification of the city eliminated the source of much of the brokerage power that these middlemen had achieved in the Republican period. While the Nationalists' own incompetence prevented them from fully taking advantage of these new circumstances, the Communists did not have the same kind of limitations. Given the transformation wrought by the Second World War, it is perhaps not surprising that Shanghai's once powerful elite was so divided in its response to the Communist takeover in 1949. Rather than resist a radical regime that threatened to attack the sources of its power and prestige, these elite middlemen chose either to cooperate with the Communists or to leave Shanghai altogether. The nationalization of industry in 1956 was an anticlimactic end to this elite's wealth and power. While a full understanding of state-building and the revolution requires examining a much wider swathe of Chinese society than just this elite, the rich view that this narrow strata provides into the Republican period suggests the potential for using social network analysis more broadly.

City and State: Comparative Implications of the Shanghai Case

This analytical approach can open up new avenues for comparative analysis that move beyond testing and adapting concepts and models derived from European history. Even with all of Shanghai's peculiarities, it can shed light on the struggle of other cities to prosper under the rule of weak or failed states in the modern world. The contrast between Shanghai and western European cities points to some possible parallels. As in western Europe, state builders and elites in Shanghai relied on very different sources and kinds of power. But unlike the European context in the early modern period, elites in Republican Shanghai had far more reason to support and promote state-building, even if it meant providing much of the resources for the new state.

As already discussed, Shanghai's elites certainly benefited from their position at the crossroads of multiple empires. But these benefits depended on a delicate balance of power, and Chinese state-building offered one of the few ways in which Shanghai's elite middlemen could hope to influence that balance of power. Contrary to the common assumption that state power tends to undermine the strength of local society, periods of state-building at the local level, such as the New Policies period in the late Qing dynasty and the mid-1930s under the Nationalist regime, were actually periods in which Shanghai's elite networks strengthened and grew more resilient.

Perhaps the reasons for this distinctive pattern of state–society relations in twentieth-century China stem from the accident of timing. Over centuries of gradual state-building in the early modern period, western European cities resisted the centralizing efforts of kings in a time when their fortifications and militias could provide some measure of protection. We can certainly see in China some parallels to these fifteenth- and sixteenth-century developments in Europe. For example, Shanghai's elite used its merchant militia and armory to seize power from the feeble Qing dynasty in 1911 (see Chapter 5). But the parallels quickly disappear; this kind of local military force was already being outstripped by professional armies in the 1920s and was a nonfactor by the time the Japanese invaded the city in the 1930s (see Chapter 6). War may have been a powerful force in Chinese state-building in the twentieth century just as it was in early modern Europe, but the nature of warfare had been fundamentally transformed in the intervening centuries.

Given this transformation, Shanghai's historical experience is arguably much more relevant to other cases of state-building in the twentieth century than any European precedents. Not only might you expect to find similar alliances of urban elites and state authorities against the forces of imperialism, you might also find other examples in which a strong society and a strong state are complementary, rather than in conflict with one another.

Networks and Social Capital in Shanghai

The concept of social capital provides another point of departure for teasing out the comparative implications of the Shanghai case. The common ground that our volume highlights can in some ways be characterized as a form of social capital, often defined as the networks, norms, and trust that foster collective action.[13] Like social capital, Shanghai's common ground certainly promoted a measure of cooperation across deep social cleavages and helped the city survive its long period of statelessness. But this common ground was also far more ambiguous than social capital, which is more often shaded with positive connotations of rational, voluntary, and even virtuous behavior. These very ambiguities can contribute to current debates over social capital.

Social capital theorists have advanced the idea that different network structures can foster or inhibit the development of social capital. Robert D. Putnam, for example has argued that social networks based on horizontal ties among peers promote social capital, whereas networks of vertical ties between superiors and inferiors have the opposite result. Republican Shanghai's elite networks were composed of both horizontal and vertical ties, making it an interesting case for exploring the impact of network structure on people's outlook and behavior. In addition, Shanghai provides a rare comparative case prominently featuring organized crime, and thus in one aspect at least provides a direct point of comparison to Putnam's seminal analysis of the role of social capital in Northern and Southern Italy.[14]

In contrast to Putnam's findings that the vertical ties of the mafia undermined trust and inhibited cooperation in Southern Italy, Shanghai's similarly structured Green Gang did not yield a tight correlation between network structure, trust, and collective action. The Green Gang certainly had an effect similar to the mafia on trust in Shanghai; the organization not only profited from the widespread uncertainty and mistrust the city was so notorious for, it also actively cultivated a climate of threat and fear.

Yet fear did not necessarily undermine collective action. Indeed, as Chapters 4 and 5 show, fear of the Green Gang's sanctions proved in many cases to be a powerful motive *for* cooperation. Putnam and his colleagues also hint at this ambiguity when they note that the mafia's core business is the provision of trust within a broader context of pervasive mistrust.[15] The prominence of darker motives for collective action in the Shanghai case suggest that the almost exclusive focus on trust in the social capital literature should be broadened to examine a wider (and arguably more realistic) range of emotions.[16]

The Shanghai case also suggests that Putnam and his colleagues may have overlooked a positive (or at least effective) aspect of the kinds of vertical ties commonly found in organized crime. In Shanghai, the Green Gang's vertical chains of patron/client relationships extended from the richest men in the city down to its most destitute beggars and transients. In a city rich with formal and informal organizations at every level in society, the Green Gang was one of the few that spanned the city's deep class divisions. This structure gave the Green Gang a decisive role in the mobilization of cross-class collective action and therefore considerable political power. Thus in the Shanghai case, as the chapters that follow will show, vertical ties could and did function as bridging relationships, which are often assumed to be only horizontal. The implications of this finding are that bridging ties may be more important for social capital than the overall structure of relationships within an organization.

The different role played by similarly structured criminal organizations in Shanghai and southern Italy suggests that the broader political context of these organizations may be as important as their internal structure in explaining their role in collective action. The more stable hostility between central state-builders and the mafia in Italy perhaps obscures the political nature of organized crime. Indeed, China's fluid political context of the 1920s and 1930s illustrates a much wider range of relationships between organized crime and the state, and this variation makes the political nature of organized crime much more readily apparent. Like the mafia, the Green Gang certainly opposed effective, centralized state power as inimical to its interests. But the Green Gang also forged a profitable relationship with the Nationalist state during the 1920s and 1930s.

Even more notable was the fact that Green Gang leaders like Du Yuesheng sacrificed their immediate economic interests for larger political goals in response to the nationalist movements of the 1930s. Ineffective regional governments in southern Italy might be a by-product of the society and culture fostered by organized crime—but it could also be the successful outcome of a deliberate political strategy (or both). Thus the findings from our Shanghai case suggest that the concept of social capital needs to be carefully contextualized because its political valence cannot be assumed.

In addition to the importance of placing social capital within its broader political context, the differences between the Shanghai and

Italian cases suggest that the complex concept of social capital needs to be unpacked to extend its comparative reach.[17] Rather than combining networks, norms, and trust into a single overarching concept, a more finely tuned approach would allow for analysis of these different sources of collective action under varying political conditions and toward varying collective goals. The role of trust in motivating and facilitating collective action mentioned earlier is just one limit to the comparative reach of the dominant conception of social capital. For example, while the focus on trust may be particularly appropriate to understanding collective action under democratic regimes, fear and distrust may be particularly important for the analysis of collective action under revolutionary conditions.

Conclusion

The simple question of what held Shanghai together may be difficult to answer, but our initial attempt has proved fruitful. Individual people and their relationship to one another may seem less sturdy and resilient than the institutions and the ideas that we usually look to in our effort to understand cooperation and cohesion. But the absence of ideas such as trust or class consciousness, or the weakness of institutions like the state in Republican Shanghai, provides a test case for the counterintuitive proposition that social networks can serve as more than a foundation for identities and institutions—in some places and times they have provided an alternative. Most often, ideas, identities, institutions, and social networks are all intertwined with one another. Shanghai's many weaknesses and divisions provide an opportunity to tease out social networks from this mix and try to understand the conditions under which they can create common ground.[18]

Scholars have long focused on Shanghai's compradors, gangsters, artists, and other border-crossers because they were so colorful and prominent in Shanghai's social landscape. Then, too, the newness and the hybridity of Shanghai's culture and Shanghainese's understanding of themselves and their place in the world have attracted considerable interest from scholars and the broader public. While understandable, this focus on Shanghai's most unusual characters and characteristics has led some people to advocate moving beyond this recent obsession with Shanghai to devote attention and resources to understanding the rest of China—the "real" China.

We certainly agree with this broader goal, but we want to suggest that Shanghai's distinctiveness is not necessarily a hurdle to drawing out larger implications and ideas for understanding China—and other parts of the world. These two preliminary explorations of the comparative implications of the Shanghai case for our understanding of state-building and social capital suggest some of the possible benefits to be gained from intensive study of important non-Western cities and countries. This potential for contributing to comparative debates suggests that further research on Republican Shanghai may serve not only to provide a fresh perspective on twentieth-century Chinese history but to help generate new theories that address the big questions of comparative politics.

At this point in the historiography of Republican Shanghai, we are just beginning to reach the critical threshold of research and scholarship to allow for comparative analysis that moves beyond testing and adapting models and theories developed for Western cases. While Shanghai may seem overstudied in comparison to other Chinese (and Third World) cities, the depth and breadth of the scholarship on Shanghai is just beginning to reach the level of scholarship on western European and North American cities. So the call to redirect attention and resources away from Shanghai studies to other parts of China also entails sacrificing the comparative potential we are just beginning to tap. We should not lose sight of the potential gains to be made by continuing this intensive effort to understand one important Chinese city. The initial choice of Shanghai as a research subject by so many scholars may well have been driven by the idiosyncrasies of the city's colorful past, but continuing down this path could yield a deeper understanding of China and our contemporary world.

PART TWO

Middlemen: Compradors, Gangsters, and Political Activists

CHAPTER 2

Huang Yanpei and the Chinese Society of Vocational Education in Shanghai Networking

WEN-HSIN YEH

SHANGHAI IN THE CENTURY after the Opium War was an immigrant city that brought together divergent populations and broke down native place insularity.[1] It is no less significant that Shanghai was where capitalism in China first emerged and, riding on the tide of patriotic nationalism, capitalist enterprises offered strong challenges to traditional cultural norms and institutional arrangements. With these changes appeared a new mercantile culture. In lifestyle and business practice, these comprador merchants set themselves apart both from old-line Chinese merchants and the gentry.[2] Some had received an early education in Confucian classics. Yet comprador fortune was hardly dependent on a mastery of classical learning. Instead, it was a new body of knowledge about the business world beyond China, inclusive of proficiency in English, that assured the successful compradors their indispensability in business transactions between cultures. Brokers in trade, the comprador merchants, thanks to the pragmatic demands of their vocation, became translators between cultures and spokespersons between different systems of value and knowledge to bridge the gap between China and the West.

It is not a matter to be taken for granted, to be sure, that mercantile wealth of a maritime nature was guaranteed to gain social legitimacy in the symbolic universe of late imperial China, which was grounded in landed wealth and bureaucratic connections. Yet between the 1860s and the 1930s, maritime trade and capitalist enterprises *did* succeed in achieving enormous prestige in coastal treaty port society.[3] Such prestige in the discursive arena—in the way words and symbols were mobilized to support mercantile enterprises—was accomplished not simply through the construction of manufacturing facilities or the development of trading practices. As the first part of this chapter shows, it involved instead an elaborate *representation* of the significance of such business enterprises and industrial undertakings as they impinged upon the dominant concerns of the day—the wealth and power of the Chinese nation.

Chinese mercantile and entrepreneurial activities in the international arena were represented as patriotic deeds that brought benefits to the Chinese nation and its people. Capitalist enterprises, thus legitimized, won the sponsorship of the state as well as the patronage of the liberal-minded gentry-elite. Shortly after the turn of the century, sons of the gentry joined those of the merchants to pursue professional training. These young men made each others' acquaintance as fellow students in colleges and universities, all seeking academic degrees in finance, economics, accounting, and corporate management, rather than the classics and history as under the civil service examinations system.

Thanks to the establishment of Western-style colleges and universities in Chinese cities, gentry networks—once sustained principally on the basis of lineage, native place ties, civil service examination rituals, and bureaucratic connections—intersected with networks of merchant guilds and associations. The rise of the "merchant gentlemen," who had been steadily in evidence since the sixteenth century, reached a high point in the first decades of the twentieth century when the merchants adopted the air of the gentlemen while the gentlemen, for their part, took up finance and industry.

This chapter argues that patterns of social interaction changed significantly alongside the reconfiguration of social prestige and symbolic representation. New patterns of sociability evolved in the late nineteenth and early twentieth centuries in China to bring different sectors of treaty-port society into collaborative or sociable contacts with each other—sectors that in an earlier time had stayed discreetly insulated in observance of normative imperatives under a different discursive system.

A principal figure in these new networks, as well as in the transformation and promotion of vocational education, was Huang Yanpei, who founded the Chinese Society of Vocational Education (CSVE). The second part of this chapter examines how the CSVE became, in the 1920s and 1930s, a new hub of networking in Shanghai that crossed traditional social and native place boundaries. The CSVE not only helped its members secure jobs and training but was capable of fashioning viewpoints and mobilizing members for mass political expression.

Social historians have long been aware of the phenomenon of Du Yuesheng, the Green Gang boss and "Al Capone" in Republican Shanghai, who led an extra-legal organization that stemmed from traditional roots and grew into a major presence in all sectors of Shanghai society.[4] Other scholars have noted the mobilization of "all Shanghai" in moments of national crisis such as the May Fourth Movement (1919) and the May Thirtieth Movement (1925), when the *entire* city presented itself in public rallies and on city streets, representing itself in terms of *all* "circles" (*jie*) of Shanghai society.[5] (See also Chapters 5 and 6 on popular protest and the National Salvation Movement, respectively.) Old-style gentry used to strive for a reputation of moral purity by refraining from social interactions with those deemed inferior in cultural accomplishment and moral cultivation. Yet by the 1920s, it became a sign of influence rather than a source of stigma for an individual to be known as a *lu lu tong*—a "fixer," so to speak—with the capacity (*tong*) to fix things through all channels (*lu lu*) in a multifaceted urban society built on multiple waves of migrants.[6]

This chapter turns attention to figures like Huang Yanpei, an educator and publicist, who was able to bridge the gap among multiple social sectors, between schools and factories, between the gentry elite and working masses. It offers three "takes" on Shanghai-based networking activities that were centered respectively on the comprador officials, the economic experts, and the vocational educators from the 1860s to the 1930s, which formed the deep background on the rise of an individual such as Huang Yanpei.

New Patterns of Social Networking

Contemporary observers and scholarly researchers alike have paid much attention to the rise of modern factories, firms, schools, political parties, charitable societies, civic associations, journalistic enterprises, theaters, publishing houses, and so forth, which emerged in Shanghai during the first half of the twentieth century. Not nearly as much attention, however, has been paid to the networking opportunities that these new institutional arrangements represented, in terms of either the discursive circumstances or the structural consequences.

Most existing social science scholarship has focused primarily on traditional Chinese networks—particularistic ties that stemmed from kinship, native place origins, and guilds. This is not to suggest that there were no further divisions within these traditional networks. Elizabeth Perry has argued that factions within native-place networks among Shanghai's industrial workers in the 1920s and 1930s contributed significantly to working-class militancy.[7] Bryna Goodman has shown, on the other hand, that although kinship and native place ties, reinforced by guild associations, provided the primary framework for various forms of identity and community, such diversity did not preclude the construction of a broader national identity on claims of uniformity.[8]

Structurally, the new styles of networking did not always require the demise or attenuation of old forms of connections. Whether the YMCA, the Red Cross, the Bankers Association, the Chamber of Commerce, the Federation of University Professors, the Shanghai branch of the Chinese Communist Party, to name but a few, these organizations called upon the resources of embedded networks and mapped onto them, through collective purpose and action, additional layers of associations. The early Chinese Communist Party in Shanghai consisted of cells of intellectuals who had shared school ties and native place origins. These individuals converted to their viewpoints textile workers and publishing house apprentices who shared native place origins and workplace connections.[9] However, working-class followers characteristically met their intellectual mentors outside the structure either of the factories or the firms, in evening schools, literacy classes, amateur theaters, and singing groups—activities that had gained cultural significance thanks to an urban environment that assigned significance to them. Such after-work social interactions were sponsored by entities such as the YMCA, the General Chamber of Commerce, or even the Chinese Nationalist Party, organizations with missions beyond those borne by the traditional guilds or native place associations.

The 1920s and 1930s, under the Nationalist government, also witnessed forceful state intervention with regard to the maintenance of traditional networks. Nationalist action ranged from political assaults on provincial elite societies (as in the case of the dissolution of the Jiangsu Provincial Educational Association in 1928) to legislative restrictions on the power of lineage elders (as stipulated in the new Marriage Law in 1931), from the Ministry of Education ban on native place associations on school campuses to Nationalist Party attempts to control the organization of local chambers of commerce (as was the case throughout the Nanjing decade, 1928–1937).

Networking activities in Shanghai in the 1920s and 1930s thus took place against dual sets of developments. New networks emerged, on the one hand, as networking activities leveraged conventional ties stemming from the provincial society. They took shape, on the other hand, within the confines of a particular social space that had been negotiated with the state. New patterns of Shanghai networking were, in a sense, results of dialectical interactions between city living and country connections, between the organizational necessities propelled by capitalist enterprises and the indigenous bonds embedded in a diverse range of immigrant communities. Neither, to be sure, was free from the legislative or normative interventions of the modernizing state. Meanwhile the new networks that had emerged in the early decades of the twentieth century straddled economic as well as social boundaries. Shanghai networking, in other words, was the outcome of three-way interactions among the state, the society, and the economy, and it is against this backdrop that we seek to understand the social and cultural making of an individual such as Huang Yanpei.

Between the Officials and the Merchants

The opening of Shanghai as a treaty port followed China's defeats in the Opium War (1839–1842). When the first party of English traders arrived in November 1843, Shanghai residents shut the gates of their city to the strangers at night, eventually forcing the latter to build a whole city on a narrow strip of land, originally a "muddy flat" of "marshes and malaria," along the waterfront. For much of the second half of the nineteenth century, maritime trade along the Chinese coast expanded in the context of armed strife and recurrent warfare. Trade, perhaps as a consequence, came to be thought of as war.

Meanwhile it became fashionable among young Chinese comprador merchants, some of them with Hong Kong educations in English schools, to cite Western practices as they contemplated their work and place in society. Chinese poverty and military defeats, they argued, were the results, first, of a general Chinese ignorance of the ways of "civilized nations," especially of the "self-governing (*zizhi*)" societies of the West. They were the results, more specifically, of Chinese ignorance of Western commerce and technology, knowledge of which required systematic study.

In addition, in conducting commerce, Chinese merchants had been hampered both by an abundance of restrictive rules at home and an inability to depend on effective state protection vis-à-vis foreign interest in treaties and in court. In China, management of mercantile affairs rested in the hands of haughty bureaucrats who were ignorant of the ways of the world. It was not enough, then, for the imperial bureaucracy to adopt policies to protect Chinese mercantile interest. It was essential that there be changes in law and reforms of institutions so as to accommodate the needs of mercantile activities.[10]

In the mid-1890s, Zheng Guanying was the most important voice on *shangzhan* (trade war) and what was to be done about it. A former comprador, an official-in-waiting, and the author of several editions of collected essays entitled *Sheng shi wei yan* (Words of Warning in a Time of Prosperity), Zheng gained national hearing in the aftermath of China's defeat in the Sino-Japanese War. Zheng affirmed the concept of *shangzhan* while attacking bureaucratic presence in the mercantile domain.[11] The issue of the moment, Zheng insisted, was not so much whether the merchants deserved the support and protection of the state but whether the old-line bureaucrats were competent enough to perform their duty.

By the end of the nineteenth century, it became a prevalent view that to succeed in new-style business enterprises, it required immersion in a new body of knowledge and skills that was best transmitted in specialized schools of commerce (*shangwu xuetang*). Success in business, in addition, required up-to-date market information and detailed familiarity with local practices across extensive regions. Such information was to be acquired and circulated through the publication of business gazettes (*shangbao*) and the organization of merchant associations (*shanghui*).[12]

It should come as no surprise that Zheng Guanying was among the first to call for new institutions that ranged from a new ministry of commerce to a large number of business schools. Other suggestions included the codification of commercial laws (*shangfa*) and the appointment of consular officers in foreign cities to coordinate mercantile affairs. Merchant demands gained success by the end of the nineteenth century. In 1899, the imperial court appointed Sheng Xuanhuai, a leading bureaucratic entrepreneur, to become the first minister of commercial treaties (*shangyue dachen*). Merchants, rather than imperial officials, began to control state administration of mercantile affairs.[13]

In the aftermath of the Boxers debacle in 1900, bureaucratic reformers and mercantile interest groups were able to push through a range of innovations concerning mercantile affairs. In 1903, a new ministry of commerce was set up—initially as part of a ministry of agriculture, industry, and commerce and later as an independent entity—to coordinate commercial affairs and assure the dissemination of information and expertise. In the same year the Imperial Law Drafting Commission, led by a team of three—including Wu Tingfang, a former comprador from Hong Kong and Qing emissary to the United States—announced a range of new laws, including commercial laws. Under the new laws, merchants in all major towns and centers in China and in Chinese towns overseas were encouraged or ordered to form chambers of commerce. These associations (*shanghui*) with elected leaderships were to help implement the new laws of the state, gather local information, and submit it up the bureaucratic channel. The newly established ministry of commerce meanwhile worked to facilitate the creation of schools of commerce and the advancement of "business learning" (*shangxue*) at all administrative and commercial centers at all levels. The ministry collected trade information, published a government gazette on commercial affairs (the *Shangwu guanbao*), and supervised the formation of local chambers of commerce. In addition, it encouraged the formation of local societies (*shangxue hui*) for the study of business knowledge.

By the first decades of the twentieth century, new-style merchants of maritime connections had succeeded not only in claiming their social respectability but also in establishing more than a mere foothold in the imperial bureaucracy. Two pieces of commercial legislation were announced in 1903: the "merchant code" (*shangren tongli*) and the "corporation code" (*gongsi lu*). Under the former, the state enumerated and recognized as "commerce" activities of twenty-some categories.[14] To be qualified for registration, they must observe in all trade practices a wide range of new laws, above all those of bookkeeping, accounting, record keeping, account balancing, and so forth, as spelled out in the various textbooks of *shangxue*.[15]

Merchant status received a major boost from such state intervention. In the 1900s, the imperial government gave orders for the organization of a multitude of local chambers of commerce. A principal charge of these organizations was the distribution, to their registered memberships, of standardized forms for record-keeping, including daily record books, monthly balance sheets, and annual total balance sheets, both by revenue and by assets. Merchant conformity to the use of these new forms was a precondition for successful applications for business registration. Proper registration with local authorities, meanwhile, was not only a precondition for a merchant's legal capacity to act but also for the legal recognition and representation of the business in court.

Business education, which taught standardized rules of record-keeping and accounting, provided the technical foundation for the implementation and enforcement of the commercial law as instituted by the imperial state. The involvement of the state in the business arena made it possible, decades after the first articulation of the notion of *shangzhan*, for maritime traders to claim respectability as the merchant-citizens of the nation. Such respectability in turn smoothed the way for networking activities between the merchants and the bureaucrats.

Between Commerce and Education

Commerce and learning, in the general order of things in traditional Chinese society, were among things that rarely mixed. In the 1900s, however, *shang* and *xue* became linked, thanks to the joint sponsorship of the imperial state and the new merchants, and *shangxue*, or "commercial learning," came to be recognized as a new category of knowledge. It no longer seemed unthinkable, that superior knowledge, instead of greed or dishonesty, should be chiefly responsible for a merchant's wealth and success. Knowledge as a factor was elevated to a critical dimension in the success or failure of commercial enterprises. Career preparation for commerce was transformed at the same time.

Just what exactly was "commercial learning" in the 1920s? The Shanghai General Chamber of Commerce, which poured resources into its library, monthly journal publications, sponsorships of books in translation and compilation, and the distribution of manuals, textbooks, newsletters, and other useful information, was a major source for the production of a certain vision.

Following trends in the United States, Chamber editorials identified two major breakthroughs in industry and commerce in the nineteenth century: an industrial revolution centered on technological innovations, and a managerial revolution that evolved around the organization of corporate structures. What Chinese businesses must acquire, in addition to technological expertise, were the managerial insights and techniques of this second revolution, which in turn was built upon an improvement in methods of accounting.

Modern firms consisted of multiple shareholders and a complex array of business involvement. Such operations relied on accounting to offer an accurate and scheduled description of the status of the operation. "Scientific management," wrote the Chicago-trained Min Zhishi, required a survey of empirical data, consultation of statistics, budget planning, inventory checks, and the like. Business decisions must never be made on the basis of an individual's impulse. Nor should matters be left in the hands of nonexperts without certified expertise in critical areas such as marketing, finance, sales, and accounting.[16] All business failures were traceable to a lack of knowledge or an insufficient application of important principles of "commercial learning."[17] The rewards of scientific management were as high as the penalties were heavy.

No fewer than a dozen journals and periodicals were in regular circulation in Shanghai in the mid-1920s to promote the "science" of commercial learning. These journals, by and large sponsored by elite banking associations in various major cities, money guilds, economics studies associations, economics or business departments of colleges or universities, and provincial bureaus of business affairs, in turn supported an editorial staff and a roster of contributors. These specialty writers often lectured either full-time or part-time in colleges of commerce, worked in government departments of finance, auditing, accounting or statistics and were generally active or prominent on the boards of various "study associations" of branches of commercial knowledge. The writers did not always author; it was not uncommon for books and articles to be the results of compilation, translation, editorial adaptation, or the labor of a hired hand. By the mid-1930s, a number of individuals were established as "grand masters" of *shangxue* and their works were accepted as authoritative in specific areas.

Take, for example, Pan Xulun, Shanghai's leading accountant in the Republican period. Pan received his master's degree from Harvard and his doctorate in commercial economics from Columbia. He chaired the Department of Accounting of Shanghai Commercial College and the Department of Commerce of Jinan University. He also held positions in the ministries of Finance and of Agriculture and Commerce and at Maritime Customs. Pan was the auditor for the Shanghai Municipal Council, the founder and director of Lixin Accounting Firm, and a member on the executive board of the Chinese Accounting Society. In the 1940s, he became Deputy Minister of Economics.

The Lixin Accounting Firm used its office space to operate an accounting school that held classes in the evenings. Pan served as the principal and chief instructor. The school published, over time, a long list of textbooks on subjects such as advanced commercial bookkeeping, advanced bookkeeping in English, accounting, corporate accounting, cost accounting, government accounting, bookkeeping and accounting, corporate finance, and corporate registration rules. Many of these titles listed Pan as their author, although often these texts were also composed with substantial contribution from his accounting staff and teaching assistants. One of these assistants, incidentally, was Gu Zhun, who began his career as an apprentice at the firm, worked his way up to become a clerk, taught as an instructor at the evening school, led an underground Chinese Communist Party cell among its vocational students, went to Yan'an during the war, and emerged in the 1950s as a leading financial cadre and economist under the People's Republic of China (PRC).

The teaching of business began in Shanghai in 1904 under a technical management program at the semipublic Nanyang College. In the next 30 years, scores of self-styled "colleges" or "universities" came into being, including 89 that folded after a negligible duration. Of these, at least 17 were "fly-by-night" operations that offered courses in commerce. By the 1930s, under the tightened rules of the Ministry of Education of the Nationalist Government, only six colleges of commerce were allowed to remain.[18]

Despite the somewhat uneven quality of some of these programs, the accredited institutions of the 1930s represented an elite sector of business education. Only a small number of students were able to afford the tuition. No more than several hundred new degrees were conferred each year in commerce. Some graduates went on to attain significant achievements. Xu Guanqun, a graduate of Shanghai College of Commerce, launched his own enterprise and assumed leadership in the "national goods movement."

In the employment market, a Shanghai diploma in commerce guaranteed neither income nor position. Still, the degree certified social status. Those who managed to obtain regular appointments as business professors or economic researchers fared relatively well, and they made money as editors, translators, and, above all, textbook compilers. The intellectualization of commerce enhanced their standing and produced new demands for their teaching. These men gave lectures, published essays, served on review boards, stated learned opinions, and embraced causes. They formed learned societies and joined professional associations to affirm vocational ties. The Chinese Accounting Association, for instance, featured a total membership of but several scores of individuals in the 1930s, and more than once elected as its president the chief government auditor under the Ministry of Finance. These associations provided opportunities for the regulators and the regulated to mingle, which might have facilitated the circulation of expert opinion but only incidentally the civic autonomy of the profession.

Huang Yenpei and Vocational Education

Western-style colleges and universities in early twentieth-century China barely provided enough space to serve the needs of the coastal elite. A large number of youths were barred from entering the system. A rough estimation showed that in the 1920s, fewer than 10 percent of Jiangsu's secondary school students entered colleges upon graduation. In Shanghai there was, alongside the professional elite, a growing sector of lower middle-class youths, of provincial as well as municipal background, who were envious of middle-class life yet frustrated about their prospects. The idea of vocational education gained support in this environment. It harped on the theme of social advancement through hard work and persistent discipline and encouraged the youthful aspirants to focus their energy on pragmatic knowledge. According to this representation, capitalist enterprises, like the old imperial bureaucracy, would reward merit and virtue, albeit of a different sort.

The principal promoter of the idea of vocational education was Huang Yanpei, a former minister of the Jiangsu provincial bureau of education and the head of the Jiangsu Provincial Educational Association. Huang was a fervent advocate of "vocational education," a position he had adopted among a wide spectrum of contending pedagogical notions that linked education to national salvation.[19] Huang envisioned a curricular program featuring business English, mathematics, accounting, and bookkeeping. Traditional literary education had trained China's youths to play with words but not to respect productive work, Huang lamented. Much in the modern economy of the new century, meanwhile, required that young talents prepare themselves with skills and education.[20]

Huang Yanpei was a native of Chuansha County and the son of a merchant. He received a classical education and earned the *juren* degree in 1904. His advancement up the ladder of bureaucratic success was thwarted the following year when the imperial court abolished the civil service examinations. Huang went to Shanghai, where he attended the Nanyang College. Nanyang, a strategic project for Sheng Xuanhuai, was to train technical and managerial executives for the state-owned communications projects under his general management. To staff and operate China's railroad lines, steamship companies, telegraph bureaus, mines, and shipyards, Nanyang offered a curriculum with an emphasis on sciences and engineering that ranged from mathematics and machinery to industrial management. Teaching materials were presented in English and Japanese before suitable texts in Chinese became available. Huang Yanpei learned Japanese along with the sciences. He also gained exposure to progressive thinkers such as Cai Yuanpei, who taught at Nanyang and introduced Huang to the Revolutionary Alliance.

Upon the creation of a Republican government in Nanjing, Cai Yuanpei was named the Minister of Education. The following year Huang Yanpei became Jiangsu's provincial minister of education. Huang Yanpei was keen on promoting his educational vision in the provincial context. He drafted a five-year educational plan that included 11 provincial secondary schools, seven county schools of agriculture, a school of commerce in Shanghai, and a higher normal school in Nanjing that eventually became, with the full support of the Jiangsu Provincial Educational Association, the Dongnan University.[21]

Huang refined his idea of "vocational education" by traveling into China's interior and visiting with the tea growers, the pottery makers, the herbal doctors, and the silk merchants. He knew from firsthand experience the usefulness of skills such as letter-writing, abacus, and bookkeeping.[22] A result of the travel was his lecture, "Learning and Career": "All business pursuits need to be based upon science; all learning must derive from facts. . . . In today's world we must work with knowledge. Whether the pursuit is political studies, commerce, engineering or something else none should be done without knowledge and learning."[23] A school, properly run, was a school that taught business and engineering matters based on scientific principles. The goal of education was not to turn schools into businesses but to close the distance between the cultured and the employed and to elevate the scientific basis of vocational pursuits.

Chinese Society of Vocational Education

Huang Yanpei's cultured man of productivity neither sported Western suits nor gave cocktail parties in garden mansions. Instead, he would shave his head and wear straw sandals. He would find frugality and self-effacement appropriate virtues for his success. Huang's formulation of modern knowledge and traditional virtues in the pragmatic cultivation of material well-being appealed to large sectors of Shanghai society. The result was the founding of the Chinese Society of Vocational Education (*Zhonghua zhiye jiaoyu she*; hereafter CSVE) in May 1917.

Huang Yanpei was the principal mover behind the creation of the society. In addition, 47 others cosigned the charter statement at the initial gathering. The founding roster was a list of national luminaries with strong roots in Shanghai. At the head of the list was Cai Yuanpei, the former minister of education who was then the president of the prestigious Peking University. Next to Cai were Fan Yuanlian, another former minister of education, and Jiang Menglin, future president of Peking University and minister of education.

Other signatories included Ma Xiangbo, the founder of the Catholic Aurora University; Yu Rizhang, the Chinese general secretary of the YMCA; Shi Liangcai, the publisher of *Shenbao*; Zhang Yuanji, the publisher of the Commercial Press; Guo Bingwen, president of the Shanghai College of Commerce; Qian Xinzhi, chairman of the Bank of Communications and president of Shanghai's General Chamber of Commerce; Song Hanzhang, the general manager of the Shanghai branch of the Bank of China; Mu Ouchu, the founder of a leading textile firm; Nie Yuntai, a liberal entrepreneur and member of Zeng Guofan's family; and scores of other college deans and university administrators. The very creation of the CSVE was both the result of and an instrument for sustained networking between Shanghai's top educators and elite merchants.

The CSVE's first order of business was the establishment of a secondary school, Chinese School of Vocational Education (*Zhonghua zhiye jiaoyu xuexiao*), that taught basic sciences, Chinese and foreign languages, business skills, and the making of machine-manufactured products. The first class, launched in July 1918, enrolled 80 students, all recent graduates of Shanghai's primary and junior high schools. In its first round of major action, the School bought acres of land beyond the Southwestern Gate of the old Nanshi and constructed several buildings with a total of fifty-some rooms. Students attended classes, went to the libraries, carried out laboratory experiments, took up residence in the dormitories, and staged dining hall riots against the kitchen staff over the quality of their meals.

In addition, they took up various assignments in school factories for training in practice. These factories manufactured machine tools, furniture, buttons, and enamel. The School ran machine tool and furniture workshops, we learned, after conducting neighborhood surveys of employment and collecting data on the employment patterns of student families of Nanshi's elementary schools. Iron works and carpentry had featured largely in these surveys. As Shanghai's master journeymen were likely to be gratified seeing their sons and nephews carrying on the family's trade in a modernized fashion, the Society ran programs to complement this wish. Buttons and enamel were selected, on the other hand, because imports of these items had dominated the Chinese market. The School taught the technical skills and proudly announced, in the 1930s, that indigenously produced buttons and enamel had succeeded in wrestling the domestic market from the foreigners.[24] To guide its graduates in the job market, the Society created a career guidance department that eventually expanded to serve a city-wide constituency. In the mid-1930s, the Chinese School of Vocational Education placed over three quarters of its graduates in an array of jobs.[25]

To provide opportunities for vocational training at an advanced level, in August 1921, Huang Yanpei entered a three-way agreement with the banker Qian Xinzhi and Guo Bingwen, an educator schooled in the United States. Both men, incidentally, were heads of state-funded modern enterprises, reporting respectively to the ministries of Communication and of Economic Affairs. The new program generated a subsidiary entity, the Shanghai Society for Supplementary Education in Commerce. The program gave vocational school students access both to college-level courses and to internship arrangements with member businesses in the Shanghai General Chamber of Commerce.[26] Sun Jianqiu interned at the Tongchang Bicycle Shop in the summer of 1936 and acquired enough grasp of the company's business dealings (importing and servicing bicycles and parts from the United States) and business management (such things as bookkeeping, accounting, accounts receivable, credit, wholesale, retail, and mail catalogs) to publish a report in the school journal.[27] Other students interned at the Xinhua Savings Bank, the Commercial Press, the Shanghai Ferry Administration, and other establishments and similarly enthused about their experiences in writing.

A third CSVE operation involved the creation of evening schools and continuing education programs aimed at Shanghai's white-collar employees. The CSVE collaborated with the Federation of Nanjing Road Merchants, a shop owner's association, and launched an after-work program for clerks and apprentices. The storeowners paid 5.00 yuan for each worker so that the latter could take courses in abacus, English, and math. Similarly, the CSVE organized a school for the clerks at Maritime Customs, National Goods Department Store, and Guanshengyuan Food Company. These programs represented a significant departure from past practices, when business "know-how" was transmitted through an apprenticeship system. The classes, furthermore, filled the leisure hours of young clerks who otherwise might be giving themselves to gambling and drinking when not confined to the insularity of their workplaces.[28]

The CSVE was the publisher of several journals, including *Education and Career* (*Jiaoyu yu zhiye*), that explored the pedagogical theories in vocational education. It published monthly reports, weekly newsletters, and series of books. The CSVE ran lecture series in multiple cities. In 1926, the CSVE collaborated with several Shanghai colleges of commerce and presented a series of public lectures on commercial law, government bonds, investment, banking, money shops, statistics, pricing, advertisement, international trade, financial institutions, and so forth.[29]

The CSVE sent delegations on study missions to the United States and Japan to observe the practice of vocational education. It dispatched investigative teams to China's interior to prepare reports on local secondary schools and vocational needs. Huang Yanpei toured Manchuria and Southeast Asia, where he inspected trade and industrial schools organized by the Japanese, the British, the French, and the Dutch.[30] In 1929, the CSVE sponsored Liu Zhan'en, president of the Shanghai Baptist College, on a much advertised visit to the United States and Japan. High-profile visits to foreign lands such as these led to many observations and reflections, which in turn supplied themes and materials for public lectures and CSVE articles.

Huang Yanpei, in short, was a tireless advocate of his beliefs, and a traveling one for much of the time. Nor did he hesitate to draw attention to the achievements of the CSVE. The CSVE was as much a sponsor of vocational educational programs as it was a proponent of the idea of vocational education. Huang Yanpei was both publicist and educator, and he succeeded in turning the CSVE into an expanding club for social activism of no less visibility than the YMCA.[31]

Organizationally, the CSVE consisted of an executive secretariat staffed by full-time employees and a board of directors elected by the fee-paying members. In 1917, there were nearly 800 individual members. Twenty years later this number grew to exceed 23,000.[32]

With the founding of the schools, the building of the workshops, the publication of the journals, the sponsorship of the travels, the organization of the annual meetings, and related activities, membership dues hardly met the Society's needs for funding. Huang Yanpei, who in the late 1910s and early 1920s had twice declined to serve as the minister of education, was able to persuade the government in Beijing to subsidize about half of the CSVE's annual expenses during the first decade of the Society's existence. Another source of support came from the Chinese Cultural and Educational Foundation (*Zhonghua wenhua jiaoyu jijin hui*) under the Ministry of Foreign Affairs. This foundation received its capital from the U.S. portion of the Boxers Indemnity Funds and was governed by a board of directors led by Liang Qichao and Hu Shi, intellectual luminaries in Beijing.[33]

A New Source of Networking and Activism

By the late 1920s, the CSVE became a vibrant entity situated at the center of a dense web of social connections and nexus of associations. It was also a civic association heavily dependent on the subsidies of the state for its continued operation.

In terms of networking, the CSVE was, first, the result of interactions between two sets of elite networks, centered respectively on the Shanghai General Chamber of Commerce and the Jiangsu Provincial Educational Association. Chambers of commerce and provincial educational associations dated their origins to the imperial edicts in the 1900s. In the early years of the Republic these elite associations exercised significant influence in the provincial assemblies under the military governors. Provincial educators and chamber leaders were among the principal advocates, for example, of a federated system of provincial self-governance.[34] As early as the 1900s, both constituencies were involved in the nationwide campaigns to promote the "national products" that had been machine-made in China.[35] The CSVE, in other words, had called upon the resources and strengths of major elite networks extending back to the late Qing dynasty. The organization and the activities of the Society, in turn, created new frameworks and conditions for emerging patterns of networking. The CSVE had consistently maintained its nonofficial status in the 1920s. It continued, at the same time, to strive for its relative autonomy vis-à-vis the state throughout the Republican period. In that sense, it was one of the strongest examples of a civic association of societal origin.

But the CSVE was made possible, from the moment of its inception, by the financial support of the state. This remained the case even after 1927, when the Nationalist Revolutionary Army marched into Shanghai, Nanjing, Wuhan, and other major Central Chinese cities and drove out the generals of the Beijing government. In the first months of Nationalist rule, the Jiangsu Provincial Educational Association was ordered to dissolve. Dongnan University, which was the Association's principal project in Nanjing, was taken over by the Nationalists and reorganized to become the Central University under the Ministry of Education.

But the CSVE, headquartered in Shanghai, weathered the transition and reemerged after a hiatus. It not only continued to operate in the open as a legally recognized civic entity but also continued to receive state subsidies. To do so, the CSVE worked out certain terms with the Nationalists. It complied with Nationalist registration requirements under the Ministry of Education. It also revised its charter. It agreed to locate its head office (*zonghui*) at the Nationalist government capital, wherever that was to be. It also agreed that no individual who had ever in any way opposed the Three Principles of the People was to be eligible for CSVE membership.[36]

The CSVE thus went to considerable lengths to assure the Nationalist authorities of its allegiance in exchange for the permission to continue its existence. But the energy and enthusiasm of the young students who converged under the various CSVE programs were beyond the control of the leaders and the regulators. In the schools and programs of the CSVE, thousands of secondary school students and white-collar workers mingled as fellow students. They met in book clubs, singing groups, amateur theaters, and English or accounting classes. They read the *Shenghuo Weekly*, the CSVE's organ and, under the editorship of Zou Taofen, one of the most popular journals with an urban lower middle-class audience.[37] In the aftermath of the Manchurian Incident in September 1931, when the Japanese military seized Manchuria, *Shenghuo Weekly* became the most vocal journal attacking the nonresistance policy of the Nationalists. At CSVE schools and programs, students organized their own military training exercises and volunteered for war efforts. In 1935, at the height of the urban mass mobilization for national salvation, "vocational youths" took part along with college students, university professors, urban professionals, and women in voicing their patriotic sentiments. Despite its indebtedness to the Nationalists, the CSVE had provided the hub that enabled—both discursively and organizationally—the urban working youths to network outside their jobs and homes and mobilize for a public cause.[38]

In the years leading up to the war, Huang Yanpei supported the pro-war sentiments of his students. He was, at the same time, cautious about antagonizing the Nationalists. In July 1937, China declared war against Japan. The following year the Nationalists moved their capital from Nanjing to Chongqing via Wuhan. The CSVE moved accordingly. In Chongqing the Government convened a Citizens' Political Participation Congress (*Guomin canzheng huiyi*) to solidify patriotic alliance, and Huang Yanpei was invited to join. As the head of the Vocational Education Faction (*zhijiao pai*), Huang was a principal architect of the Democratic Alliance (*Minzhu tongmeng*) that was to bring, under one umbrella, an array of political activists from Confucian-style village reconstructionists to English-educated liberal constitutionalists.

In its ability to address the petty urbanites, to mobilize mass patriotism, and to participate in parliamentary discussions during the war, the CSVE had demonstrated a networking capacity that reached beyond old-fashioned elite networks and interpersonal relationships. Yet once the war broke out, the CSVE also found itself relocated away from its established base. It was further strained of resources thanks to wartime inflation. In Chongqing, the CSVE had no recourse but to fall upon the assistance of the Ministry of Education and the Central Military Council, which was chaired by none other than Chiang Kai-shek.

Earlier, under the sponsorship of the CSVE, a School for Wireless Communications had been set up in the International Settlement in Shanghai. In December 1941, Japanese troops moved into the concessions. Shortly thereafter, Japanese military police took into custody the top administrators of the communications school and subjected these men to torture. In its plea with the Central Military Council, the CSVE drew attention to the heroic sacrifice sustained by its staff in the occupied zone.[39] The equipment used at the CSVE's Shanghai school had been American imports. Japanese military suspected that the school had been working with Nationalist intelligence services to train agents, a suspicion more or less confirmed in postwar Chinese memoirs.

After the war the CSVE followed the Nationalists back to Nanjing. In 1947, the CSVE celebrated its thirtieth anniversary in Shanghai. Huang Yanpei and his colleagues reviewed the decades through wars and revolutions. In the late 1940s, the CSVE oversaw the active operation of nearly one hundred cultural and educational enterprises. It listed over ten thousand former students among its alumni. It had produced a significant number of graduates—including Gu Zhun at the Lixin Accounting Firm—who joined the Communist forces in northern Jiangsu and Yan'an during the war. It had trained an equal number of accountants, bookkeepers, machinists, and others who took up various positions in Nationalist-controlled areas.

As the Nationalists and the Communists engaged in a full-scale civil war (1947–1949), Huang Yanpei resolutely steered the middle course of democratic consultation. He worked gingerly to broker a precarious peace and appeared to carry much weight as an opinion leader in the Democratic Alliance. But the CSVE, despite its regional offices, national operations, long rosters, and dense networks, was no political party. Under the general secretariat there were neither political cells nor mass organizations. Neither were there legal protections or economic resources to sustain its autonomous development as a civic entity.

When the Communists took power in late 1949, the new authorities honored Huang Yanpei with a ministerial appointment. They also disbanded the CSVE. In its heyday before the Sino-Japanese War, the CSVE had been an important arena for Shanghai's educational and entrepreneurial elite to address the issue of lower middle-class aspirations for upward mobility. The Communist shutdown in a way brought a fitting point of closure to more than a half century of middle-class networking and bourgeois mobilizations. It was not until the late 1980s, in the economic reforms that brought new life back to the cities, that Chinese scholars, albeit from a different perspective, rescued the memories of the CSVE from the fate of historical oblivion.

Conclusion

With Huang Yanpei and the Chinese Society of Vocational Education, networking in Shanghai reached a new level of complexity and sophistication. Tens of thousands from divergent places of origin and social backgrounds became part of an extended network, getting jobs, receiving training, and organizing leisure. Beyond that, they shared aspirations, fashioned viewpoints, and participated in organizations that were capable of mass political expression.

But the CSVE was not a political party, least of all a revolutionary party intent on the toppling of the existing political authorities. It carried out its teaching and organizing activities in the open and called upon the state to supply resources for its continued operation. As in the case with the comprador officials of the late Qing dynasty and the certified professionals of the Republican decades, mutual accommodation with the state sustained the CSVE while at the same time constraining its possibilities.

Under the Nationalists, the collaboration between the CSVE and the state was a transaction that had often worked to mutual advantage. Through the provincial educators and the new entrepreneurs, the Nationalist Party found a way to reach the emerging stratum of the white-collar workers, which otherwise would have remained disparate and disorganized, working in firms with fewer than 10 people. The CSVE, on the other hand, scored in the crucial arena of prestige as a result of its association with the state, whether as an entity receiving official subsidies or as a voice opposing state policies on stated principles.

Shanghai networking in the first half of the twentieth century was thus a matter of structure as well as of circumstances, of organizations as well as of politics. Social elites came to the fore at a time of weakened central political authority, responding to the new needs of a changing economy by devising new modes of social interaction. They called upon the resources of the state, the society, and the economy to perform new functions and to institutionalize such endeavors.

From comprador officials to vocational educators, the newly enriched and the old-line educated together built new organizations that were to change preexisting patterns of networking. In equal measure, none was able to escape the power of the state and the powerful undercurrents in party politics.

The reach of capitalism was admittedly limited in China in the first half of the twentieth century. But as comprador merchants became imperial officials, accountants received state-certified professional prestige, and educators trained white-color employees in collaboration with the entrepreneurs, important lines in social divisions were being crossed in city after city, community after community, on the imperatives of economic rationality. Even though no democracy had emerged in the form of electoral politics or individual representation, capitalism as such had acted as an important force, transforming the patterns of social interaction in Chinese cities. It had forcefully rearranged societal priorities and reconstructed ethical codes. It elevated the prestige of economic pursuits and placed wealth, along with power, on the national agenda.

It is in the changing patterns of Shanghai networking in the first half of the twentieth century that we find tangible evidence of the institutionalization and the reconfiguration of such values and priorities.

CHAPTER 3

Wang Yiting in the Social Networks of 1910s–1930s Shanghai

KUIYI SHEN

IN THE FOURTH EDITION of *Who's Who in China*, published in Shanghai in 1931, Wang Yiting (1867–1938) was introduced as "chairman of the board of directors of Wah Cheng Fire and Marine Insurance Company; director of the Chinese Electric Power Company; chairman of the Shanghai City Chamber of Commerce; vice chairman of the General Chamber of Commerce; chairman of the board of directors of the Bureau of Municipal Affairs for Shanghai City; in charge of communications and of Agriculture, Labor, and Commerce under Dr. Sun Yat-sen's regime in the first year of the Republic; founder of the Lung Hua Orphanage; and member and/or chairman of the Anti-Kidnapping Society, China Philanthropic Association, China Red Cross Association, Shanghai Public Benevolent Cemetery, Zung Tsi Tang, China International Famine Relief Association, Lester Hospital, Government Famine Relief Commission, Huai Ho Conservancy, Buddhist Laymen's Society, Pure Karma Buddhist Association, and about 15 other minor institutions of charity and 40 institutions of education, including Great China University, the Bureau of Municipal Affairs, and the Municipality of Greater Shanghai."[1]

From this list, it is not difficult to see that Wang Yiting was an extremely successful businessman, was actively involved in and sponsored the Republican revolution of the 1900s and 1910s, and participated in major charitable and religious activities. This long list, however, only accounts for a small number of the titles Wang Yiting held in numerous charitable and business organizations, Buddhist societies, and municipal administrative organs. Moreover, it does not even include any titles

Wang Yiting, known as a famous painter and patron of the Shanghai School, had in more than 20 painting societies and artists associations, where he served either as chairman or board member.

During the 1910s and 1920s, the international metropolis of Shanghai was in a very special situation. On the one hand, a large part of Shanghai's territory, the concessions, was under the nominal control of foreign powers. The remainder was in a state of near political vacuum because of the unstable governmental control that characterized the warlord period. In these very special circumstances, Shanghai's Chinese social elite, along with the various organizations they formed, wove a social net that became an alternative site of political power and that dominated the city's social, cultural, and economic functions.

Wang Yiting, one of the most notable activists in the Shanghai social networks, played crucial roles at various times on Shanghai's political, economic, cultural, and social stages. His rich and complicated life, with his connections to important colleagues in many fields of endeavor, perfectly exemplifies the unique network of social, economic, cultural, philanthropic, and religious ties among prominent citizens of early Republican Shanghai. During a critical period for the young Chinese Republic, Wang Yiting, a modest apprentice-turned-comprador, was able to rise quickly in Shanghai society to lead many elite institutions and organizations and successfully cut across boundaries between the native and the foreign.[2]

Ascent from Humble Origins

Wang Yiting was born in 1867, the sixth year of the Tongzhi reign of the Qing dynasty, in the Shanghai suburb of Zhoupu. His original name was Wang Zhen, but he is best known as Wang Yiting. He also used other names, such as Meihua guanzhu and Haiyun louzhu. After the age of 40, he took another name, Bailong shanren, but in Buddhist circles he also used names such as Jueqi and Kuxingtoutuo.

Wang Yiting grew up in a quite poor family. Only with the help of his relatives, and particularly one local scholar known to historians only as Jiang Xiucai, was he able to enter a private academy run by the retired *daotai*, Mr. Zhu. In 1881, after eight years of study, he was sent into the city to be an apprentice at the art shop Yichuntang.[3] Although he stayed there only one year, Yichuntang provided him opportunities to see and study many paintings and calligraphy pieces, which people sent to the store for mounting, and also gave him a chance to meet two very important people in his life, Ren Yi, more commonly known as Ren Bonian (1840–1896), and Li Weizhuang.[4] Ren Bonian, the leading master of the Shanghai School of painting, became his teacher and introduced him into the Shanghai art world. Li Weizhuang recommended him for entrance to the Shenyu qianzhuang,[5] a traditional Chinese bank, which set a foundation for his future business career in Shanghai. Li Weizhuang, from a wealthy family in Ningbo, was a successful businessman and owned several banks in Shanghai at the time. He was also an art lover and collector, so he often sent paintings and calligraphy to Yichuntang for mounting. Li saw Wang as very smart and eager to learn, so recommended him to work in the bank. During his period as an apprentice in Shenyu qianzhuang, Wang Yiting still practiced painting and calligraphy and used his evenings to go to Yichuntang to study and copy master paintings. It is said that he also went to Guangfangyanguan to learn English.[6] His language study would seem to indicate an ambition to expand his associations not only outside Shanghai but outside China itself.

Three years later, after he finished training at Shenyu qianzhuang, he was sent to another bank, Hengtai qianzhuang, for further study. In 1886, Li Weizhuang appointed Wang as *paojie* (bank representative) of Tianyuhao bank. It was very unusual that a staff member was appointed to such an important position at the age of only 20. Because of his excellent performance, Wang was soon promoted to the position of manager and put in charge of the shipping business of the Li family.

By the beginning of the twentieth century, when Wang was in his early thirties, he was already an important person in the Shanghai business world, tying his activities into a variety of interlinked social networks, investing in the fields of banking, commerce, and industry, befriending men of culture, and doing business with Japanese.

As a Businessman

Wang Yiting's entrée into Shanghai society was initially based on his ties of friendship, business, and art to influential patrons such as Li Weizhuang. He soon accumulated fabulous wealth in his business dealings, rising to the apogee of East Asian society. Yet, he retained a lifelong sympathy for people with modest backgrounds like his own, which he expressed through his accomplishments in charity, education, and culture.

The turning point in Wang Yiting's business career came in 1902. He became a comprador of the Japanese firm Osaka Shipping Company in Shanghai,[7] establishing close, long-term relationships with Japanese business circles from then on. He kept working as comprador for numerous Japanese companies until 1931, by which time almost every Japanese in Shanghai would know Wang Yiting.[8] In 1907, he was invited to be comprador of the Nisshin Steamboat Shipping Company. In the same year, along with Gu Xinyi, Ye Hongyin, Yuan Baosheng, Li Pingshu, and Shen Manyun, Wang Yiting established Lida Flour Mill. In 1910, he and his friends opened a new flour mill, Shenda mianfengchang. During this period, he established a collaborative relationship with comprador Li Zhifang, who worked for the Mitsubishi Bank. Because the Mitsubishi-owned shipping companies controlled the international shipping business and Wang's employer, the Nisshin Steamboat Shipping Company, specialized in domestic shipping, the two compradors quickly controlled much of the shipping business in Shanghai and accumulated a great amount of capital. Later, Wang was appointed comprador of Osaka Packet Shipping Company, which was in charge of the shipping business between Shanghai and Tianjin, Dalian, and Jilong. He was also the president of the Shanghai Spun Silk Company (*Shanghai zhizao juansi she*), which was owned by Mitsui Bank,[9] and a board member of Dayou Flour Mill, Huashang Electric Appliances Company, Dada Shipping Company, and many other companies and factories.

After he opened Tongtai qianzhuang with other friends in 1908, Wang Yiting started to spread his influence in the banking industry. In 1920, he established two banks, Dafeng Commercial Savings Bank (*Dafeng shangye chuxu yinhang*) with Zhu Lanhang and Gu Xinyi, and Huada Commercial Savings Bank (*Huada shangye chuxu yinhang*) with Gu Disan and Rong Zongjing. Two years later, Jiangnan Bank, was opened in Shanghai with Wang as a board member. Wang also sat on the boards of Zhonghua Bank, Xincheng Bank, and others. In 1918, when the Japanese Stock Exchange opened its office in Shanghai, Wang Yiting and other two Chinese, Jin Xizhi and Hu Meian, were appointed as board members.

From as early as 1904, Wang Yiting participated in organizing many major commercial societies. When the Shanghai General Chamber of Commerce was established in May of that year, Wang was elected a board member. He was also the manager of the South Shanghai Chamber of Commerce (*Hunan shangwu zonghui*) at the time. In 1908, he organized the Shanghai Nanshi Chamber of Commerce Federation (*Shanghai *nanshi shangtuan zonghui*), and he was elected general secretary of the Shanghai Industry Association (*Shanghai chupinsuo*) in the following year. In 1920, Wang became the chairman of the board of the newly established Shanghai Flour Exchange. Three years later he was elected chairman of the Shanghai General Chamber of Commerce.

In May of 1927, after Chiang Kai-shek crushed the Communist-led workers' uprising and took control of Shanghai, the Shanghai Commercial Federation (*Shanghai shangye lianhehui*) was established, and Wang, Yu Xiaqing, and Wu Yunzhai were elected cochairmen. The Federation included more than 60 societies, such as Shanghai County Chamber of Commerce, Zhabei Chamber of Commerce, and Shanghai Bankers Association.[10] By the end of the 1920s, with his increasingly widespread social networks and vast wealth, Wang Yiting had reached unimaginable heights in the Shanghai business world.

As a Revolutionary

Obviously, Wang Yiting was a great success in the business world and took a leadership role in Shanghai. His great accomplishments, however, were achieved in the very special circumstances of the time and should be viewed not in isolation but as part of a larger network of social and political relationships. As a powerhouse of China's modern transformation, Shanghai was a city of tremendous complexity. Perhaps the most obvious among these complexities was the fact that a large part of Shanghai consisted of foreign concessions. The Taiping Rebellion further restructured the political map of Shanghai. The self-government movement initiated by the Qing court, based on local pressures from 1905 to 1911, actually created an opportunity for an increasingly active, commercialized, and differentiated local leadership to challenge the imperial dynasty and ultimately contributed to its overthrow.[11]

The business success of Wang Yiting also benefited from his close relationship with local elites and the friendship of local politicians. As early as 1905, Wang Yiting started to actively involve himself in local politics. In that year, when Li Pingshu and other local gentry organized the new General Bureau of Engineering for Shanghai City (*Shanghai chengxiang neiwai zong gongchengju*),[12] a prototype for an autonomous government of the Chinese territory in Shanghai, Wang joined the committee. In 1908, Wang was elected to the board of directors. The Bureau's stated goal was to develop municipal works and increase the quality of life in the Chinese city to reach a level equivalent to that of the concession areas. Within six years, it built and repaired more than 100 streets, 60 bridges, 9 city gates, and 16 wharfs.[13] In 1909, in response to the Qing court's newly issued *Regulations for Local Self-government*, the Shanghai Self-Government Office (*Shanghai chengxiang neiwai zizhi gongsuo*) was established, based on the former General Bureau of Engineering for Shanghai City. Wang Yiting continued as a member of the board of directors.[14] The new office started to organize a local merchants' militia for the purpose of defense.

In 1906, when the Shanghai Chinese Merchants Association (*Shanghai huashang gongyihui*) was formed, Wang Yiting, a key member of the Shanghai Chamber of Commerce, on which the association was founded two years earlier, naturally became one of 41 board members of the new organization.

In December of 1906, when the Constitution Preparation Committee (*Yubei lixian gonghui*) was founded in Shanghai following the Qing court's call to draw up a constitution, Wang was elected a board member.[15] Wang was also elected a member of the Shanghai County Council in 1909 with other merchants, such as Li Pingshu, Zhu Baosan, and Zhang Jianian.[16]

In the winter of 1910, with deep disappointment at the failure of the Qing court's constitutional reform, Wang Yiting turned to the anti-Qing movement and joined the Revolutionary Alliance (*Zhongguo Tongmenhui*) with Shen Manyun and Ye Huijun. As the head of the finance department of the Shanghai headquarters of the Revolutionary Alliance, Wang was in charge of budget and expenses. He himself also donated 500,000 yuan to help publish the journal of the society, *Minzhu bao* (Democracy News). On October 27, 1911, in response to the anti-Qing uprising in Wuchang, Li Pingshu met Chen Qimei (1878–1916)[17] through Wang Yiting. Chen was the head of the Revolutionary Alliance in Shanghai and helped to incite defection among the army and police of Shanghai.[18]

On November 3, 1911, uprisings broke out in Shanghai. The Revolutionary Army quickly seized the northern part and old city region of Shanghai. But the stronghold of the imperial garrison at the Jiangnan Arsenal (*Jiangnan zhizhaoju*), led by its director, Zhang Chubao, stubbornly resisted. In an act of desperate bravery, the leader of the Revolutionary Army, Chen Qimei, entered the Qing army's headquarters alone to urge Zhang Chubao to surrender but instead was detained by Zhang. To rescue Chen, Wang Yiting called his son, Wang Mengnan, who had just returned to Shanghai from Japan, to organize a dare-to-die corps.

Wang Mengnan led this corps with Chiang Kai-shek[19] and with its help the forces of the uprising defeated the Qing army and rescued Chen Qimei. [20] After that, Wang Yiting and Chen became bosom friends.[21] On November 4, 1911, an autonomous local government, *Hujun dudufu*, was established in Shanghai by the Revolutionary Alliance and local elites, with Chen Qimei as the chief. Wang Yiting was appointed as the head of the Transportation Department but later switched to the Commerce Department. Wang Yiting's Xincheng Bank acted as the new government's bank. He used the commercial and political networks he had established in previous years to ask local elites to donate money and even borrowed 350,000 yuan from the Mitsui Bank under his own name to support the new government.

In 1912, the Nationalist Party (KMT) established its Shanghai branch. Wang Yiting was the director, with Zhu Baosan and Shen Maozhao as deputies, and Gu Lügui was head of the finance department.[22] Wang Yiting was extremely active in the political sphere in Shanghai until the middle of 1913 when Yuan Shikai issued warrants for his arrest.

On April 1, 1912, Sun Yat-sen was forced to resign as temporary president of the new Republic of China, but Wang Yiting remained a loyal supporter. When Sun Yat-sen's closest ally, Song Jiaoren, was assassinated at Shanghai railway station on March 20, 1913, on the orders of the power-hungry warlord Yuan Shikai, Wang Yiting was standing by Song's side. In this period, Sun Yat-sen was in charge of China's railroad construction and planning for industrial and commercial development, which he undertook despite severe budget shortfalls. With the help of prominent Shanghai businessmen and bankers, such as Wang Yiting, Zhu Baosan, Zhang Jingjiang, and Shen Manyun, Sun established the China Bank of Industry and Commerce and the Sino-Japanese joint venture China Xinye Bank to raise money for railway construction.

Sun Yat-sen launched a "Second Revolution" against Yuan Shikai in 1913, but it soon collapsed because of lack of military support. Wang Yiting and many other Sun Yat-sen supporters were placed on a wanted list by Yuan Shikai. On July 26, Sun Yat-sen, Chen Qimei, Huang Xing, Li Pingshu, Cen Chunhuan, Shen Manyun, and Yang Xinzhi were deported by the International Concession authorities. Sun Yat-sen, Chen Qimei, and others fled to Japan. Wang Yiting, whose residence was in the Chinese city, chose to stay in Shanghai.

What circumstances permitted Wang Yiting and the other Shanghainese revolutionaries to safely remain in the city while the others fled is not known, but it is likely that their strong networks in Shanghai society protected them. In Wang Yiting's case, his strong connections in the Japanese business world may also have carried weight. He subsequently avoided direct political activities but supported his causes through the power of his wealth.

As a Philanthropist

This period of rapid change saw China's local leaders both reacting to and capitalizing on ever new sets of political relationships within a constantly changing national context.[23] This period, between 1913 and 1927, was the golden age of local elite leadership. Following the collapse of the Qing dynasty, continuous political and military battles between warlords resulted in a political vacuum in Shanghai and provided a new "public" sphere for the local elites' activity. Local elite leaders devoted their energy to building up their own areas. The result was a burst of municipal works, such as road building, hospital construction, land surveying, new business ventures, and other projects.

"Local public welfare," which was a new idea, emerged in the self-government movement of the late Qing period. This kind of public service may be traced to the traditional charity of the local gentry but also received organizational influence from foreign cultural forms. In early Republican Shanghai, the diverse activities of associations contributed to this development of activities related to local service. In this process, the Shanghai elites, with businessmen such as Wang Yiting at their center, came to play a leading role.[24]

Although, after 1913, he gradually faded out of the Shanghai political scene, Wang Yiting turned his energy to philanthropy, public welfare, education, and art. As one of the most influential men of the local elite, and a powerful businessman with political and social networks established over several decades, Wang Yiting continued to play a decisive role in Shanghai society until his death in 1938.

Based on recorded sources from the late 1920s and early 1930s, there were about 200 philanthropic societies and institutions in Shanghai. In that period, Wang Yiting was listed as founder, cofounder, or executive officer of eighteen societies and institutions. Among them were philanthropic societies, such as *Shanghai cishantuan, Shanghai youmin xiqinsuo, Hunan shishanhui, Renji shantang, Zhongguo jiuji furu zonghui,* and *Shanghai cishan tuanti lianhehui.*[25]

Wang Yiting's documented involvement in philanthropy may be

traced to as early as 1906. In that year, together with Li Pingshu and Gao Fengci, he founded the Shanghai Orphanage in the old Chinese city, Nanshi. It moved in 1910 to the southwest suburb, near Longhua Temple. The orphanage, which accepted children from the ages of 6 to 18, ran an elementary school and a crafts workshop. Boys were taught carpentry and rattan-working; girls learned sewing, cooking, drawing, and embroidery.[26]

Shanghai cishantuan (Shanghai Philanthropic Association) was founded in 1912 on Meijia Street, Nanshi, by Wang Yingting and Lin Jichun, and included Tongren fuyuantang and five other subsocieties. They sent relief to disaster areas and provided food and established schools for refugees.

In 1919, floods broke out in five provinces, Henan, Hubei, Anhui, Jiangsu, and Zhejiang. Several million people in more than 60 counties suffered in the disaster. On December 19, *Henan yizhenhui* was established in Shanghai to help the relief work. Businessman and philanthropist Zhu Baosan was elected as Honorary Chairman and Xu Ganlin and Wang Yiting as Director and Deputy Director, respectively. In the same year, Wang Yiting also established *Hunan shishanhui,* sending food, medicine, and clothing to the disaster areas and organizing relief workers to give smallpox vaccinations to refugees.

On May 9, 1920, the Chinese Society for Assistance to Women and Children (*Zhongguo jiuji furu zonghui*) held its seventh national meeting and celebrated completion of construction of its new headquarters in Shanghai. Over 10,000 people attended the meeting. At this meeting, Zhu Baosan and Wang Yiting were elected chairman and vice chairman of the society. The society adopted 225 orphans and took in 127 women that year.[27] A few months later, on September 25, Wang Yiting, with Tang Shaoyi and others, founded *Huayang yizhenhui*, a charitable group aimed at collecting local and foreign donations for Chinese refugees. Because of the urgent and serious condition of the disaster areas, they immediately raised funds of 5 million yuan for the affected region. Wang Yiting also collaborated with his teacher and friend Wu Changshi (1844–1927) to paint a work entitled *Liumin tu* (Refugees) for donation to the society.[28] When the Chinese Red Cross Epidemic Disease Hospital was founded in 1922, he and Tang Luyuan were appointed as directors.

In 1927, when the Shanghai Charitable Group Alliance (*Shanghai cishan tuanti lianhehui*) was established, Wang Yiting was elected Chairman of the Executive Board. The standing committee of this group included

Huang Hanzhi, head of the Shanghai Firefighters and former district judge in Shanghai, Wang Xiaolai, representative of the Shanghai General Chamber of Commerce, and Mo Xilun, director of the Shanghai county council (yihui).[29] This organization also played a crucial political role during the multiple power switches between the warlords, local elites, Communists, and Nationalists in 1927.

Between July and September of 1931, heavy rains caused flooding along the Yangzi, Yellow, Pearl, and Songhua Rivers. Seventeen provinces were affected, and 80 million people, almost a quarter of China's total population, suffered in the floods' devastation. In early August, Jiangsu province established a Committee for Charitable Flood Relief. Wang Yiting was appointed director of the Shanghai branch. Among other committee members were Du Yuesheng, Zhang Xiaolin, Huang Jinrong (see Chapter 4), and Yu Xiaqing. To handle the influx of desperate and homeless refugees, these elites from different but overlapping networks founded temporary refugee centers, facilitated adoption of orphans, and distributed donated clothing, medicine, and food to survivors.[30]

At the same time, on August 6, the Shanghai Chamber of Commerce established the Committee to Solicit Donations for Flood Relief. Yu Xiaqing, Wang Yiting, and Wang Xiaolai were elected as executive officers, and Wang Yiting served as vice chairman.[31] The Chamber of Commerce committee was active in various forms of fundraising, using horse races and theatrical performances as charitable events.[32] They even asked city landlords to donate two months' rent receipts to the cause of flood relief.[33] On September 11, 1931, Wang Yiting, again with other Shanghai celebrities that included Du Yuesheng, Yu Xiaqing, Zhang Xiaolin, and Wang Xiaolai, organized a charitable game festival at Yeyuan Garden. All admission fees collected during the five-day event were donated to philanthropic projects.[34]

On April 10, 1934, Wang Yiting and Huang Yanpei (see Chapter 2) founded the Shanghai Beggars Assistance Society (*Shanghai jiugaihui*). In response to another summer of widespread natural disasters, on October 14, 1934, it was deemed necessary to establish a Committee to Collect Donations for Drought Areas (*Shanghai gejie choumu gesheng hanzai yizhenhui*). Lin Sen was elected as the Honorable Chairman, Kong Xiangxi as Chairman, and Wang Yiting as Vice Chairman.

This lifetime of philanthropy was recognized in 1936 when Wang Yiting reached the age of 70. The Shanghai municipal government organized a birthday celebration to honor him for his public service. Beyond publicizing his good works in many of the major newspapers, the government announced plans to build a new road called "Wang Yiting lu" between the orphanage he founded and the Longhua Temple. Because of the war, it was not completed.

As a Lay Buddhist Activist

The 1910s to 1930s were an era of Buddhist revival in China. In the metropolis of Shanghai, the adherents of Buddhism were particularly active. Many Buddhist laymen were well-known intellectuals who had close relations with the political and commercial worlds. Wang Yiting was one of the four most famous Buddhist laymen in Shanghai, one of a group called the "Three *Zhi*s and One *Ting*" (Guan Jiongzhi, Shi Shengzhi, Huang Huanzhi, and Wang Yiting). In 1922, Wang Yiting was elected chairman of the China Buddhist Society (*Zhongguo fojiaohui*). As the chairman, he led the Chinese Buddhist delegation to attend the East Asian Buddhist Meeting in Japan in 1925. He founded many Buddhist societies and turned most of them to charitable work. For example, *Puji shanhui*, established in 1912, offered medicine, clothes, and food to refugees and helped hospital workers to give smallpox vaccinations. He and Wang Junsheng founded *Pushan shanzhuang* in 1914.[35] It gave relief food, clothes, and medicine to disaster areas, provided coffins and offered funeral services for the deceased, and built schools and hospitals for refugees. In the autumn of 1917, Wang Yiting, with Yu Xiaqing, Di Chuqing, and Zhu Baosan, founded *Fojiao cibei yizhenhui* to provide relief to people in the disaster areas of Tianjin and Beijing.

Wang Yiting's activist charity work extended beyond China. Perhaps because of his many business dealings with the Japanese, he was quick to react when on September 1, 1923, Japan suffered the Great Tokyo Earthquake. Wang Yiting heard the news at the first moment because his second son, Wang Shuxian, was doing business in Tokyo at the time. Wang Yiting immediately organized relief work. On September 5, he called a meeting of Shanghai elites and merchants.[36] Two days later, the Chinese Voluntary Relief Association for Japanese Disasters (*Zhongguo xieji rizai yizhen hui*) was established, and Zhu Baosan and Wang Yiting were nominated as chairman and vice chairman.[37] They raised 180,000 yuan of donations that day, then immediately bought emergency goods and rented a ship, *Xinminhao*. On September 12, the first batch of relief goods arrived in Kobe from Shanghai. In October, they organized another two lots of relief goods to send to Japan. As a

Buddhist, Wang Yiting also founded the Buddhist Society for Relieving Japanese Disasters (*Fojiao puji rizai hui*) and organized 49 day Buddhist ceremonies at Emei, Jiuhua, Wutai, and Putuo, four famous mountain temples, for Japanese victims. He also donated a bronze bell to Japan to express the charity of the Chinese. This relief work earned Wang Yiting a great reputation in Japan and also a closer relationship with the Japanese community in Shanghai. In 1931, the Japanese built a tower called Disaster Relief Memorial in Tokyo for the bell. Since then, every year the Japanese have held a ceremony at this place to memorialize the earthquake.

In 1926, *Shijie fojiao jushilin* (World Buddhist Layman's Grove) was established. Wang Yiting was the chairman of this lay Buddhist society, which opened schools, hospitals, and libraries for refugees and poor people and provided coffins when the destitute died. With Guan Jiongzhi, Shi Shengzhi, and Huang Huanzhi, Wang also organized the Shanghai Society to Preserve Buddhism (*Shanghai fojiao weichihui*) in 1928.

In 1929, when a new Chinese Buddhist Society was established, Wang was elected a member of the executive board. Using his personal relationship, Wang Yiting led Di Chuqing, Xie Zhucheng, and several other board members to see Chiang Kai-shek to ask for his support and request the government's approval of the new Society's registration. In 1933, Wang Yiting and Xu Shiying went to see Chiang Kai-shek again, asking Chiang's help to establish West Lake in Hangzhou as a special place for Buddhists engaged in the religious practice of freeing captive fish. Chiang helped them and called the Zhejiang provincial government to take care of the matter.

When the *Shanghai fojiao ciyou yuan* (Shanghai Buddhist Orphanage) was established by the Chinese Buddhist Society in 1933, Wang Yiting was nominated as the chair of the board of directors, while another famous layman, Guan Jiongzhi, became the director. Their mission was to adopt orphans and educate them to become useful members of society. In their first enrollment, they had 37 students. In June 1935, the society opened another elementary school for the public.[38]

One of his contemporaries praised Wang as follows in the publication *Shen Bao*:

In Shanghai there were no charities without Master's involvement. If his name was not found in the trustee's list of any charity, it would not be persuasive enough to call for people's support. By and large, charitable groups were not well financed. Yet, in their attempts [to render aid] often they strove for the utmost. As a result, their income was not able to meet the expenses and they had to turn to Master for help . . . Master used to say that "in charitable activities, people naturally are willing to contribute money." On those occasions when [charitable organizations] could not raise funds, Master would come up with his own paintings and calligraphy and raise huge sums of money for them.[39]

As an Artist

As Ren Yi and Wu Changshi's student and friend and one of the most important Shanghai School painters in the early twentieth century, Wang Yiting also took a leadership role in the Shanghai art world. In the period from the 1910s to the 1930s, he enthusiastically participated in many important activities, especially as an organizer and sponsor for artistic societies. Artistic societies, like other privately organized Shanghai groups, were essential parts of Shanghai's social network, enabling individuals to connect with one another in a variety of ways. Wang Yiting was a major artist of his time, but his contribution to the prominent painting societies to which he belonged was not solely artistic.

Wang Yiting was an outstanding painter. He was proficient in painting figures, birds, flowers, animals, and landscapes and was particularly renowned for his Buddhist figures and his dragons and cranes. His brushwork was executed with a fluent and calligraphic style. In his early years, he studied painting with Xu Xiaocang and Ren Yi. Later, after Wu Changshi eventually settled in Shanghai in 1913, he started to study with Wu. Some of his work shows the gracefulness and richness of Ren Yi, some the simplicity and vigor of Wu Changshi.[40] Yet Wang was also a Buddhist philanthropist and a political and social activist who often used his own paintings to help people. Many of his paintings expressed his strong concern about social problems of the time, as well as his Buddhist beliefs and compassions. The preface Wang Yiting wrote for his album of paintings *The Homeless* typically reflects his anxiety. As a leader of many charitable societies and social organizations, he shared many responsibilities with the local government for the city's water projects at the time. The preface reads:

This is extremely urgent and thus only a temporary solution for the area. If one considers the sources of the northern and southern provinces' yearly calamities and heavy rains, one finds that although natural disasters may be forthcoming, people have not yet exhausted their means of addressing these problems. For a long time no province has researched water projects. If we desire to stop the floods, [we must] first control their sources; that which can end the anxiety of a hundred generations can only be water projects![41]

Another pair of figure paintings, *Fate*, painted in 1922, which feature fluid, free, and spontaneous lines, best represent the characteristics of his figure style.[42] The plebeian subjects are not new, and the theme of solitary street characters may be traced back to the Ming painter Zhou Chen or the Qing Yangzhou painters. Even his contemporary, Chen Hengque, painted an album of street people entitled *Beijing Customs* (*Beijing fengsu*) a few years earlier, in 1914–1915.[43] But the admonitory inscriptions by himself and Wu Changshi on these paintings show his Buddhist beliefs.

As an artist and social celebrity, Wang Yiting also strongly supported art education. He was one of the most important sponsors of art schools in Shanghai. He sat on the board of trustees of many art schools, such as Shanghai Art School (*Shanghai Meizhuan*),[44] Shanghai Women's Aesthetic College (*Shanghai nüzi shenmei xueyuan*), and Changming Art School (*Changming yishu zhuanke xuexiao*). In 1929, when the Ministry of Education organized the first national art exhibition, Wang Yiting, along with Lin Fengmian, Liu Haisu, and Xu Beihong, was asked to join the general administrative committee.

Equally, if not more important, Wang Yiting used his social network to lead fellow artists into the broader Shanghai society. By involving themselves in charitable, social, and even political activities, Shanghai artists increased their consciousness of participation in public service, expanded the social space of their activities, and raised their social visibility. Art societies also played active roles in the public sphere.

The dramatically altered function of painting societies can be traced to the commercial dynamic in Shanghai. Unlike gatherings of painters held in earlier generations, as in eighteenth-century Yangzhou, which were informal and for the purpose of exchanging painting skills and making friendly contacts, painting groups were gradually transformed into something like guild organizations. Few characteristics of the scholar-official ideal remained by the end of the Qing dynasty, as the artists coordinated their sales and commercial activities for mutual benefit. In the early and mid-nineteenth century, there were several active painting clubs in Shanghai to which professional painters belonged.[45] By the second half of the nineteenth century, the commercial function of the societies became more evident. The new societies differed from scholarly gatherings of the past by broadening their membership to all artists, without earlier concerns for social status and learning.[46]

The first organized calligraphy and painting society may have been the Seal-carving, Calligraphy, and Painting Institute of the Tijin Hall of Shanghai (*Haishang tijin guan shuhuahui*). Wang Yiting was always a leading member and became its vice director in 1915. Based on the activities of its first director, Wang Xun (?–1915),[47] it is estimated that the group was founded in the 1890s in the mid-Guangxu era. After 1911, when many retired Qing officials moved to Shanghai, calligraphy and painting were popular and the Haishang Tijinguan became like a club, especially in the evenings. Painters newly arrived in Shanghai would often present themselves to these socially prominent gentlemen in order to establish a price list and to obtain their backing. The group established an important economic function by maintaining a price list for each member and serving as an agent for painting and calligraphy sales. It also provided a place where members might study and trade old paintings and antiques. It is said that more than 100 painters, calligraphers, and seal carvers joined the group. Funding for the society was said to have come from the wealthy official and businessman Sheng Xuanhuai. After Wang Xun died in 1915, he was succeeded as director by Wu Changshi, and Ha Shaofu and Wang Yiting became vice directors of the group.

If cultural attainment was one means of entering Shanghai's social elite, charitable giving was the best demonstration of having arrived at society's peak. Moreover, as Shanghai's social elite sought to change society, they sought to do so through charitable work. As described earlier, Wang Yiting and other elites led many specific disaster relief efforts and charitable organizations. In 1909, Wang Yiting helped to found the Yu Garden Calligraphy and Painting Charitable Society (*Yuyuan Shuhua Shanhui*), an important Shanghai art society that expressly brought together the seemingly different worlds of charity and art. Headquartered at the Deyuelou of the Yu Garden in Shanghai, this artistic and literary group soon became a quasi-commercial cooperative organization with a formal written charter, which reads:

> In Shanghai there are many societies, perhaps more than anywhere in China. We have seen, among them, many philanthropists use their wealth and generosity to aid the needy and help the poor and many notables promote *fengya* [cultural pursuits] and preserve the national essence. We painters, however, only tend to our brushes and ink, and conscientiously cultivate the fields of our inkstones. We are not able to help these notables to reform society; we also

are not able to help support the poor people. We live in the same city, so we feel shame. Although big buildings and overcoats can help people avoid wind and rain, fine dust and drops of dew can also help to supplement the mountains and sea. Although the degree of power differs, they are all magnanimous. This is a responsibility we should not decline to shoulder. That is why we have gathered like-minded colleagues to establish this Calligraphy and Painting Charitable Society and have rented the second floor of the Deyuelou at Yuyuan as our headquarters. After painting and writing, we can use the place to discuss ancient and modern affairs, and also to educate the younger generation. The society has established a price list for members that we attach as an appendix to our charter. Half the income from sales goes to the society and is deposited in *qianzhuang* [Chinese-style banks] to earn interest. If we want to do some charitable work, we will discuss how to use this money and demonstrate our charitable intent . . .[48]

The name of the group, Calligraphy and Painting Charitable Society, was selected because half the price of work sold was returned to the artists; the other half was invested and the interest used for charitable purposes. The cause to which the money would be contributed was decided by a meeting of the group. In winter they usually bought rice and in summer purchased medicine. They donated to areas of Gansu, Zhejiang, Shandong, and Henan that suffered from floods or droughts.[49] In a meeting held on March 3, 1909, Gao Yong was selected director. He, however, modestly declined and recommended Qian Huian for the position. Other directors included Yang Baoguang, Ma Ruixi, Shen Xinhai, Wang Yiting, and Wang Xun. The society's manifesto explicitly called upon artists to assist Shanghai's elite to reform society, preserve the national essence, help the poor, and promote cultural pursuits, suggesting that artists have the capability to do good works in society as well as in art.

Many important Shanghai painters participated throughout their lives in the activities of these art societies and, in the twentieth century, in their group exhibitions. As one of the founders of the Yu Garden Charitable Society, and with his special position in Shanghai society, Wang Yiting consistently encouraged artists to participate in public service and philanthropic works. His connections to Shanghai's economic elite, along with his willingness to call upon the generosity of both artists and his business friends, guaranteed philanthropic buyers for paintings sold at charitable exhibitions.

One letter written by Wang Yiting to Ha Shaofu, another active member of the charitable society, showed that Wang Yiting also recruited Wu Changshi to participate in these activities:

Thank you very much for displaying the paintings and calligraphy in recent days. I still have more than twenty pieces at my place, which include Fouweng's [Wu Changshi's] painting. I will ask people to send them to you.[50]

A letter to Wang Yiting by famous calligrapher Zeng Xi also indicated Wang's effort to invite Zeng to participate in the charitable society's activity.[51]

Wang Yiting was also the founder or cofounder of the Shanghai Calligraphy and Painting Research Society (*Shanghai shuhua yanjiuhui*, established in 1910), the Shanghai Chinese Calligraphy and Painting Preservation Society (*Shanghai Zhongguo shuhua baocunhui*),[52] the Qingyuan Art Society (*Qingyuan yishe*, 1929), the Guanhai Art Club (*Guanhai tanyishe*, 1930), and the Li Society (*Lishe*, 1936). He was also a board member of many painting societies, such as the very important Heavenly Horse Society (*Tianmahui*, 1919), the Shanghai Calligraphy and Painting Society (*Shanghai shuhuahui*, 1922), the Shanghai Calligraphy and Painting Alliance (*Haishang shuhua lianhehui*),[53] the Bee Painting Society (*Mifeng huahui*),[54] and the Chinese Painting Society (*Zhongguo huahui*);[55] he was a major member of the Yiyuan Painting Group (*Yiyuan huaji*, 1895), the Suyue Painting Society (*Suyue huashe*),[56] the Yiyuan Painting Research Center (*Yiyuan huihua yanjiusuo*, 1928), the Yifeng Society (*Yifengshe*, 1933), and other art societies.

In these societies, with his financial strength and high social status, Wang Yiting played a key role in organizing numerous exhibitions for international exchange, charitable works, and patriotic activities.[57] He was also an important patron for many artists and art societies whenever they needed support.

As with relief efforts, Wang's artistic reach and influence extended to Japan. With his help, the Sino-Japanese Art Society (*Zhong-Ri meishu xiehui*) was founded in 1922. From 1922 to 1931, Wang Yiting organized five joint exhibitions in Shanghai, Nagasaki, and Tokyo. In 1930, he founded the Sino-Japanese Art Colleagues Association (*Zhong-Ri yishu tongzhihui*).[58] He led several groups of Chinese artists to visit Japan and participate in the exhibitions.[59]

He was also the most important promoter of his teacher and friend Wu Changshi's art in Japan. With his networks in the Japanese community of Shanghai, as well as in Japan, Wang Yiting introduced many Japanese scholars, artists, and businessmen to Wu Changshi and organized numerous exhibitions for him in both Shanghai and Japan. For example, in 1914, Wu Changshi held an exhibition facilitated by Wang at Rokusanen, a Japanese garden restaurant located in the

Japanese-dominated part of Shanghai's international concession. The owner, Shiraishi Rokusaburo, later became an enthusiastic promoter of Wu's art. Many of Wang's Japanese friends also helped to organize Wu Changshi's exhibitions in Tokyo, Osaka, and Nagasaki, spreading Wu's name in Japan.[60]

Although he maintained close personal friendships with many Japanese, when the Sino-Japanese War broke out in 1931 and the Japanese army invaded the northeastern provinces of China, Wang Yiting resigned all his positions in Japanese companies, ceased his work as a comprador, and joined the National Salvation Movement (see Chapter 6). He organized painters to donate paintings in a series of fund-raising exhibitions to support the volunteer army and the hundreds of thousands of refugees fleeing the Japanese annexation of Manchuria. An All-China Artists Society to Support the Northeast Volunteers was established on December 16, 1932, with Wang Yiting as chairman. On January 1, 1933, the *Lake Society Monthly* (*Hushe yuekan*) published an announcement:

> The famous Shanghai painter, Mr. Wang Yiting, and others are organizing a Painting and Calligraphy Exhibition to Support the Northeast Volunteers, in order to collect donations from the art world. The organizing office is in the Chinese Federation of Salvation Societies, Zhongshe, Room 4, 150 Weihaiwei Road, the British Concession, Shanghai. We are now collecting art works. We welcome artists' donations.[61]

On February 5 of the same year, Wang Yiting, along with He Xiangning, Wang Jiyuan, Zhang Shanzhi, Zhang Daqian, Huang Binhong, Pang Xunqin, and Chen Xiaodie, donated more than 40 paintings and held an exhibition, "Modern Masters' Small Ink Painting Show," on Nanjing Road. The money they collected was all donated to the refugees from the northeastern provinces.

Conclusion

How could such a figure as Wang Yiting appear? The nature of his activities may have been unique to his period, made possible by the political power vacuum in the late Qing and early Republican era. The power vacuum had two principal causes, the weakness of the Qing regime, which led it to launch the local self-government movement and eventually led to the collapse of the court itself, and the ongoing warlord battles of the early Republican era. Shanghai's Chinese territory thus had no stable city government, and in this politically chaotic situation, different *shetuan* or societies emerged. The phenomenon began with the local autonomy movement, but warlordism continued to provide a stage for the action of such groups. When authority was formally loosened in response to the actual Qing loss of control, *shetuan* took over many governmental functions, such as public works. Over the course of the late Qing and early Republican periods, Shanghai developed in a unique way as a commercial metropolis, and the newly wealthy merchants came to enjoy a social status previously monopolized by those with Confucian degrees. The sphere of action opened up by the local autonomy movement in Shanghai brought businessmen like Wang Yiting, gangsters like Du Yuesheng (see Chapter 4), and former Confucian officials like Li Pingshu together for quasi-governmental communal action. In the context of the treaty-port environment, foreign models were emulated for Chinese development, particularly in forming a new social structure and in developing public works. Businessmen came to play a larger role in public service, but this involvement gradually shifted to a more political role, as the commercial societies became prototypes for local government, or in a sense functioned as shadow governments.

Finally, the personal character of Wang Yiting, the man, played a large role in establishing and maintaining certain social networks. He was modest and kind, and by all accounts he must also have been a very friendly person, one able to effectively reach people in a range of social and professional worlds. His character, then, helped to establish his social networks and further strengthen his social status, thus increasing his influence in a range of different fields.

By 1927, Wang Yiting had been retired from politics for more than 15 years, when the Northern Expedition Troops crushed the Communist-led workers' uprising in Shanghai and established a Nationalist government in Shanghai. The Nationalists then called upon Wang Yiting to assume the chairmanship of the Shanghai Advisory Council. Although it proved an empty and powerless title, this episode shows that the Nationalist Party (KMT) sought to use Wang Yiting's reputation to legitimize itself. One undeniable connection to which this can be attributed is the early friendship between Chiang Kai-shek and the Wang family.

Similarly, in 1937, after the Sino-Japanese War had expanded to most parts of China, a rumor began circulating that the Japanese wanted Wang to serve as mayor of a Shanghai puppet government.[62] Although Wang Yiting fled to Hong Kong to avoid this situation, and did not survive to resolve it, it demonstrates that the invading Japanese also hoped to use his social networks to control Shanghai. Upon Wang's death in 1938, Chiang Kai-shek sent a boldly brushed couplet, which was hung in the center of the funeral hall. It explicitly praised Wang Yiting's stubborn refusal to cooperate with the Japanese, despite the physical frailty and illness that ultimately took his life. Chiang wrote:

> In the midst of buffeting wind and rain, you still stood straight and firm.
>
> After the country is returned to order and peace, I will return to mourn you again.[63]

Wang Yiting's story seems to combine a Confucian model of meritocracy with a Horatio Alger story of rags to riches. Indeed, his social networks and the times in which he lived exemplify just such a divide between worldview and practical reality, one that he was remarkably able to bridge in his own career and social activities. Educated and given an opportunity to rise from his modest beginnings through the kindness of a powerful man who recognized his talent and character, his story begins like that of a Ming dynasty scholar-artist—such as Dong Qichang, whose stellar performance on the civil service examinations ultimately led to an appointment as tutor to the heir apparent.[64] As such, it is a case of success through merit that personifies the Confucian ideal and, though rarely acknowledged as such, was part of the faith that held the system together.

Wang Yiting's story, including his many good works, could be the beginning of a tale about a benevolent Confucian in a premodern Chinese social network. However, the circumstances of Wang Yiting's life and times, both geographically and chronologically, provided a much larger stage for his activities and produced a more significant impact on the many social groups with which he associated. While this chapter is intended as a contribution to our collective thinking about social networks, it is hard to avoid wondering what would have happened if this particular individual had not possessed the talent, education, and personal qualities he had. He was both a product of an unusual time and, equally important, a powerful architect of the new Shanghai in which he lived.

CHAPTER 4

Du Yuesheng, the French Concession, and Social Networks in Shanghai

BRIAN G. MARTIN

THE GREEN GANG was ubiquitous in Republican Shanghai. Its influence touched the lives of nearly everyone in the city: marginalized beggars, industrial workers, office clerks, and captains of commerce and industry. Estimation of its power formed a regular part of the calculations of Chinese political parties and foreign authorities.

The Green Gang's rise was no accident.[1] It reflected the peculiar economic and structural opportunities offered by Shanghai in the first two decades of the twentieth century. Opium and later narcotics smuggling provided both the financial resources and the initial contacts with Chinese business elite that facilitated the growth of the French Concession Green Gang.

The political and social turmoil that came in the wake of the 1911 Revolution and the collapse of the traditional political order created opportunities for previously marginalized groups, such as secret societies, to move to political center stage. At the same time, the peculiar colonial setting of Shanghai with political and administrative authority divided among three separate sovereignties—the Chinese city, the International Settlement, and the French Concession—provided an ideal environment for the Green Gang to pursue its illicit activities and for its leaders to emerge as local political fixers.

The emergence of the French Concession Green Gang to a position of preeminence among the gangs of Shanghai also required strong and ambitious leaders who could make the most of these opportunities. Huang Jinrong laid the foundations for its rise, but it was Du Yuesheng, in the 1920s and 1930s, who refashioned the French Concession

Green Gang into an instrument for the promotion of his economic, political, and social power in Shanghai. There were three elements in this transformation: forging closer links with the new Nationalist Government and becoming an important element in its corporatist structure in Shanghai; using the profits from opium and narcotics to finance the expansion of Du's interest in the world of legitimate business; and developing his own personal organization to bring together his various legitimate interests. In this way, Du transformed the Green Gang's relations with the local Chinese business and political elites, while at the same time transcending his gangster origins to become a respected and significant political player in Shanghai. As a result, by the mid-1930s, his organization operated at a fairly high level, ensuring a degree of predictability and a form of order in a city where political authority was diffused among foreign powers and a weak Chinese state.

In setting out its argument, this chapter deals first with the gangster origins of the Green Gang and the opportunities provided by the political and social developments in Shanghai in the first three decades of the twentieth century that allowed it to prosper. The chapter will then discuss how its leaders, particularly Du Yuesheng, sought to legitimize their activities and to integrate their gangster systems with the new political and economic structures developed by the Guomindang state. This process culminated in the creation by Du of an extensive personal organization, the *Heng She*, which brought together his various political, financial, and social interests in Shanghai. This was a first for a Green Gang leader and was quickly imitated by others.

Background: The Gangster Origins of the Green Gang and Its Links with the Shanghai Polity

From its inception the Green Gang had a relationship with the Chinese commercial world. Its progenitors in the eighteenth and nineteenth centuries among the sailors of the Grand Canal grain fleets cooperated with local Jiangnan merchants in smuggling goods on their own accounts on the grain boats. With the demise of the Grand Canal grain route in the mid-nineteenth century, some of these ex-sailors turned to salt smuggling in the Jiangbei. They formed business associations with those salt merchants who sought to increase their profits by circumventing the official state monopoly on salt.[2]

By the turn of the nineteenth and twentieth centuries, the various groups of the Green Gang that operated in Shanghai interacted with the broader society mainly through criminal structures. Armed robbery was a constant hazard for the businesses and property of the Chinese bourgeoisie, whose members lived in fear of ruthless kidnapping gangs that operated in the Shanghai region. Extortion and intimidation were rife. These were favorite pursuits of Shanghai's various beggar gangs, each with its own "territory." They would levy a protection fee on local shopkeepers and those who refused to pay would find beggars crowding the doorways of their shops, intimidating their customers and destroying their businesses.[3]

The Green Gang also engaged in certain enterprises that could be easily run as extortion rackets. Huang Jinrong's common-law wife, for example, controlled the night-soil monopoly in the French Concession. Her customers queried her charges at their peril! Building on their historic links with the former grain fleet sailors, Green Gang bosses controlled the stevedores on the Shanghai wharves as well the sailors who worked for the coastal and inland shipping companies, such as the China Merchants' Steam Navigation Company. According to a Shanghai adage: "Good men do not eat dock rice. If you want to eat dock rice then you must submit to an 'old man' (*laotou*, that is, a gangster boss)."[4] So the proprietors of Shanghai's major stevedoring companies, such as Liu Hongsheng, who owned the China Docks Company (*Zhonghua Matou Gongsi*), considered it essential to the smooth running of their businesses to reach mutually beneficial accommodations with local Green Gang bosses.

Political developments also served to strengthen the role of Green Gang bosses in Shanghai society. The most significant event in this regard was the 1911 Revolution and its aftermath. Elements of the local Green Gang participated in all the upheavals of the revolutionary period in Shanghai: the 1911 Revolution itself, the Second Revolution of 1913, and the movement against Yuan Shikai in 1916. The Tongmenghui considered the various Chinese secret societies as useful allies in fomenting anti-Qing rebellions and, as a result, these societies gained a certain newfound legitimacy in the Republican era. In Shanghai, Green Gang groups were organized into the Mutual Progress Association of the Chinese Republic (*Zhonghua Minguo Gongjin Hui*) and formed an important element of the power base of the revolutionary military governor, Chen Qimei. Chen, himself, became a member of the Green Gang to bind its local leaders even more tightly to his political cause.[5] The period of the 1911 Revolution, therefore, witnessed the first tentative cooperation between the Green Gang and the revolutionary parties of the new Republic.

The colonial structures of the Shanghai foreign settlements also enabled the Green Gang bosses to widen their political connections and so increase their influence over the Chinese population of the settlements. Preoccupied with ensuring control over their burgeoning Chinese populations, the settlement authorities adopted the strategy of co-opting certain gang bosses into their Chinese detective squads. These authorities entered into an implicit bargain with their selected gang bosses: in return for helping to maintain order among the settlements' Chinese populations, the authorities would turn a blind eye to the illicit activities of these gang bosses/detective chiefs. This phenomenon was greatly enhanced by the outbreak of the First World War when large numbers of European police personnel left Shanghai to volunteer for war service, thus providing unexpected career opportunities for Chinese members of the police forces. Beginning in the mid-1910s, selected gang bosses became, in effect, "compradors of violence," hired to enforce the coercive authority of the colonial state by "Chinese methods" over the Chinese residents of the settlements. As the British Consul General observed of the situation in the French Concession in 1930, the Green Gang bosses were "extremely useful intermediaries in dealing, by Chinese methods, with any Chinese troubles which arise, whether political . . . , industrial . . . , or even [those affecting] peace and good order. They can continue their opium dealings just so long as the concession benefits—very materially—and is spared much of the trouble to which foreign authorities in China are so often heirs."[6]

A prime example of the gang boss-cum-detective chief was Huang Jinrong, the chief of the Chinese detective squad of the French Concession. He successfully used his official position to further his own criminal interests, although he ensured deniability by running his illicit businesses through his common-law wife, Miss Gui, or trusted henchmen, such as Du Yuesheng. Huang's official position gave him enormous influence among the Chinese of the concession, who sought out his good offices when dealing with the French authorities.[7] Huang was not unique. Even though this situation was less pronounced in the International Settlement, it also had its quota of Chinese police officers who doubled as gang bosses. A notable example in the 1930s was Lu Liankui (1889–1938). Known to his British associates as "Lolly Lo" because of his girth, he had a meteoric rise in the Shanghai Municipal Police (SMP) Chinese detective squad from the late 1920s through the 1930s, reaching the rank of Superintendent by 1937. In the course of his rise through the ranks, Lolly Lo eventually received over

100 commendations and two Shanghai Municipal Council medals for his police work. Lu was also a major Green Gang boss, being a disciple of Ji Yunqing, one of the eight leaders of the Big Eight Mob that operated in the International Settlement through the early 1920s—one Japanese source, indeed, alleged that Lu's rise in the SMP was due to the influence of Du Yuesheng.[8] Throughout the 1920s and 1930s, many Chinese members of the SMP were accused of colluding with gangsters: John Pal, a former Shanghai journalist, observed that "almost every Chinese detective on the [SMP] force had a criminal record", and a former British member of the SMP noted that in the 1930s corruption was widespread in the SMP's Chinese detective branch, especially concerning contraband opium.[9]

As for Huang Jinrong, one of his most important illicit activities was involvement in opium trafficking. In addition to providing most of the financial resources for the French Concession Green Gang, opium was also the means by which Huang and his colleagues Du Yuesheng and Zhang Xiaolin deepened their relations with the Cantonese (Chaozhou) opium merchants, local warlords, and corrupt members of the French administration. By the mid-1920s, the three French Concession Green Gang leaders had set up their own distribution company, the Three Prosperities Company (*Sanxin Gongsi*), worked closely with the Chaozhou opium merchants, and established profitable relations with a succession of local warlord regimes, including local representatives of the Anfu Clique and Sun Chuanfang. They also entered into a mutually beneficial corrupt compact with key members of the French administration, including the chief of police, Captain E. Fiori, and the Concession's chief administrative officer, M. Verdier, who agreed to look the other way in return for sizeable monthly payments.[10] These arrangements distinguished the French Concession Green Gang from other Green Gang groups in Shanghai and gave it a direct interest in supporting the prevailing political arrangements in the city.[11]

The Search for Legitimacy and Du's Transformation of the Green Gang

As their power and influence grew in the mid-1920s, the three Green Gang bosses sought ways to legitimize themselves in the eyes of the Shanghai population. An important development in this regard was their success in gaining control of the organization that looked after

Shanghai's tutelary deity. In November 1924, they took over the association that handled the affairs of Shanghai's City God Temple (*Yimiao Dongshihui*). The temple's fortunes had declined over the previous decade, especially after a couple of serious fires in the early 1920s. After the three gang bosses gained control, they spent considerable sums in refurbishing the temple and in bringing new life to the temple environs. Since many small businesses in the Chinese City were established around the City God's Temple, and felt the impact of the temple's decline, the gang bosses' refurbishment program also strengthened their links, for good and ill, with these small business interests.[12]

Philanthropic Activities

Another means by which the French Concession Green Gang bosses tried to gain popular legitimacy was by engaging in philanthropic activities. Acts of charity were a key element in popular Buddhism and an important means by which local notables gained standing with and acceptance by the populace. (For the importance of philanthropy and the role of the *tongxianghui*, see Chapter 8 of this volume.) Gang bosses, such as Huang Jinrong and Du Yuesheng, wanted desperately to achieve popular acceptance as local notables and saw philanthropy as a key means of doing so. At the same time, their criminal connections were an important means in preparing the ground for such a role. Both Huang and Du parlayed their links to armed robbers and kidnapping gangs into influential roles with Shanghai's bourgeoisie. They acted as mediators, or brokers, between these gangs and their victims, with family members or businessmen approaching Huang or Du to negotiate the return of their relatives or property. This also applied to foreign residents. In one instance, Huang Jinrong used his Green Gang connections to obtain the release of the wife of a senior French official who had been kidnapped by bandits in the Lake Tai region. And Huang was also part of the negotiating team that sought the release of those foreigners kidnapped from the Shanghai-Beijing Blue Express by the Shandong bandit and Green Gang leader Sun Meiyao in 1923.[13] The high point in the institutionalization of this role was reached when Du became a member of the board of directors of the Anti-Kidnapping Society in 1935.[14]

With the outbreak of the Jiangsu-Zhejiang War in 1924 a large number of refugees fled to the foreign areas of Shanghai, and the three gang bosses contributed to the relief efforts.[15] Du Yuesheng engaged in similar refugee relief efforts during the brief Sino-Japanese conflict in Shanghai in early 1932, and he also contributed funds for the relief of victims of the devastating Yangtze floods in Central China in 1931 (see Chapter 3 on social networks). Extremely conscious of his own lack of education, Du set up and funded the Zhenshi Middle School in the 1930s, which provided a free education for boys from poor families and was run by one of his cronies, the right-wing Guomindang politician Chen Qun. Quite a number of boys graduated from this school and went on to have successful careers in Shanghai. Beholden to Du for their start in life, the Zhenshi Middle School graduates formed another important strand in his network of influence in Shanghai.[16]

Du was regularly described as a "great philanthropist," and philanthropic activities became institutionalized within the new Guomindang state when Du Yuesheng was appointed chairman of the Chinese Red Cross Society. In 1928, for example, the Shanghai and Wusong Benevolent Institution presented Du with a silver medal "for his deep interest in philanthropic work".[17]

As a native of Gaoqiao in Pudong, Du also sought to help the people of his native district, which was then a rural backwater. Among other good works, he established the Gaoqiao Rural Progress Association (*Gaoqiao Nongcun Gaijinhui*) in 1934, which engaged in a number of reconstruction projects, including tree planting, irrigation, and the provision of a credit society and a primary school.[18]

Such philanthropy, however, had its limits and was carefully calculated for its political effect. Other philanthropic organizations, such as the Anti-Kidnapping Society and the Door of Hope, sought to provide protection to those people who fell victim to the more predatory activities of the Green Gang system (see Chapter 8).

Du Yuesheng and the Guomindang State

The accommodation of the French Concession Green Gang, on the initiative of Du Yuesheng, with the new Chinese state power of the Guomindang was fundamental to the expansion of its power and influence. The key event was its involvement in Chiang Kai-shek's purge of his erstwhile communist allies in April 1927, which led eventually to Chiang's incorporation of Du's gangster cohorts into his system of power in Shanghai. This was underscored by the assistance that Du and his colleagues gave the Chinese forces during the Sino-Japanese conflict of early 1932. During the 1930s, Du developed close relations with the Guomindang's CC Clique that controlled the Shanghai municipal Government and was the principal player in the city's politics. This became Du's most important political relationship, and over time his political fortunes became inextricably entangled with those of the CC Clique (see Chapter 7).[19]

Organized labor was an important element in the politics of Shanghai, and Du played a key role in the Guomindang's system of labor control. He built on his successes in establishing his control over the French Tramways Union (1928–1932), in the process eradicating communist influence in the union, and in recruiting into his Green Gang system two leading Guomindang trade unionists, Lu Jingshi and Zhu Xuefan. Both Lu and Zhu were senior officials of the Shanghai Postal Workers' Union who used Du's assistance to establish their authority in the union and were instrumental in reorganizing the city's peak trade union organization, the Shanghai General Labor Union. Zhu later went on to become China's representative at the International Labour Organization in Geneva, and Lu became Du's most trusted lieutenant and his conduit to the CC Clique. Du's influence in labor circles reinforced his value to the Guomindang who came to regard him as its "fixer" in Shanghai. And his power over the official trade unions increased his influence with Shanghai's Chinese industrialists, who regularly solicited his services to mediate contentious labor disputes in the 1930s.[20]

Even Du's opium interests became entwined with the institutions of the Guomindang state. When the Guomindang government introduced its phased suppression of opium over a six-year period in 1934, Du was appointed one of the three heads of the Shanghai Municipal Opium Suppression Committee (*Shanghai Shi Jinyan Weiyuanhui*). Du, therefore, was able to continue his operations quite openly within the framework of phased suppression, which was essentially a de facto monopoly.[21]

By the mid-1930s, therefore, Du derived much of his influence in Shanghai from his association with the Guomindang's state-building efforts and, in particular, from his personal relationship with Chiang Kai-shek. He behaved, indeed, like a politician. In mid-1936, for example, he initiated a fund-raising campaign to purchase military aircraft for presentation to Chiang on the latter's fiftieth birthday.[22] When Chiang's government faced serious challenges from those advocating a stronger stand against Japan, Du was chief among those to whom it turned for help. In December 1935, during the student demonstrations calling for immediate resistance to Japan, the Shanghai municipal government sought Du's advice, and he gave his support to Mayor Wu Tiecheng's decision to forbid Shanghai students from going to Nanjing to petition the government. Another example was the arrest of the National Salvation Association's "seven gentlemen" in November 1936. During their incarceration Du helped to break the impasse in discussions between the seven and the Guomindang government by visiting them with letters from Chiang Kai-shek and Guomindang Secretary General Ye Chucang.[23] (For more on the politics of the National Salvation Movement, see Chapter 6.) When the Nanjing government faced one of its gravest crises with Chiang Kai-shek's arrest by Zhang Xueliang in Xi'an in December 1936, Du sent Zhang an urgent telegram offering to go himself to Xi'an as a hostage in return for Chiang's release.[24] Du's act of loyalty contrasted sharply with the actions of some senior members of the government at the time.

Du Yuesheng and Shanghai Business Interests

Du's efforts to gain respectability as a local notable through his philanthropic activities were motivated in part by his desire to penetrate Shanghai's legitimate business world after 1927. Using the proceeds from opium and gambling operations, in 1929, Du set up a modern-style bank, the Zhonghui Bank, which became the center of his business operations. In establishing the bank, Du used his contacts in the financial world. Both Xu Maotang, the comprador of the P&O Banking Corporation, and Zhu Rushan, the Chinese manager of the Union Mobiliére Societé Française de Banque et de Placement, were indebted to Du for past favors and reluctantly agreed to provide an important part of the Zhonghui Bank's initial capitalization. In the course of the 1930s, Du acquired an interest in a number of other modern-style banks, including the Minfu Union Commercial Bank (*Minfu Shangye Chuxu Yinhang*), the China Investment Bank (*Guoxin Yinhang*), the Pudong Commercial Bank (*Pudong Shangye Chuxu Yinhang*), and the Bank of Asia (*Yazhou Yinhang*).[25]

Du also used his political contacts to expand his interests in Shanghai's modern banking sector. In 1935, he played an important role in the Guomindang Government's takeover of the three major Chinese banks: Bank of China, the Central Bank of China, and the Bank of Communications. In this operation Du's connections in the Shanghai financial world and his ability to intimidate opponents proved very useful to the

Minister of Finance, Kong Xiangxi, in effecting the takeover. According to an SMP Special Branch report, Kong requested that Du negotiate with the shareholders of the Bank of China and the Bank of Communications because these "shareholders were on friendly terms with Mr. Tu [Mr. Du], in whom they had much confidence . . .".[26]

In a parallel government takeover of three leading commercial banks, Du gained effective control of one of these, the venerable Commercial Bank of China (*Zhonghua Tongshang Yinhang*).[27] The unseating of the Commercial Bank's managing director, Fu Xiao'an, a prominent member of the Zhejiang financial clique who had had difficult relations with Chiang Kai-shek's government after he became one of its principal targets in 1927 because of his close association with the regime of the warlord Sun Chuanfang, revealed the vulnerability of even the most powerful financiers who lacked strong political connections. It also underscored the pivotal role Du had acquired in mediating the worlds of politics and high finance.

As part of this mediation Du also put himself forward as a "political" representative of Shanghai's business interests with the national and local authorities. He had already developed this role in the French Concession when he and his two confreres, Huang Jinrong and Zhang Xiaolin, helped set up the French Concession Chinese Ratepayers' Association (*Fazujie Nashui Huaren Hui*) in January 1927. Through their control of this body, the three Green Gang bosses negotiated rates issues directly with the French authorities and argued its alleged "representative" nature to gain seats for Du and Zhang on the French Concession's Provisional Commission (which had replaced the former Council in 1927). Through his astute use of the Chinese Ratepayers' Association, Du was able to increase his political influence in the French Concession and to gain effective control over the Chinese representatives on the Provisional Commission by 1930 to 1931.[28]

The political and military crisis provoked by the Sino-Japanese conflict of early 1932 provided Du with a further opportunity to represent the political interests of the Shanghai bourgeois elite. He played a prominent role in the activities of the Shanghai Citizens' Maintenance Association (*Shanghai Shimin Difang Weichihui*), which was set up during the crisis by the Shanghai bourgeoisie to deal with numerous administrative, financial, and troop support issues, and with its successor the Shanghai Civic Association (*Shanghai Shi Difang Xiehui*, or SCA). After the 1934 assassination of the SCA's first chairman, Shi Liangcai, Du took over as chairman and worked to promote cooperation between the Shanghai bourgeoisie and the Guomindang government. In 1936 and 1937, he involved the SCA in the government's efforts to organize elections for the proposed National People's Congress (*Guomin Dahui*) and the concomitant citizenship registration campaign.

By 1936, Du also had succeeded in gaining effective control of the Shanghai Chamber of Commerce. In a convoluted political struggle, Du ensured that his business crony Wang Xiaolai gained the chairmanship of the Chamber, and Du, himself, emerged as a member of the Chamber's Standing Committee. By the outbreak of the Sino-Japanese War, therefore, Du was already, in effect, a major Shanghai politician whom both the national and municipal governments consulted regularly as the spokesman for the interests of Shanghai's capitalists. At the same time, however, Du continued to rely on gangster techniques when necessary to further his business interests. He and his colleague Zhang Xiaolin used carefully orchestrated intimidation to gain seats on the board of directors of the Shanghai Cotton Goods Exchange (*Shanghai Huashang Shabu Jiaoyisuo*) in 1930 and so obtain a share of the exchange's lucrative business.

Again, in 1932 to 1933, part of Du's tactics for seizing control of the Da Da Steam Navigation Company (*Da Da Lunchuan Gongsi*) was the sustained intimidation of its board of directors. Among other measures, he ordered his Green Gang followers to create a fracas on the company's Shanghai dock to ensure its closure by the police, thus placing unacceptable financial costs on the company.[29] Du's persuasive combination of gangster coercion and political influence made him irresistible to Shanghai's Chinese business elite. They therefore vied with one another to invite him to join their boards of directors.

The opening in early 1936 of Du's new art deco premises for the Pudong Native Place Association (*Pudong Tongxianghui*) on the Avenue Edward VII symbolized the preeminence Du had achieved in Shanghai's leading economic and political circles. The opening ceremony was extremely grand and attended by leading Shanghai capitalists such as Yu Xiaqing, Wang Xiaolai, and Zhang Jia'ao; senior figures in the Guomindang and Nationalist government like Kong Xiangxi, Lin Sen, and Sun Ke; as well as local Shanghai politicians such as Pan Gongzhan and Mayor Wu Tiecheng. Du had established the Pudong Native Place Association in January 1932 to look after the interests of Pudong natives resident in Shanghai. Du's association with Pudong gave "face" to this backward district in urban Shanghai and, by 1935, the Association had

18,000 members. Du himself derived significant standing in Shanghai's elite circles as the patron of one of the largest native place associations in Shanghai.[30] (For further detail on the Pudong Native Place Association, see Chapter 8.)

Heng She: Du Yuesheng's Personal Organization

In November 1932, on the advice of his key lieutenant, Lu Jingshi, Du set up his Perseverance Society (*Heng She*) as a means of bringing together his various Shanghai interests. To achieve this, Lu—in conjunction with Tang Shichang, the editor of Shanghai's leading Chinese language newspaper, *Shen Bao*—deliberately structured the Perseverance Society as a public "social organization (*shetuan*)," which was legally recognized by the Guomindang state.[31] Its purpose was to promote Du's interests with the local Chinese political, economic, and social establishment. And so its membership was restricted to politicians, government and military officials, industrialists, financiers, and professionals. Stressing the precept of emphasizing quality rather than quantity, membership was restricted to capitalists who were at least directors or chairmen of enterprises, to bureaucrats of section chief (*kezhang*) and above, and to military officers of the rank of major (*shaoxiao*) and above.[32] Du intended to keep the Society distinct from his regular Green Gang organization, and so the majority of his gangster coterie was excluded from membership. Although Perseverance Society members underwent a membership ceremony similar to that of a secret society and they acknowledged Du as their "master," they were not inducted into the Green Gang, and Du did not instruct them in the secret language of the Green Gang.[33]

The Perseverance Society, therefore, provided an informal forum where those local capitalists and politicians who were linked to Du could come together to discuss important local issues, seal business deals, and settle disputes. According to the Society's regulations, its purpose was to "maintain friendly contacts and to provide mutual support" among members.[34] Its clublike atmosphere provided a relaxed environment that allowed its members to discuss business and politics and to finalize various deals. This was remarked on by Zhang Songjiao, the manager of the Ningbo Commercial and Savings Bank and member of the Society's executive committee, in a speech he made to the Society's Third Congress in 1936: "The Perseverance Society as an organization, when glimpsed at, appears to be no more than a place where men of affairs can relax at their leisure. In reality it is not so. When one is engaged in major plans in the world of politics and business a common practice is to complete the matter over tea or drinks; if the matter is not pressing it is easier to deal with it over a chat, and this is frequently what leisure time is used for."[35]

Du, himself, of course, also used the Perseverance Society as a means by which he kept his finger on the pulse of the Shanghai elite and through which he could informally press his own views and influence decisions. As discussed next, the Perseverance Society was a personal organization and it did not take any formal positions on the issues of the day. Nevertheless, by canvassing the views of its members, Du kept himself well informed of the political currents circulating among the local elite. This allowed him to act effectively on behalf of Chiang Kai-shek when called upon to do so, as discussed in the previous section.

Although relatively small in numbers, the Society experienced a remarkable expansion in the years immediately before the outbreak of the Sino-Japanese War. Between 1933 and 1937, membership increased fourfold, from 130 to 564 members. Recruitment efforts increased in the late 1930s as evidenced by the 91 new members admitted to the Perseverance Society in the six-month period from November 1936 to April 1937, according to figures provided in the Society's journal, the *Heng She Yuekan*.[36] The three main categories were businessmen and industrialists (54%), followed by politicians and government officials (24%), and then professionals (i.e., lawyers, journalists, medical practitioners, and educators, 13%). The balance was made up of small numbers of trade union officials (6%) and military officers (3%). Over 80 percent of these members lived and worked in Shanghai.[37]

Leading Shanghai notables, such as Yu Xiaqing, Wang Yiting, and Huang Yanpei, had well-developed, close personal connections with Du, but they were not members of the Perseverance Society. Their preexisting standing in Shanghai society precluded their membership in Du's personal organization. The capitalist members of the Society were of a secondary order, though still important figures in Shanghai's financial and industrial worlds. They included Xu Maotang, the comprador of the P&O Bank; Hong Yanbin, head of the Shipping Section of the China Merchants' Steam Navigation Company; Zhang Songjiao, manager of the Ningbo Commercial and Savings Bank; Cai Futang, compradore and proprietor of the Chanfeng Real Estate Company; Wang Shuhe, manager of the Guoxin Bank; Wang Demin, owner of the Anle

Textile Mill; Hou Guohua, general manager of Fuxing Industries; Hu Yuyu, compradore of the International Settlement Tramways Company; and Zhang Jianhui, general manager and proprietor of the China Marine Engineering Works.[38]

The Society looked after its members, especially those facing economic hardship. In 1935, for example, the Perseverance Society set up its own employment section under Lu Jingshi in response to growing concern about unemployment among Society members. In the 12 months from November 1935 to November 1936, 40 members sought employment through this section. Of these, 21 found employment through the services of the section in such agencies as the Stamp, Tobacco, and Wine Tax Office, the Shanghai Municipality's Opium Prohibition Committee, the Shanghai Municipal Fish Market, the Wusong-Shanghai Defense Commissioner's Headquarters, and the Da Xin Theater. The Society's journal, the *Heng She Yuekan*, also ran an employment column for those members seeking work. In May 1937, there were six members seeking employment through this column, consisting of three ex-policemen, a former director of Butterfield and Swire's Wucheng Shipyard, a restaurateur, and a former rice hong owner.[39]

The *Heng She Yuekan* began publication in January 1936 and was published every month until April 1937 when it went over to a bimonthly format. After the outbreak of the Sino-Japanese War, it appeared only intermittently. The journal published a wide range of items, many written by members of the Society, including essays on politics and social issues, short stories, discussions of Beijing Opera, and travelogues. It also chronicled the Society's affairs, publishing the minutes of executive committee meetings and the Society's annual accounts, together with reports of the banquets hosted by the Society.[40] Banquets were a major Society activity. Between January 1936 and April 1937, the Perseverance Society held a total of 41 banquets, or an average of three a month. Most of these were hosted by key figures in the Society, such as Lu Jingshi or Hong Yanbin, and some were major events involving over 200 guests, such as the celebration of Du's birthday, the annual summer banquet cruise on the Huangpu River, and the farewell banquet for Zhu Xuefan on going to Geneva to represent China at the ILO.[41] Additionally, some major events organized by Du's followers were also attended by business and political leaders, such as the dedication of Du's Family Temple in Pudong in 1931 and Du's sixtieth birthday celebrations in 1947.

The Perseverance Society had its own formal organizational structure, consisting of a nine-man standing committee, a 19-member executive committee, and regular congresses. The standing committee was the Society's highest decision-making body, its membership between 1934 and 1936 consisting of Lu Jingshi, Cai Futang, Zhang Kechang, Xu Maotang, Zhang Rongchu, Zhang Zilian, E Shen, Zhang Shichuan, and Chen Dazai. The executive committee supervised a total of 18 sections (*zu*) covering such activities as planning, entertainment, theater, banquets, economics, travel, social functions, education, legal affairs, and employment. In an attempt to encourage greater involvement by Society members, an Advisory Council (*Pingyihui*) consisting of 50 members, roughly 10 percent of the Society's total membership, was set up in 1936. The revised regulations of the Perseverance Society of May 1937 set out this organizational structure in some detail. According to these regulations the standing committee met every fortnight, the executive committee met once a month and was summoned by the standing committee, the advisory council met every two months and was summoned by its head, and the congress met every six months at the request of the executive committee.[42]

Despite this formal structure, the Perseverance Society remained Du's personal organization—he selected all the office-holders and directed how the members would vote. In his speech to the Society's Third Anniversary Congress, Lu Jingshi underscored this fact when he said that Du was the one leader and one center of the Society and that its members had to "serve Mister Du like dogs and horses".[43] The Society's very insignia symbolized the fact that it was Du's personal organization: a circle in the center of which was a copper bell imprinted with a crescent moon. The bell represented the source of sound, the character for "sound" being a homophone for *sheng*, the second character of Du's given name, while the crescent moon formed its first character, *yue*, the combination giving "Yuesheng."[44]

By providing the Perseverance Society with a formal organizational structure that mimicked a political party, Du and his aides were stressing both its modernity and its identification with the goals of the Guomindang state. Leading Society members took up the Guomindang government's refrain that the only means to save the nation in its time of trouble was to create modern and rational organizations, along the lines of the Perseverance Society. Lu Jingshi, for his part, believed that the Perseverance Society by modernizing (*xiandaihua*) and rationalizing (*helihua*) itself would have an important role to play in achieving the Guomindang's nation-building ambitions: in strengthening mass organization, building up society, and rejuvenating the nation. As he stated at the Society's Third Anniversary Congress in November 1936:

> In my opinion the key to whether the nation and the race survives or perishes is directly related to the degree of national organizational strength. The weakness of our fellow-countrymen's organizational capacity has already been a major stain on [our] history. Although over the years the various types of organization within our nation have appeared formally to be vigorous, yet if one studies their reality none of them was equipped with the proper requirements, so that they were unable to develop a genuine and solid strength. What are these so-called proper requirements? They are nothing more than to have a [clearly defined] center (*zhongxin*) and constancy [of purpose] (*hengxin*) [in other words the proclaimed characteristics of the Perseverance Society] . . . if we have a centralised leadership (*zhongxin lingchou*) and steadfast cadres (*hengxin zhi fenzi*) then we can begin to speak of a modern and rational organization (*xiandaihua helihuazhi zuzhi*). If this can be achieved and it is permanent then we can begin to take on the heavy responsibility of activating (*zhenzuo*) the organizational strength of the race.[45]

In other words, Lu argued that the Perseverance Society was just the type of modern and rational organization needed to strengthen the nation. Others endorsed this view. Wang Xiaolai, Chairman of the Shanghai Chinese Chamber of Commerce and an important crony of Du Yuesheng, also spoke at the Third Congress. Noting that China was in the throes of a national crisis, Wang stated that all Chinese had to knuckle down and endure (*heng*) all kinds of hardships and that economic production was a key means of saving the nation. He observed that Perseverance Society members were just the kind of people needed to build the nation and achieve national salvation.[46]

The creation of a personal organization like the Perseverance Society was a new departure for a Green Gang boss, and other Green Gang bosses who sought social acceptability quickly imitated Du's initiative. Zhang Renkui—the doyen of Green Gang elders in the 1930s—set up his own Benevolence Association (*Ren She*) in 1935. Du's mentor, Huang Jinrong, followed with his own personal organization in 1936, the Fidelity Society (*Zhongxin She*), as did Du's Green Gang associate Jin Tinsong, with his *Ming She*. Even some of Du's Shanghai cronies associated with the Perseverance Society set up their own organizations, such as Yang Hu with his Revive China Study Association (*XingZhong Xuehui*) in 1936 and Wang Xiaolai with his Ascendant Society (*Sheng She*). Du's followers also followed his example and set up their own personal organizations, such as Lu Jingshi's Tranquillity Society (*Jing She*) and Zhu Xuefan's Resolute Society (*Yi She*). None of these imitative associations, however, rivaled Du's organization in the extent of its social, political, and economic influence.[47]

During the war years, with Du living first in Hong Kong and then in Chongqing, the Perseverance Society languished. In these years Du did try to ensure a continuing role for the Perseverance Society, for example, by appointing a couple of its members in 1940 to the secretariat of the Shanghai United Committee (*Shanghai Shi Tongyi Weiyuanhui*) set up to coordinate Guomindang underground resistance in the Jiangnan. He also established new branches of the Society in unoccupied China. Nevertheless, the Japanese occupation of Shanghai not only cut Du off from the Society's core area, it also created severe tensions within the Society as many of its members threw in their lot with the puppet governments created under Japanese auspices.[48]

The Perseverance Society, however, was so central to Du's system of power in Shanghai that the first thing he did after his return in 1945 was to reestablish it. Lu Jingshi was as important to the re-creation of the Society after the Sino-Japanese War as he had been to its founding. Indeed, Du recognized Lu's contribution when he expressed his gratitude to him at the 1948 Congress, referring to him as a "model member of the Perseverance Society" and going on to say:

> Within our society [the Perseverance Society] comrade Lu Jingshi is a person who not only has made strenuous contributions both to society and the nation, but also has taken on extraordinary responsibilities for the Perseverance Society. I hope that each member of the Perseverance Society can imitate comrade Lu Jingshi by making similar efforts and taking on similar responsibilities, so that our society can develop and have bright prospects.[49]

Membership rose markedly in the early postwar years, standing at 1,500 in 1947, and the Society was able to hold two congresses in 1947 and 1948. With its victory in the Civil War, the Chinese Communist Party terminated the mainland operations of the Perseverance Society. It continued to exist on Taiwan, thanks to the efforts of Lu Jingshi, and it published two commemorative volumes after Du's death. The Society's glory days, however, lay behind it.[50]

Limitations and Decline

The transformation achieved by Du Yuesheng in the Green Gang's relations with Shanghai's society, though impressive, was never complete. Fear remained the ultimate sanction for Du and his fellow Green Gang bosses. In negotiations with these gangster bosses, local businessmen knew that, no matter how benign the gang bosses were, they would be subject to increasing levels of intimidation and threats of violence if they failed to reach agreement on the bosses' terms. If they crossed these Green Gang leaders, they could pay with their lives. To cite one example, in the 1980s, the last Chinese manager of Jardine Matheson operations in Shanghai still remembered with great bitterness the murder of his uncle by Zhang Xiaolin because his uncle had refused to sell Zhang a piece of real estate that the latter coveted.[51] Du could be equally ruthless. During the negotiations over the 1935 "banking coup," Du sent an unambiguous warning to Zhang Jia'ao, the long-serving general manager of the Bank of China, that his life would be in danger if he attempted to oppose the government's takeover of the Bank of China.[52]

Du's influence and power among Shanghai's bourgeoisie also depended on a particular concatenation of political circumstances. When these changed, his power was greatly weakened. The semicolonial status of Shanghai was of paramount importance in providing Du with the ability to leverage his influence by playing off the foreign and Chinese authorities, creating among them a belief in his indispensability. The war years ended all that, especially after the outbreak of the Pacific War in December 1941 and the Japanese Army's occupation of the International Settlement. Although a Vichy-administered French Concession continued its separate existence for a few more years, it was a compliant partner of both the Japanese and the Wang Jingwei regime. The war changed the political complexion of Shanghai. To give "face" to its ally, the Wang Jingwei regime, the Japanese government formally returned the International Settlement to Chinese control following a declaration of its intent in January 1943, and Vichy agreed to return the French Concession by mid-year. Not to be outdone, both Britain and the United States signed agreements with Chiang's government in the same month, surrendering their extraterritorial rights.[53] These developments ensured that with the end of hostilities Chinese authorities would enjoy full sovereign rights in Shanghai for the first time. As a result, Du's "mediator" role between the Chinese and foreign authorities became redundant, and he therefore lost much of his utility to Chinese officials.

Du's efforts to craft a new political strategy to take account of the postwar environment met with indifferent success.[54] His two attempts to gain formal political office in Shanghai both failed. In September 1945, Du lobbied hard for the post of mayor of Shanghai, but in the end it went to the head of Chiang Kai-shek's personal office. And in August 1946, he sought the position of president (speaker) of the newly elected Shanghai Municipal Council. However, in a convoluted deal with the CC Clique, Du enjoyed the position for only a few minutes, being replaced on the grounds of "ill health" by the CC Clique's candidate Pan Gongzhan. So, even those Guomindang factions to whom he had been closest, like the CC Clique, began to distance themselves from him. With the end of the Sino-Japanese War and the descent into civil war, the political mood of the Guomindang changed, becoming more moralistic and even puritanical. Those political groups that epitomized this change, such as the Three People's Principles Youth Corps and close associates of Jiang Jingguo (the powerful son of Chiang Kai-shek) were in the ascendant. They adopted a "root and branch" approach to reforming the Guomindang, determined to rid it of those corrupt and "feudal" features that allowed political fixers like Du to flourish. Faced with this increasingly hostile environment, Du had largely retired from the political arena by late 1948. His influence with Shanghai business leaders also had declined by then. Du's increasing inability to influence the Guomindang authorities in the interests of Shanghai business had weakened his ability to manipulate the Shanghai bourgeoisie.

Du's moment, when he had played a central role in the politics and economy of Shanghai, was over. Du himself, however, did not fully realize this. Throughout 1949 and 1950, he engaged in protracted secret discussions with communist representatives in Shanghai and Hong Kong seeking to protect his assets in return for not opposing the communist takeover, even considering a new role for himself in a communist-dominated Shanghai. These overtures ended only with Du's death in 1951.

PART THREE

Network Dynamics: Political Movements and Social Networks

CHAPTER 5

Popular Protest in Shanghai, 1919–1927: Social Networks, Collective Identities, and Political Parties

ELIZABETH J. PERRY

SOCIAL NETWORKS are the basic building blocks of collective action. As students of contentious politics generally recognize, the mobilization of large-scale protest movements requires the activation of ongoing relationships.[1] The key to this process lies in organizers' ability to encourage participation in terms that make sense to potential recruits, based on their preexisting social connections. Sociologist Roger Gould explains: "An appeal to solidarity will only succeed to the degree that the collective identity it invokes classifies people in a way that plausibly corresponds to their concrete experience of social ties to others."[2] Whether movement organizers make their pitch on the basis of class, nation, religion, or any number of other possible appeals, those targeted "must be able to see their own social connections as concrete instances of the abstract model implied by an ideology; they must also perceive the social connections of their putative peers as equivalent to their own."[3] Central to this argument is what network theorists call "structural equivalence"—or the grouping of individuals in ways that are understood to be parallel to other groupings, regardless of whether or not the groups themselves are connected to one another.[4]

In tracing Parisian protest from the Revolution of 1848 to the Commune of 1871, Gould detects a fundamental shift in the underlying social networks—and attendant identities of the participants—from one movement to the next. Parisians, he argues, participated in 1848 as members of a working-class struggle for labor rights, whereas in 1871 they joined the Commune as citizens fighting for urban autonomy. The basis of "insurgent identity" had expanded from class to community, reflecting changes in the character of social networks in mid-nineteenth century Paris. This transformation, according to Gould, was largely the result of Baron Haussmann's massive urban renovation projects of 1852 to 1868, which relocated workers from the city center to newly annexed districts. In outlying neighborhoods, residence (or "community") overshadowed occupation (or "class") in structuring social networks. The enlargement of collective identity was facilitated by the emergence of formal organizations that permitted a "jump in mobilizational scale."

This chapter explores the changing role of social networks and collective identities during China's most dynamic period of urban protest (1919–1927) in its most vibrant city: Shanghai. The transformations that occurred in this period were arguably as profound and politically influential as those that took place in Haussmann's Paris, yet the origins and outcomes could hardly have been more different. In Shanghai, networks and identities were altered not by urban renewal projects and attendant shifts in demographic concentration,[5] but by the emergence of modern political institutions—political parties in particular—seeking a popular constituency. Although these new entities espoused expansive collective identities of citizenship, they were constrained by the nature of preexisting social relations. The outcome of this clash between political aspirations and social realities invites us to reconsider some standard assumptions of network theory in light of the Chinese experience.

The following survey of popular protest in early Republican Shanghai will, as movement theorists would expect, illustrate the centrality of social networks in facilitating mobilization: preexisting interpersonal connections constituted the basic building blocks of participation. At the same time, however, the Shanghai example points to the importance of issues about which available theory offers little guidance. While new formal organizations expanded the scale at which previous networks operated, in the end these organizations were themselves comprised of, and limited by, more enduring patterns of interaction. The Shanghai case highlights the salience of networks not only for *mobilization* but for *demobilization* as well. Moreover, the protests under consideration here challenge conventional sociological accounts that see a jump in mobilizational scale as dependent upon a commensurate enlargement of collective identities.

The May Fourth Movement

The May Fourth Movement of 1919 occurred two years prior to the founding of the Chinese Communist Party, and five years before a fundamental reorganization (along Bolshevik principles) of the Nationalist Party that would commit it to the task of mass mobilization. May Fourth thus serves as an instructive baseline from which to gauge the political developments that subsequently transpired.

In stark contrast to the movements that followed in its wake, May Fourth unfolded without overt direction from political parties. As Joseph Chen observes, "Sun [Yat-sen] and the Kuomintang exerted little or no political influence as far as the Movement was concerned."[6] Although Sun was residing in Shanghai at the time, he was an observer rather than an organizer of the events that transpired. Some KMT (Nationalist Party) members (e.g., Shao Lizi) played an active part in the movement, but they did so as individuals rather than as party members.

This is not to say, however, that the May Fourth Movement in Shanghai was unorganized. In fact, its rapid growth bespoke an impressive infrastructure of mobilizing networks—some of which predated May Fourth and others of which emerged during the course of the movement itself. The most powerful networks (in terms of their capacity to mobilize people who might otherwise have remained uninvolved in the events of the day) were those connected to organizations that had a longstanding history of political activism in the city: native place groups and secret societies in particular. Such associations had played a key role in Shanghai's rendition of the 1911 Revolution, and their leaders evinced a continuing interest in political developments under the new republic.

In view of the salience of preexisting networks in the May Fourth Movement, it may be helpful to begin with a bit of historical background. The revolution that overturned monarchical rule in 1911 was facilitated in Shanghai by a remarkable degree of elite cohesion. This "social fusion" had assumed political expression before the revolution in what Mark Elvin describes as the "first formally democratic political institution in China"—a city council established in the Chinese section of Shanghai in 1905.[7] Drawing upon a tradition of guild, charity, and public works activities, the Shanghai city council presided over a "limited welfare state" and, according to Elvin, one in which political corruption was virtually absent, issues were openly debated at public meetings, and decisions were taken by majority vote.[8]

In the 1911 Revolution, the city council and its armed merchant militias (whose combined membership numbered some 3,000 troops) threw their united support behind the revolutionary cause.[9] With the militias playing the key role in the fall of the local imperial government, it was little wonder that city council leaders inherited the posts vacated by officials of the ancien régime. When revolutionary leader Chen Qimei resigned in July of 1912, council notables gained control of the new military administration as well.[10] Militia director Li Pingshu, for example, became Minister of Civil Affairs.[11]

The cordial and cooperative relations that prevailed among members of the Shanghai elite, some of whom issued from gentry backgrounds and the majority of whom were merchants, was in large measure due to shared native place, guild, and secret society connections. These networks not only bred familiarity and trust in economic affairs, they also facilitated political engagement. More than eighty political parties were active in Shanghai around the time of the 1911 Revolution; although they advocated public (*gong*) service, most were based on cozy constellations of fellow provincials.[12] In 1911, connections between *Tongmenghui* revolutionary Chen Qimei (who was also a Green Gang leader in addition to belonging to this precursor of the political party in China) and entrepreneurs from Chen's home province of Zhejiang provided the basic foundation for revolutionary action in the city. Shanghai businessmen Yu Xiaqing and Wang Yiting (see Chapter 3)—both of whom hailed originally from Zhejiang—were close associates of Chen Qimei.[13]

Native place groups boasted a record of confrontational activity in Shanghai dating back to nineteenth-century territorial disputes with the French authorities.[14] In 1905, native place organizations sponsored a merchant boycott of American goods to protest mistreatment of Chinese in the United States. A decade later, they helped launch a boycott of Japanese products to signal their disapproval of the Twenty-One Demands. Thus it was not surprising that these groups also assumed major mobilizing responsibilities during the May Fourth Movement. As Bryna Goodman has noted, "In the May Fourth Movement in Shanghai, native place groups clearly acted as units for the organization, expression, and dissemination of nationalist ideology. Without these groups, it is difficult to imagine how such effective social mobilization could have occurred."[15] Networks of fellow provincials, Goodman explains, provided the "component elements" of the better known "modern" organizations (e.g., student unions and merchant associations) usually credited with organizing the May Fourth Movement.[16] Such ties were critical to the cooperation and coordination of otherwise diverse groups of workers, students, and merchants that was a defining feature of the movement.

This is not to suggest that May Fourth—often considered to mark the beginning of "modern" politics in China—was merely the product of static "traditional" institutions. In fact, native place groups were themselves undergoing important alterations at this time, as "modern" *tongxianghui* emerged to replace older *huiguan*. The newer organizations represented a growing commitment to political action and social mobilization, the results of which would become quite clear just a few years later in the May Thirtieth Movement of 1925.[17]

Another institution that was entering the throes of a major transformation at this time was the Shanghai Green Gang. As an organization that targeted recent immigrants to the city, the Gang was profoundly influenced by demographic developments and attendant changes in native place associations. Moreover, 1919 was the year in which Chiang Kai-shek reportedly became a disciple of Green Gang "godfather" Huang Jinrong, through the introduction of Shanghai businessman Yu Xiaqing.[18] This connection augured an enhanced political role for the Gang that would come to fruition eight years later in Chiang's stunning April 12 coup against the Communists.

The changes under way in native place and secret society relations around the time of the May Fourth Movement were indicative of a gradual diminution in the cohesion that had characterized elite relations in Shanghai from the late Qing dynasty through the 1911 Revolution. During the revolution and its immediate aftermath, a small and interconnected group of local notables dominated the city's guilds, chambers of commerce, merchant militia, and urban administration. Crystalized politically in the institution of the city council, elite cohesion was seriously eroded by the disbandment of the council on orders from Yuan Shikai. In 1913, Yuan dissolved the national parliament and outlawed the KMT; the following year he abolished the local and provincial assemblies (including the Shanghai city council) that had been established as part of the late Qing reforms.[19] In so doing, Yuan helped to create an alienated Shanghai elite, poised to play a catalytic role in the massive urban protests that would erupt a few years later.[20]

The decline of elite cohesion was accompanied by a growing level of generational, ideological, and organizational contestation. Within the ranks of the bourgeoisie, an activist minority of "younger, more innovative entrepreneurs of radical inclination" was arising on the eve of the May Fourth Movement.[21] Excluded from the Shanghai Chamber of Commerce, these "Young Turks" founded the Shanghai Commercial Federation in March 1919 to press for democratic political reforms. Representing 53 groups of merchants, organized outside of the entrepreneurial establishment, the Federation would play an influential part in the May Fourth and May Thirtieth Movements and the inauguration of Nationalist rule in Shanghai.[22]

The May Fourth Movement, in other words, occurred during the midst of a more general political ferment in which new actors and institutions were gaining an influential voice. Even so, as social network theory would predict, new entrants to the political arena drew heavily upon preexisting ties in mounting their challenge to the status quo. Marie-Claire Bergere points out that the influence exerted by May Fourth activists derived not only from the general mass nationalism of the day but even more from the close connections that this group retained with the reformist elite of the late Imperial period.[23] Native place allegiances and secret society affiliations constituted flexible bonds, capable of linking different cohorts and classes in a common patriotic cause. The fact that a large percentage of Shanghai students came from merchant families further solidified the relationship between these key constituencies.[24]

The outcome, as Joseph Chen has characterized it, was "the first *total* popular movement in Chinese history"—with students, merchants, workers, and ordinary citizens closing ranks in opposition to the imperialist threat.[25] Native place groups convened meetings, sent telegrams of protest, and served as conduits of information that spanned academic, commercial, and industrial circles.[26] Such networks touched the educated and affluent elite and, to a lesser degree, members of the proletariat and lumpen proletariat as well. Among skilled workers, guilds and native place associations were key vehicles of mobilization. For unskilled workers, factory foremen—many of whom were gang leaders who had recruited workers from their own native places—served as critical intermediaries. Thanks to gang directives, even beggars, pickpockets, and prostitutes refrained from plying their trades during the May Fourth general strike.[27]

Native place and gang connections, important as they were, were not the sole bases of preexisting ties among May Fourth activists. Jeffrey

Wasserstrom finds that many of the student leaders, a disproportionate share of whom were from Fudan University, "knew each other and in some important cases had worked together in the past."[28] Participation in a recent lecture campaign, organized by Fudan students to encourage morality and hygiene in the surrounding countryside, was a common experience shared by many student leaders.[29]

Of course, the May Fourth Movement did not simply rely upon preexisting networks; it also spawned its own mobilizing groups. Wasserstrom writes of students establishing a "complex hierarchy of interconnected organizations, all of which played some role in coordinating youth protest activities."[30] Following the example of merchants, students founded 10-person groups (*shiren tuan*) whose members swore a collective oath to boycott Japanese goods and to ensure that their fellow members remained faithful to the cause. All recruits pledged to convert others to the movement as well. In theory, each member was expected to mobilize nine additional participants, thereby generating 10 new groups of 10.[31] These informal arrangements did not outlive the movement itself, but a number of formal organizations (from student unions to merchant federations) did persist, constituting important bases of mobilization in subsequent movements.

Taken as a whole, May Fourth organizational activity presented a serious challenge to government control. Wasserstrom highlights the tendency of students to mimic and usurp official roles, resulting in a "protest bureaucracy run almost exclusively by students."[32] The foreigners in Shanghai, alarmed by the threat posed by these various groups, sought to blunt their popular authority. On June 8, 1919, the Shanghai Municipal Council issued a notice prohibiting ordinary citizens from "appearing on the streets or in any public place, in uniform or wearing any distinctive dress or badge or headgear signifying membership in any particular organization, association, or body."[33] The trappings of officialdom, in other words, were to be reserved for officials of the International Settlement. Chinese authorities in Shanghai, especially worried about the heterogeneous, cross-cutting character of May Fourth participation, took steps to prevent planning meetings between students and merchants.[34] Despite efforts at repression by foreign and Chinese officials alike, May Fourth activists were able to organize and sustain a powerful "triple stoppage" (*sanba*) that included store closures by merchants, class boycotts by students, and a general strike by workers.

What "collective identity" served to link these diverse groups in common struggle? While the various constituencies harbored disparate concerns, they were all moved by the distressing prospect of national extinction (*wangguo*) to join hands in calling for the preservation of national sovereignty and repudiation of the terms of the Versailles Treaty. The May Fourth Movement is often seen as the beginning of modern Chinese nationalism, but the term *wangguo* was an ancient one, dating back at least to the Warring States Period (fifth to third centuries B.C.), which had gained currency following the Mongol and Manchu invasions of the thirteenth and seventeenth centuries.[35] It was resuscitated during May Fourth in a new call for all "citizens" (*guomin*) to participate in the struggle to save the nation from extinction. As the founding manifesto of the Shanghai Students' Union expressed its objectives: "Awaken the citizens' patriotic spirit, using practical means to rescue [the nation] from peril" (*Huanqi guomin zhi aiguoxin, yong qieshi fangfa, wanjiu weiwang*).[36]

The protest repertoires adopted by May Fourth participants also indicated an admixture of old and new patterns of contention. After attending a citizens' meeting (*guomin dahui*) on June 29 to decry the Versailles Treaty, the crowd of thousands marched in the pouring rain to the military governor's office to present its demands. When soldiers with bayonets sallied forth to halt the protesters, the crowd knelt down on the muddy road and kowtowed. The age-old tactic was evidently persuasive: "abashed, [the soldiers] lowered their rifles."[37]

The May Fourth Movement drew upon familiar social networks, political concepts, and protest practices in mobilizing a disparate constituency. The result was a powerful movement that endured for nearly two months and succeeded in attaining its central demand of rejecting the Paris Peace Treaty. Remarkable as this display of activism was, however, it did not represent a newfound homogeneity among the Shanghai citizenry. At a *guomin dahui* attended by 80,000 to 100,000 people on July 1, for example, each group "was assigned to a station according to its vocation or social class."[38] Although Shanghai's movement—in contrast to Beijing's—involved all social strata, they participated in segmented fashion. Even the union of students and merchants that constituted the backbone of the movement was temporary and conditional: "They formed alliances but only on an ad hoc basis. Between the two groups, there was neither any degree of substantial, lasting political cohesiveness and stability nor any basic common interest that would presage a lasting bond between them after the movement."[39]

The May Thirtieth Movement

While the May Fourth Movement proceeded without partisan inspiration and supervision, this was certainly not the case for the May Thirtieth Movement that broke out six years later. Both the KMT and the CCP (Chinese Communist Party) played prominent roles in the events of May 1925, contributing to a movement that was noticeably more politically ambitious than its forerunner. Whereas protesters in 1919 had largely limited their purview to the noxious provisions of the Treaty of Versailles, six years later they would raise general demands for an end to imperialism and warlordism along with the implementation of fundamental political reform. All countrymen (*tongbao*) were enjoined to participate in this struggle for liberation.

May Thirtieth exhibited an increase in ideological sophistication along with a greater capacity for mobilization, particularly among workers. Some 60,000 Shanghai workers had participated in the May Fourth general strike, while on May Thirtieth the number skyrocketed to 200,000. Moreover, the speed of this mobilizing process had also increased markedly: in 1919, it took over a month to organize a general strike in the city; in 1925, less than a week elapsed between the May Thirtieth incident and the start of the general strike.[40]

The principal leadership organ of the May Thirtieth Movement was a group, called the Federation of Workers, Merchants, and Students (*gongshangxue lianhehui*), that was established on June 4, 1925, with the explicit purpose of providing unified direction to the protest. Unlike the organization with a similar name that had formed for a similar purpose during the May Fourth Movement, the May Thirtieth federation was from the beginning a highly partisan—and highly effective—body. As CCP leader Qu Qiubai noted, the federation would serve Shanghai "virtually as a local government" for the next two months.[41] Although the Chamber of Commerce refused to join it, other major sectoral organizations (e.g., the Shanghai Federation of Street Unions, the All-China Students' Union, the Shanghai Students' Union, the Shanghai General Labor Union) were active constituents. The dominant voice in the federation was unquestionably that of the CCP, speaking through the General Labor Union and its energetic director, Li Lisan.[42] But the federation was not simply a Communist mouthpiece; issues were debated and reformulated in the course of its deliberations.[43]

While both the KMT and the CCP sought to capture and channel the mass indignation evoked by the May Thirtieth Incident, in which Chinese students were killed by British police, the Communists proved considerably more skillful in this effort. As Wasserstrom observes, the May Thirtieth Movement can even be said to have "made" the Chinese Communist Party, thanks to its adroit handling of the opportunities presented by the bloody confrontation on Nanjing Road.[44] At the start of the Movement, the CCP claimed a national membership of around 900; by the end of 1925, it boasted a roster of some 10,000 members.[45] Although KMT membership was much larger, numbering 147,000, it was widely acknowledged that "nine out of ten local [KMT] organizations were led by Communists or left-wingers."[46] Nowhere was this more true than in Shanghai.

The Communists' relative success was due to several factors. For one thing, at the time most of the top leadership of the CCP was concentrated in Shanghai, whereas the KMT was still centered in Guangzhou. For another, the KMT was bedeviled by deep internal divisions. Left-wing and right-wing factions within the KMT argued vociferously about how vigorously to pursue certain mass constituencies.[47] The principal KMT organizer in Shanghai, Ma Chaojun, had recently been sent to the city from Guangzhou as a representative of the right-wing. His mission was to counter growing Communist influence by founding conservative "Sun Yat-sen-ism societies" among the youth of Shanghai.[48] Although in his memoirs Ma claims a leading role in instigating the May Thirtieth Movement, historian Richard Rigby concludes convincingly that Ma's part "must have been a fairly minor one."[49]

Yet one should not draw too stark a distinction between KMT and CCP initiatives at this time. Thanks to the united front inaugurated the previous year at the instigation of the Comintern, the two political parties were formally pledged to a policy of cooperation. This partnership allowed individual Communists to join the KMT and established umbrella organizations (under the KMT) to supervise joint mobilizing efforts directed at workers, merchants, peasants, women, and youth. For both parties, students and workers were primary targets of recruitment; activists in Shanghai universities and factories often enjoyed concurrent membership in both parties. Of the 165 representatives who attended the first national congress of the KMT in January 1924, some 25 delegates were also leading members of the CCP (including Communist Party co-founders Li Dazhao and Chen Duxiu, as well as Mao Zedong).[50] The first secretary (*mishu*) of the Shanghai branch of the KMT, established in February 1924, was none other than Mao Zedong.[51] The radical campus of Shanghai University represented in essence a KMT-CCP joint venture from which the Shanghai labor movement drew many of its most able organizers, especially among students from Zhejiang (indicating the continuing salience of native place links).[52]

Despite important differences in ideology and practice, both political parties were committed to building broader and more powerful political organizations and identities capable of sustaining more ambitious and influential mass movements. As Nicholas Clifford characterizes them, the KMT and CCP in 1925 were "new nationalists" anxious to create "new institutions that would transcend provincial and regional lines and provide China with precisely the kind of disciplined and well organized leadership that had been so lacking in the May Fourth Movement of 1919."[53] Both parties called upon their fellow countrymen (*tongbao*) to join them in this national crusade.

The speed and size of the May Thirtieth mobilization process bears witness to the organizational success of these party-sponsored initiatives. Following the advice of Comintern agents, both the KMT and the CCP established "front" organizations among various sectors of Shanghai society.[54] Roger Gould has observed that formal organizations, including political parties and their ancillary offshoots, can exert great influence on the scale at which group identities are convincing to potential participants. Formal organizations, Gould notes, create social ties that encourage the recognition of commonalities on a broader level than would be expected on the basis of informal social networks alone. By establishing contacts that cut across the boundaries of everyday life, these new groups permit a "jump in scale," thereby facilitating more inclusive identities and insurrections.[55] The Federation of Workers, Merchants, and Students, which provided overall direction for the May Thirtieth Movement, bears out Gould's point. This new organization formally linked the worlds of labor, commerce, and education and raised demands for fundamental political change to liberate China from the twin scourges of imperialism and warlordism.[56]

Critical as formal organizations were to the development of the May Thirtieth Movement, they did not supplant preexisting bases of involvement. Secret society connections proved crucial as the Green Gang forged relationships with both the KMT and CCP. Although, as Brian Martin emphasizes, these alliances were "essentially pragmatic,"[57] they afforded the political parties access to otherwise inhospitable realms of Shanghai society. The CCP, within weeks of its establishment, authorized the infiltration of gang networks in order to make headway in the labor movement.[58] Not long thereafter, Green Gang strongman Du Yuesheng developed contacts with Chen Lifu and other key KMT leaders. The role of the Green Gang in the May Thirtieth Movement was complex and contradictory. On the one hand, Communist labor leader Li Lisan struck deals with gang chieftains to facilitate the mobilization of a general strike.[59] On the other hand, Du Yuesheng worked closely with KMT representatives in Shanghai to try to restrain the burgeoning movement.[60]

While formal organizations facilitated a broader mobilization effort, relations both within and among such organizations were mediated by key individuals. In a manner that resembled the machinations of Shanghai elites in earlier periods, these "central nodes" wielded decisive influence over their personal webs of association and allegiance. On the night of May Thirtieth, Ma Chaojun and other KMT leaders repaired to their Shanghai headquarters to discuss how to respond to the chilling events of the day. Du Yuesheng also attended the meeting, as did Yun Daiying—a CCP member who served concurrently as secretary of the Youth Department of the Shanghai KMT. As soon as the meeting had adjourned, Yun went directly to the home of Zhang Guotao (a founding member of the CCP), where leaders of the CCP Central Committee (including Chen Duxiu, Li Lisan, Liu Shaoqi, and Cai Hesen) had gathered. Yun shared with his fellow Communists the news that the KMT had called for a triple strike, a policy that the CCP was quick to embrace.[61]

Political parties were major players in the May Thirtieth Movement, particularly in its early stages, but over time the determining influence of particular individuals became increasingly apparent. The most important such individual was businessman Yu Xiaqing, who at this time held no party affiliation. Active in patriotic struggles since the Ningbo guild's confrontation with French authorities in 1898, Yu had become Shanghai's "quintessential middleman."[62] Although Yu was away from the city at the time of the May Thirtieth Incident, he returned to play a critical part in the ensuing movement. Yu Xiaqing's prominent position among the Shanghai merchant class was rooted in his Ningbo origins, but his rise (from poverty) was emblematic of a new basis of elite leadership in which achievement figured as importantly as native place ties.[63]

In contrast to some of the more conservative members of the Shanghai business elite, Yu Xiaqing enjoyed close ties with Du Yuesheng and the Green Gang. Having entered political life as a protégé of Chen Qimei, Yu appreciated the contribution of secret society support to broader political causes. Founder of the merchant militia that had spearheaded the 1911 Revolution, Yu was also no stranger to armed struggle. After his return to Shanghai during the May Thirtieth Movement, Yu turned to the Green Gang to channel the protest in directions he preferred. Although Yu was wary of the radical labor movement that was developing under CCP inspiration, he realized that it might serve a useful purpose in pressuring the International Settlement on issues such as Chinese representation on the Shanghai Municipal Council and the return of the Mixed Court to Chinese control, matters about which he cared deeply. Distrusted by the Communists and the foreign authorities alike, Yu sought a middle ground in his effort to leverage political concessions.[64]

Having established—within the Chamber of Commerce—a special commission to administer the May Thirtieth strike funds, Yu Xiaqing wielded substantial financial power over the movement. As money poured in from around the globe to sustain the hundreds of thousands of hungry strikers, Yu's commission controlled the lifeline of the protest.[65] Mediating between the conservatives in the Chamber of Commerce and the more radically inclined merchants who comprised the Federation of Commercial Groups and the Shanghai Federation of Street Associations, Yu acted as a pivotal figure both within the business community and beyond. When he reached the conclusion that the dangers of mass mobilization outweighed the prospects for political reform, he called upon Du Yuesheng to break the general strike.[66] With the chief brokers of both financial and coercive power now united against it, the movement could not be sustained. Once Yu and Du withdrew their support, the fragile alliance that had knit together the CCP, the KMT, gangsters, workers, merchants, and students quickly unraveled.

May Thirtieth departed significantly from May Fourth in the prominent involvement of political parties and, relatedly, the more strident calls for fundamental political reform. Thanks to the plethora of formal organizations—many of which were affiliated with the KMT and/or CCP—that had recently emerged in Shanghai, mobilization was rapid and comprehensive. Due especially to the efforts of the Communists and their newly established General Labor Union, workers played a more central role than had been the case six years before. But continuities between the two movements were also apparent. For one thing, most of the new developments were a direct product of the earlier May

Fourth experience. Disappointment over the failure of May Fourth to bring about fundamental political change inspired many of the organizational efforts of the 1920s. For another thing, familiar networks based upon native place and gang affiliations were the glue that held together many of the new organizations. And, in the end, personal prestige and persuasion—as demonstrated by the interventions of Yu Xiaqing in particular—proved more powerful than new organizations in determining the ultimate outcome of the movement.

The Workers' Three Armed Uprisings

The armed uprisings of 1926 through 1927, which rid Shanghai of warlord rule and delivered the city to the National Revolutionary Army, are often seen as the apogee of the Communist-inspired labor movement. An astounding 800,000 people participated in the general strike that accompanied the third, victorious uprising in March of 1927. The insurrections were the fullest—and final—expression of the first united front between the KMT and CCP. Under the protection afforded by this partisan cooperation, a major wave of association building swept the city over the course of the three uprisings.[67] A citizens' meeting (*shimin dahui*) convened on March 22, shortly after the third uprising, drew nearly 500,000 representatives from more than 1,000 different organizations.[68]

Political parties and formal organizations of various stripes played a visible and vital role in the mobilizing activity of the day. More than either May Fourth or May Thirtieth, the three armed uprisings were accompanied by concrete demands that reflected a growing political sophistication on the part of parties and professional associations alike. CCP and KMT cadres convened numerous meetings with business leaders and other interested citizens to develop a detailed blueprint for a new "Shanghai citizens' revolutionary government" (*Shanghai shimin geming zhengfu*). In the end, however, the bloody denouement that occurred with Chiang Kai-shek's April Twelfth massacre was less a product of institutional or ideological imperatives than of decisions by influential individuals relying upon longstanding social networks to advance their particular agendas.[69]

With advice and assistance from the Comintern, the CCP was certainly the principal instigator of the armed uprisings.[70] Hoping to replace warlord rule with a new political order, the Communists reached out to all urban citizens (*shimin*) in their insurrectionary quest. First merchants and then workers were targeted as the critical force of the struggle. To attract these and other elements, the Communists worked closely with various power brokers, most notably the KMT, business associations, and the Green Gang. But eventually, of course, it was the leaders of these very groups who would betray them, drawing upon personal connections that long predated the formation of the CCP.

Preparations for the first uprising in October 1926 focused on business circles, inasmuch as the CCP at this point was advocating a "bourgeois revolution" to topple warlord governance and usher in a new, more democratic rule. The disarray surrounding the first attempt at insurrection, which was quickly quashed by warlord forces, convinced party leaders of the desirability of relying upon workers, rather than merchants, as the mainstay of the struggle. Yet, even though the Communists' control of the General Labor Union afforded them an advantage when it came to labor organizing, mounting a general strike still required the cooperation of influential elites in the city. Communist labor leaders Zhao Shiyan, Wang Shouhua, and Luo Yinong met repeatedly with KMT representative Niu Yongjian, Green Gang strongman Du Yuesheng, and business notables Yu Xiaqing and Wang Xiaolai in an effort to muster the widest possible support for their enterprise.[71]

Niu Yongjian had been quietly dispatched to Shanghai in 1926 by the centrist faction of the KMT to carry out underground preparations for the Northern Expedition's advance on the city. A native of Shanghai, Niu had been associated with Chen Qimei in the revolutions of 1911 and 1913 and enjoyed extensive contacts with the Shanghai elite.[72] Niu's assignment was to use these networks to facilitate a peaceful takeover of the city by the KMT. In this mission he found himself increasingly at odds with the Communists, who were wedded to the process of armed struggle.[73]

As Niu Yongjian became more concerned about Communist intentions, his interest in secret society and merchant alliances intensified. Niu's initial success in developing links with these elements came with his promotion of a Shanghai "citizens' assembly" (*shimin gonghui*) to preserve the city from the threat of civil war.[74] Activating a web of connections that dated back many years, Niu then proceeded to put local Shanghai power holders in touch with his boss—Chiang Kai-shek. Chiang himself had served as aide to Chen Qimei during the 1911 Revolution and, as we have seen, pledged discipleship to Shanghai Green Gang "godfather" Huang Jinrong around the time of the May Fourth

Movement. Chiang's introduction to Huang had apparently been arranged by Yu Xiaqing, who served as a director of the Shanghai Stock Exchange during Chiang Kai-shek's brief tenure there.[75] In November 1926, after a hiatus of some seven years, Chiang resumed contact with his Green Gang "teacher." At this time the Shanghai Green Gang had recently undergone a major restructuring that rendered it more cohesive and politically influential and thus of greater importance to outside parties. The next four months saw a period of intense negotiations between KMT centrists and the Green Gang, as the two sides discussed what it would take to realize their mutual interest in a non-Communist Shanghai. According to Brian Martin, by the end of February 1927, the Green Gang—whose bosses had been appointed as Chiang Kai-shek's special agents in Shanghai—was fully committed to the KMT. Concerned about the Communist labor movement and calculating that Sun Chuanfang's warlord government was already on the ropes, Gang chieftains bet on the KMT as offering the most promising political future. This turn of events, Martin suggests, helps to explain the abrupt failure of the general strike during the Communists' second attempt at armed insurgency in late February 1927.[76]

Martin is certainly correct to stress the growing partnership between the Green Gang and the KMT. But, at least from the Communists' perspective, the prospect of enlisting both secret society and KMT assistance in their insurrectionary ambitions remained very much alive as they geared up for yet a third armed uprising the following month. On numerous occasions between the abortive second uprising and the successful third uprising, CCP operatives reported on meetings with Du Yuesheng at which the gang leader pledged continuing protection for their labor organizing initiatives.[77] A strike of the magnitude that accompanied the third uprising—with its 800,000 participants—would surely have been impossible had the Green Gang chieftain overtly opposed it.

Once the Communist-sponsored insurgency had rid Shanghai of warlord rule, however, the Green Gang was quick to press its advantage with the KMT. The first to call upon Chiang Kai-shek when he arrived in Shanghai shortly after the third uprising was Huang Jinrong.[78] Soon thereafter, a delegation of the Shanghai Federation of Commerce and Industry organized by Yu Xiaqing (along with Wang Yiting and other business notables sympathetic to Chiang Kai-shek) offered Chiang a 3 million dollar loan for the purpose of breaking the power of the Communist trade unions.[79] With the Green Gang poised to provide the muscle for just such an operation, the die was cast. Before daybreak on April 12, 1927, hundreds of gangsters descended on Communist strongholds to disarm the workers. The "white terror" that ensued sent the Communists packing and converted their movement from a proletarian to a peasant revolution. In 1920s Shanghai, elite networks—transformed though they were by the political developments of the era—remained too resilient to permit a Communist takeover of the city.

Mobilization and Demobilization

Popular protest in early Republican Shanghai affirms the centrality of social networks, while pointing to some further analytical challenges for students of collective action. The topic of demobilization remains largely unexplored by either network or social movement theorists, who have generally been content to ascribe a movement's decline either to "state repression" or to "movement fatigue" among participants. Influenced by a rational choice perspective that views collective action as an unusual phenomenon, the explanation for which requires special attention to the manner in which "free rider" problems are overcome and mobilization achieved, theorists have devoted scant attention to the equally challenging question of demobilization.

The Shanghai case suggests that networks may also play a crucial role in the process of demobilization. Neither state repression (which was limited by multiple sovereignty and warlord rule) nor movement fatigue (in this period of impassioned nationalistic fervor) can explain the unraveling of May Fourth, May Thirtieth, or—most dramatically—the three armed uprisings. Rather, in each instance demobilization followed upon the decisions of key network leaders (e.g., Yu Xiaqing, Du Yuesheng, Chiang Kai-shek) to reconstitute and reconfigure the loyalties of their associates in ways that undermined the ongoing movement. Protests are undone, it would seem, not by government brutality alone or by the frailty of followers, but sometimes by the repositioning of the original parties to the mobilizing coalition. Networks hold the potential not only to build movements but to destroy them.

A second issue on which the Shanghai experience may indicate a need for further analysis concerns the relationship between "insurgent identity" and scale of mobilization. Gould's pioneering work suggests an intuitively obvious linkage between a more comprehensive participatory appeal (citizenship rather than class, for example) and a broader mobilization outcome (the Paris Commune as opposed to 1848). Yet when we examine the basis of participation in Shanghai over the initial decades of the twentieth century, another—rather surprising—scenario presents itself. Although the size and scale of collective action grew exponentially in this period, the basis upon which recruitment appeals were made appears to have narrowed.

From the Revolution of 1911 through the three armed uprisings, movement participants in Shanghai responded consistently to claims of "citizenship." There are, however, multiple Chinese terms for what is universally translated into English as "citizenship."[80] The different Chinese terms, moreover, indicate alternative understandings of the political community to which one owes allegiance. At the time of the 1911 Revolution, the all-encompassing *gongmin* (or "person of the public") was the most common way of phrasing an appeal for political participation. At this time, various "citizens' assemblies" (*gongmin hui*) were established in the Chinese sections of Shanghai. In 1913, a "national citizens' assembly" (*quanmin gongmin hui*) emerged in Shanghai, only to be banned the following year by Yuan Shikai's blanket edict prohibiting all local councils and assemblies. Although we do not know the precise size or composition of these bodies, historian Xu Xiaoqun surmises that they must have been made up mainly of local merchants, since these were the people with the greatest stake in maintaining order and managing local affairs.[81] We have seen that merchants played a leading role in bringing about the 1911 Revolution in Shanghai.

The term *gongmin* (borrowed from the Japanese neologism *komin* as an equivalent for the Western term *citizen*) had been used by late Qing reformer Kang Youwei in his influential essays on citizen self-rule (*gongmin zizhi*), published between 1902 and 1903. Kang was at this time advocating political changes along the lines of Japan's Meiji Reform. Some Chinese interpreted Kang Youwei's proposed model as a license for local autonomy, whereas others saw it as advocating a centralized system.[82] As Frederic Wakeman has explained, Kang himself did not enthusiastically endorse local self-rule but valued constitutional government because it was "more *kung* [*gong*], more public, than the selfishness of pure autocracy."[83] In any case, despite the broad term for *citizenship,* those being tapped for participation were in fact limited to the educated and affluent urban elite.

During the May Fourth Movement, a somewhat narrower term for citizen—*guomin,* or "people of the nation-state"—came into vogue.[84] Now the political community to which "citizens" were rallied was not an expansive public (*gong*) but a particular nation–state (*guo*). As citizens of the Republic of China, patriots owed their allegiance to their newly constituted polity. When business and educational leaders in Shanghai formed a local council during the May Fourth Movement, they dubbed it a *guomin dahui*.[85]

In the May Thirtieth Movement of 1925, a yet more parochial term and one tinged with racial connotations, *tongbao* (referring literally to those born of the same womb), became the favored address in recruiting participants. Suggesting an intimacy that was possible only among people who shared a common bloodline, the term was often accompanied by other kinship designations. Communist manifestos during the May Thirtieth Movement were addressed to "brothers and sisters from the same womb" (*tongbao xiongdi jiemei men*).[86] Not an abstract polity but an extended family was the community to which participants were called.

The three armed uprisings were mobilized on the basis of a seemingly even narrower identity. Now people were asked to participate not for the sake of the public, the nation–state, or the race, but simply as urbanites (*shimin*). It was, in other words, neither as world citizens nor as Chinese citizens but as citizens of Shanghai that potential recruits were rallied to the cause. As the first manifesto issued in conjunction with the uprisings put it: "Shanghai belongs to the Shanghai residents themselves!" (*Shanghai shi Shanghai shimin zijide!*)[87] And yet this narrowest identity proved most attractive of all. In contrast to the 60,000 strikers of May Fourth and 200,000 of May Thirtieth, the second and third uprisings brought first 350,000 and then 800,000 strikers out onto the streets.[88]

If my speculation about the contraction of collective identities is correct (and, in the absence of evidence establishing that strikers were actually responding to the terms by which movement organizers addressed them, it remains at best a plausible hypothesis), then what is the implication for network theory? Perhaps it is not the broadest but rather the narrowest common denominator that holds the greatest potential for mobilizing disparate social networks to undertake unified action in pursuit of ambitious political goals.

Conclusion

The emergence of political parties in Republican Shanghai did promote a more ideological agenda, as reflected in organizers' demands for an end to warlordism and imperialism. Yet, in the end, mass passions seem to have been less excited by calls to defend the public or the nation than by more familiar appeals as fellow kinsmen or local residents. By the time of the armed uprisings, Communist cadres had come to appreciate the importance of linking their national party to local concerns. As they explained in an open letter to Shanghai citizens (*shimin*):

You don't know where the Chinese Communist Party is and who its members are, do you? Actually the CCP is still secret and cannot easily reveal its organization, but the party's organization extends across the entire country. Members of the CCP are constantly around you and are giving their all for you.

The Shanghai district committee of the CCP is the party's organization in Shanghai. Its responsibility is precisely to serve the interests of the Shanghai masses. Since the May Thirtieth massacre, its resolve and determination have been made clear. You mustn't think that CCP members are only active in convening citizen assemblies. You should know that in your very midst, members of this party are ceaselessly engaged in ordinary revolutionary struggles. Thus we alert the citizens of Shanghai to the following demands on their behalf:

Residents of the foreign concessions should all enjoy equal rights to participate in city government
Unconditionally take back the Mixed Court . . .
Promulgate a Shanghai municipal labor insurance law
Reduce the price of rice . . .
Oppose the property tax
Oppose the household registration fee
Oppose the tobacco levy . . .

Only if these demands are met can 'humiliated Shanghai' become 'revolutionary Shanghai,' and a Shanghai self-governed by the citizens of Shanghai be established.[89]

Specific demands such as these, which appealed to the citizenry of Shanghai as residents, laborers, consumers, and taxpayers, resonated with members of many different networks, whose internal connections were after all based upon mundane, everyday interactions.

Yet, in the end, influential patrons quickly proved able to dismantle even as impressive a movement as that which coalesced during the three armed uprisings. The Janus-faced character of networks in Republican Shanghai, capable of effecting both rapid mobilization and demobilization, is consistent with more general observations often made about the nature of Chinese social relations. As more than a few anthropologists have remarked, mainstream Chinese values tend to place a higher premium on interpersonal relations (*guanxi*) than on commitment to abstract causes or ideologies.[90] Mayfair Yang, in her study of social relations in contemporary China, explains that *guanxi* involves a "sense of 'social connections,' dyadic relationships that are based implicitly (rather than explicitly) on mutual interest and benefit."[91]

Thanks to what Yang characterizes as the "primacy and binding power of personal relationships,"[92] we can appreciate why individual Chinese might be quick to shift allegiances when influential members of their networks (*guanxiwang*) signal that it is appropriate to do so. The political implications of various *guanxiwang* are difficult to forecast, because as Lucian Pye emphasizes: "the particularistic basis of a relationship does not in itself provide a clear clue for predicting the purposes for which the relationship might be directed. People might be associated with each other, for example, because they came from the same town or province, but this would almost never mean that they would therefore work together for the interests of that place."[93] To translate this insight into the language of network theory, *guanxiwang* would appear to militate against "structural equivalence," or the recognition of a specific set of relationships as part of a more general pattern.

The practice of *guanxi*, by personalizing social relationships, has been portrayed by some China scholars as operating differently from the ways in which sociologists have characterized social networks in general. *Guanxi* is depicted in these accounts as an exception to Mark Granovetter's famous "strength of weak ties" hypothesis, which suggested that weak ties (i.e., those involving less commitment of time, emotional intensity, intimacy, and reciprocity) may be more likely than strong ties to serve as conduits of information and influence. Weak ties, Granovetter proposes, can function as bridges between otherwise fragmented groups, thereby facilitating concerted community action.[94] Similarly, Roger Gould's argument about a "jump in scale" with the establishment of formal organizations posits a relatively powerful mobilizing role for more distant, less intimate relationships. In the Chinese context, however, Bian Yanjie has recently argued that strong ties (i.e., those based on substantial mutual knowledge and trust, or *guanxi*) are typically the means through which influence is exercised in the contemporary job market.[95] Amy Hanser sums up the distinction: "Contrasting the concept of *guanxi* . . . with that of tie strength generates two insights: First, there *is* something different about *guanxi* relative to Granovetter's concept of tie strength. There is more reciprocity involved, a greater sense of trust and obligation than is captured in the notion of a simple 'social tie.' Second, social ties can and do work differently in different contexts."[96]

Early twentieth-century Shanghai was a highly unstable context, marked by extraordinary demographic, political, and social change. The dangers and uncertainties inherent in such a fluid environment contributed directly to the centrality of native place and secret society networks. The power of these groups lay both in the close one-on-one relationships through which new members were recruited and retained and in the capacity of these *guanxiwang* to provide protection, procure employment, proffer introductions, and perform other key services. But *guanxi*, like social ties more generally, comes in strong and weak flavors. A person may, for example, claim "*guanxi*" with a fellow provincial or gang member even when their actual relationship is intermittent and emotionally thin. In a society like China, where human behavior is generally understood as an outgrowth of social relationships rather than a reflection of individual interests, there may well be a tendency on the part of informants and analysts alike to exaggerate the level of reciprocity and intimacy involved in such relationships. Nevertheless, whether we choose to think of *guanxi* as something singularly Chinese or not, its institutional expression in native place associations and secret society gangs was a defining feature of early twentieth-century Shanghai.

When the KMT and CCP tried to navigate the treacherous waters of Republican-era Shanghai, they naturally sought to enlist the assistance of these influential entities. But modern political parties—which are established to articulate and aggregate interests in accord with an abstract ideological vision—operate by principles very different from *guanxiwang*. Whether we date the origin of China's political parties to Sun Yat-sen's founding of the Xingzhonghui in Honolulu in 1894 or to his establishment eleven years later of the Tongmenghui in Japan, political parties were a foreign implant in modern China. The political history of 1920s Shanghai is largely the story of how the two major parties attempted to transcend their alien origins by adapting to the realities of Chinese society. The narrowing of participatory identity, to better capture the lived experience of ordinary Shanghai residents, was but one manifestation of this larger process.

The partisan contest between the KMT and CCP was not conducted on a level playing field, however. Despite the CCP's increasing ideological flexibility and willingness to do business with all manner of potential collaborators, the Communists at this time lacked the personal connections—or *guanxi*—upon which KMT leaders were able to draw. These ties, in some cases stretching back two decades to the late Qing period, linked men such as Chiang Kai-shek, Huang Jinrong, Du

Yuesheng, Yu Xiaqing, and Niu Yongjian in bonds of reciprocity that proved stronger than the fervor of mass nationalism, let alone any abstract appeal of communism. Round one in this contest thus went to the KMT—or, more precisely, to that wing of the KMT (led by Chiang Kai-shek) that was especially adept at converting *guanxi* into political capital. It would take the CCP another two decades to develop the requisite connections (and military capacity) to score an even more resounding comeback.

CHAPTER 6

The National Salvation Movement and Social Networks in Republican Shanghai

PARKS M. COBLE

THE NATIONAL SALVATION movement was perhaps the largest popular movement not directly tied to a political party during China's Nanjing era. Although it lacked the violence and scale of the upheavals surrounding the armed uprisings from 1926 to 1927, the salvation movement built on the linkages among students and urbanites formed in the May Thirtieth Movement and became a major political force during the 1930s. As a general term, "national salvation movement" refers to a wide range of groups and organizations that formed during the 1930s to address the issue of Japanese aggression in China. Much of this activity was political, attempting to force the Chiang Kai-shek government to adopt a stronger stand against Japan. Much also involved raising funds for Chinese forces who were actually fighting the Japanese (such as the Nineteenth Route Army in Shanghai in 1932) or were thought to be doing so (such as General Ma Zhanshan in Manchuria). As a specific term, the National Salvation Movement usually refers to the organizations that formed at the time of the December Ninth movement of 1935. These included the Shanghai Cultural Circles National Salvation Association (*Shanghai wenhua jie jiuguo hui*), which issued its manifesto on December 12, 1935, calling for resistance to Japan, and the All-Shanghai National Salvation Association League (*Shanghai gejie jiuguo lianhe hui*), which held its first rally on January 28, 1936, the fourth anniversary of the fighting at Shanghai.[1]

The salvation movement was a product of the aggressive assaults on Chinese sovereignty by Japan during the 1930s. Although the mid-1920s had witnessed an upsurge of political activity associated with the

May Thirtieth movement and the Northern Expedition, Chiang Kai-shek's "White Terror" had silenced much of this. The Japanese seizure of northeast China following the Manchurian Incident of September 18, 1931, reactivated public opinion in China. National outrage was widespread, at least among the urban dwellers and student population. Whereas the anti-imperialist movement of the 1910s and 1920s targeted virtually all of the treaty powers, particularly Britain, Japan's actions in the 1930s made it the sole focus. Japanese aggression also eclipsed many of the social issues as well. To be certain, the vast majority of Chinese were illiterate, rural peasants largely uninvolved in social issues. But for millions of students, workers, and urban professionals, the Japanese attacks galvanized them into action. Students from all over China, including Shanghai, poured into Nanjing, demanding that the Chinese government resist the Japanese. Violent clashes between police and students occurred in mid-December 1931, with thousands arrested. Shanghai businessmen joined in, organizing an anti-Japanese boycott.[2] Labor unions largely quiescent since Chiang's repression took on new life. Seventy unions in Shanghai sent petitions to Nanjing demanding resistance to Japan, and on September 24, 1931, nearly 30,000 Chinese workers in Japanese factories in Shanghai went on strike.[3]

Yet for all of the significance of the Manchurian Incident, it was perhaps the outbreak of conflict in Shanghai itself on January 28, 1932, that most affected public opinion in the city. While the Manchurian Incident led to Japanese control of a vast territory with a population of at least 30 million, the area was quite distant for Shanghai; few of the activists in the city had ever seen the place. The six weeks of fighting in 1932 in Shanghai, however, was right in their midst. Entire sections of Shanghai (such as Zhabei) were in flames. Factories were destroyed, the famous library of the Commercial Press was deliberately burned, and many schools and colleges were targeted.[4] Salvation groups already mobilized since September 1931 stepped up their activities with the new fighting. Now they could become directly involved in the conflict.

In Chapter 5 of this volume, Elizabeth Perry suggests that the basis of mobilization from May Fourth to May Thirtieth to the three armed uprisings became increasingly narrow. By the last movement, people were being mobilized as urbanites not as world citizens or even Chinese citizens. The 1932 fighting, in part, reversed this trend by putting renewed emphasis on being a citizen of the nation. Yet the specific fighting that developed in Shanghai focused on the city itself. Saving Shanghai from

Japanese aggression was a real, tangible issue that mobilized all segments of this divided city.

On January 31, 1932, student, labor, women's, and business groups established the Federation of Anti-Japanese National Salvation Associations (*Shanghai shi gejie kangRi jiuguo hui*) to unite their efforts. The Shanghai Civic Association (*Shanghai difang xiehui*), led by Green Gang figure Du Yuesheng, assisted Chinese forces with gang members based in the foreign concessions where they could monitor Japanese activity. The Refugees Aid Society (*Zhandi nanmin linshi jiuji hui*) attempted to cope with the civilian victims of the fighting. These groups raised over 40 million yuan to aid the Chinese troops. Students formed drama and singing groups to assist troop morale, and nearly 800 joined the fighting.[5] The spring of 1932 created the most vigorous popular movement in Shanghai since the suppression of April 1927.

Salvation activities always had a political edge. Although directed against the Japanese, they also targeted Chiang Kai-shek and other Chinese thought guilty of nonresistance. Nanjing's lack of resistance following the Manchurian Incident and the conclusion of the truce ending the conflict at Shanghai led salvationist organizations to demand political change. Zou Taofen and his journal *Shenghuo* (Life) led the charge directly attacking Chiang Kai-shek's announced policy of "first internal pacification (i.e., eliminating the communists), then external resistance." Chiang responded by closing publications like *Shenghuo*, arresting those considered subversive, and authorizing the assassinations of intellectuals and journalists deemed to be a threat.[6]

Yet Chiang's actions failed to quash the movement, for which the Japanese bear the blame. Had Japanese aggression ceased with the creation of the puppet state Manchukuo (*Manzhouguo*), perhaps more Chinese would have accepted Chiang's policy of nonresistance. But that was not to be. Japan provoked a series of conflicts and incidents over the next five years that kept the Japanese problem on the front page of newspapers virtually every day.[7] In the summer of 1932, Japanese forces attacked and overran Rehe province (now northern Hebei and eastern Inner Mongolia), which was added to Manchukuo. The conflict spread and a fairly intense war erupted along the Great Wall in the spring of 1933, with China suffering at least 30,000 casualties. Chiang dispatched Huang Fu to negotiate the Tanggu Truce in May 1933, the terms of which seriously weakened Nanjing's position in the north. In April 1934, an official of the Japanese foreign ministry, Amo Eiji, proclaimed Japan's "hands off China" statement, stating Japan's objections to China's involvement with other countries. In July 1934, under pressure from Tokyo, Nanjing lowered China's tariffs on key commodities of interest to Japan. Moves by the Japanese Guandong (Kanto) army into Inner Mongolia in early 1935 precipitated a new crisis and two additional "understandings" between China and Japan—the He-Umezu Agreement and the Qin-Doihara Agreement—both of which undercut Nanjing's authority in the north. Nanjing was also required to issue the Goodwill Mandate (*dunmu bangjiao ling*) on June 10, 1935, prohibiting provocative acts or speeches aimed at "friendly neighbors." The Japanese issue would not go away and each action further inflamed public opinion and undercut support for Chiang's nonresistance policy.

The salvation movement itself became the center of contention between Nanjing and Tokyo, with the latter demanding that Chiang suppress anti-Japanese thought in China. As Sei Jeong Chin details in Chapter 7 of this volume, when the salvationist journal *Xin shenghuo* (*New Life*), edited by Du Zhongyuan, published an article deemed derogatory of the Japanese emperor, Tokyo's consul in Shanghai demanded that Du be arrested and anti-Japanese groups be curtailed. Du's sentence of fourteen months in prison on July 9, 1935, further inflamed the salvationists. Every attempt by Nanjing to calm public opinion was usually countered by a new Japanese provocation.

On September 24, 1935, the Japanese commander of the North China Garrison held a press conference in which he called for "autonomy" from Nanjing for the five key provinces of north China. Under Japanese leadership, Tada proclaimed, north China would become a "paradise" for all, a new Manchukuo. Nor was all activity confined to the north. In early October 1935, Japan dispatched six destroyers to Xiamen to protest a customs incident. Almost simultaneously, eight gunboats were sent to Wuhan because of alleged anti-Japanese activity by the local military commander.

In late 1935, Japanese military leader Doihara Kenji actively pressured militarists in north China to declare their independence of Nanjing. When Chinese leaders appeared to be wavering on the issue, the result was the outburst of demonstrations usually called the December Ninth Movement. Even inland Sichuan was involved. When Japan attempted to open a consulate in Chengdu in August 1936, a riot led by students from West China Union University resulted in the deaths of two Japanese. Japan's minister to China presented Nanjing with a long list of demands to settle the matter, and Tokyo dispatched two additional warships to Wuhan.

Meanwhile two separate clashes had occurred at Fengtai near Beiping (as Beijing was then known), with Japan using these as a pretext to pressure north China commander Song Zheyuan to declare "autonomy" from Nanjing. Lt. Colonel Tanaka Ryukichi, intelligence staff officer of the Japanese Guandong army, had already begun organizing a mercenary force of 6,000 to invade Suiyuan province in Inner Mongolia to "liberate" it from Chinese rule. A brief war developed in November and December 1936 between this force and Chinese commander Fu Zuoyi. By the time Chiang Kai-shek left for Xi'an and his kidnapping by Zhang Xueliang, Sino-Japanese relations were at a crisis point and Chiang's policy of "first pacification, then resistance" was widely disparaged.

Japanese provocations therefore kept the issue of resistance on the front page throughout this period. Despite assassinations, arrests, and edicts, Nanjing could not silence national salvation activity. The final frenzy of organizing developed in the latter part of 1935 when the north China autonomy movement seemed a fait accompli. The December Ninth demonstrations fired up students all over China. Activity spread from northern to southern cities, including Shanghai, Nanjing, Guangzhou, and the Wuhan area. By the end of December, student groups had organized the National Salvation Union (*Jiuguo lianhe hui*) in Shanghai, which linked student groups with other salvationist organizations. Nanjing responded with repression. On December 19, Minister of Education Wang Shijie banned further demonstrations, and two days later Nanjing proclaimed martial law in the Shanghai–Nanjing area.[8]

Despite the government's efforts, the Japanese push for north China "autonomy" and the resulting December Ninth movement further activated public opinion in China. The move by the Chinese Communist Party (CCP) to endorse a united front approach further strengthened the salvationist cause. Well-known leftist figures, such as Madame Sun Yat-sen (Song Qingling), joined the movement and called for unity between the Guomindang and the CCP and for resistance to Japan. Zou Taofen, who had been forced to travel abroad when Chiang cracked down on the movement, returned from America to Shanghai in August 1935. Although his major journals had been suspended by Nanking, Zou still had a base of operations in his Shenghuo Book Store located in Shanghai. He also established a new weekly journal, *Dazhong shenghuo* (Life of the Masses) on November 16, 1935, sales of which reached almost 200,000 per issue.[9]

When the Shanghai Cultural Circles National Salvation Association formed on December 12, 1935, its manifesto was signed by over

200 prominent intellectuals, led by the elderly Ma Liang, founder of Furen University and one of China's most prominent Roman Catholics. Other signatories included Zou Taofen; Tao Xingzhi, a student of John Dewey at Columbia University who had for many years been an activist in the mass education movement; Wang Zaoshi, a lawyer in Shanghai who had earned a Ph.D. in political science at the University of Wisconsin; and Shen Junru, another prominent lawyer in Shanghai.[10]

On December 21, He Xiangning (widow of Liao Zhongkai) and Shi Liang (a Shanghai lawyer with close ties to Madame Sun Yat-sen) launched the Shanghai Women's National Salvation Association (*Shanghai funujie jiuguo hui*). Other like-minded groups included Shanghai newspaper reporters, who called for an open press, and a group from the movie industry. Later Sha Qianli, a Shanghai lawyer, organized a professional workers' salvation group. The primary goal of these groups was to block any further concessions in north China. This activity culminated in the organization of the All-Shanghai National Salvation Association League, which was kicked off with a rally of several thousand people.[11]

The salvation movement outraged Chiang Kai-shek, who considered it a communist front. In fact, the movement was led by many sympathetic to the communist cause and was definitely exploiting the intense public anger at Japan and at Chiang's appeasement policy. But Chiang faced a dilemma. He distrusted the salvationist movement and his appeasement policy required that he suppress anti-Japanese activity. Yet repression of the movement often backfired, increasing public support. When Nanjing ordered the journal *Tazhong Shenghuo* suspended in late February 1936, Zou Taofen immediately began publishing a new journal, *Yongsheng* (Eternal Life), which was an instant success. When, in February 1936, Nanjing issued new emergency laws to curb demonstrations, the salvationists responded with a large protest in Shanghai. On May 31, 1936, the All-China League of National Salvation Associations (*Quanguo gejie jiuguo lianhe hui*) met in Shanghai and issued its proclamation. "Since September 18th China has experienced four years and eight months of suffering," the manifesto read. During that time, Japan seized "a territory of 1,680,000 square kilometers, covering six provinces, enslaving sixty million of our people and killing more than 300,000." The only solution is that "all military units of this country should put an end to civil war . . . and take prompt action to fight the enemy."[12] The movement flourished during the spring of 1936. As Paul

Linebarger has observed, "the National Salvation (*chiu-kuo*) movement is third in point of size and influence [after the Guomindang and CCP]. Genuinely a movement, it had no membership books, no formal or systematic organization. . . . The movement spread like wildfire." Ultimately, he concluded "most literate persons not already committed to formal Kuomintang [Guomindang] or Communist membership fell under the influence of the movement."[13]

The National Salvation Movement and Social Networks

Clearly, Japanese aggression had inflamed Chinese public opinion in 1935 and 1936. But how did the salvation movement achieve such a public presence and influence so quickly? The answer is that the movement plugged into an existing set of social networks that had developed over the first decades of the twentieth century and had been the foundation of many previous political movements. The "national" salvation organization formed in Shanghai was not a monolithic group that opened its membership to individuals. Instead, it was a coalition of constituent organizations, each based on profession and status. Cultural workers, newspaper reporters, clerks, bankers, lawyers, student groups, YMCA supporters—each formed their own individual group that then became part of the coalition.

The first three decades of the twentieth century were a "golden age" for the formation of nongovernmental organizations in Shanghai. Several factors contributed to this trend. Shanghai was China's largest trading port, most international city, and dominant in the new industrial and commercial economy. The media—newspapers, journals, book publishing, movies, and popular art—were all centered in Shanghai. The divided jurisdiction of the city—the International Settlement, French Concession, and Chinese city—ensured weak law enforcement and made it difficult for Chinese authorities such as Chiang Kai-shek to crack down on autonomous organizations. Some of these groups were "traditional" organizations that assumed new roles in changing Shanghai. Bryna Goodman's work on native place associations reveals how these groups played new and surprising roles in the changing environment of the city. Andrea McElderry demonstrated how "native banks" (*qianzhuang*) were really evolving with the growth of foreign trade, while Western-style modern banks became a fixture by the 1920s. Both the Shanghai Bankers Association (representing the modern banks) and Shanghai Native Bankers Association were important public groups in Republican Shanghai. They were joined by religious organizations, students associations, alumni organizations, chambers of commerce—the list is almost endless. Even criminal elements flourished in the new conditions. Du Yuesheng and the Shanghai Green Gang were an integral part of the social fabric of the city, as Brian Martin shows in Chapter 4 of this volume.[14] Similarly, we see in Elizabeth Perry's Chapter 5 that these associations and the links among them were key to the mobilization of Shanghai during the May Fourth and May Thirtieth movements and the three armed uprisings.

This array of nongovernmental organizations might not strike the Western reader as particularly extraordinary, but it was a relatively new phenomenon in China and one which would not last. The outbreak of war in 1937 and the occupation by Japan of the Chinese city (and the International Settlement in December 1941) was the beginning of the end. Neither the Japanese overlords nor the victorious Guomindang in 1945 were open to politically and socially active groups not under government control. When Chairman Mao and the Chinese Communist Party took over, they eliminated all vestiges of nonparty associations. Only today are such groups gradually emerging in China, but they are still far less active than in the 1930s.

During these early decades of the twentieth century, Shanghai indeed had a rich network of professional and associational groups that provided organizational links for the salvation movement. Most of these groups were formed for reasons unrelated to political causes; yet, they often served as the foundation for political action. Xiaoqun Xu, in his study of the rise of the professions in Shanghai, details the development of the Shanghai Bar Association. An outgrowth of the development of the legal profession, this organization was strongly influenced by the Western model. The major goals of the bar association were professional and, in fact, its bylaws prohibited the group from engaging in political issues unrelated to professional matters. Yet Xu points out that with the Manchurian Incident and the intense fighting in Shanghai itself from 1931 to 1932, the Shanghai Bar Association violated its own rules and became intensely involved in the resistance movement. The group telegraphed China's Ministry of Foreign Affairs, demanding a hard line against Japan; supported Ma Zhanshan, the Chinese commander who appeared to be resisting the Japanese in Manchuria, and voted a 3,000 yuan donation for the Nineteenth Route Army fighting the Japanese at Shanghai without, many argued, the support of Chiang Kai-shek. In other words, the newly formed professional organization became one of the mechanisms for organizing pro-resistance activity during this period of crisis.[15]

Nor were the lawyers alone. The rich texture of groups and associations in Shanghai provided the networks for political work. Xu points out that in the aftermath of the Manchurian Incident, "public associations and newly founded national salvation societies in Shanghai held no less than 138 public rallies and issued at least 532 declarations and circular telegrams. . . . Of those statements and telegrams, 217 were from the industrial and commercial sectors, 94 from students, 61 from workers, 40 from educators, and 18 from the culture circle."[16]

The native place associations (*tongxiang hui*) became active in the resistance from 1931 to 1932. As Bryna Goodman notes, "Responding to the explosive events in Manchuria and Shanghai in the fall and winter of 1931 to 1932, Shanghai native place associations published strident criticisms of Zhang Xueliang and rallied considerable financial support for Ma Zhanshan."[17] In addition, they often provided office space to various salvation groups. In 1937, for instance, eight anti-Japanese groups found shelter in the Pudong association, and others housed such organizations as the Shanghai Young Writers' National Salvation Propaganda Group and the National Salvation Workers' Institute. Native place groups were also active in refugee relief, though usually helping those from the home community. Thus when thousands fled from the Chinese city into the foreign zones after August 13, 1937, the Guangdong native place group provided shelter for 50,000 displaced Cantonese and the Ningbo group for 25,000 of their fellows.[18] The National Salvation Movement simply could not have developed with the speed and power it did in the late 1930s had it not been for the array of nongovernmental organizations that formed during the early decades of the century and the rich experience of previous political movements, especially the crisis from 1931 to 1932.

Yet organizations were not the whole story; perhaps not even the main story. Most salvation manifestos contained not only the names of the various groups supporting the movement but also the names of leaders. Lists of donors were often published as well. It was the personal network of connections that was as critical to jump-starting the salvationist campaign as enlisting formal organizations. No complete chart of the web of personal ties among the Shanghai elite is possible, but it is clear that even in a city the size of Shanghai, the dominant players in every sector often interacted with one another in settings such as the Chinese Ratepayers Association, the alumni association of the prestigious St. John's Academy, chambers of commerce, and so forth. Elsewhere in this volume we have seen how Shanghai leaders such as the merchant Yu Xiaqing, the comprador Wang Yiting, the educator and activist Huang Yanpei, and others had complex links within Shanghai society. All played crucial roles in earlier mobilizations. So an individual such as Green Gang leader Du Yuesheng appeared on the board of directors of many respectable groups, including the Pudong Native Place Association (*Pudong tongxiang hui*), the Shanghai Northeast Refugees Relief Association (*Shanghai dongbei nanmin jiuji hui*) set up in fall 1931, the Shanghai Civic Association, the Bank of China, and the Central Bank of China.[19] He became a crucial node in the networks linking Shanghai elites and made possible movements like the salvationists.

Some personal ties went back to the early years of the century when the late Qing reforms unleashed new social energy. In 1906, for instance, a group of intellectuals in Shanghai formed the Research Society for Constitutional Government (*Xiangzheng yanjiu hui*). Among the group were Huang Yanpei, Shi Liangcai, Chen Leng, and Di Chuqing. Shi eventually owned the influential newspaper *Shen Bao* and along with Huang Yanpei was active in the Shanghai Civic Association headed by Du Yuesheng. Di and Chen were associated with the *Shi Bao*, while Huang Yanpei formed the Chinese Vocational Education Society (*Zhonghua zhiye jiaoyu she*; see Chapter 2 of this volume). Their early association gave these individuals a connection that facilitated their working together in later movements. Younger activists often formed client–patron relationships with these more senior figures and could sometimes connect with their patrons' network when organizing a political movement. Huang would start a journal to promote vocational education and, in 1923, hired a young graduate of St. John's University, Zou Taofen. The young man had a genius for editing a journal, creating a lively letters-to-the-editor column and a huge circulation for Huang's journal. As noted previously, Zou became increasingly active in the anti-Japanese movement and his journals became the major outlet for salvationist writing. Zou could often use the name of his patron, Huang Yanpei, to forge new ties. Du Zhongyuan, who wrote the article on the Japanese emperor that so annoyed the Japanese, was a refugee industrialist from Manchuria who arrived in Shanghai with an introduction to Huang Yanpei. That connection linked him to Zou and the *Shenghuo* group. Zou increasingly developed his own network. For instance, he became close to Zhang Naiqi who worked for banker Li Ming at the Zhejiang Industrial Bank. Zhang eventually was forced out of the bank by Guomindang pressure and devoted his full time to writing for salvationist journals.[20]

Tracking down the complete web of personal ties among the Shanghai elite is impossible, but sufficient links are evident that it becomes clear how different organizations and individuals could be so quickly brought together. Sufficient people from different groups—educators, lawyers, bank managers, publishers, and even gangsters—had worked together in the past to allow rapid formation of new coalitions. For instance, the Manchurian Incident and fighting at Shanghai had forged a strong series of connections among the anti-Japanese activists in Shanghai. In turn, these connections were used in January 1933, when a number of intellectuals became concerned about the use of arrests and assassinations by the Chiang government to silence opposition to his appeasement policy. They formed the League for the Protection of Civil Rights (*Minquan baozhang tongmeng*). Leaders of this group were Madame Sun Yat-sen, Cai Yuanpei, Lin Yutang, Hu Yuzhi, Lu Xun, Yu Dafu, Wang Zaoshi, Shen Junru, and Zou Taofen. Cai was perhaps China's most famous educator; Lu Xun, Lin Yutang, and Yu Dafu among the best-known writers. Hu Yuzhi was an editor for *Dongfang zazhi* (Eastern Miscellany), one of China's best-known journals, and for Zou Taofen's *Shenghuo* as well. The League was not entirely successful, because a leading member, Yang Xingfo, was gunned down in Shanghai in June 1933. Yang had been vice president of Academia Sinica and an alumnus of Cornell and Harvard.[21] Yet the league facilitated new connections among Shanghai's intellectuals and publishers, connections essential to the formation of the salvation movement in 1935 and 1936.

When new salvation groups were formed, publishing the leaders' names served as a public signal to followers that this was a cause worth fighting for. In effect, it drew on the networks of these leaders to strengthen its numbers. For example, when the Shanghai Cultural Circles salvation group issued its proclamation on December 12, 1935, to support the students in Beiping, the name at the top of the list was the venerable Ma Liang. His name on the manifesto was a signal to the many people who had worked with him over the decades that they should join the cause.[22] The other marquee name, of course, was Song Qingling (Madame Sun Yat-sen), widow of the father of the Republic and sister-in-law to Chiang Kai-shek himself. Madame Sun's association with the Guomindang left and Chinese Communist Party meant that her name on a manifesto signaled to her supporters that they should join in. Since the formal organization of the left-GMD and the

CCP in Shanghai had largely been destroyed by Chiang's agents, Madame Sun's public stance was crucial in communicating political positions to stranded activists.

Japanese aggression provided the fuel for the explosive growth of the National Salvation Movement in the period from 1935 to 1937, but existing networks allowed its rapid organization. The large number of nongovernmental bodies—whether lawyers, clerks, students, or factory owners—facilitated the rapid organization of salvation activity. The complex web of personal connections between so many leading activists in Shanghai, from the elderly Ma Liang, to the famous Madame Sun Yat-sen, to Zou Taofen, Wang Zaoshi, and Zhang Naiqi, allowed for these constituent groups to move with remarkable speed.

Why Shanghai?

The National Salvation Movement was by far stronger in Shanghai than any other area in China. This was not surprising since Shanghai had such a dominant role in the modern sector of the economy, in the publishing and media industries, and as a center of contact with foreign influences. The divided political situation in Shanghai, what with the International Settlement, French Concession, and Chinese city, also afforded the opportunity for action. Chiang's Guomindang forces could not act at will in the foreign sectors of Shanghai. The Japanese were constrained by the presence of other foreign powers. These conditions did not pertain in most other cities in China in 1936, at least not to the same degree as in Shanghai. Ironically, the 1936 movement had really been kicked off by the December 9, 1935, demonstrations, which were organized in Beiping. Indeed, student actions, strikes, and marches spread to Tianjin and north China before coming south.[23]

Yet it was much more difficult to sustain the movement in the north because of Japanese pressure. Beiping had no International Settlement such as Shanghai to offer a zone of protection. The foreign sectors in Tianjin were divided and small; Japan's position was substantial. Concessions made in the earlier Tanggu Truce and by He Yinqin and Qin Dechun in 1935 left north China vulnerable to Japanese influence. Remaining Chinese authorities in the area, such as Song Zheyuan, head of the twenty-ninth army, were under intense pressure to restrain all anti-Japanese activity. On December 23, bowing to Japanese demands, Song ordered all schools in Beiping and Tianjin to close for vacation. It is sometimes argued that the demonstrations had actually strengthened

Song's hand in dealing with the Japanese but the overall atmosphere in the north made the type of salvationist activity found in Shanghai impossible. Later, in May 1936, the Japanese increased the strength of their garrison in Tianjin, in part to counter the influence of the salvationist movement, and in December Tokyo dispatched marines to Qingdao to curb anti-Japanese labor unrest.[24]

A number of southern leaders had been far more open to the anti-Japanese line, perhaps in part because they wished to embarrass and weaken Chiang Kai-shek so as to retain as much autonomy as possible. By late 1936, however, Chiang had largely destroyed these southern leaders, save for the Guangxi Clique. Cai Tingkai had made Fujian a bastion of anti-Japanese sentiment but, in January 1934, the Fujian Rebellion had been soundly defeated by Chiang. Then in the summer of 1936, Chiang outmaneuvered the quasi-independent leader of Guangdong province, General Chen Jitang, bringing that southern polity under his tight control. Salvationist groups therefore found the going tough in these areas. Resistance sentiment was stronger in Guangxi province, but this remote and impoverished area could not support the type of visible movement associated with Shanghai. The metropolis was the key center for the salvation movement.

Arrest of the Seven Gentlemen

On July 15, 1936, four leaders of the salvation movement, Zou Taofen, Zhang Naiqi, Shen Junru, and Tao Xingzhi, issued a platform for the group, "A Number of Essential Conditions and Minimum Demands for a United Resistance to Invasion," which specifically noted the CCP's adoption of a united front approach and called for cooperation between the two parties to resist Japan. Chiang's policy of appeasement had clearly failed, they stated, but if he would resist Japan, all would rally to support him. Chiang saw this as proof that the National Salvation Association was a Communist front organization, and the Guomindang denounced it as an unregistered, illegal, and "reactionary" body.[25] Meanwhile a series of labor strikes against textile mills in Shanghai owned by Japanese led to a showdown. By mid-November 1936, the strikes involved over 20,000 workers and began to spread to other cities. While they began over wages and working conditions, the strikes quickly took on an anti-Japanese tone, with the National Salvation Association providing financial support. Japanese authorities blamed the salvationists for the labor unrest and when violence erupted at the

Toyoda textile mill in Shanghai on November 17, 1936, the Japanese consul general demanded that Nanjing arrest leaders of the association.[26]

During the night of November 22, 1936, Chinese police arrested seven key leaders of the association—Zou Taofen, Zhang Naiqi, Shen Junru, Sha Qianli, Li Gongpu, Wang Zaoshi, and Shi Liang. The arrests were made in the International Settlement and the French Concession in Shanghai and required the cooperation of the foreign authorities. Of the major leaders of the movement, only Madame Sun Yat-sen, He Xiangning (Madame Liao Zhongkai), and Ma Liang (then 97 years old) were spared.[27] Nanjing attempted to keep the case quiet, but the arrests created a sensation. The press quickly dubbed these the "Seven Gentlemen" (*Qi junzi*). In an attempt to dampen publicity, Nanjing authorities moved the seven to Suzhou on December 4, 1936, where their trial would begin in the spring of 1937. The arrest of the Seven Gentlemen shifted the focus of the salvationist movement; efforts to pressure Chiang to release the leaders became the immediate goal, although always attached to the resistance issue. As Madame Sun Yat-sen told reporters, "Seven leaders of the National Salvation Association have been arrested, but there are still 400,000,000 Chinese people whose patriotic wrath and righteous indignation cannot be suppressed! Let the Japanese militarists beware! They may cause the arrest of seven leaders, but they must still reckon with the Chinese people."[28]

The arrest of the Seven Gentlemen revealed the wide-ranging social networks that the salvationist leaders had developed. The Seven had ties to education, publishing, the legal profession, and banking—their political networks were extensive and a wide assortment of leaders voiced support for their release. Green Gang leader Du Yuesheng visited them in prison, as did banker Qian Yongming and prominent business leaders Wang Xiaolai and Yu Xiaqing, both stalwarts of the chamber of commerce. Newspaper stories detailed the family background of the Seven, portraying them as heroes, and their arrests invigorated the protest movement. As the historian Ch'ien Tuan-sheng observed, "Their arrest so boosted the number of adherents and sympathizers that they actually became the third most powerful party, next to the Kuomintang and the Communist Party."[29]

Four of the Seven were members of the Shanghai Bar Association (SBA), and a team of 21 prominent lawyers from Shanghai volunteered to serve as the defense team. Interestingly, the SBA itself did not take a public position on the matter in sharp contrast to its active role from 1931 to 1932. As Xiaoqun Xu's study makes clear, Chiang Kai-shek had put enormous pressure on the group after the earlier involvement to refrain from political activity. In the 1936 salvationist wave, the SBA did not take stands as a public body but allowed its members to do so as individuals. Thus, in February 5, 1936, the group decided that its members could join the federation of salvation societies but the body itself would not.[30]

Perhaps the most important supporters of the Seven Gentlemen were the two military commanders at Xi'an, Zhang Xueliang and Yang Hucheng. Both would make release of the Seven a key demand in the Xi'an incident. Zhang had gone to Luoyang on December 3, 1936, to personally urge Chiang to release the leaders. Even after Chiang won his freedom at Xi'an and returned to Nanjing with Zhang Xueliang in tow, the salvationists remained in prison. The Seven were indicted by a Jiangsu court on April 3, 1937, charged with "endangering the nation." In June 1937, the case went to trial. Both the legal team from Shanghai and the lawyers among the Seven pleaded their case. Yet, ultimately, the trial was political. When asked by the prosecution, "Is not the slogan resist Japan and save the nation (*kangRi jiuguo*) a Chinese Communist slogan?" Shen replied, "The Communist Party eats, I also eat. Is it possible that if the Communist Party resists Japan, then we cannot resist Japan?"[31]

The salvationists also tried to elicit international support to force release of the Seven Gentlemen. Wang Zaoshi was traveling overseas when the arrests occurred, promoting the salvationist cause among overseas Chinese. Wang was able to get the support of well-known Westerners, including Albert Einstein and John Dewey, who sent a telegram to Nanjing on February 5, 1937, urging release of the Seven.[32]

Meanwhile, Madame Sun Yat-sen led a protest at the trial. On July 5, 1937, she arrived in Suzhou with a delegation of 30 to 40 people to demonstrate in front of the Jiangsu Court building, demanding to be arrested. Calling the movement "Go to prison to save the nation," Madame Sun stated that if the Seven were guilty of the "crime" of patriotism, then she and her compatriots were likewise guilty. The demonstration was designed to embarrass Chiang Kai-shek and to pressure Nanjing to release the leaders.[33] When the Marco Polo Bridge Incident occurred only two days later, the movement had suddenly to shift gears. Although continuing to press for the release of their leaders (which finally occurred on July 31), salvationists now had to direct their energies to the immediate crisis.

War

Although the Marco Polo Bridge Incident, of July 7, 1937, is now considered the official start of the Sino-Japanese war, it achieved this status only in retrospect. At the time, it was not immediately clear that China would resist. Song Zheyuan, commander of Chinese forces in Hebei province, in fact, arranged for a cease fire. Only with stiffened Chinese resistance in the north and the outbreak of fighting in Shanghai, on August 13, 1937, did Chiang Kai-shek's determination become clear. In the five weeks between Marco Polo and the eruption of fighting at Shanghai, salvationist leaders worked frantically to ensure that China would fight. Salvationist groups fired off telegrams to commanders in north China urging them to be strong; they collected money to assist the northern troops. Their fear was that Chiang would sign another agreement such as the Tanggu Truce that would surrender Beiping and Tianjin to the Japanese without a fight.

Salvationist writer Wang Yunsheng, writing on July 12, 1937, warned against such a move: "The fire that has burst forth in the north heralds the coming of the great age in East Asia." After describing the fighting at the Marco Polo Bridge and Wanping, he noted that the Japanese had already violated the cease fire and the situation resembled that on the eve of the Manchurian Incident of September 18, 1931. "This spark is our warning. We must quickly use blood to extinguish it. If we let it continue to burn, it will destroy our nation," he warned. "The Chinese people are a people who deeply love peace . . . however the time has come to use war to support peace."[34]

The salvationist intellectuals greeted the battle of Shanghai with near euphoria. Although surprising in retrospect, it must be remembered that until the outbreak of fighting on August 13, most salvationists were skeptical that Chiang Kai-shek would resist. Although today it is often said that Chiang agreed to resist Japan as part of the settlement of the Xi'an Incident of December 1936, Chiang publicly proclaimed that he had made no deals at Xi'an and made no public statement indicating any change in the policy of nonresistance. Against this backdrop, the salvationist intellectuals greeted the outbreak of war as a liberating event. The outbreak of fighting at Shanghai actually fulfilled the major goals of the salvation movement, namely to get Chiang Kai-shek to abandon his policy of appeasement, to resist further concessions to Japan, and to accept a united front with the CCP. Chiang in fact did all of these, putting the bulk of his forces into the fierce battle in and around Shanghai and accepting an alliance with the CCP in part to gain assistance from the Soviet Union.

With these political goals achieved, the salvationists shifted into two further types of activity. The first involved assisting the troops on the battlefield by raising funds, food, and clothing and performing auxiliary work. The salvationists used the same types of strategies they had pursued in 1932 when fighting erupted in Shanghai. Just five years earlier, the lessons of that fighting provided a dress rehearsal for 1937. The second activity of the salvationists was propaganda, which they deemed essential for the war effort. These were both activities that benefited from the vast social networks of the key salvationist leaders.

On July 22, the Shanghai salvationists had reorganized under the name Association to Save the Nation from Extinction (*Jiuwang xiehui*), a title they felt demonstrated the now military nature of the struggle with Japan. The outbreak of fighting in Shanghai, where the salvationist movement had been concentrated, provided the movement with an opportunity for even more direct action, including fund-raising drives to aid wounded soldiers and refugees, assist in transporting wounded from the front, and foster volunteer work in hospitals. In late September, 100,000 jackets were collected for soldiers at the front.[35]

Several leaders of the Shanghai Civic Association, including Du Yuesheng, Wang Xiaolai (of the chamber of commerce), Huang Yanpei, and Xu Xinliu (head of the National Commercial Bank of Shanghai), organized a coalition of business and banking groups, including the chamber of commerce and native place groups, to provide assistance to military. Taking the name the Association of Various Shanghai Circles in the Rear to Aid in Resisting the Enemy (*Shanghai shi gejie kangdi hou yuanhui*), it added Shen Junru to its board after his release and return to Shanghai. The group actually used many of Du Yuesheng's gangster connections to assist in its work, much as had been done in earlier movements. Among the tasks was helping Chinese hardware stores in sectors of Shanghai being seized by the Japanese to move their materials to a safe haven in the foreign sectors.[36] Du also chaired a meeting of 50 bankers on July 28, convened to help raise funds for the military effort and to press for a firm stand against the Japanese. Representatives of the Shanghai Bankers Association, Native Bankers Association, and numerous individual banks participated, including Qin Runqing, Shanghai's most prominent native banker, Song Hanzhang and Bei Zuyi (father of architect I. M. Pei), both key officials with the Bank of

China in Shanghai, and bankers Xu Jiqing and Xu Xinliu. The bankers raised funds and collected clothing and shoes for soldiers as well.[37]

The salvationist intellectuals began the campaign of wartime propaganda. Production of journals and newspapers increased, including the *Jiuwang ribao* (Salvation Daily) and *Kangzhan sanri kan* (War of Resistance, published every third day). The censorship that had so hampered the movement before was now eased. On August 14, the Shanghai Cultural Circles Salvation Association, led now by Cai Yuanpei, Pan Gongzha, Mao Dun, and Hu Yuzhi, among others, held writing and drama workshops to assist members in creating and publishing resistance literature. To shore up the morale of soldiers and civilians, they organized teams to present resistance propaganda through songs, speeches, and dramas. These propaganda groups performed on street corners, in hospitals, and even near the battlefront.[38]

Despite their euphoria at China's heroic stand at Shanghai, the reality of war was sobering. The salvationists were confronted with a level of carnage unequaled since World War I. Nor could they easily escape this violence. Even though most moved to the security of the International Settlement, none were more than a few blocks from the killing. Within the settlement itself, scores died when Chinese airplanes accidentally dropped bombs on the busy Nanjing Road and in front of the Great World Entertainment Center. Salvationist writers tried to turn their sense of outrage at the barbarity of war against the Japanese. Glossing over the bombings by Chinese, they focused instead on the Japanese air attack on the south railway station in Shanghai on August 28. Although the Japanese claimed that Chinese soldiers were occupying the station, most Chinese and international observers said it contained only civilian refugees. Western sources listed 200 dead and 250 wounded in the attack. Salvationist literature used the war atrocity to rally the Chinese. The noted author Ba Jin wrote a moving description of the carnage, listing 600 to 700 dead and calling it the most shameful page in Japanese history. Only refugees, mostly women and children, were in the south station, he wrote. "This is not warfare, this is murder! What the Japanese air force showed to the world was not its power but its cruel insanity."[39]

Yet, the salvationist writers still had to confront the cold reality of defeat. Although China inflicted a high cost on Japan in the Shanghai area, the Japanese army advanced in both north and central China, and nothing could disguise this. One approach was to acknowledge Japan's success but still term the situation a Chinese victory. Hu Yuzhi, writing in late October, called the period from August 13 until the present a mere prologue to the real war to come. He noted that China had already taught Japan a lesson, because the Japanese warlords had assumed that a small force would be sufficient to intimidate China. Now they had seen that a major war would be required to subdue China, and this escalation had isolated Japan internationally. China must enter a new phase of resistance, he wrote, making plans for long-term resistance.[40] But it was hard to mask the pessimism that developed about the military situation with the retreat of the Chinese army from Shanghai and then Nanjing.

End of the Salvationist Movement and Its Social Networks

Most treatments of the National Salvation Movement of the 1930s focus on political issues, the role of the movement in the Guomindang-CCP struggle. Indeed studies done in the People's Republic of China often emphasize the importance of communist leadership in the salvationist movement. In fact, many key leaders of the cause were associated with the CCP and the Guomindang left, for example, Song Qingling and Zou Taofen. Yet the movement can be read in a different way. The salvationist cause can be interpreted as a rapid mobilization of social forces in urban, Republican China through organizational and personal networks. Groups rallied for both political reasons (to force the Nanjing government to adopt a tougher stand against Japanese aggression) and for direct action (raising money and equipment for troops or directly aiding in the fighting). The style of the organization was to draw on specific groups, such as students, cultural workers, women, business leaders, professional workers, and the like, and then form umbrella organizations. In this way, the salvationist movement could move out into the community and utilize a vast web of networks to mobilize individuals for protests, fund-raising, and other activities.

To function in this way, the salvationist movement required certain conditions. The first was motivation, provided in this case by Japanese aggression. The second was public space for freedom of the press and assembly. Although Republican Shanghai was hardly a free society, the complexities of the treaty port environment provided a degree of shelter (see Chapter 7). As Nara Dillon and Jean Oi noted in Chapter 1 of this volume, Shanghai was a divided city that came close to being stateless. Salvationist journals such as those of Zou Taofen's could usually publish for an extended period before being closed and later reopening under a different title. In this manner, news of Japanese provocations could be disseminated rapidly. Salvationist rallies could usually be held before police intervened. To control the foreign concessions, Nanjing either had to use illicit means (such as the assassinations directed by Dai Li) or go through negotiations with foreign powers. The latter was done when the Seven Gentlemen were arrested, but this could be arranged only because the Japanese pressured the treaty powers to act.

Finally, there was the city of Shanghai itself—its international status, its wealth as a trading center, its large industrial base, its financial power, its dominant position in publishing, motion pictures, and the arts. This gave birth to the large body of organizations, chambers of commerce, bar associations, cultural groups, and criminal gangs, many of which had overlapping memberships and which formed the basis for the salvation movement.

Chiang Kai-shek's defeat at Shanghai and retreat inland marked the beginning of the end of the salvation movement and its social networks. The battle for Shanghai left the lower Yangzi region in tatters—tens of thousands dead, factories burned, railroad tracks torn asunder. The Japanese closed the Yangzi to commercial traffic and imposed a harsh occupation on the Chinese city and its environs. There was an element of ambiguity in the occupation because much of the International Settlement was not seized until December 1941, becoming an "isolated island (*gudao*)" surrounded by Japanese-held territory. Some intellectuals and many businessmen continued to operate out of this zone, which permitted a degree of freedom in the midst of war. Nonetheless, the networks that had made the rapid formation of the salvation movement possible collapsed with the Japanese occupation.

Those networks rested in large part on Shanghai's role as an international city, a wealthy treaty port, an industrial and financial center, and the dominant force in Chinese publishing and cultural production. Occupied Shanghai would be only a shell of its former self. Pearl Harbor led both to the complete Japanese occupation of the metropolis (although the Vichy-controlled French Concession retained limited autonomy until July 1943) and to the isolation of Shanghai from the Western world.[41] The Japanese imposed rigid political and economic controls over the population. The wide range of nongovernmental associations that were the underlying networks of the salvationist movement were destroyed by the war. In his study of Shanghai intellectuals living under the Japanese occupation, Po-shek Fu postulates three responses: passivity, collaboration, and resistance. The first required intellectuals to suspend activity and attempt to survive the war in anonymity. The second usually provided an income but forced intellectuals into Japanese-sponsored projects and organizations. The last, resistance, usually meant leaving Shanghai for the interior.[42]

And scatter they did. Many left for the interior, either unoccupied China in the southwest or the CCP areas. Zou Taofen, for instance, moved with the Guomindang government to the interior until political pressure led him to flee to Hong Kong. After the Japanese occupied the colony in December 1941, Zou returned to interior China. Serious illness late in the war forced him to travel incognito to occupied Shanghai to seek medical treatment, where he died on July 24, 1944.[43] A few, such as Shen Junru, would spend the entire war in Guomindang China, but remaining aboveground and active in occupied China was impossible.

When the war ended, the Guomindang returned to a Shanghai much altered by the war. The economy had been shattered by fighting and hyperinflation. The end of extraterritoriality during the war eliminated the "neutral zones" that had given the many nongovernmental organizations a degree of autonomy when confronting the Nanjing leaders. Yet it would be Maoist China that would destroy the networks so essential to the salvation movement. The types of organizations important in 1930s Shanghai—student groups, chambers of commerce, banking associations, bar associations, the YMCA, and even the Green Gang—were all either eliminated or replaced by those controlled by the CCP. Autonomous, nonparty groups were not tolerated.

The Chinese Communist Party had used the National Salvation Movement to push its united front agenda during the 1930s. Although most of the salvationists were not communists, the group endorsed policies favored by the CCP. Its rapid emergence and influence came from two sources, the popularity of the idea of resisting the Japanese and the well-developed organizational and personal networks essential to its formation. The CCP leadership was well aware of how potent this combination could be. Perhaps that explains in part the rigid crackdown on autonomous groups. No matter how innocuous these groups might appear to be—alumni associations, literary societies, or business guilds—they held the potential for people to organize for taking political action.

CHAPTER 7

Politics of Trial, the News Media, and Social Networks in Nationalist China: The *New Life Weekly* Case, 1935

SEI JEONG CHIN

ON JULY 1, 1935, MAJOR newspapers in Shanghai reported that Du Zhongyuan, the publisher of the *New Life Weekly* (*Xinsheng zhoukan*), had been charged with the crime of "obstructing foreign relations." The Japanese Consulate in Shanghai had demanded that the Nationalist government charge Du Zhongyuan with this offense for his publication of an allegedly disrespectful article about the Japanese emperor. Right after Du Zhongyuan was sentenced to 14 months with the denial of an appeal, public discussions on the case appeared in the major newspapers. Relegating to the background more sensitive issues that might damage the legitimacy of the state, the public discussions focused on the illegality of the court's denial of the appeal. Even though the sentence ultimately was not revoked, the court responded to the public discussions and an appeal of the case was approved by the Supreme Court. These public discussions appearing in the Shanghai daily newspapers, limited as they may have been, had considerable influence on judicial decision making.

Without analyzing the role of the media, the *New Life Weekly* case of 1935 has been interpreted by Chinese scholars as an illustration of the Nationalist government's repression of anti-Japanese activities and the humiliating capitulation of Chinese courts to Japanese imperialism.[1] This view assumes that the state–society relations were antagonistic and that the Nationalist government possessed strong state power to impose total control over the public opinion. However, despite the seeming antagonism between the state and politically vocal elites in Shanghai over China's foreign policy in the 1930s, it was the social networks among government officials, elites, and the news media, formed during the national crisis that followed the Manchurian Incident of 1931, that enabled them to cooperate and further mutual interests over the course of Du Zhongyuan's trial. The social networks among them not only enabled the state to prevent public discussion of the case from damaging state legitimacy but also enabled elites and the news media to publicize their own position in the major newspapers, thereby influencing judicial decision making. Thus, by focusing on the role of social networks in the construction of public opinion during the political trial, this study of the *New Life Weekly* case will shed new light on state–society relations in China during the Nanjing decade (1927–1937).

Despite the state's efforts to prevent it, public opinion mediated by the news media was an important factor in judicial decision making in China. As early as the nineteenth century, as William Alford's study of late Qing criminal cases has rightly pointed out, media-generated publicity about trials had already become one of the most important factors in the legal process.[2] Eugenia Lean's recent study on the Shi Jianqiao case effectively shows how public sentiment influenced the judicial system with the burgeoning of the mass media and the reading public's growing preference for melodrama.[3] However, without analyzing the practice of news production, these analyses fail to effectively show how public opinion was constructed and gained power to influence judicial decision making.

In contrast to the civil society paradigm in which state–society relations were assumed as antagonistic, my study of the role of the media in judicial decision making reveals that the relations among state officials, local elites, and the news media were interdependent. In the 1930s, Nationalist government officials, the news media, and the local elites of Shanghai gradually grew intimate through social networks forged in the face of the national crisis ignited by the Manchurian Incident in 1931. Social networks that evolved between the state and the news media made their relations more cooperative. This gave the news media an important role as a political space for contestation and negotiation. Consequently, the practice of news media production in Republican China reveals a complex pattern of negotiation among the state, elites, and the news media itself.

Shanghai News Media and the State in the 1930s

The preoccupation with civil society and the public sphere in existing scholarship on the Chinese news media has led historians to search for an independent news media that could have served as an alternative to a state-dominated political culture. This framework assumes the relation between the state and the news media to be antagonistic, partly because of preconceptions of the authoritarian nature of the Nationalist government's press control.[4] However, relations between the state and the news media became interdependent through the social networks formed historically in the context of the national crisis and nation-building.

The Japanese invasion of Manchuria in 1931 immediately ignited ever more intensive anti-Japanese sentiment and the advocacy of the resistance policy promoted particularly by Shanghai newspapers under the influence of local elites. However, the Nationalist government advocated a nonresistance policy against the Japanese invasion in order to focus on its extermination campaign against the CCP (Chinese Communist Party). Local notables organized various anti-Japanese associations to promote the resistance policy and criticize the Nationalist government's nonresistance policy.

As the Shanghai news media dominated the national news market, it was imperative for the Nationalist government to get control of the Shanghai news media. In late nineteenth and early twentieth centuries, Shanghai had become a center for publications that were distributed and read nationwide. Shanghai's reading public never lacked a diverse press. There were major newspapers, tabloids, various weekly or monthly magazines, as well as the foreign press. Among all of these publication types, major daily newspapers such as *Shen bao, Xinwen bao, Shi bao, Shishi xinbao,* and *Da wanbao* were considered the most influential. They also had the biggest circulations, reaching out to a local and nationwide readership in 1930s China. Daily circulation of *Shen bao* and *Xinwen bao* was 150,000 and *Shi bao* and *Shishi xinbao* sold 80,000 and 54,000, respectively.[5] These major Shanghai newspapers enjoyed an unsurpassed position in the national newspaper market during the 1930s because of the rise of self-conscious professionalism among journalists, the development of the post service and transportation in Shanghai, its vicinity to the capital city of Nanjing, adoption of Western-style management by Chinese newspapers, and the import of Western technology.[6]

Chiang Kai-shek was extremely conscious of the anti-Japanese sentiment growing in Shanghai and attempted to control public opinion through various institutional constraints, such as press law and censorship. The Japanese military also continued condemning the anti-Japanese activities and the publications, exerting pressure on the Nationalist government to get control over them. Since the news media was perceived as a powerful political institution, the Nationalist party-state, which was astutely aware of the power of the press, was eager to control the news media.[7]

One of the most distinct features of media culture in the 1930s was the increasing role of the state in the operation of the news media. The Nationalist government's press law was promulgated in December 1930. This law forbade publications containing items intended to "undermine the KMT [Nationalist Party] or violate the Three People's Principles." Censorship was enforced in Shanghai through various organizations.[8] The government established the censorship bureau for newspapers, which was composed of representatives from the Shanghai municipal government, the municipal KMT party bureau, and the military. Thus, the Nanjing government was the first modern state in China to attempt a centralized censorship system.

However, with relatively weak state power the Nationalist government had to resort to government officials' social networks with the news media to enforce its press law and censor the news media in Shanghai. Officials in charge of controlling newspapers also needed to seek cooperation with newspapers because there was no way they could control whole newspapers with their limited bureaucratic apparatus. By using personal connections of officials and editors or publishers of newspapers, the government attempted to draw out their voluntary cooperation with the government in publicizing official versions of political events or to negotiate what could or could not be published. At the news censorship conference held in Nanjing by the Central Propaganda Department on February 28, 1934, Chen Kecheng, head of the Shanghai News Censorship Office, reported that because of the complicated nature of the Shanghai newspaper world, it was difficult to enforce press control unless a person had considerable personal empathy (*ganqing*) with the newspaper world and had considerable means (*shouduan*) at their disposal.[9] The Shanghai KMT Party branch recommended in 1935 that party members make use of personal relationships with influential publishers to control newspapers.[10] If we analyze the careers of officials who were in charge of press control, they all had rich experience and social networks in the field of journalism. For example, Pan Gongzhan,[11] who was a member of the CC Clique and an influential party official in Shanghai, had extensive social networks within the newspaper world, as he was a former journalist for *Shangbao* and *Shen bao*. Chen Dezheng,[12] a former editor-in-chief of the *Minguo ribao*, was appointed as a head of the Publicity Bureau of the Shanghai

KMT Party branch, which was in charge of controlling the press. Such officials relied on their networks with the news media to elicit voluntary cooperation with the government.

Beginning in the mid-1930s, the Nationalist government also gained control over the Shanghai news media by building social networks, gradually taking over bureaucratic funding and staffing of the commercial news media. Party-run news media, which had existed from the 1920s, could not survive in the competitive newspaper market. Thus, the party-state started to seek a way to appropriate commercial news media to pursue its agendas. The government was not only controlling the news media but also actively using commercial dailies for its own publicity. Some of the high-ranking officials in the Nationalist government set up their own newspapers in Shanghai to facilitate the enforcement of their favored policies. Wang Jingwei, after taking his position as prime minister in January 1932, sent his secretary Lin Bosheng[13] to found *Zhonghua ribao* in Shanghai on April 11, 1932.[14] Pan Gongzhan, a member of the CC Clique and head of Education Bureau in the Shanghai municipal government, launched the newspaper *Chen bao* in Shanghai in 1932.[15] Finally, Kong Xiangxi, the Nationalist government's Minister of Finance, took over major daily newspapers such as *Shishi xinbao, Da wanbao,* and the *China Press.*[16]

On the other hand, the social networks between government officials and the Shanghai news media became even stronger because the Shanghai news media could not function without depending on government support, given the institutional constraints set by the Nanjing regime. First, in terms of financial stability, the publishers of newspapers constantly sought subsidies and political patronage from the state. Various government institutions also subsidized Shanghai newspapers for their own publicity. For example, *Chen bao,* founded by Pan Gongzhan in 1932, received a monthly subsidy of 6,000 yuan from the Central Propaganda Department. The *China Press,* an English-language newspaper, gained monthly subsidies of 1,000 yuan from the Central Propaganda Department and 2,000 yuan from the Ministry of Foreign Affairs.[17]

Second, it was imperative for newspapers to seek cooperation with officials, who would guarantee the efficient gathering of news sources, the ability to pass the censorship bureau, and the efficient publication and distribution of newspapers. Hence, news media in the 1930s sought personal connections with the state to make the newspaper business more predictable. Accordingly, public opinion in Republican

China cannot be considered as developing independently from the state. In the Chinese case, newspapers that expressed public opinion needed social networks that connected it with state authority to obtain the power to influence government policy making.

Rising Tension: State, Elites, and Anti-Japanese Publications

The *New Life Weekly*, a sequel to the famous journal the *Life Weekly* (*Shenghuo zhoukan*), had a circulation of 150,000 and was the most popular weekly magazine in Shanghai in the 1930s. The *New Life Weekly* also held a relatively staunch anti-Japanese and anti-imperialist stance and was highly critical of the Nationalist government's policy of not resisting Japan following the Manchurian Incident.

Behind the publication of the *New Life Weekly* there were thick networks of anti-Japanese entrepreneurs, financiers, publishers, and urban professionals in Shanghai. Anti-Japanese sentiment was promoted through various publications and activities led by these Shanghai elites. This group of Shanghai elites, who were politically vocal, emerged after the Shanghai Incident with the organization of the Shanghai Civic Association (*Shanghai shi difang xiehui*) chaired by Shi Liangcai, a proprietor of the newspaper *Shen bao*.[18] This organization was formed in June of 1932 to undertake a comprehensive range of administrative, financial, and troop-support functions throughout the conflict in Shanghai that had taken place earlier in that year.[19] Members of the Association included entrepreneurs, such as Liu Hongsheng and Mu Ouchu; financiers Lin Kanghou, Xu Xinliu, Zhang Gongquan, and Qin Runqing; Shanghai gang leaders Du Yuesheng and Zhang Xiaolin (see Chapter 4 of this volume); Huang Yanpei, a leader of the Jiangsu educational world (see Chapter 2); and the Shanghai newspaper publishers Shi Liangcai and Wang Boqi. Capitalists and publishers shared common interest in mobilizing the public for the cause of nationalism and resistance against Japanese imperialism. Capitalists were anxious to mobilize the populace in support of domestically produced commodities, and publishers found that the theme of resistance against the Japanese invasion sold quite well in urban China.[20] Furthermore, those urban professionals closely connected with capitalists as well as publishers were enthusiastic in giving support to the anti-Japanese cause as well.[21]

Major Shanghai daily newspapers, which had maintained a neutral stance on political issues, underwent politicization after the Manchurian Incident and the Shanghai Incident. This politicization of the news media was led by Shi Liangcai, who was chairman of the provisional municipal council established in 1932 and head of the Shanghai Civic Association. As head of the Shanghai Daily Newspaper Association, which was composed of *Shen bao, Xinwen bao, Shibao, Shishi xinbao, Minguo ribao,* Shi could exert influence over those newspapers. Moreover, after Shi bought 50 percent of *Xinwen bao* in 1929, he could exert even more influence over that paper. Most of the major newspapers of Shanghai maintained an editorial stance that advocated resistance to the Japanese invasion before 1934. After Shi Liangcai was assassinated in November 1934 on the order of the head of the Nationalist secret service, Dai Li, for his anti-Japanese position, Shi's leadership position in the Shanghai Civic Association was taken over by Du Yuesheng, a leader of the Shanghai Green Gang.[22] According to the Japanese newspaper *Shanghai Mainichi,* in 1935, all anti-Japanese magazines, papers, and mosquito papers (tabloids mainly covering sensational and entertainment news) were subsidized by the Shanghai Civic Association.[23]

The Nationalist government was in a delicate position after June 10, 1935, when the Goodwill Mandate with Japan prohibiting anti-Japanese activities was enacted. This edict forbade anti-Japanese activity without specifically identifying Japan. "The cultivation of goodwill with our neighbors being of prime importance," the edict read, "the central government has repeatedly ordered that all citizens should observe proper amenities toward friendly nations, and not indulge in discriminatory or provocative speeches or acts."[24] Before the Mandate, the most common object of Nationalist censorship was Communist publications. The Nationalist government could easily get cooperation from the Shanghai Municipal Police in confiscating Communist-related publications and arresting their writers or publishers. Now the government found itself in charge of controlling anti-Japanese publications, albeit with greater difficulty in justifying such censorship. To complicate matters, the local Nationalist Party branch in Shanghai was generally becoming involved with the anti-Japanese movement as well.

Du Zhongyuan's[25] the *New Life Weekly* should be understood in this political context. The *New Life Weekly* was one of the few anti-Japanese and anti-imperialist mainstream magazines in Shanghai. Du Zhongyuan's editorials starkly promoted resistance against Japan. The periodical reprinted songs used by resistance fighters in Manchuria, which referred to the Japanese as "devils" and "insects."[26] Phrases such as "militaristic," "fascist," and "imperialistic" were regularly used to describe the Japanese government. Du also directly criticized the appeasement policy of the Nanjing government and expressed mistrust of government-led patriotism, arguing that the responsibility of resistance to Japan belonged to the masses.[27]

The *New Life Weekly* was a sequel to *Life Weekly (Shenghuo zhoukan)*, which had been published by Zou Taofen. *Life Weekly*, which obtained a circulation of nearly 150,000, also supported the cause of resistance against Japanese military encroachment. *Life Weekly* was originally an organ of the Chinese Society of Vocational Education (*Zhonghua zhiye jiaoyu she*), which was founded in 1913 by Jiangnan gentry leaders and Shanghai entrepreneurs such as the cotton magnate Mu Ouchu and Huang Yanpei, the head of the Jiangsu Provincial Educational Association and advocate of educational reform and economic modernization for the strengthening of the nation (see Chapter 2). Huang Yanpei associated with Shi Liangcai and worked for *Shen bao*, while Mu Ouchu was also a leading capitalist. These two people were core members of the Shanghai Civic Association and constituted an important part of the social networks of the politically vocal elites of Shanghai, who emerged after the Manchurian Incident and the Shanghai Incident.

As *Life Weekly* became a target of the state's press control, the *New Life* group sought a new publisher who had political networks with high officials to protect the journal. When publication of *Life Weekly* was suspended in December 1933 and Zou Taofen left Shanghai, Zou Taofen's colleagues Hu Yuzhi, Xu Boxin, and Ai Hansong discussed publishing a new journal; Hu Yuzhi recommended Du Zhongyuan, a refugee entrepreneur from the city of Shenyang in Manchuria, as editor-in chief as well as publisher.[28] After meeting with Zou Taofen in 1930, Du Zhongyuan had become an important writer for *Life Weekly*. He was also a member of the board of directors of the Life Bookstore (*Shenghuo chuban hezuo she*), which was established in July 1933. Du Zhongyuan started to publish *New Life Weekly*[29] as a successor to *Life Weekly* in February 1934.

If we closely examine Du Zhongyuan's political networks, we see that the decision to appoint him as publisher and editor-in-chief of the journal was a strategic one. In reality, Ai Hansong[30] was in charge of the journal; Du Zhongyuan seems to have been merely a figurehead. Because Du had a porcelain factory in Jiangxi, when he was busy he sometimes let other people write his editorials for him.[31] Du

Zhongyuan, in fact, managed to maintain close relationships both with the local elites of Shanghai and with high KMT officials.

Du Zhongyuan came to Shanghai after the Manchurian Incident and, with his connection to Zhang Xueliang[32] and high KMT officials, he was instantly connected with Shanghai elites. He joined the Shanghai Civic Association in August 1932 and actively associated with Shanghai elites such as Shi Liangcai and Mu Ouchu.[33] Du Zhongyuan was also a chairman for the Chinese National Products Production and Marketing Cooperative Associations established after 1931, which cooperated with the Shanghai Civic Association to promote the national products movement.[34]

Du's activity in Shanghai was actually part of his propaganda work for the Northeast National Salvation Association (*Dongbei minzhong kang Ri jiuguo hui*). After the Manchurian Incident, Du became joint head of propaganda in the Northeast National Salvation Association, which was organized under the permission of Zhang Xueliang on September 16, 1931.[35] Du traveled to various places along the Yangzi River to give speeches to propagandize the anti-Japanese cause from the winter of 1931 to the spring of 1932.[36] He was sent to Shanghai in January 1932 by the Northeast National Salvation Association and as a representative of Ma Zhanshan to support the Nineteenth Route Army in Shanghai.[37] Du Zhongyuan introduced Ma Zhanshan in a meeting of Chinese National Products Production and Marketing Cooperative Associations on July 7, 1933.[38] He also reported on the war in Manchuria in October 1932 at a meeting of the Shanghai Civic Association and attempted to mobilize Shanghai capitalists for war support.[39]

Du Zhongyuan's close relationship with Zhang Xueliang likely helped him to associate with the head of Shanghai's Green Gang, Du Yuesheng. Du Yuesheng had a long-established relationship with Zhang Xueliang, since he had had business dealings involving contraband opium with Zhang in the past.[40] According to the memoirs of Du Zhongyuan's son, Du Yuesheng had associated with Du Zhongyuan and protected him during the anti-Japanese movement.[41] A patron such as Du Yuesheng was invaluable for anyone involved in the publishing business. In addition to taking over the leadership of the Shanghai Civic Association, which was known to support anti-Japanese publications, he was even on the board of directors of major Shanghai daily newspapers, such as *Shishi xinbao*, by 1935.[42]

According to the *China Press*, *New Life Weekly* had formerly been subsidized by Zhang Xueliang but had later been taken over by the Shanghai Civic Association, of which Du Yuesheng was the chairman.[43] It is entirely likely that Du Yuesheng, as the chairman of the anti-Japanese Shanghai Civic Association, subsidized *New Life Weekly*. Brian Martin argues that Du Yuesheng, with his close connection with Chiang Kai-shek, participated fully in the new "corporatist" state system created by the Nanjing government. As in many other aspects of their relationship, however, Du was quite autonomous and he openly broke with Nationalist regime on the issue of Japan. Whatever his motives, Du's sympathy to the anti-Japanese cause also enhanced his political and economic power at the local level.

Further, Du Yuesheng, as a native of Pudong, maintained close relations with Huang Yanpei, who was also from Pudong. After being persuaded by Huang Yanpei to participate in the anti-Japanese activities, Du Yuesheng joined the Shanghai Civic Association.[44] As discussed, the Shanghai Civic Association had been subsidizing anti-Japanese publications, including *New Life Weekly*. From this perspective, we see that Du Yuesheng clearly did not always cooperate with Chiang Kai-shek's corporatist state.

Du Zhongyuan's political networks explain why *New Life Weekly* could contain such strong anti-Japanese sentiment and harsh criticisms of the Nanjing regime and continue to be published in the midst of the allegedly stringent censorship of the Nationalist government. The political patronage from Du Yuesheng allowed the journal to easily pass the censors because Du Yuesheng had a close relationship with members of the CC Clique such as Pan Gongzhan and Wu Kaixian, who controlled the censorship of books and magazines.[45] The success of the journal seems to have been achieved because of its ties with patrons who could guarantee protection from censorship or other kinds of control by the Nationalist regime. Therefore, in spite of its harsh criticism toward the Nationalist government's appeasement policy, *New Life Weekly* escaped the postal ban on its distribution until the Japanese consul general took issue with an article published in May of 1935.

This analysis also questions previous studies of the anti-Japanese movement that dichotomize the government's repression of growing anti-Japanese sentiment and local elite resistance against government suppression, suggesting that the two sides maintained antagonistic relations. The operation of *New Life* shows that elites involved in the anti-Japanese movement had close ties and used their social networks with state officials to guarantee the stability of their businesses, including those openly critical of the regime.

The Making of a Public Trial

The trial of Du Zhongyuan in 1935 was a political one, the proceedings of which experienced direct interference from the Chinese state and pressure from Japanese authorities. An article entitled "Idle Talk On Emperors" (*Xianhua huangdi*) was published in the *New Life Weekly* on May 4, 1935. The content of the article was as follows:

> Today, most emperors have only the name but not the substance; i.e., they are emperors in name, but not emperors in power. As far as we know, the emperor of Japan is a biologist . . . He lacks the real power, though everything is done in his name . . . The Japanese militarists and capitalistic class are the real rulers of Japan. As it has been mentioned above, the present Emperor of Japan is interested in studying biology . . . It is said that he has made many discoveries in biology. And yet, contemporary Japan would not give up her antique—the "emperor" . . . The British regard their emperor as noble figurehead . . . which is different from Japanese case . . . In fact, [the Japanese emperor] is a puppet of the real rulers of modern times.[46]

This article, written by a writer pen-named Yi Shui, discussed the general world trend towards the weakening power of emperors and suggested that the Japanese emperor's rulership was merely empty. The article did not cause an immediate reaction, but Japanese hard-liners seized the matter as a test case for the Goodwill Mandate and a further method of pressuring Nanjing. The article was reprinted in *Da bao* in Tianjin for three days, from June 11 to 13. When the article was discovered by the Japanese, the newspaper was closed after negotiation between the Tianjin mayor and the Japanese consul general.[47] After the article became known in Shanghai, the Japanese consul general, Suma Yakichirō, met with Shanghai mayor Wu Tiecheng on June 24 and protested the article. The Japanese demanded the punishment of the publisher and the writer of the article, the suspension of the publication of the *New Life Weekly*, and a "fundamental" solution to all anti-Japanese activities. Wu Tiecheng agreed[48] to accept most of the Japanese demands.[49] Further, on July 7, the head of the Central Propaganda Bureau of the KMT, Ye Chucang, telegraphed all provincial party headquarters prohibiting anew all anti-Japanese activity by party groups.[50]

Now the Nationalist government had to ensure that the trial of Du Zhongyuan would proceed without further provoking Japan. In order to do that, the Nationalist government needed to seek cooperation from the defendants. The real dilemma for the Nationalist government was that the Shanghai Book and Magazine Censorship Committee (*Shanghai tushu zazhi shencha weiyuan hui*),[51] known to be under the control of the CC Clique in Shanghai, passed the article and issued a certificate of censorship.[52] It was critical for the KMT Party that Du Zhongyuan not testify that the censorship bureau had actually passed the disputed magazine. Otherwise, the Japanese would certainly hold the Nationalist government accountable. Furthermore, the Party was aware that the proceedings of the trial were subject to intense media coverage. Members of the Shanghai KMT Party branch in charge of the censorship committee, such as Pan Gongzhan, and Tong Xingbai, came to the *New Life* office and asked for the return of the certificate of censorship issued by the Shanghai Books and Magazine Censorship Committee. They also asked the publisher not to admit when he testified in court that the issue of the journal in question had passed censorship.[53] Pan Gongzhan, a former journalist of *Shen bao* and *Shangbao*, might have been specifically chosen because he could make use of his own social networks in Shanghai newspaper circles to carry out this plan.

The Nationalist government also had to arrest Du Zhongyuan and the writer of the article. Yi Shui was actually a pen name of Ai Hansong, who was in charge of the publication of *New Life Weekly* during the absence of Du Zhongyuan.[54] However, as Yi Shui's identity was not known to the public, the court could not summon the writer of the article and could only summon Du Zhongyuan. Instead of arresting Du Zhongyuan by force, government officials attempted to persuade him to voluntarily appear for trial. Wu Kaixian, a member of the standing committee of the Shanghai branch of the KMT, visited Du Zhongyuan to convince him that as long as he appeared he would get only a fine, which the party would cover. Wu Tiecheng also invited Du Zhongyuan for a meal, guaranteeing that as long as he appeared in court there would be no charges brought against him.[55]

Different from other civil or criminal trials, archival records show that the Nationalist authorities actively interfered in judicial decision making in this case. The Public Security Bureau, after receiving a secret order from the Shanghai municipal government, sent a secret letter to the Second Branch of the Jiangsu High Court to investigate and deal with the person responsible for writing the article on June 26.[56]

At first a prosecutor in the Second Branch of the Jiangsu High Court rejected the request for an indictment, as the grounds for the case were dubious. However, the Shanghai municipal government urged the court for an indictment.[57] Moreover, the Ministry of Judicial Administration[58] was asked by the Ministry of Foreign Affairs to indict Du

Zhongyuan.[59] The Ministry of Judicial Administration, to which the Second Branch of Jiangsu High Court was directly subordinate, sent a secret telegram on June 29 ordering it to try the case.[60] Under these pressures, the court finally decided to indict Du Zhongyuan for "Obstructing Foreign Relations" after a hearing on July 2.[61]

Du Zhongyuan was brought to trial on July 9 and charged with insulting the head of a friendly state under Articles 310 and 116 of the New Criminal Code (Article 325 of the Old Criminal Code).[62] In the end, President Judge Yu Hua of the Second Branch of the Jiangsu High Court sentenced Du to 14 months imprisonment.[63] The defense lawyer Wu Kaisheng made two points: first, Du Zhongyuan was not responsible for the article since he was not in Shanghai when it was published on May 4, 1935, and did not read the article before publication; second, the article was not insulting to the Japanese emperor being merely a scholarly discussion of the general phenomenon of the weakening of monarchical power.[64] Du Zhongyuan claimed that the magazine did not have any grievance against the Japanese emperor, although the magazine stood for anti-imperialism.[65]

A boisterous scene took place in the court after the announcement of the sentence. When Du's attorney asked for a suspended sentence and a retrial, Judge Yu rejected the appeal. Judge Yu's ruling caused a storm of protest. Du Zhongyuan banged his fists on the railing and shouted: "China's law has been conquered by the Japanese!" The exclamation brought an echo from the spectators, who shouted: "Down with the Nanjing Government! Down with Japanese Imperialists!" and denounced government leaders. Handbills of an "inflammatory nature" were scattered about the courtroom; they read "advocate the anti-imperialist and anti-Japanese *New Life Weekly*."[66]

Because Japanese newspapers were covering the case closely, it was impossible for the Nationalist government to prohibit Chinese newspapers from covering it as well. However, due to negotiations between the mayor of Shanghai and the Japanese consulate to the public trial, the coverage in major Shanghai newspapers was mostly limited to the same news releases coming from the Central News Agency and to documents and letters written by the court, the KMT, or the defendants. Newspapers did not report the case until July 1, 1935, when Du Zhongyuan was summoned to the court, and this coverage consisted of a dry description of the trial proceedings only. Because the case concerned Sino-Japanese relations, a central issue in Chinese politics at the time, the Nationalist government closely regulated coverage of the trial in the press. No editorial comments on the case were published in major Shanghai newspapers. As we have seen from the KMT Party members' meeting with Du Zhongyuan about the certificate of censorship, the state initiated informal negotiations with the defendants and the news media to influence how the public trial was presented to the Chinese—as well as the Japanese—public.

Negotiated Public Opinion: State, Elites, and the News Media

Attorneys found no means to contest the sentence in the courtroom, especially after Du Zhongyuan's appeal was denied. Therefore, Du Zhongyuan and Shanghai elites sought to contest the court decision outside the courtroom. Their strategy was to have their interpretation of the legal issues that underlay the case publicized in the major Shanghai commercial newspapers to mobilize support for Du's cause. Right after the public trial on July 9, the Du Case Support Group (*Du'an houyuanhui*) was organized by Shanghai publishers.[67] Bi Yuncheng, a close friend of Zou Taofen who worked for the *New Life Weekly*, was active in mobilizing support from Shanghai elites sympathetic to anti-Japanese activities.

Discussions in major Shanghai newspapers after the trial reveal that public opinion generated through negotiations between the state, social elites, and news media had considerable influence over judicial decision making in the *New Life Weekly* case. Major Shanghai commercial newspapers such as *Shen bao, Xinwen bao, Shi bao, Shishi xinbao, Min bao, Da wanbao,* and *Damei wanbao* functioned as important avenues for political communication among various government agencies and so wielded considerable influence. It was common practice for government institutions or social organizations to publish letters and other communications in the newspapers in order to represent them to the public. Although the point is often neglected, Chinese officials and social organizations also constituted a significant component of newspaper readership. In this sense, newspapers were an important means for political communication between officials, government agencies, and social organizations in Republican China.

Mu Ouchu,[68] with whom Du Zhongyuan had a personal connection, advocated in the newspapers for an appeal in the *New Life Weekly* case. Rather than writing a formal editorial, however, Mu publicized in *Shen bao, Xinwen bao,* and other major newspapers a letter he had sent to the Shanghai Chamber of Commerce in defense of the appeal.[69] The letter discussed the illegality of the court's denial of the appeal, its undue punishment for Du Zhongyuan, and its refusal to suspend his sentence, which Mu argued went against human feelings (*renqing*). Mu claimed that the current situation was a threat to the legal protection of Shanghai citizens and to all Chinese.

Mu Ouchu could take this daring public position because of his own standing within the Shanghai elite network that promoted the anti-Japanese activities. He was one of the founders of the Shanghai Civic Association, along with Shi Liangcai and Huang Yanpei. Probably owing to his association with Shi Liangcai, Mu often published his articles in *Shen bao* and the *Shen bao Monthly*.[70] Mu Ouchu was president of Chinese Cotton Goods Exchange, so his letter's publication in the Shanghai newspapers drew considerable public attention. Further, Mu Ouchu had served as standing Vice Minister of Industry and Commerce at the invitation of Kong Xiangxi and Minister of Industry and Commerce from 1928 to 1930, so he was well connected with central government officials as well.

Mu's letter to the Shanghai Chamber of Commerce was transferred to the Shanghai Bar Association for deliberation. The Bar Association published its reply to the Shanghai Chamber of Commerce in *Shen bao* on July 23, stating that they had decided to petition to the Judicial Yuan regarding the illegality of the denial of appeal by the Second Branch of the Jiangsu High Court. As the issue of Du's appeal took center stage, the full text of the defense attorney Hou Yuzhi's appeal and complaint were first published by Shanghai newspapers on July 22 and July 23.

As the issue became more controversial, the court needed to publicize its legal justification for denying the appeal to make it acceptable to the public. Hence, the announcement of the denial of Du's appeal by the Second Branch of the Jiangsu High Court on July 19 followed, and the legal basis for the court's decision[71] was also published in the major newspapers.[72]

After publishing the letter by Mu Ouchu, the newspaper *Damei wanbao* was at the center of public discussion of the case. Since the newspaper was registered under American nationality and managed by Zhang Sixu, a former official in the Shanghai Branch of the Ministry of Foreign Affairs, *Damei wanbao* enjoyed relative autonomy from governmental interference in their editorials. Indeed, it was in the pages of *Damei wanbao* that Zhao Chen, member of the Legislative Yuan, announced publicly that Du's appeal should be accepted.[73] Public discussion advocating the court's acceptance of an appeal became influential after Zhao Chen's editorial on the *New Life Weekly* case was published in *Damei wanbao* on July 21.

Zhao compared the *New Life* trial with a similar Japanese case in which the Japanese judiciary upheld its independence against the Ministry of Foreign Affairs' request to prosecute a murder attempt on a Russian prince by a Japanese in 1892. He urged the judiciary to uphold judicial independence from foreign powers.[74] As one of the authors of Criminal Procedure Code, Zhao asked the judiciary to accept the appeal in an interview published in *Damei wanbao* on July 24.[75] Zhao Chen had been a lawyer in Shanghai, from 1928 until 1933, before he was appointed as a member of the Legislative Yuan. As a legislator, Zhao's arguments in Shanghai newspapers on behalf of Du Zhongyuan carried considerable authority.

Qu Yue, a lawyer, also had his editorial on the issue of Du's appeal published in *Damei wanbao* on July 26. He argued that the appeal should be accepted to uphold judicial independence and that revoking the original sentence would not harm the court's authority. He also claimed that law should not be sacrificed in favor of foreign relations. *Damei wanbao* further published an editorial entitled "Whether Chinese Law Was Conquered" from the Hong Kong newspaper *Xunhuan ribao* on August 1. The article argued that the appeal should be accepted to uphold judicial independence and to correct the current situation in which Chinese law was being "conquered" by the Japanese.

The Nationalist government could not but respond to these public discussions, particularly Mu Ouchu's letter published in the Shanghai newspapers. The Control Yuan proclaimed that the denial of the appeal by the judge in the Second Branch of the Jiangsu High Court needed to be investigated further. Members of the Control Yuan decided to send personnel to the court to investigate the sentence, dispatching a petition to its president to decide on the appropriate measures.[76] In the meantime, Hou Yuzhi also petitioned the Control Yuan to impeach the judges of the Second Branch of the Jiangsu High Court claiming they had perverted the law to flatter foreign powers by denying the appeal. In response to Hou's petition, a member of the Control Yuan, Zheng Luosheng,[77] sent his own petition to the president of the Control Yuan, Yu Youren (1879–1964).[78] On August 14, Yu Youren, known for his support for anti-Japanese activities, sent a letter to the Supreme Court to deal with the case.

With the rise in support for Du's appeal expressed in major Shanghai newspapers, the Judicial Yuan had to respond to this public discussion. After receiving a letter sent by the Shanghai Bar Association, the Judicial Yuan ordered the president of the Second Branch of the Jiangsu High Court to investigate the matter. Du Zhongyuan's case was soon brought to the Supreme Court for appeal. The Supreme Court finally revoked the denial of appeal issued by the Second Branch of the Jiangsu High Court, although Du Zhongyuan's sentence was not actually revoked.[79] Du Zhongyuan was released on September 9, 1936, after serving 14 months.

Public discussion of the issue of Du's appeal in the influential Shanghai dailies generated power to influence the judicial decision. The social network of Mu Ouchu, with its connections to the major Shanghai newspapers such as *Shen bao*, provided access to the news media. However, because these Shanghai newspapers were in turn interdependent on government officials in the process of news production, publicity necessarily had to be limited. Public discussion of the *New Life Weekly* case and coverage of the trial in major Shanghai commercial newspapers was limited to the issue of judicial independence from foreign powers, particularly Japan. In this way, newspapers relegated to the background other more sensitive issues, such as the Nationalist government's interference with the court decision, the potential implications of that government's political suppression of the anti-Japanese movement, and freedom of the press. Public opinion as mediated by the mainstream commercial newspapers need not come into direct conflict with state interests. Discussion of the more sensitive issues was limited to other media outlets such as foreign newspapers, magazines, and handbills.

Alternative Public Opinion and Media Spectacle

In contrast to the moderate public discussions in major Shanghai newspapers centered on Du Zhongyuan's appeal, other media outlets contained a much broader range of public discussion about the case. Foreign newspapers and magazines, Chinese magazines, mosquito papers, and even handbills carried contents that had the potential to undermine the Nationalist government's position. These media outlets held less authority in policymaking, but they enjoyed relative autonomy from the state compared to the mainstream Shanghai newspapers and could therefore offer alternative coverage of Du Zhongyuan's case.

Even though the major newspapers saw themselves as remaining moderate in their discussion of Du Zhongyuan's case, the reading public had a different interpretation of the coverage. Eighty Chinese youths reportedly held demonstrations in the French Concession on July 30, shouting anti-KMT and anti-imperialist slogans concerning the suppression of the *New Life Weekly*.[80] *New Life's* Reader's Association sent a letter to subscribers that demanded restoring publication of the anti-Japanese and anti-imperialist *New Life Weekly*, immediate release of the anti-Japanese patriot Du Zhongyuan, and freedom for the common people's anti-Japanese activities and anti-Japanese press.[81] Shanghai police intelligence reports also stated that *New Life* subscribers received handbills expressing strong anti-Japanese and anti-government sentiments and criticizing the "treacherous government" for oppressing the liberties of the people.[82]

The Chinese publications involved in promoting anti-Japanese sentiments were aware of the significance of the *New Life* case in furthering the resistance cause. For this reason, they turned the case into a spectacle that could attract public attention. Du Zhongyuan had once complained that "modern" women in Shanghai were too busy eating Western food, watching movies, and listening to the radio to care about the nation.[83] According to this reasoning, the anti-Japanese movement needed to find ways to attract the public's attention. Zhang Xueliang had a shrewd perspective on the *New Life* case as a spectacle that would draw national as well as international attention. When asked by Lu Guangji to assist in the release efforts on Du Zhongyuan's behalf, Zhang stated that "we should let all China and the world see Du Zhongyuan imprisoned for the cause of anti-Japanese national salvation. That will be his glory."[84] Similarly, one of the Chinese readers of *China Weekly Review*, in praising the journal's critical editorial stance on the *New Life* case, claimed that "it seems to me that one of the most effective weapons against Japan's present maneuver in this country is publicity and more publicity."[85]

Zou Taofen also took advantage of the Du Zhongyuan case as a chance to mobilize anti-Japanese and nationalist sentiment. Zou's journal *The Life of the Masses* (*Dazhong shenghuo*), first published November 16, 1935, featured a column by Du Zhongyuan entitled "Random Thoughts in Prison (*Yuzhong zagan*)". Although Du was circumspect in discussing his imprisonment and its causes, he called for resistance against the nation's enemies and severely criticized Hu Shi, who largely supported the Nanjing government's nonresistance stance against the Japanese. The appearance of the column served to remind readers of

Du Zhongyuan's fate for his stance against Japan.[86] Later in November 1936, Zou Taofen published a book, also entitled *Random Thoughts in Prison* (*Yuzhong zagan*), composed of Du Zhongyuan's writings and featuring a heroic photograph of Du standing proudly in front of the jail.

The foreign press took on an even more strident tone in its coverage of the case. Since English-language newspapers and magazines did not come under Chinese government censorship, they played an important role in making news out of the *New Life* case. These newspapers attracted Chinese readers seeking sources for news other than Shanghai's Chinese newspapers. The English-language publication *The China Weekly Review*[87] was perhaps the most active in publishing editorials on the case. The publisher and editor-in-chief of the magazine, J. B. Powell,[88] was sympathetic to the anti-Japanese movement and criticized Japanese imperialism as well as Nationalist government censorship after the Manchurian Incident.[89] *The China Weekly Review* was mostly read by Americans, but Chinese intellectuals also constituted some of the publication's readers. A number of Chinese readers sent letters supporting the journal's "frank and outspoken" editorial stance on the *New Life Weekly* case.[90] *The China Weekly Review* published many editorials that directly criticized the arrest of Du Zhongyuan and the court's denial of his appeal. Meng Changyong argued that Du's publication of the controversial article was not a crime. Meng maintained that "Idle Talk On Emperors" did not constitute an instance of "obstructing the friendly relations" between China and Japan, because it lacked "criminal intention" on the part of the editor and writer of the article. Moreover, he suggested that what the article said about the emperor was quite true. Meng argued that according to the laws of Criminal Procedure, Du's appeal should have been granted.[91]

Another editorial argued that Du Zhongyuan was sent to prison not because his writing was illegal under Chinese law, but because the "warlords" of Imperial Japan were looking for something to use to force their demands upon a militarily weak Chinese government.[92] The writers compared the *New Life* case with an earlier article in the U.S.-published *Vanity Fair* magazine, which had represented the Emperor of Japan drawing a cart. The writer pointed out that in the United States the Japanese merely lodged a protest, but in China the Japanese were successful in intimidating government authorities into savagely punishing the supposed offender.

Du Zhongyuan's case also instigated and mobilized public discussion of the problem of censorship and the Nationalist government's press law. The *China Weekly Review* published an article entitled "Censorship Should Be Conducted Intelligently or Abolished Entirely." The writer pointed out that after the national crisis in Manchuria, censorship became more stringent, arguing that this was due to Japanese pressure on Chinese officials to prevent the publication of news and articles that the Japanese government wished to keep from public view. The article also quoted an article by Professor Hubert S. Liang, a member of the faculty of the School of Journalism at Yenching University in Beiping. Liang's article stated:

> Broadly speaking, the Chinese publishers and editors, realistic as they are, do not claim unfettered freedom of the press. That is, they accept censorship as a temporary necessity, considering the peculiar situation in which China finds herself today. What they strongly object and resent is the haphazard and unintelligent way in which censorship is sometime exercised . . . Most of the censors are untrained for their task and not infrequently they themselves cannot wisely distinguish what should or should not be published in the interest of the country . . . Also there is the frequent duplication or even conflict of orders by the different parties that are supposed to be interested in a certain particular item of news.[93]

The famous author Lu Xun sarcastically commented on the censorship in the *New Life* case as well, writing that the punishment for the violation of the "Goodwill Mandate" was more severe than the punishment applied to the "reactionary (*fandong*)"—that is, Communist—press. Discussing censorship, Lu Xun quoted an article in *Zhonghua ribao* stating that in the absence of a special organization for censorship, book distribution was often suspended after publication but that after the censorship committee was established publication became more efficient. In this way, Lu sarcastically observed that because the censorship committee was abolished after the *New Life Weekly* case, the distribution of books and magazines was not guaranteed for publishers.[94]

The case also helped stimulate the growth of the student movement in north China. On November 1, 1935, student groups in Beiping petitioned the KMT to grant freedom of speech, press, and assembly. In their petition, they denounced the Nationalist government and the Japanese military invasion. Student groups complained that the Nationalist government could brand any activities undertaken on the part of the people as a crime. Previously this was done under the pretext of eradicating the "Red Danger" and now it was done under the pretext of maintaining the Nationalist government's international relations. As one example, student groups mentioned Du Zhongyuan as a patriot who had been subjected to trial under criminal law simply because of "injuring international friendship."[95]

It is noteworthy that the Legislative Yuan passed a revised version of the press law on July 12, 1935, only three days after the trial of Du Zhongyuan. During deliberations in the Legislative Yuan, one of the discussants insisted that it was urgent to revise the press law after observing the *New Life* case.[96] The revised law stipulated that court cases should not be criticized in the press before judgment was rendered.[97] Moreover, under the revised press law, newspapers and magazines could only be published following registration, which was stricter than the old law stipulating that newspapers and magazines could be published while applying for registration.

These alternative public discussions appearing in magazines, handbills, foreign news media, and so forth show that the government's attempt to control public opinion was far from complete. Compared to the major newspapers in Shanghai, which developed intimate social networks with local notables as well as government officials, these other kinds of news media flourishing in Shanghai enjoyed relative autonomy from external pressure. However, there was a trade-off. Even though they could be used more effectively for public mobilization, these media could impose less influence on government policy making.

Conclusion

The *New Life Weekly* case demonstrates how social networks among the state, local elites, and the news media were an important factor in constructing public opinion and giving it influence on judicial decision making. Public opinion as a cultural artifact—constructed through negotiation within this complex network of personal connections—arbitrated political issues and social reality. Although the interference of the Nationalist government with judicial decision making was noted by elites, the issue was not discussed as such in the mainstream newspapers, since it might have undermined Chinese state authority in national politics as well as international relations. Rather, the more indirect issues of appeal and judicial independence from foreign power were the topics of discourse in the major newspapers.

Accordingly, the position of mainstream Shanghai newspapers on the *New Life Weekly* case remained moderate. The social networks that evolved among the state, local elites, and the news media led to the creation of public opinion that would not significantly undermine either state power or the power of the local elites and the news media. Although divided over foreign policy, the state, elites, and the media still had some room to negotiate thanks to social networks that allowed them to maintain interdependent relations throughout much of the 1930s.

More radical public opinion had to find other outlets, such as magazines, foreign news media, tabloids, or handbills, which were less influential among government officials and the Chinese public. As the media spectacle surrounding the *New Life Weekly* generated the message that anti-Japanese publication and activities were being suppressed by the state in defense of Japanese imperialism, the anti-Japanese movement began targeting the Nationalist government in December 1935. Although social networks among the state, local elites, and the news media created a public space to negotiate and enhance mutual interests, it did not guarantee full security for any of them to maintain their own power and authority.

PART FOUR

Networks in Action: Charity and Welfare in Republican Shanghai

CHAPTER 8

What Is In a Network? Local, Personal, and Public Loyalties in the Context of Changing Conceptions of the State and Social Welfare

---

BRYNA GOODMAN

NETWORKS OF ALL TYPES, both personal connections (*guanxi*) and larger, structural cliques and affiliations, marked Chinese society and politics in the Republican era, but what did they mean? This chapter analyzes the shifting social assumptions and behaviors underlying one of the most apparently natural types of Shanghai social networks, those based on common native place origins, customs, and dialects. Formal native place associations (*huiguan, gongsuo,* and *tongxianghui*) and informal native place networks pervaded urban social intercourse and urban management in the early Republican period.[1] Although native place ties and the loyalties they expressed were almost ubiquitous, they were by no means automatic or imbued with stable meanings.[2] Like culture, social networks are not fixed but are dynamic, changing, and contingent. If ubiquitous, native place ties were by no means exclusive. Rather, native place networks and institutions were strands and nodes in an expanding web, or patchwork, of urban services and functions that encompassed as well commercial, secret society, religious, private philanthropic, and governmental institutions. These multiple providers of social services worked more often in overlapping or parallel than in oppositional roles. Because of their pervasiveness and relative flexibility, native place associations provide a useful window onto Republican-era social networks, one that may be particularly revealing because of the ways that native place ties threaded their way through other institutions, networks, and social formations of the time.

This chapter examines the shifting social practices and social valuations of native place networks, formal and informal, in association with shifts in political structures and ideology, particularly in regard to transformations in notions of the public (*gong*) and the people (*gongzhong*). The social welfare activities of native place associations in the Republican era and the role of native place networks within charitable organizations are central to this discussion. From their inception, native place associations—as associations of outsiders in cities—needed to justify their existence as embodying not just private networks, but a broader public good (*gongyi*).[3] In this regard, the prominent social welfare practices of these associations may be understood not simply as a means of serving their respective sojourner communities, but as a strategic mechanism that helped to diffuse both the hostility of the Qing state toward private associations and the hostility of locals toward outsiders. Social welfare is a particularly fertile arena for examining networks and ideas of the public, since welfare practices express norms of social responsibility, connect haves to have-nots, and constitute boundaries and definitions of community.

The last decades of the Qing dynasty (1644–1911) were marked by an expanding emphasis on public print (newspapers and journals) and public spaces (for meetings and leisure recreation), together with an expansion in the numbers of people who constituted an imagined political public.[4] After the 1911 revolution, the creation of a new Chinese republic based on notions of popular sovereignty deepened these trends, as public associations and public print emphasized the twin civic imperatives of being of the people and representing the people.[5] Republican values called for new, activist models of public citizenship that went beyond late Qing precedents. Public welfare activity was fundamental to a widely felt cultural imperative for social organizations to serve the public if they were to be legitimate. Insofar as native place networks risked public castigation for promoting the private or narrow interests of one regional group or faction, the associations that formalized these networks took public works quite seriously.

Social welfare, then, was a crucial strategy for both the constitution and legitimation of native place networks, particularly in view of the growing social problems of the new era, problems exacerbated by the failings of new structures of government. Concern for the broad social welfare of society was also crucial for the public reputations of leading social figures in the Republican era—the directors of native place associations among them—who were called upon as public citizens (*guomin*) to transcend the limits of the personal networks with which they were associated and embrace a larger public identity. In practice this meant that public figures multiplied their public identities and affiliations.

In the early Republican era, in the wake of the formation of a Chinese republic and in the public ferment surrounding the May Fourth Movement, public associations and urban media grew rapidly in numbers and expressed considerable diversity. In a political context that was increasingly marked by a multiplicity of voices and a growing popular politics, it was possible for new leaders to emerge into public influence through popular networking. In contrast to this efflorescence of voluntary associations and initiatives in the early Republican era, the Nanjing decade (1927–1937) saw the progressively stronger exercise of power by agents of Chiang Kai-shek's government, in combination with the rising power of the Green Gang. The changed political context was reflected in an increasing concentration of social influence in a smaller number of social notables with very substantial business, political, and institutional ties, and possibly gang connections as well.[6] Transformations in the political climate were mirrored in the shifting social roles, functions, and legitimation strategies of social networks. Although native place associations and networks were important in both the early Republican era and in the Nanjing decade, their public manifestations were different. Whereas the more politically open early Republican era saw a great increase in the numbers of associations, the Nanjing decade saw the developing concentration of a small group of large and powerful associations, headed by especially well-connected leaders.

The first section of this chapter briefly outlines the social welfare practices of native place associations in the Republican era as an introduction to the formal functioning of native place networks in the developing public realm. The second section examines the role of native place associations and ties in charitable concerns that went beyond the boundaries of native place community and were organized in terms of a broader public—on a city-wide or national basis—to show the expanding importance of native place networks in wider social transactions. The third section of this chapter examines the dynamic logic of Republican-era social networking: the concurrent multiple affiliations of most leaders, who characteristically combined a range of business, charitable, civic, and often religious leadership positions into a potent public persona. These multiple positions and the networks they conveyed increased these individuals' leadership authority as well as the efficacy of their public interventions. The careers of two prominent leaders of native place associations, one from the May Fourth era and the other from the 1930s, serve in this section to illuminate the different social meanings of these leaders' networks and the changing politics of the public in each time period. In conclusion, I reflect on the enduring utility but changing social and political meanings of native place networks following the political winds and constraints of the Republican era.

Expansive Social Welfare Practices in the Republican Era

In the Republican era, Shanghai native place associations engaged increasingly in social welfare activities.[7] The range of these practices both extended the philanthropic activism associated with merchant guilds in the late Qing and redefined public activism in accordance with changing definitions of both public governance and the constitution of public associations.[8] Late Qing *huiguan* and *gongsuo* assisted with temporary coffin storage and transportation (permitting sojourners to fulfill the ritual requirement that the dead be buried in ancestral soil in the native place), provided occasional help to poor or runaway sojourners, returned indigents to the native place, and occasionally funded small-scale rice-gruel stations, charitable schools, and hospitals. In the Republican era, native place associations, often newly constituted as modern *tongxianghui*,[9] equipped themselves financially and bureaucratically to administer a wider variety of services for growing numbers of people.

Some of the expansion in philanthropic work by native place associations may be attributed to the limitations of local government in the warlord era and the declining social order of Shanghai sojourners' home areas. The Shanghai Chaozhou Huiguan, for example, acted like a local administration in exile, managing relief in the face of catastrophic flooding in Chaozhou in August 1922, funding and directing a local Shantou benevolent institution to investigate local conditions, care for orphans, and arrange for adoptions. From Shanghai the *huiguan* directed the repair of local dikes, deflecting the attempts of local Chaozhou officials to divert the Shanghai *huiguan* money to their own uses. If the scope of the Shanghai Chaozhou Huiguan social welfare work in Chaozhou is striking, it was hardly unique. Although Ningbo suffered fewer natural and man-made disasters in the same time period, the Ningbo Tongxianghui collected and contributed 74,000 yuan for burials and refugee relief in response to flooding in the Ningbo area in August 1921.[10]

In Shanghai, as in the native place, Shanghai sojourner associations invested increasingly in social welfare services for their communities.

As the population of Ningbo people in Shanghai increased, between 1918 and 1922 the Siming Gongsuo engaged in a frenzy of mortuary building, collecting a sum of 520,000 yuan for the refurbishment of older mortuaries and the construction of new ones. By the end of this period the Siming Gongsuo managed five mortuaries and a hospital for Ningbo sojourners. Although the scale of the Ningbo coffin repository and shipment network was unique, most moderately sized native place associations provided their communities with some assistance in the costly matters of temporary coffin storage in Shanghai, charitable cemeteries, and shipment back to the native place. Sojourner mortuary growth in the Republican era, a reflection of immigration to Shanghai, is reflected in the numbers of such mortuaries listed in successive guidebooks to Shanghai: 20 in 1914, 33 in 1919, 41 in 1931.[11]

In her survey of late imperial philanthropy, Angela Leung has suggested that late Qing philanthropy was fundamentally conservative and expressed a moralizing status quo, if a robust social dynamism.[12] In the context of weak and divided local government administration, Shanghai *huiguan* and *gongsuo* leaders at the end of the Qing dynasty played an important role in urban management and in what might be considered socially conservative social welfare practices, as they constituted themselves at the moral pinnacle of hierarchical native place communities. Such practices expanded in the Republican era, but were joined, in a process of community redefinition, by a new range of social welfare activities and altered understandings of the power dynamics of moral community that reflected new ideals of citizenship. The social welfare programs of early Republican *tongxianghui* often developed in opposition to older community hierarchies, emphasizing a more democratic populism (with public meetings and voting) and redefining charity to promote the health and education of larger numbers of nonelite members of the community. The new administrative activism of Republican-era associations frequently emerged in the context of power struggles within native place communities, struggles that reflected both older and newer understandings of associational values and governing structures. As the political climate shifted, so did the ideological and material basis for community welfare.

This process may be illustrated through the example of the Guang-Zhao Gongsuo, the association of Guangdong sojourners from Guangzhou and Zhaoqing prefectures. In 1918, a split developed within the *gongsuo* between a conservative faction and a "new style" reform faction that demanded both quantitatively *more* charitable activity and new *types* of charitable activity. At this time the Guang-Zhao Gongsuo was already operating a coffin repository and cemetery, a charitable hospital and two charitable schools. Reformers wanted to substantially increase the overall financial commitment to poor sojourners by regularizing contributions from all *gongsuo* directors. They also advocated a shift in charitable emphasis from what they termed negative, or inactive welfare (*xiaoji cishan*), which involved traditional concerns for burial functions and caring for the dead, to positive, active welfare (*jiji cishan*), which involved increasing relative *gongsuo* investment in charitable education and medical services.[13]

The Guang-Zhao reformers' tactics in this power struggle also involved a conceptual departure in *gongsuo* management, shaking up the oligarchic rule of *gongsuo* elders with the introduction of a mass meeting. By calling a large public meeting and unveiling a plan to substantially tax the rich to help the poor, the reformers were able to mobilize sufficient popular support to displace the old *gongsuo* leadership. By means of their successful ability to appeal to a large population of their fellow-provincials, the reformers won the battle, took over the leadership of the *gongsuo*, and quickly established six new charitable schools, including a night school for workers. These were funded largely by contributions from leading reform-faction businessmen, including Huo Shouhua, Feng Shaoshan, and Lu Weichang.[14] By their acts of benevolence the new association leaders solidified their patronage bonds with their newly mobilized constituency, bonds of public support that served the leaders well in the public relations struggle in the Shanghai media that surrounded the reform of the native place association. The public nature of the split within the Guang-Zhao community was striking, but other major native place communities similarly developed their investments in the direction of a more populist modern civic welfare, focused on education and public health, in addition to their more traditional charitable functions.[15]

The reform of the Guang-Zhao *gongsuo*, its reconstitution as a more inclusive and more populist organization, and the redirection of its public welfare activities were all linked to the new politics of the public that emerged in Shanghai in the early Republican era and intensified in the nationalist and associational ferment surrounding the May Fourth movement. Internally, influential sojourner groups reformulated their governing structures with constitutions and improvised public elections. Externally, associations legitimated themselves by demonstrating that they represented the public (*gongzhong*) through charitable activities, public works, public meetings, and the publication of announcements and meeting minutes on the pages of the daily newspapers.[16] This reorientation of associational habits is evident in the development of the largest and most powerful of the early Republican sojourner associations, for example, the Ningbo Tongxianghui, as well as somewhat smaller, but nonetheless substantial sojourner associations like the Shaoxing Tongxianghui, or the Hu She, an association of Huzhou sojourners.[17]

The expanding administrative structures of these associations in the Republican era reflected the broad quasi-governmental scope of their activities. In a departure from the small, generalist administrative core of a few managers and a secretary that characterized late Qing *huiguan* and *gongsuo*, the new *tongxianghui* constitutions of the 1920s and 1930s often detailed vast committee structures, with specialized administrative positions for committee members who handled legal services, public works, housing issues, investigation, job introductions, social surveys, statistics, schools, hospitals, and so on. In this sense, native place associations in this period adopted a new kind of governmental rationality that they associated with the ideals of appropriate organization of the new Chinese republic, reflecting new notions of a public constituted by a citizenry with civic responsibilities.

The scale of the new social welfare activities embraced by these reformulated native place communities depended to a large degree on the financial and social capital of association leaders. The expansion of welfare activities was made possible by Shanghai's commercial growth. Because not all sojourning communities boasted prosperous Shanghai capitalists among their members, it was by no means the case that all sojourners in Shanghai could look to their native place associations for assistance. Native place associations depended on a combination of financial resources and influential leaders. Sojourning groups that lacked such economic and human resources failed to develop efficacious associations through which to constitute native place community. In such cases, there was little or no native place safety net for the rescue of impoverished sojourners.

Relief Networks, Native Place Ties, and Multiple, Overlapping Institutions

At the same time that native place associations increased their social welfare activities, modeling their expanded practices on notions of republican citizenship, the reach of native place networks extended into social welfare organizations that were not defined on the basis of native place. To some extent this was simply a function of the pervasiveness of native place ties as a mechanism of urban alignment and identity. In other cases, it was a function of the expansive public practices of native place associations that recognized an imperative in the Republican era to go beyond the boundaries of narrow native place community. In the process, we may observe how native place associations took the initiative to combine, creating new forms of charitable associations that connected people from different native place groups.[18]

The protean nature of formal and informal native place networks and their tendency to infuse social welfare functions beyond the native place community may be illustrated through the examples of two charitable concerns. Both emerged in the double context of the expansive new ideals of a republican civic order and the urgent and alarming social disorders of the early Republic. That is, these institutional developments were not simply responses to reconceptualizations of the public realm, they were practical solutions to problems posed by the increasing ineffectiveness of government in this period. Both of the new charitable concerns discussed next defined themselves on a city-wide or even national basis. The records of these charities and the records of native place associations testify to areas of overlap, interaction, and interdependency.

Serving as our first example is the Shanghai Shelter for the Disabled (*Canji yuan*), an organization with no direct connection to native place networks, aside from the fact that the leading founder—the wealthy businessman, philanthropist, Buddhist, and painter, Wang Yiting—was also a director of the Hu She, the Shanghai Huzhou sojourner's association, among his numerous public affiliations (see Chapter 3).[19] The Shelter for the Disabled was established in May 1919. Kōhama Masako has examined the shelter's records in order to analyze the social networks that led individuals to receive charity.[20] Kōhama's study makes visible a common principle in the practice of charity and indeed many social and business transactions in the Republican era: needy individuals who wished to gain entrance and receive services from the charity could not register without letters of introduction from guarantors. This requirement tended to enforce the importance of native place affiliations as a relatively accessible type of social connection that aspirants for assistance might use to their benefit.

The register and letters of introduction in the Shelter for the Disabled archives reveal the social networks that led individuals to the shelter. Many of the individual guarantors were shelter directors, usually prominent businessmen whose many contacts knew of their charitable connections and sent people to them. Numerous letters were also written by the Green Gang figure Huang Jinrong, who was similarly asked by his contacts to write letters of introduction on behalf of third parties. Huang was also an officer of the Disabled Shelter. Other guarantors were corporate, though more commonly in the form of social organizations rather than police or public security offices. Here one finds listed various native place associations, among them the Guangdong and the Ningbo *tongxianghui,* together with various charities, businesses, and other corporate concerns. At times the most prominent leaders of native place associations, men like Yu Xiaqing, signed letters of introduction, their names virtually ensuring the efficacy of the letter.[21] The records reveal the variety of private connections that could lead individuals to charitable associations. Needy individuals clearly claimed whatever connections they could. But the requirement by charitable concerns for guarantors enforced the importance of all social networks and social connections. Individuals with no such connections were far less likely to gain access to charity.[22]

The example of the Shanghai Shelter for the Disabled reveals the underlying importance of a variety of social networks, native place networks prominent among them, to new charitable institutions that were not organized on the basis of native place. In contrast, the Anti-Kidnapping Society (*Zhongguo furu jiuji zonghui,* literally "Chinese Society for the Rescue of Women and Children," or CSRWC) provides a second example, this one representing a new collective initiative undertaken by native place associations that mobilized their social networks to confront new social problems.[23] This organization was established at the beginning of the Republican era by three Shanghai *tongxianghui* (Shaoxing, Ningbo, and Huzhou) and was initially housed in the Shaoxing Tongxianghui. Yu Xiaqing and Wang Yiting, leaders of the Ningbo and Huzhou sojourning communities, respectively, were also at the head of the CSRWC. The collaborative project was no doubt facilitated by the fact that the founding *tongxianghui* were all associations of sojourners from Zhejiang province, albeit associations representing distinctive dialects and local cultures. The new philanthropic organization, which soon expanded its focus to include people from Jiangsu province, was created to deal with a problem of increasing concern in Shanghai, the rise of kidnapping, trafficking, and the disappearance of women and children in the Republican urban environment. The CSRWC had branch offices in various Chinese cities, not just Shanghai, since its work often involved tracking individuals down in distant cities like Tianjin.

Native place networks were fundamental to the charitable rescue initiatives undertaken by this association. Much of the work of kidnapping detection took place on steamboats. CSRWC investigators on the boats began their efforts by listening to the accents of passengers who were traveling with women and children. Because the most commonplace social bonds and groupings reflected native place affinities, suspicions of kidnapping arose when the regional accents of adults and children did not match. Shipping company compradors were conferred titles of "honorary investigators" of the CSRWC in order to encourage their support. Conveniently, several prominent shipping compradors were leaders of the major Zhejiang and Jiangsu native place associations and were among the members of the CSRWC. In his study of kidnapping networks and rescue mechanisms, Iwama Kazuhiro highlights the native place ties that led businessmen from victims' hometowns to become involved in kidnapping rescue efforts. When kidnapping victims from the south found themselves in northern cities and appealed for help, their regional dialects identified them as southerners. Concerned private individuals and local public security bureaus to which victims appealed both turned to businessmen from the south who happened to be working in the north. Such fellow provincials often helped to temporarily house victims while using their native place networks back home to locate the victims' relatives. These businessmen stood to gain in reputation from the publicity that would result from their benevolent actions. In certain respects, the emergence of the CSRWC may be understood as an institutional formalization of these social inclinations.[24]

In the functioning of the CSRWC and the administration of rescue, it is important to note the interaction among government offices, public nongovernment associations (both the CSRWC and various native place associations), and informal private native place networks. In practice, government offices and the police counted on and coordinated their actions with these native place networks. In many cases, such coordination was facilitated by the fact that native place networks interpenetrated the government. In the case of the Hu She, one association for which there is an extant list of individual members' occupations, 179 members were listed in 1937 as employed in the Guomindang and government (*dang-zheng*). Another 69 were employed in military, police, or judicial positions (*jun-jing, sifa*).[25]

Because the networks of sojourner associations also linked sojourners in various cities (the branches of the Hu She, for example, linked together Huzhou people in Shanghai, Nanjing, Wuhan, Suzhou, and Jiaxing), sojourner networks were useful in coordinating activities that spanned several localities. *Tongxianghui* records, particularly those of Zhejiang and Jiangsu organizations from the 1920s and 1930s, show careful, steady cooperation between *tongxianghui* officials, sojourning communities in other cities, the CSRWC, and various local public security bureaus, all working for the safe return of individual children and women. These records suggest that, in general, family members of victims did not normally go directly to the police. They commonly appealed to their native place associations, which acted as brokers or go-betweens with the CSRWC and relevant local authorities.[26] When individuals did go directly to the CSRWC, as Christian Henriot has observed, this may have been because they saw the CSRWC as "an extension of the native place association."[27]

Indeed, at times, local government officials appeared as extensions of the native place association. The overlapping nature of these ties may be illustrated by a not atypical case. In 1920, a girl with the surname Chen was kidnapped from the south and forced to work in a brothel in Heilongjiang. Her family, working with the Shanghai CSRWC, raised funds to pay the girl's debts to the brothel and approached the CSRWC branch office in Heilongjiang. Their own funds were insufficient, howsever, and their success depended on a contribution from an official serving in Heilongjiang who was from Shaoxing. Not only did his Shaoxing connection motivate him to work with the CSRWC and to contribute financially, but he also arranged safe housing for the girl until her successful return home.[28]

In the case of the CSRWC, we see the development in the early Republican era of a new form of specialized public welfare organization, in which several native place associations combined forces in a broad gesture of civic welfare to address a new social problem of national scope. The formal creation of a new type of functionally distinct welfare organization enabled integration of personnel resources and public and private networks that often went beyond the scope or abilities of a single native place network. But the new charity was not conceived to work independently of native place associations and necessarily relied on their human resources to facilitate rescue efforts. By the

1920s, the activities of the CSRWC were regularized and assimilated into the welfare work of many native place associations. The records of native place associations also document their financial contributions to the CSRWC, both to the organization in Shanghai and to branches in home areas.[29] Given the coordination that was necessary to contact families, gain the assistance of local police, locate missing individuals, and arrange safe transportation home, the CSRWC relied heavily on the networks of influential and capable *tongxianghui* to resolve the complex cases before it. Individuals without access to competent *tongxianghui* with networks that could monitor and coordinate activities across several cities were considerably less likely to recover lost family members.

If the CSRWC was conceived as a national civic organization, it was always dominated by people from Zhejiang and Jiangsu. The CSRWC did not restrict its activities to victims and families from Zhejiang and Jiangsu, but people from these areas were nonetheless its primary concern, and it served them better than it served people from other communities. Although native place networks facilitated the work of the charity in many respects, they were sometimes an obstacle to its harmonious functioning because of tense relationships between particular native place groups. In the early years of the CSRWC, for example, Ningbo functionaries of the charity harassed Guangdong sojourners, suspecting the worst of Guangdong travelers, and dragged their wives and children off boats. Efforts to establish CSRWC offices in the Pearl River delta failed.[30]

The document trails of native place associations and the CSRWC suggest that the practical mechanisms of charitable rescue and their success or failure were determined, above all, by the relative strength and resources of particular organizational networks at any given time. This is particularly evident in the sudden significance of the Pudong Tongxianghui in charity work during the 1930s. In 1935, the powerful Pudong Tongxianghui, only just established in 1933, already handled a load of five to twenty CSRWC cases per month for individuals from Pudong and Shanghai (which from the administrative reach of the *tongxianghui* appeared as part of Pudong). At times the Pudong association even handled the safe return of individuals of other native place origins, like Shaoxing, for reasons that are not clear, aside from the relative strength and efficacy of the Pudong association.[31] Given the limitations of government social services and the political and social complexities of the Republican period (both in the warlord era and under the Guomindang), the flexibility of native place associations and networks in bridging the boundaries between public and private provided considerable and enduring utility—even if the nature of these associations and the relative value of different native place networks shifted with the temper of the times.

Multiple Networks and the Shifting Politics of the Public

The multiform practices of charity, as discussed earlier, reflect the ways in which the individuals who constituted the urban elite of the Republican era tended to hold several concurrent social leadership positions. For those individuals who helped to link needy people with charitable organizations, multiple and overlapping connections enriched their ability to serve as patrons and guarantors, enhancing their leadership authority. In the Republican era, the numbers and forms of voluntary and quasi-representative associations in Shanghai increased in number. This development may be partially attributed to the growth and increasing complexity of Shanghai's population and economy and partially to changes in popular political consciousness associated with growing nationalism and the establishment of a republican form of government. In this context, native place association heads multiplied their leadership roles in the growing pool of Shanghai voluntary groups, clubs, political circles, charitable ventures, and civic institutions.[32] Through these multiple public leadership roles, association leaders broadened their patronage networks, increased their constituencies, and magnified their standing as public figures. This in turn enhanced the efficacy of their social interventions.

Rather than formally separate their roles, such individuals tended to blend their multiple social functions, including charity work, assuming the persona of potent public patrons. The multiplicity of their positions conveyed access to a variety of social networks. The density of the networks embodied in individuals increased their ability to connect, mediate, and function across different realms of public activity.

This tendency for prominent social leaders to embody multiple network connections remained continuous throughout the Republican period; however, the politics of the public and the public meanings of networks worked differently at different moments. The greater spontaneity of social organizations in the May Fourth era and the emphasis, in May Fourth rhetoric and media, on public democracy give the impression of looser networks and greater potential for social mobility through the vehicle of populist politics. In contrast, in the Nanjing decade, power concentrated increasingly in a few key social players, with comparatively greater overlap of networks of social, financial, and state power. Public understanding of and aspirations for native place networks adapted to and reinforced this altered political context.

Occasionally, as will be illustrated shortly, at moments when behaviors challenged convention and embroiled leaders in controversy, or when new and somewhat unusual associations formed, it is possible to locate public articulation and discussion of the normative values and appropriate use of networks. At such moments, native place networks—always poised between negatively charged private loyalties and the public good—became denaturalized, delegitimated, or in need of exceptional justification.

The shifting politics of the public, as well as public understandings of the networks formalized in native place associations, may be illustrated by two examples, each in its way characteristic of the political imperatives and constraints of its time and each revealing some of the limits and contradictions of native place networks. The first such example reflects the public politics of the May Fourth era of relative economic prosperity and popular associational ferment. The second is taken from what Brian Martin has termed the Guomindang corporatist environment of the mid-1930s.[33] These examples of multilayered social networks and what might be called the politics of constituting the public are chosen, not so much as representative of native place associations in each time period, but rather as provocative indicators of some of the distinctive formations and politics of networks in each era. Insofar as each case indicates the multiple and overlapping networks embodied by association leaders whose power and reputation derived from the way they brought together a density of interlinked networks, these examples express the concerns of the broader climate of public culture in each period.

Our initial example involves one of the Guang-Zhao Gongsuo reformers of 1918, Tang Jiezhi. Reform of his native place association was a part of his engagement in a broad movement to reform Chinese institutions in a more democratic and inclusive fashion. As a new leader of the Guang-Zhao Gongsuo, Tang became active in power struggles across a range of Shanghai civic institutions. He was an early leader of the Shanghai Commercial Federation, which initiated the early merchant mobilization associated with the May Fourth Movement in Shanghai and challenged the elitist and oligarchic structure of the Shanghai General Chamber of Commerce.[34] His agitation for democratic reform bore fruit when the newly swelled membership of the Chamber elected him—together with his Guang-Zhao Gongsuo reformer-compatriots whose names appeared earlier in this chapter, Feng Shaoshan and Huo Shouhua—to the new board of directors.

Along with Feng and Huo, Tang was involved in the contemporaneous emergence of a grassroots movement for a "commoner's chamber of commerce" through the organization of smaller merchants and shop owners into commercial street unions. By January 1920, the commercial street unions could claim a total constituency of 10,000 shops. Tang, Feng, and Huo, together with leaders of the reformulated Ningbo Tongxianghui and 41 of the commercial street unions, were also at the core of an August 1920 preparatory committee for a National Citizens' Assembly. In September 1921, a new Federation of Commercial Street Unions was created and it elected Tang as president. All of this reform agitation was based on the articulation of a new language of republican citizenship and popular representation.

In Tang's activism, it is possible to observe the process by which a newly risen native place association leader came to be associated with a broad number of public organizations, becoming a highly public figure.[35] Because of controversy surrounding a legal case in which Tang became entangled in 1922, it is possible, additionally, to observe some of the public uses and understandings of associational networks and identities at the time, as well as some of the possibilities and limitations of such social networks. After his secretary, Xi Shangzhen, committed suicide at Tang's office, Tang was arrested and charged with defrauding her of money.[36] Newspaper coverage of the case illustrates well the importance conveyed by an individual's social networks. In the court of public opinion, the moral probity of the two principals in the case was demonstrated through the public statements and activities of the associations with which they were connected.

On the side of Xi Shangzhen, the first association to publish a statement in the newspapers on Xi's behalf was the Dongting Dongshan Tongxianghui. Other groups quickly joined in the effort to stir public opinion in sympathy for Xi and against Tang, including teachers and students from Xi's alma mater, the East City Women's School, three additional native place associations from Xi's home province of Jiangsu, a women's professional association, and an office workers' association.[37]

Commenting on the network of associations that provided public testimonials on Xi's behalf, one commentator challenged Tang's associational backers, making clear the public expectation that these associations (placed in the position of moral guarantors) should speak to the issue of Tang's credibility:

> For several days running, newspapers have featured articles about the Xi-Tang case. These testify that it is a major incident in society. . . . Now the women's circles and each public association have also spoken. . . . Tang's fellow sojourners selected him as their director, manager, board member and supervisor [of their various organizations]. . . . They should investigate the facts and judge Tang's rights and wrongs. If [Tang's] . . . behavior corresponds to what has been reported in the newspapers, they should protect their reputation and quickly expel this mad horse from their organizations. If investigation . . . reveals that Tang is untainted, that he acted out of human kindness and has been slandered, they should intervene to protect his reputation and their own.[38]

This public challenge—which held the associational network responsible for investigating and attesting to the conduct of the individual and for maintaining the morality of the whole—did not go unmet. In the course of Tang's trial, the social networks he had painstakingly built in his swift rise as a public figure emerged to forcefully intervene on his behalf. After his second court hearing but prior to the court's verdict, representatives of 24 public associations (including five native place associations, a self-government society, a workers' mutual aid society, thirteen commercial street associations, a trade association, and two workers' unions) convened a public "indignation meeting."[39] The minutes of this meeting, published in the daily papers, cast Tang as a victim of systemic judicial abuses in Shanghai and pronounced the public goal of rectifying the judiciary to protect human rights. Significantly, the participants declared that their actions were not just about Tang but had the wider, civic purpose of "saving the spirit of judicial process . . . and protecting [China's] status internationally."[40]

The roster of the meeting revealed the strengths and limitations of Tang's personal network of connections. Though Tang's social affiliations were extensive, they were short-lived, and his political ambitions and activism had easily created as many enemies within these organizations as they had gained him friends. Unlike many associational leaders who made their fortunes first and then were pressed into leadership roles because of their evident resources, Tang did not possess a large fortune to match his many social obligations and projects. Indeed, his arrest had touched off deep controversies within several of the organizations with which he was connected in a leadership role. The Chamber of Commerce, for example, was pressured from both within and without to take a public stance on the case but the directors decided to remain silent to avoid controversy.[41] The actions of those association leaders who did choose to publicly align with Tang—using their association's name—did not go uncontested. Members of some groups immediately protested their leaders' actions, pointing out that the association as a whole did not necessarily support Tang. This bickering forced some of Tang's supporters (including representatives from the Ningbo Tongxianghui) to withdraw the names of their associations from public statements of support. The following day representatives of a slightly reduced group of 20 associations initiated a judicial reform movement, documenting their commitment to civic, rather than personal loyalties.[42]

Despite the efforts of Tang's defenders to constitute their action as broadly based and in the public interest, Tang's attackers denounced the personal networks that lay behind the judicial reform movement. In an article entitled, "Private Friendships Are Not Public Opinion," one of Tang's critics argued:

> If a minority of people because of their private relations (*sijiao*) conduct a public demonstration falsely in the name of public opinion (*gonglun*) this destroys the credibility of the masses. All of the people should rise up and question this minority that calls itself the representative of the people. Each organization, for the sake of private friendship, attempts to rescue Tang Jiezhi . . . This doesn't legitimate disguising private friendship as public opinion. How much more so when you can't necessarily say the majority in each association in fact enjoy a friendship with Tang. If you want to save Tang, do it in your own names. Why should you use the collective name of the group? A social pillar of philanthropy has [fallen] . . . Did the deceased really do things for the public good? You gentlemen in the majority of each organization! . . . How is it that you can be dragged to accompany a coffin to the grave on another's behalf, without opening your mouths in protest?[43]

The comment plays on the ambiguities of public and private ties that accompanied the bundling of public identities and networks in individual leaders, a blurring of public and private loyalties that was characteristic of native place networks at this time. The author effectively deploys the new democratic rhetoric of the May Fourth era, with its emphasis on the majority and the masses, to raise questions of hierarchy and the contradictions of the unequal power relations between leaders and memberships of associations that purported to represent the public. The circulation of these ideas marked the politics of the public at this time. In order to convey public authority or to speak in the voice of public opinion, leaders sympathetic to Tang needed to wrap their own sympathies in the cloak of public associations. At the same time, the democratic rhetoric provided a language for dissent within these associations, raising questions about the contradictions between leaders and ordinary members. Members who were not consulted did not necessarily feel the same ties to Tang that their leaders did. Their complaints of private manipulations bore a sting since Tang's group had publicly introduced the language of public democracy into *gongsuo* politics in the 1918 struggle to unseat the old *gongsuo* oligarchy. When that dispute broke into the daily newspapers, this rhetoric pierced the public solidarity of the native place association. If native place associations had never commanded absolute loyalty, a politics of unquestioned hierarchy and consensus vis-à-vis the outside had prevailed in the late Qing era.[44] As the associational ground shifted in the May Fourth era, contending groups deployed the new rhetoric against each other, exposing the fickleness of networks that were based, not so much on a commonality of ideas or interests, as upon an idealized sentiment of native place community.

The radically transformed political terrain of the 1930s is apparent in our second example of multilayered networks and the politics of the public. Here we turn to the formation of the Pudong Tongxianghui in 1932. The abrupt emergence of this powerful new *tongxianghui* challenged normative ideas of native place associations. In contrast to other powerful *tongxianghui*, all of which had a long-term institutional presence in the city that naturalized the native place group, the Pudong Tongxianghui sprang massively into being as the preeminent Green Gang leader Du Yuesheng rose to the peak of his influence. As Du rose, Pudong people—and anyone who could claim Pudong identity—quickly mobilized to create the association and become beneficiaries of Du's influence. The Pudong Tongxianghui hoisted Du—already prominent in a range of civic affiliations and legitimate business enterprises—into an institutional position of local patronage, together with other influential Pudong leaders of quite different political, economic, and intellectual backgrounds. Most notable among these were the tireless proponent of vocational education, Huang Yanpei (see Chapter 2), the cotton entrepreneur and Buddhist activist Mu Ouchu (Mu Xiangyue), and the businessman Wang Yiting (whose varied associations with the Hu She, the Shanghai Shelter for the Disabled, the CSRWC, and Buddhist circles have already been noted; see also Chapter 3 of this volume). Du, of course, stood to benefit from the legitimacy conveyed by service to his native place community as well as the additional loyalties that could be generated through the institutionalization of native place sentiment.

Du's prominence was, indeed, the stimulus to the rediscovery or renaissance of Pudong native place sentiment and its formalization in a native place association. Except for the small and ephemeral Pudong Fellows Association created by Li Pingshu in 1905, Pudong had not historically had a native place association.[45] Nor were all of the Pudong Tongxianghui members, or even its leaders, clearly Pudong natives. Wang Yiting provides a case in point. Wang's ancestral home was in Huzhou, Zhejiang, and he was a well-known activist in the Huzhou association (Hu She), but his birthplace was Pudong. This accident of birth location, not traditionally relevant to native place identity (which was ancestral), enabled him to luxuriate in the benefit of dual native place identity and embrace a new, more flexible, and strategic use of the term.

In other respects, the Pudong Tongxianghui inspired similar creativity, fueled by overwhelming desire to establish legitimate connections with Du Yuesheng and deploy his influence for a variety of useful purposes. In a 1931 membership drive manifesto for the creation of the new *tongxianghui*, Huang, Du, Mu, and Wang noted that, in contrast to other native place associations in Shanghai, Pudong people were not exactly sojourners: "It is fortunate that our people are only a thin strip of water away from Shanghai, different from the sojourning condition of people from other areas."[46] This was no obstacle to the formation of a sojourners' association, however, and the organizers leapt to action, establishing more than 73 membership registration and collection teams.

Some of these teams were organized conventionally enough on the basis of district (Baoshan, Nanhui, Chuansha, and so forth), with Du Yuesheng in charge of the Shanghai team. But the other teams were organized by *jie* (occupational circle) and their reach revealed Du's extensive networks throughout the fabric of urban society: party, military, government (two teams), city government, communications (three teams), banks, insurance, the stock market (two teams), lawyers, newspapers, police (two teams), traditional medicine, and philanthropy circles, together with all of the major trades, including Du's old trade, fruit-selling. Wang Yiting headed the membership enlistment and collection team for philanthropic circles.[47] By October 1931, these teams had already collected a total of 54,445 yuan. By the next year, the Pudong Tongxianghui had attracted nearly 20,000 members, just slightly fewer than the most powerful and long-established Ningbo Tongxianghui. Within just a few more years, nearly 600,000 yuan had been collected, enough for the construction of a striking new modern building, the grandest of all *tongxianghui* buildings, on Avenue Edward VII.[48]

Pudong Tongxianghui leaders often stressed the civic-mindedness, indeed universality, that resulted in the creation of their new association, comparing it to older *tongxianghui*: "This one is for the benefit of mankind, not just the benefit of people from one locality. What virtue!"[49] Such protests of virtue should be understood as a response to lingering concerns for the public, to the now unvoiced but obvious questions raised by the identification of the *tongxianghui* with Du Yuesheng, whose civic works were vast but not untainted by his gangster enterprises and networks.

If Pudong Tongxianghui proponents emphasized their association's public and civic purposes, the public politics of the 1930s revolved nonetheless around powerful figures and networks of personal loyalties. In the case of the Pudong Tongxianghui, we can see little of the early Republican-era concern about clothing personal loyalties in public guise, which was observable in public discussion of the Tang case.[50] The Pudong Tongxianghui collection network depended more on Du Yuesheng's networks of influence than on native place identity. The association itself featured Du Yuesheng everywhere. The inaugural celebration of the new Tongxianghui building in 1936, which gathered on stage all of the Shanghai elite without reference to native place, was held in the new Du Hall; the characters "*Du ting*" appeared above the heads of Du and Wu Tiecheng, the Cantonese mayor of Shanghai who shared the podium; and a large photograph of Du was positioned between the two. Du's calligraphy graced the covers of Pudong Tongxianghui publications, and his name appeared on all correspondence dealing with difficult matters.

Even if the universal Pudong Tongxianghui was in many ways a public monument to Du (whose extensive connections contributed to its universal importance), this does not mean we should pass lightly over the serious charitable and civic functions of this institution. Rather than viewing the Pudong Tongxianghui as a front organization for a gang boss, it would be more accurate to understand it as an important charitable association, perched on the back of an especially powerful embodiment of multilayered networks, deriving its resources and sustenance from its ability to claim those connections.

Indeed, the charitable resources and institutional efficacy of the

Pudong Tongxianghui were impressive. After the Japanese attack on Shanghai on January 28, 1932, the Pudong Tongxianghui sent out a notice that all Pudong people who were homeless could register and receive assistance. It quickly constructed refugee centers in Zhoupu and Yangsi *zhen* and established six stations for the distribution of rice, at a total cost of 15,540 yuan.[51] In September 1933, when typhoons struck the coastal areas, the *tongxianghui* collected 366,563 yuan for relief. In 1937, the Pudong Tongxianghui organized rescue teams and established 12 refugee centers that operated until March 1939, sheltering a total of 4,186 people. Male refugees were introduced to employment; women were given embroidery work. Special medical services were provided for pregnant women.[52] At the same time, as war disastrously affected the livelihood of people in the cotton-producing area of Pudong by disrupting the market, the Pudong Tongxianghui established a Cotton Transportation and Sales Society that raised 1 million yuan to purchase Pudong cotton, transport it across the Huangpu River by convoy, and store it safely in the French Concession.[53]

Conclusion

The question posed in the chapter title—What Is In a Network?—is not to be answered simply. The illustrations provided for discussion here have highlighted the ways in which it could be imperative for members of Shanghai society to claim connection to publicly recognized social organizations and individuals. Networks were necessary for charitable assistance; networks could provide for character witnesses in times of legal troubles. At moments of political mobilization like the May Fourth Movement, networks also served to create a public, speaking on behalf of individuals. Native place ties and native place associations were important for these functions, as were the numerous other networks with legitimate social standing with which they were generally intertwined.

But native place associations, which encompassed personal ties and affections but extended them to a larger, impersonal, imagined community, were a particular kind of network, poised as they were between private ties and a larger public. In the late Qing period, *huiguan* and *gongsuo* in many respects served quasi-governmental functions in the city, maintaining order (and occasionally organizing protest) among their sojourning populations. By the end of the nineteenth century, through their merchant elite leaders, these networks often made strategic connections across different sectors of the Chinese population of the city or with foreign authorities in the city.

The performance of social welfare functions was essential to the construction of native place community and to the authority that legitimated hierarchy within the community. Over the Republican period, native place associations endured as institutional expressions of social networks that were extremely useful, flexible, and adaptive to changing circumstances. As China declared itself a republic, native place networks served as important conduits of information, organization, and mobilization in movements characterized by popular nationalism and civic activism. In the context of evolving notions of the public, the leaders of native place associations came under greater pressure both to include a larger portion of the sojourning population in their associations and to attend to the broad native place community through public welfare functions (*gongyi*).

In the early Republican era, in the context of a fragmented Chinese government and a city of divided jurisdictions, and later in the Nanjing decade, in the context of a predatory state and war with Japan, these welfare functions helped (albeit in a partial and uneven way) to mitigate some of the imperfections and limitations of the state. Under the circumstances, maintaining these networks of community wherever there were resources to maintain them was of great mutual benefit to leaders and sojourning communities alike. In the Nanjing decade—marked by an increasingly corrupt, intrusive, extractive, brutal, and at times indifferent government—native place associations served an important function, protecting their sojourning communities, negotiating, and sometimes rebuking agents of the state.[54]

The fundamental importance of native place associations to the maintenance of Shanghai social order was perhaps most obvious in wartime, when native place associations made up for the limited ability of the Shanghai municipal government to deal with the catastrophic bombing of Hongkou and Zhabei in August 1937. Twenty-one native place associations immediately mobilized their resources to assist their communities. Among these (in addition to the already mentioned work of the Pudong Tongxianghui), the Guangdong Tongxianghui managed five refugee centers and the Ningbo Tongxianghui maintained 14 centers and arranged boat transportation for 200,000 people to Ningbo (one-third to two-fifths of the entire Shanghai Ningbo population). At this time of life and death, maintaining the native place tie provided many Shanghai residents with an alternate home to flee to when life in Shanghai became untenable.[55]

The question remains of how to categorize these networks and associations. Native place ties, unlike many other bases for social networks, did not convey a precise platform of beliefs or elaborate an ideology, unlike popular movements, political parties, or religious communities. Native place ties—ever present as an idea—were in many respects more potential than real, certainly in terms of the larger sojourning community. Native place networks were commonly realized among small groups of like-minded individuals at all levels of social, political, and economic institutions. Among the large sojourning community, they were more ephemeral, symbolized by the architectural presence in the city of the native place association but only concretized in a patchwork fashion by charitable and other public works that extended to a larger community or were occasionally visible in public meetings or other events that evoked large-scale native place loyalty and identity. If Republican-era innovations (like the Guang-Zhao reformers' efforts to provide schools to poorer sojourners) helped to broaden the popular base of support for particular associations, such efforts nonetheless fell far short of encompassing the entire potential constituency.

Native place sentiment created the possibility of a social network and of social assistance on the basis of the evocation of common referents of regional culture. Native place associations were created as a remedy to the understood traumas of sojourning, a situation of social and territorial displacement in which individuals were understood to suffer from the lack of the normal networks that protected them in their home areas. Native place associations were not class organizations, nor were they restricted by occupation. In many ways, if quite instrumental in their social operations, native place ties were particularly useful precisely because their relative emptiness of meaning meant they could be turned to many purposes or combined with other affiliations. Because the communities they evoked could be quite sizeable and because the native place tie cut across social classes, native place associations were particularly effective conduits of mobilization for popular movements.[56] Through their numbers and the range of people they brought together, in an era concerned—in different ways at different times—with representations of the public and the people, native place associations (in the absence of representative organizations or mechanisms of government) could at times create a compelling likeness of "the people" that so many so desperately wished to call into being.

At the same time, even as native place associations constituted themselves as building blocks of the larger public, and even as they may have historically served to some extent, in the Republican period, as laboratories for the creation of national citizens,[57] their basic inclination to favor one group over others created an uneven public, made up of unequal groupings—as opposed to equal citizens. Some groups were necessarily more influential than others. People from relatively poor or underrepresented native place groups, those without the resources to invest in and construct influential networks, were marginalized, left outside of the kind of corporate citizenship necessitated by the realpolitik of the era. Similar contradictions existed at the level of the Shanghai city government constituted in the Nanjing decade, as successive mayors filled their administrations with subordinates from their own native places, since all potential appointees were not, after all, equal.[58]

Although formal and informal native place ties ran through the fabric of the city, these ties did not automatically create networks: they did so when such networks were mutually beneficial to those concerned. This depended on resources and relations of patronage and hierarchy, even in the context of the growing inclusiveness of these associations and their increasingly populist and, at moments, democratic rhetoric. At their most democratic, in the early 1920s, native place communities experienced their greatest internal divisions. Attempts by progressive activists to create populist associations that would challenge the status quo resulted in sharp ideological divisions that could not be soothed by native place affections, in some cases temporarily sundering networks formerly characterized by group solidarity. The mass meetings and elections that were part of the new politics of the 1918 reformed Guang-Zhao Gongsuo, for example, led to the splitting off of a conservative faction, which formed its own association.[59] Significantly, such moments led, not to the repudiation of the native place framework by any of the parties, but to the creation of multiple competing native place associations, each vying to capture the name of the group, and the "public" represented by the group, for their purposes.

In the 1930s, native place associations increasingly interpenetrated with the state. The leaders of native place associations now included in their number not simply business elites but in some cases the most powerful gang leaders as well. These shifts necessarily altered the social character of these associations and the power relations that infused them. Though in many respects beneficial for their memberships, and although they at times provided outlets for civic activism in an increasingly constrained political environment, the super-sized *tongxianghui* of the 1930s were, at core, authoritarian and fundamentally conservative associations dependent on the status quo that provided the basis for the financial resources and influence of their multiply affiliated leaders.

CHAPTER 9

The Politics of Philanthropy: Social Networks and Refugee Relief in Shanghai, 1932–1949

NARA DILLON

WHILE SHANGHAI was notorious for its extreme poverty in the Republican period (1911–1949), it was at the same time an important center of Chinese philanthropy.[1] Shanghai's wealthy citizens supported hundreds of charitable organizations and launched major fund-raising drives in response to humanitarian crises, whether in Shanghai or any other part of China. For members of Shanghai's elite, these charitable activities enhanced their social prestige, built a foundation for political power, and helped meet their spiritual needs. For the rest of Shanghai, these charitable organizations comprised an important part of a large, lively voluntary sector that was vital to the functioning of the city. Coming out of a relatively strong tradition of local self-rule, Shanghai's private voluntary sector often actively engaged in the kind of work performed by governments elsewhere.[2]

For most of the Republican period, for example, private charities and native place associations took the lead in responding to the problems of Shanghai's poor, especially when those problems threatened social and political order in the city. The Chinese state was a relatively minor player in social welfare in Shanghai up through the 1930s, operating small pilot programs and occasionally stepping in to subsidize and help coordinate private initiatives.[3] (The municipal governments in the French and Anglo-American colonial districts of the city were even less active than their Chinese counterpart in regard to social welfare.) In the 1940s, however, the respective roles of state and society began to change in social welfare, and in the arena of refugee relief, they underwent a complete reversal. After the Second World War, the Chinese state became the dominant service provider for Shanghai's refugees, and private organizations took on the role of supplementing the state program.

The broad contours of this transformation match patterns of state-building in other parts of the world, where state services expanded in the face of social crises that were too large in scope for private organizations to handle effectively. Industrialization, urbanization, and war have been viewed as forces that undermined traditional forms of social protection and prompted the creation and expansion of the welfare state in Europe and other advanced industrial countries.[4] While Chinese state-building in the Republican period was more preliminary and tentative than in these European welfare states, most scholars have viewed Chinese civil society (or the Chinese voluntary sector, to use a more neutral term) as being even weaker than the fledgling Chinese state.[5] As a result, this transformation in the roles of the public and private sector in 1940s Shanghai evokes little surprise, whether viewed from a comparative or a historical perspective.

But a closer examination of the Shanghai case raises some puzzling questions. At least in Shanghai, if not the rest of China, this reversal of roles between state and society was not a straightforward process of cumulative state expansion at the expense of a weakening civil society. Instead, the process was marked by sharp discontinuities and a distinct pattern of state and societal capabilities waxing and waning together, rather than in opposition to one another. Tracing this pattern across the discontinuities of the late Republican period provides some insight into the nature of Nationalist state-building efforts in Shanghai, as well as China as a whole, and also raises questions about the commonly held assumption that the state is more effective than civil society in coping with major social crises.

The wars of the 1930s and 1940s brought major, repeated humanitarian crises to Shanghai. The hard-fought but ultimately unsuccessful Japanese invasion of Shanghai in 1932 was followed by a much larger Japanese invasion and occupation of the city in 1937. Both battles destroyed large swathes of the city and created massive refugee crises, displacing hundreds of thousands of people in the 1932 fighting and as many as a million during the 1937 battle. Even after the Second World War finally came to an end in 1945, the economic and political dislocations of the Chinese Civil War (1946–49) contributed to a smaller-scale but endemic refugee problem in the late 1940s. Comparing the joint public/private refugee relief responses mounted in reaction to these crises provides a window into the changes in state-society relations that took place in the late Republican period. Social networks were the primary force that held these refugee relief initiatives together, and their transformation helps to explain the development of a large, ambitious, but very weak Chinese state in the late Republican period.

Shanghai's 1932 Refugee Crisis

The Japanese invasion of Shanghai in January 1932 forced more than 200,000 people to flee the fighting and search for safety. The battle lasted several weeks, but the damage inflicted was so significant that the refugee crisis lasted into the following summer. Although this 1932 refugee crisis was larger and longer than previous relief efforts, the response followed long-standing patterns of state-society relations and therefore provides a useful baseline for analyzing the changes of the late 1930s and 1940s.

Shanghai had long experience with refugees, since their problems demanded attention almost every winter, as well as during periodic crises such as floods. Private charities and native place associations responded to these emergencies by distributing free food and clothing, providing temporary shelter, and arranging transportation back to the countryside for rural migrants. Many of these voluntary associations were located in the foreign concessions, but their activities extended across Shanghai's many political divisions. Usually, these private organizations operated relatively independently from one another, but when the need arose, they managed to create mechanisms to coordinate their activities, whether through informal cooperation by their directors or by creating more formal interagency organizations. For example, the charities that regularly provided winter relief to refugees cooperated with one another by sharing information and informally dividing up responsibility for different parts of the city. After the Nationalist regime was established in 1928, the Shanghai municipal government sought to insert itself into these private initiatives, providing another mechanism for coordination and often offering government subsidies as well.[6]

Following these long-standing patterns, Shanghai's private charities and native place associations responded to the 1932 refugee crisis spontaneously and independently. Soon after the invasion began, the Shanghai Federation of Charities, Chinese Red Cross, Red Swastika Society, and numerous native place associations set up refugee shelters, soup kitchens, temporary medical clinics, and burial services. More than

70 shelters were quickly established in schools, police stations, and other buildings and empty lots around the city.[7]

The Shanghai municipal government was hard hit in the battle, especially since its offices were destroyed and its revenue collection ground to a halt. Mayor Wu Tiecheng (who had only recently been appointed after a leadership crisis) and his top officials were forced to set up temporary headquarters in the foreign concessions, where their political authority was dubious at best. Although they were not directly under attack, Shanghai's other two municipal governments in the International Settlement and the French Concession did not take the initiative in caring for the refugees who were crowding into their territories. In fact, their initial response was to set up barricades to try to avoid being overrun.[8]

In contrast, even though the 1932 crisis was much bigger in scale than previous refugee problems, Shanghai's private voluntary associations were not overwhelmed by it. Immediately after the fighting began, seven wealthy businessmen active in charity and local politics held an emergency meeting in the Renji Benevolent Hall (*Renji Shantang*), one of Shanghai's leading charities. These men decided to send the Chairman of the Shanghai Federation of Charities, Wang Yiting (see Chapter 3), to negotiate with the International Settlement's Shanghai Municipal Council to open the concession to the refugees. After Wang gained the foreigners' cooperation, he and the other activists organized the Shanghai War Zone Provisional Refugee Relief Committee (*Shanghai zhanqu nanmin linshi jiuji hui*). The committee eventually had 42 members, including representatives from organizations involved in the relief effort, municipal officials, and prominent members of the local elite. Working closely with the newly established Shanghai Local Preservation Society (*Shanghai difang weichihui*), the Shanghai War Zone Refugee Relief Committee helped raise funds and coordinate care for the refugees.[9]

Early on in the crisis, state officials and the private philanthropists on the War Zone Relief Committee had conflicting visions of the roles that state and society should play in the refugee relief effort. At a meeting of the War Zone Relief Committee, an official from the Shanghai Bureau of Social Affairs, Chen Lengzeng, announced that the municipal government had ordered its staff to draw up plans for a comprehensive state refugee relief program. Businessman Wen Lanting countered that the government should play only a supplementary role in refugee relief. He went on to argue that because the war affected all the people, refugee relief should also be the responsibility of all the people.[10] The issue was essentially settled when the Refugee Relief Committee voted to invite all organizations in the city to participate in the committee's work. Another indication of the War Zone Relief Committee's relative autonomy from the municipal government was the fact that prominent critics of the KMT (Nationalist Party) and Chiang Kai-shek, such as Lin Kanghou, became members of the committee.[11]

The differences in these visions of state and society were more rhetorical than real in 1932. The Shanghai municipal government contributed what it could to refugee relief, including policing shelters, inoculating refugees, organizing special classes, and sending staff from the Bureau of Social Affairs to work with the War Zone Refugee Relief Committee. Although it also donated 30,000 yuan to the refugee relief effort, the Shanghai municipal government did not have the resources to match its ambition of caring for the refugees on its own in 1932.[12] In fact, when hundreds of unemployed workers demonstrated in front of the municipal government's temporary headquarters demanding relief during the battle, the police had to be brought in to break up the protest, because the Bureau of Social Affairs had nothing to give them.[13] The difference in the scale of the resources that Shanghai's elite businessmen could mobilize in this kind of crisis is readily apparent in the 3 million yuan they donated to the Nationalist troops who were struggling to defend the city from the Japanese invasion.[14]

Of course, having the resources to respond to a major crisis does not automatically ensure that they are used effectively. The key reason for the relative effectiveness of Shanghai's voluntary associations was the strength of the elite networks that helped coordinate their activities. In the early 1930s, the social networks these philanthropists had forged over decades of public service were quite narrow but also dense and multilayered. They encompassed only a thin slice of society—Chinese men of Shanghai's upper elite—and excluded most foreigners, women, and other social classes. Most members of the Shanghai War Zone Refugee Relief Committee were wealthy businessmen of various kinds, including compradors, merchants, industrialists, investors, and people who combined some or all of these roles. There were also a handful of prominent gangsters. (Although the gangsters certainly were in a different social class than these elite bourgeois men, the differences were blurry since the gangsters also operated legal businesses and were active philanthropists; see Chapter 4 of this volume.)

Although these networks may have been narrow in scope, the men who formed them had strong bonds with one another that combined multiple layers of personal, school, business, native place, religious, and political ties. The native place held most in common was Zhejiang, especially the Ningbo area, although there was also a significant contingent from southern Jiangsu. Buddhism was their most common religious affiliation. Many of these men had been active in public affairs since the late imperial period, including serving in Shanghai's first municipal government, participating in the 1911 Revolution, and leading many of the subsequent political movements that swept through the city in the 1910s and 1920s. When the Nationalist Party gained control of Shanghai in 1927, many of these men forged connections to General Chiang Kai-shek and some gained positions on the Shanghai Municipal Council.[15] Their common backgrounds and especially their shared experiences gave these men strong connections to one another.

Perhaps the best way to unravel the social networks incorporated into the War Zone Relief Committee is to focus on one of its most central members, Wang Yiting. As detailed in Chapter 3 of this volume, Wang had multiple, overlapping connections to more than one-third of the members of the Shanghai War Zone Refugee Relief Committee. Through these friends and colleagues, Wang ultimately had indirect connections to most of the rest of the committee. Wang Yiting made his fortune as a comprador, which he used to sustain an active artistic, spiritual, and public life.

Since the 1910s, Wang Yiting had devoted considerable energy and money to charity, which he considered a part of his spiritual practice as a lay Buddhist. In Chapter 3, we saw listed the more than dozen private charities that Wang founded. We know that he served as chairman of the Shanghai Federation of Charities since its organization in 1927. Through serving on the board of directors of the dozens of different private charities, and through their interlocking boards, Wang had connections to nine other members of the Refugee Relief Committee, including men like Green Gang leader Huang Jinrong and chamber of commerce activist Wang Xiaolai. [16]

To choose one of these charities to illustrate, Wang Yiting was chairman of the board of the Renji Benevolent Hall (*Renji Shantang*). Renji was one of the largest charities in the city, with an orphanage, income support programs for widows and the elderly, and programs to distribute free food, medicine, and clothes to the poor.[17] Eight other members of the War Zone Refugee Relief Committee also served on the board of the Renji Benevolent Hall. Many members of the Renji board were Buddhists and, like Wang Yiting, they were also members of the Shanghai Buddhist Preservation Association (*Shanghai fojiao weichi hui*).[18]

This survey of just Wang Yiting's charity networks illustrates the dense overlapping of the social networks underpinning the Shanghai War Zone Refugee Relief Committee. Examining the nature of his relationship with one of the other leading committee members reveals how complex these ties were. Yu Xiaqing was one of the best-known members of the Shanghai War Zone Refugee Relief Committee, and his relationship to Wang Yiting dates back at least as far as the brief Chen Qimei government established in the wake of the 1911 Revolution (see Chapter 5 on popular protest). They also served together on the 1927 Shanghai Municipal Council and were leaders in the 1931 anti-Japanese boycott movement. In addition, they both served on the board of the Shanghai Federation of Charities. Their business relationships were equally complex, since both held leadership positions in the Shanghai Chamber of Commerce and both served on the boards of numerous corporations.[19]

Green Gang leader Du Yuesheng was another central figure of the 1932 Refugee Relief Committee (see Chapter 4). Prominent in Shanghai's charity and relief efforts since the 1920s, Du brought a different kind of personal network to the committee. Du certainly had the same kinds of business relationships that Wang enjoyed with many other committee members, serving on the boards of directors of multiple companies. But Du Yuesheng also had close connections to the other gangsters, Huang Jinrong and Zhang Xiaolin, and the government officials on the committee.[20] More significant, Du's personal network reached far beyond the confines of Shanghai's elite. Through the Green Gang, Du's networks reached out to industrial workers and down to the lowest levels of Shanghai society. He also cultivated connections in the French Concession's municipal government and to the highest levels of the Nationalist regime in Nanjing. The reach of these networks gave Du Yuesheng a unique position on the 1932 War Zone Relief Committee that more ordinary businessmen like Wang Yiting could not match.

The Chinese state was linked to this network through men such as Pan Gongzhan, one of three Shanghai officials who served on the 1932 War Zone Refugee Relief Committee. In addition to his official positions as a high-ranking member of the local KMT branch and the former director of the Shanghai Bureau of Social Affairs, Pan was a Shanghai native and in many ways also a member of these elite networks. Like many members of the War Zone Relief Committee, Pan claimed Zhejiang as his native place. He attended St. John's University in Shanghai, as did several other committee members, and then worked as a journalist and editor for another committee member, Shi Liangcai, publisher of *Shen Bao*.[21] Moreover, the 1932 War Zone Relief Committee was not the first time that Pan had served as a bridge between the party and Shanghai's elite. In the first few years of KMT rule, when the party and the leadership of the Shanghai Chamber of Commerce were fighting for control over the influential organization, Pan emerged as a moderate within the party and served as an intermediary between the local elite and the more radical factions of the Shanghai KMT branch.[22] The role played by public officials such as Pan Gongzhan on the War Zone Relief Committee illustrates how social networks blurred the division between state and society even as they facilitated effective cooperation.

The War Zone Relief Committee provided a vehicle for a joint fundraising drive as well as a forum where the organizations caring for refugees could seek help from one another.[23] What made the formal organization work effectively in a context where it was so new and the wartime conditions so difficult was the informal social networks among its members and their shared experience in previous refugee crises. Since these networks encompassed both state and society, they also provided a basis for effective public/private cooperation. Although state officials had ambitions to do more, the balance between private and public provision of social welfare services in the refugee relief drive was clearly tilted toward the private sector in 1932. Even with this tension, the relationship between state and society was marked by cooperation rather than competition. The War Zone Refugee Relief Committee dissolved itself in the summer of 1932 after the last refugee camps were shut down. Although the committee was short-lived, it provided a template for the crises that followed.

The 1937 Refugee Crisis

Shanghai's 1937 refugee crisis dwarfed the 1932 crisis, with more than 1 million refugees fleeing a larger and more devastating Japanese invasion.[24] This invasion was Shanghai's most severe crisis of the twentieth century, and while it led to the retreat of the Nationalist government in defeat, it did not shatter the city's large but fragmented voluntary sector. Despite the enormous scale of the suffering, the people of Shanghai were once again able to mobilize massive resources and channel them into an effective relief effort. Why did the refugee relief effort succeed even though the war itself was lost? Four factors help explain this confounding outcome. Three were already apparent in the 1932 campaign:

the spontaneous initiatives of hundreds of organizations and individuals in the face of the crisis, the strength of the informal social networks linking their efforts together, and effective cooperation between the state and civil society. A fourth factor was new and just as critical to the outcome: the mobilization of resources and volunteers from a much wider swathe of Shanghai society than had ever been achieved before.

As in the past, the spontaneous and rapid response of organizations and individuals to the emergency was the first key to the successful 1937 refugee relief campaign. The organizations that led the 1932 refugee campaign were among the first to respond to the new crisis, but they were by no means alone. This time, several hundred temporary shelters and camps were established during the battle, ranging in size from small shelters housing a few dozen refugees in restaurants to major camps sheltering tens of thousands of refugees in huge reed huts. On the first day of the invasion, for example, tens of thousands of refugees gathered on the narrow street in front of the Renji Benevolent Hall, pleading with the staff trapped inside for shelter from the bombing. Renji staff led the refugees to any and all shelter they could find in the International Settlement, including theaters, dance halls, and their own native place associations.[25]

Native place associations also responded to the crisis on their own, establishing shelters, providing emergency health care, and arranging transportation for their fellow provincials out of the war zone. For example, the Cantonese population of Shanghai was particularly hard hit by the bombing, and the Cantonese Native Place Association (*Guangdong tongxianghui*) and the Cantonese Guild (*Guangzhao gongsuo*) moved quickly to recruit Cantonese businessmen to turn their restaurants and factories into emergency shelters. These organizations went on to establish more permanent refugee shelters and an emergency refugee hospital, ultimately sheltering approximately 50,000 refugees over the course of the crisis.[26]

Numerous charities established their own refugee shelters, such as the Chinese Child Welfare Association (*Zhongguo ciyou hui*), the YWCA (*Jidujiao nuqingnian hui*), and the Red Swastika Society (*Shijie hongwangzi hui*). The Red Swastika Society was one of the most active organizations, setting up relief teams, eight refugee camps, four temporary refugee hospitals, and two medical clinics. While the Red Swastika Society had considerable experience in providing disaster relief around the country, the Chinese Child Welfare Association and the YWCA had no such background in relief work. Prior to the war, the Chinese Child

Welfare Association operated a small orphanage and several day-care centers, while the YWCA operated night schools for women workers. Lack of experience, staff, or funding did not deter them from assuming responsibility for hundreds of refugees.[27]

Other organizations were forced into taking action. For example, when the northern districts of Shanghai were torched by retreating Chinese troops in early October 1937, tens of thousands of refugees fled south, only to find themselves under attack by the Japanese from the air. In the melee, Jiaotong University's president threw open the campus gates to the refugees, hoping the crowds would save the university from the bombing raid. The tactic saved the university from the bombing, but it created a whole new set of problems. As many as 17,000 refugees crowded into the suburban campus, taking over classroom buildings and erecting crude shelters on athletic fields. Food, clothing, and medical care were scarce, if available at all. Fearing riots, university officials struggled to bring in supplies and impose order on the crowds, but they were simply overwhelmed by the sheer numbers. After several days of pleading, university officials were finally able to convince the Salvation Army to step in and organize a camp on their campus even though it also had no previous experience with refugee relief.[28]

These individual decisions, whether made reluctantly or enthusiastically, were the foundation of the massive relief effort. For charities and native place associations that had been carrying out relief programs for victims of floods and winter weather for decades, the new services fit with long-standing practices. As in the 1932 crisis, there was no need to consult organization leaders, much less convene a meeting of the board of directors, to assume responsibility for the refugees. For groups such as the YWCA and Salvation Army the decision was more difficult, but the example of so many other voluntary associations immediately taking action no doubt influenced their decisions to tackle such an ambitious task.

The same elite networks from the 1932 refugee relief campaign provided the key links that made this spontaneous, decentralized response work. In the five years between the two invasions, the social networks among Shanghai's philanthropists grew stronger as these men continued to play prominent roles in the public arena. Six members of the 1932 War Zone Refugee Relief Committee were appointed to the new Shanghai Municipal Council in 1932, including Wang Yiting, Du Yuesheng, and Pan Gongzhan.[29] In addition, the Shanghai Local Preservation Society, a voluntary association founded at the same time as the War

Zone Relief Committee, was reestablished as a permanent organization in 1932 to continue mobilizing against Japanese imperialism and responding to the city's problems. Shi Liangcai was the chairman of the renamed Shanghai Civic Association, and Wang Yiting, Du Yuesheng, and several other leaders of the refugee relief campaign served on the board of directors. After Shi was assassinated in 1934, Du Yuesheng took over leadership of the organization.[30]

Du Yuesheng's newfound respectability was also enhanced by establishing a new Pudong Native Place Association in the fall of 1932. Both Wang Yiting and Huang Hanzhi served as board members of the new organization.[31] When the organization opened its new eight-story building in 1936, the occasion was important enough that the mayor and other prominent people from other native places sought to join in the public celebration. KMT leader Pan Gongzhan contributed his own calligraphy to the celebration, and Yu Xiaqing and Wang Xiaolai gave speeches to the crowds.[32] These are just a few examples of how the relationships among these elite activists continued to grow and deepen in the early to mid-1930s.

In the 1937 invasion, these elite networks were once again incorporated into new, ad hoc coordinating committees organized in the heat of the crisis. This time, however, three committees were established, in contrast to the single committee that led the 1932 campaign. While having three coordinating committees could be a source of confusion, overlapping membership helped provide a measure of informal cooperation to the coordination effort. In addition, some continuity with the earlier campaign was provided by the 15 committee members who again volunteered to serve on committees in 1937. Six of these returnees served on multiple committees in the 1937 refugee relief effort and formed a core group: Wang Yiting, Du Yuesheng, Pan Gongzhan, Wen Lanting, Huang Hanzhi, and Qu Wenliu.[33]

All six of these core members served on the Shanghai Federation of Charities Disaster Relief Committee (*Shanghai shi cishan tuanti lianhehui jiuzai hui*), which proved to be the longest lasting of the three coordinating committees. The Charity Federation Committee was originally founded in early 1937 by the Shanghai municipal government and the Shanghai Federation of Charities to raise funds for refugees in Northern China. As tensions increased in the Yangzi region in the summer of 1937, the committee began preparing for refugee problems closer to home by leasing trucks and organizing relief teams. Over the course of the Battle of Shanghai in the fall of 1937, the Shanghai Federation of Charities Refugee Relief Committee assumed responsibility for 98 shelters housing an average of 50,000 refugees per month.[34]

If confusion was a potential liability of multiple coordinating committees, the benefit was drawing a wider range of organizations and people into the refugee relief effort. While the Charity Federation Committee largely brought together the same groups and individuals who had been involved in the 1932 crisis, the other two committees were more diverse. The Shanghai municipal government established the second coordinating committee on the eve of the invasion in August 1937: the Shanghai Municipal Relief Committee (*Shanghai shi jiuji weiyuanhui*). The new committee reached beyond the traditional charities to include representatives from native place associations, the Shanghai Chamber of Commerce, and the Shanghai Civic Association, among others. Housed in the new Pudong Native Place Association building, this committee's refugee relief effort soon rivaled the Charity Federation's efforts, establishing 104 shelters over the first six weeks of the Battle of Shanghai.[35]

The third committee, the Shanghai International Relief Committee (*Shanghai guoji jiuji weiyuanhui*), was founded soon after the battle began and included both foreign and Chinese members. In addition to the civil and military leaders of the foreign concessions, the committee included some of the most prominent members of Shanghai society, such as diplomats, university presidents, physicians, Christian ministers, Buddhist monks, and representatives from most of the major religious charities in the city. In contrast to the Buddhist dominance of the Charity Federation Committee, the International Committee also included Catholic and Protestant missionaries, Chinese Christians, and new, heterodox Chinese religions such as the Red Swastika Society's *daoyuan* beliefs. Another notable feature of the International Committee's diversity was the inclusion of two women, both of whom were Chinese.[36] The International Committee operated six shelters of its own and launched an international fund-raising drive to raise funds for all the refugee shelters in Shanghai. Foreign residents also established the Shanghai International Red Cross Society to help the beleaguered Chinese Red Cross raise funds and provide food and medical care to all the refugee camps in the city.[37]

The state and party were also actively involved in the 1937 relief campaign. Both the Shanghai municipal government and the national government provided funding, staff, and other resources to support the private-led relief effort. The Bureau of Social Affairs provided some staff to help the coordinating committees get up and running. Police helped provide security for the camps, public health workers set up temporary medical clinics, and KMT cadres organized patriotic educational activities for the refugees. The central government's contribution at this stage of the war was to donate 20,000 yuan for refugee relief to the Charity Federation Committee.[38]

Although this kind of direct involvement by party and government officials came to an end when the Battle of Shanghai was lost, public/private cooperation continued long after the Japanese military seized control of the city in November 1937. In fact, in financial terms, the Nationalist government contributed far more to Shanghai's refugee relief programs after the Battle of Shanghai was lost than beforehand. By the spring of 1939, the central government was contributing 100,000 yuan per month to Shanghai's refugee relief effort, channeled through international charitable organizations.[39] As the KMT retreated further and further west under the Japanese onslaught, these refugee relief funds provided tangible evidence of the regime's continued resistance.

But even the broader reach of these committees and the higher levels of funding provided by the Nationalist government do not account for the numbers of volunteers and vast sums of money raised in 1937. The contrast in scale between the 1932 and 1937 refugee relief campaigns helps put the fund-raising problem in perspective. The 1937 refugee relief effort not only involved five times the number of refugees, but the 1937 Battle of Shanghai lasted three months, rather than weeks, and the refugees lingered without jobs or homes for years, rather than months.

While data are not available for the overall campaign, partial financial reports from these committees give a sense of the scale of the resources the citizens of Shanghai managed to mobilize during the crisis. As already noted, the Shanghai Charity Federation Refugee Relief Committee operated 98 emergency shelters housing an average of 50,000 refugees and thus comprised almost half of the overall campaign. In the six months following the invasion, the Charity Federation Committee spent 1.38 million yuan to house and feed its refugees.[40] This amount comes to more than 10 times the budget for the Shanghai Bureau of Social Affairs for a comparable period in fiscal year 1935–36 (the last full year available).[41] Almost all of this funding came from voluntary donations by Shanghai residents.

Thus the 1937 refugee relief effort demanded far greater resources from a wider range of people than this core network of elite philanthropists had ever reached before. This dramatic expansion in donors and volunteers was more than a spontaneous outpouring of support for resistance against a foreign invasion, although patriotism and fear of a common enemy were certainly important in motivating people to come forward and participate. Political mobilization was also important—the National Salvation Movement was a key factor in rousing Shanghainese from all walks of life to participate in the refugee relief campaign.

The revival of the National Salvation Movement had its origins in Beijing, where students led the December Ninth protests of 1935 against Japanese imperialism, but the movement spread quickly and in 1936 Shanghai emerged as another center of anti-Japanese mobilization (see Chapter 6). Groups of students, journalists, professionals, women, filmmakers, professors, businessmen, workers, and others organized dozens of national salvation associations in Shanghai. This organizational drive built up to the founding of the All-Shanghai National Salvation Association League on January 28, 1936, and then culminated in the creation of the All-China League of National Salvation Associations on May 31, 1936.[42]

The National Salvation Movement adopted an inclusionary mobilization strategy, seeking to incorporate as broad a swathe of Chinese society as possible. Movement leaders argued that the movement should be open to all Chinese who opposed Japanese aggression in China, regardless of status, occupation, or party affiliation. Movement activist Zou Taofan even advocated embracing people who had previously been accommodating toward the Japanese. This inclusive brand of nationalism was not an empty promise. It allowed men like Wang Yiting, a comprador with extensive business, religious, and artistic connections to Japan, to recast himself as a nationalist and continue to play a prominent public role in the 1930s. An even more telling example of the pragmatic political flexibility that marked this political movement was the cooperation that developed between foreigners and Chinese in forums such as the Shanghai International Relief Committee (see Chapter 10 on transnational networks).

Once the Japanese invasion began, Shanghai's national salvation associations sought to mobilize the city to support the war effort in every way possible. Movement leaders framed the refugee relief initiative as one of the ways patriotic citizens could participate in the war, as important as joining the fighting or helping to care for wounded soldiers on the front lines. Popularizing the slogan, "Those with money, give money; those with strength give strength," the national salvation associations encouraged people in all walks of life to contribute whatever they could to the effort. To publicize this message, 113 national salvation associations in the city cooperated in launching a propaganda drive that organized more than 4,500 people into 930 propaganda teams.[43]

Their message was heard. The national salvation associations for the employees of banks, insurance companies, and department stores each organized fund-raising teams to go door to door soliciting donations. Prompted by their own national salvation associations, industrial workers voted to donate their company welfare funds to the refugee relief effort, even though many of them had been laid off once the fighting began. Others were inspired to volunteer. For example, one young reporter found his way through the chaos to the Cultural Workers' National Salvation Association (*Wenhuajie jiuguo weiyuanhui*), looking for a way to support the war effort. The organization's leaders sent him to a refugee camp being set up by the Shanghai International Relief Committee, where he was immediately put to work building huts. He stayed for several years after the construction was finished and eventually became a top administrator in the refugee camp.[44] These examples are just a few of the ways the national salvation associations mobilized groups such as middle-class professionals and industrial workers to participate in charity for the first time.

As part of its efforts to promote the National Salvation Movement, the Chinese Communist Party (CCP) also became actively involved in the refugee relief effort. This role represented a departure for the CCP. In the 1932 Japanese invasion, the Party ordered its members not to participate in relief work, because it was considered too bourgeois. In 1937, however, the Party's commitment to the united front policy and the National Salvation Movement led to a reversal on CCP policy toward bourgeois charity. The Shanghai branch placed a high priority on refugee work and assigned more than one-fourth of its underground cadres to work on refugee relief during the Battle of Shanghai.[45]

The National Salvation Movement provided the link between the CCP and the elite network helping to coordinate the refugee relief campaign. Underground Communist cadres working in the National Salvation Movement befriended Zhao Puchu, a young lay Buddhist activist and founder of the Chinese Buddhist National Salvation Association. At the beginning of the Battle of Shanghai, Wang Yiting and Huang Hanzhi put Zhao Puchu in charge of the Shelter Division in the Shanghai Federation of Charities Refugee Relief Committee. Responsible for staffing almost 100 refugee shelters, Zhao turned to his contacts in the National

Salvation Movement to recruit volunteers. Through these connections, more than 30 Communist cadres were given positions as managers and teachers in the Charity Federation refugee shelters, where they conducted propaganda and recruited volunteers for Communist guerilla units being formed in the countryside outside Shanghai.[46] The National Salvation mobilized volunteers and donations across the many divisions in Shanghai society, including national, ethnic, religious, class, gender, and political lines. Without this massive outpouring of support, caring for up to 1 million refugees would have been impossible.

Just as impressive as the scale of the campaign, however, is the fact that it was sustained for several years after the battle was lost. After the Japanese military took over Shanghai, donations to the refugee committees began a gradual decline.[47] The defeat dealt a serious blow to the morale of the Shanghai residents left behind to face the Japanese occupation. Furthermore, the National Salvation Movement was forced to retreat to the foreign concessions and then go underground.[48] Many of the national salvation associations managed to survive despite Japanese efforts to repress them, however, most redirected their energies inward. For example, the National Salvation Association of Shanghai Banks and Money Guilds reorganized itself into the Shanghai Banking Employees' Association in the International Settlement, and while it continued to make charitable contributions, it focused on establishing welfare funds and consumer cooperatives to help its own members survive the war.[49]

Although the Charity Federation and the International Refugee Relief Committees consolidated camps repeatedly as refugees left the Shanghai area or returned to work, by the spring of 1938 more than 70,000 refugees still remained, but funding was running short. The new Chinese municipal government established under the authority of the Japanese military gradually opened some small welfare programs such as orphanages and homes for the disabled, but nothing on a scale that could resolve the refugee problem.[50] Similarly, while the International Settlement's government levied new taxes to help care for refugees, it preferred turning these revenues over to private charities rather than to provide direct services.[51] By the fall of 1938, the Charity Federation Refugee Relief Committee was forced to forge on alone, reorganizing itself into the Shanghai Refugee Relief Association and renewing its fund-raising efforts.[52] Hong Kong philanthropists and the Nationalist government provided new sources of funding, and the refugee relief program was able to continue.

The Battle of Shanghai in the fall of 1937 probably represents the peak of private philanthropy in the city's history. The number of people served and the scale of the resources mobilized in such a short period of time were unprecedented. The spontaneous initiatives of countless voluntary associations and individual activists, combined with active support from the Chinese municipal government and the central state, were critical in getting the campaign off the ground. The mobilization of donations and volunteers by the National Salvation Movement was just as vital for quickly expanding these new programs to meet the huge demand. The participation of the Communists was probably the most striking example of the broad reach of this mobilization effort. All of these ingredients came together through the preexisting core network of wealthy philanthropists and state officials who provided the linkages to put these enormous new resources to use and ensure that they were not simply wasted. Although the Nationalist army lost the Battle of Shanghai, for the three months prior to that loss, the capacities of both state and society increased by leaps and bounds. Furthermore, after that crushing defeat, Shanghai's voluntary sector proved to be resilient enough to sustain the largest social welfare program of the Republican period for several years.

Refugee Relief During the Civil War, 1945–1949

Despite the achievements of the wartime refugee relief campaign, it failed to lay a foundation for the ambitious relief programs launched by the Nationalist government when it returned to Shanghai after the war finally ended in 1945. A few elements of the 1930s relief efforts, such as the public/private coordinating committees, were standardized and incorporated into the postwar program, but underneath the similarities in formal institutions, there were profound discontinuities. Where prewar refugee relief efforts were broad-based campaigns involving dozens, and sometimes hundreds, of public and private organizations, including the efforts of the KMT and CCP, the postwar program was the work of a single government agency.

Two wartime changes contributed to this transformation. One change was the fragmentation of the elite networks that had helped coordinate public and private relief initiatives in the 1930s. As a result, there was less pressure from charity leaders to coordinate their activities, and there was little resistance to state initiatives in refugee relief. Probably more important were the wartime changes in the KMT, especially its new ambitions in the realm of social policy. The KMT came back to Shanghai in 1945 with the intent of making the state a major social service provider and showed relatively little concern for cooperating with the voluntary sector. These changes in social networks and the party-state shaped a very different refugee relief program in the late 1940s.

The social networks bonding Shanghai's philanthropists together began to fragment during the eight-year-long Japanese occupation. One problem was the death of central figures in these networks during wartime, when there were fewer people with the same kinds of resources and connections to replace them. For example, Lu Baihong, a prominent Catholic businessman and philanthropist who was a member of both the 1932 and 1937 refugee relief committees, was murdered in late 1937. While his wife took his place on the Shanghai International Relief Committee and tried to carry on her husband's initiative to establish a new charity for street children, she simply could not replace the rich web of business, political, and social relationships he had forged with other members of Shanghai's elite in his decades of public service.[53]

Four other philanthropists active in the refugee relief efforts of the 1930s died during the war, including Wang Yiting. Given his central role in Shanghai philanthropy for more than 20 years, he was not easily replaced. Several of his longtime associates from Buddhist groups like the Shanghai Buddhist Preservation Society stepped forward to try to fill his shoes, but none had the scope of connections to take over all of Wang's roles. Huang Hanzhi, who had long been actively involved in the Renji Benevolent Hall, inherited many of Wang Yiting's leadership positions, such as Chairman of the Charity Federation and Executive Director of the Renji Benevolent Hall.

Another Buddhist businessman, Wen Lanting, became board chairman for many of the other charities that Wang Yiting had founded. Qu Wenliu took on Wang Yiting's central role in fund-raising, including making repeated trips to Hong Kong to solicit donations.[54] Zhao Puchu, the young activist put in charge of the Charity Federation shelters, represented the new generation being drawn into this long-standing network of Buddhist philanthropists. None of these men, however, matched Wang's dense and expansive connections to the rest of Shanghai's elite that would allow them to step into his role as a central broker within those networks. Shanghai's network of philanthropists survived and adapted to these changes, but it also became increasingly fragmented.

The politics of the occupation had an even bigger impact on these networks. The inclusive politics of the National Salvation Movement gave way to the polarizing politics of collaboration and resistance. Both the Nationalists and the Communists politicized the ambiguous question of collaboration, redefining retreat from Shanghai as a form of resistance. The Communists recruited people to join their guerilla units in the countryside, while the Nationalists exhorted all patriotic citizens to leave occupied areas and move into the interior. They especially encouraged industrialists to move their factories to the wartime KMT capital to aid the resistance. While relatively few businessmen moved their companies, many did have the resources to escape the Japanese occupation. At least nine of the elite philanthropists who led the 1937 refugee relief effort chose to leave Shanghai during the war, including Green Gang boss Du Yuesheng.[55] These departures left major holes in Shanghai's elite networks for the remainder of the occupation, putting even greater pressure on the philanthropists left behind to continue to raise funds and care for the refugees.

The decision to stay behind was a dangerous one. Even as the occupation stretched into eight years, underground KMT and CCP agents sought to discourage any kind of cooperation with the Japanese by attacking and assassinating collaborators.[56] Most of the philanthropists in the Shanghai Refugee Relief Association sought to avoid collaboration, but the politics of the refugee relief effort became increasingly murky and ambiguous over the course of the war. Their resistance consisted of refusing official positions in the collaborator governments established by the Japanese military. But of course the task of caring for the victims of the war required at least the tacit consent of the troops who were waging it.

Pearl Harbor removed the veil over the unspoken cooperation that had emerged between the Refugee Relief Association, Shanghai's collaborator governments, and the Japanese military. With the American declaration of war, the Japanese took control of the Anglo-American and French Concessions, eliminating the fragile autonomy of the Refugee Relief Association. At that point, the Director of the Refugee Relief Association, Huang Hanzhi, was arrested.[57] The other members of the organization were forced to declare their allegiances. Most continued to avoid collaboration, but several prominent leaders did decide to switch sides. Wen Lanting joined the collaborators and was rewarded with important positions in the fledgling economic management bureaucracy of the national collaborator regime.

Two other prominent philanthropists who had been members of the 1932 and 1937 refugee relief efforts, Lin Kanghou and Yuan Ludeng, also decided to collaborate and assumed increasingly prominent roles in Shanghai's charities in the latter half of the war.[58] As food shortages worsened and more of the economy came under government control, this kind of open collaboration became increasingly important to the refugee relief effort, as well as to carrying out any other kind of charity work under the occupation.

After the Japanese surrender in 1945, KMT officials and philanthropists like Du Yuesheng, Wang Xiaolai, and Liu Hongsheng rushed back to Shanghai to try to reclaim their former lives. But their eagerness to return did not heal the political divisions that had grown within Shanghai's elite between those who retreated and those who stayed behind. Although the KMT was slow to punish collaborators in many parts of China, it did move quickly and decisively against collaborators in Shanghai. Wen Lanting, Lin Kanghou, and Yuan Ludeng were all arrested for treason and given prison sentences ranging from six to eight years. Those who avoided collaboration but stayed behind came under suspicion as well, even though some of them had worked closely with the Nationalist government to sustain the relief effort after the KMT retreat. For example, Huang Hanzhi came under suspicion because he managed to secure his release from prison after Pearl Harbor. Some of the returnees speculated that he had struck a deal to collaborate secretly in order to get out of prison. Huang managed to avoid prosecution and return to public life, but his reputation never fully recovered.[59] These wartime divisions left holes in Shanghai's elite networks that were not repaired quickly or easily. Just as the political decisions made during the war proved to be irrevocable for the individuals who made them, the damage done to Shanghai's philanthropic networks proved to be long lasting.

The war also changed the KMT and the Nationalist government. Even though factionalism and corruption weakened the party-state in many ways, the KMT grew much more ambitious in the realm of social policy over the course of the war.[60] The Nationalist government established a new Ministry of Social Affairs in 1940, which then enacted a series of new laws to tighten state regulation of private charity, to create new social welfare institutions to care for orphans, the disabled, and the elderly, and also to establish state-operated winter relief programs for refugees and the homeless.[61] Even though the prewar refugee relief model had proved to be successful in extremely difficult circumstances, Nationalist policy makers abandoned the practice of encouraging and supporting these kinds of spontaneous, decentralized private initiatives. Instead, the Nationalist government sought to build up a new government bureaucracy to provide refugee relief services directly.

Staff from the Bureau of Social Affairs and other agencies of the Shanghai municipal government operated the shelters, soup kitchens, and medical clinics that comprised the Winter Relief program.[62] As the name suggests, the postwar Winter Relief program was originally intended to be seasonal, but economic and political conditions deteriorated to the point that it evolved into ongoing, year-round operation by the winter of 1947–48.[63] The new program's shelters housed an average of 24,000 refugees and its soup kitchens fed another 30,000 people outside the shelters each day. Although the postwar program was smaller than the services mounted in the campaigns of the 1930s, it was the largest social welfare program operated by the state.[64]

The one holdover from the campaigns of the 1930s was the creation of a joint public/private committee: the Shanghai Winter Relief Committee (*Shanghai shi dongling jiuji weiyuanhui*). Chaired by the mayor, the Winter Relief Committee included another 55 members who were all appointed by the municipal government. Besides one returning KMT member, only six commission members had been part of the 1937 refugee relief effort.[65] Among that small group, it was the longtime philanthropists who had left Shanghai during the war who were rewarded with the best positions. For example, Green Gang leader Du Yuesheng was appointed Chairman of the Fund-raising Subcommittee, which was the most influential position on the commission granted to someone outside the party.[66]

In comparison to the coordinating committees of the 1930s, the single biggest change in the membership of the Winter Relief Committee was the inclusion of 16 KMT and city officials. These officials not only comprised a significant bloc within the committee (as opposed to a few liaisons), they also dominated the leadership of the organization. Another key difference lay in their connections to the rest of the committee. Unlike the earlier relief operations, these officials were appointed to the committee based on their formal positions in the municipal bureaucracy rather than their relationship to the rest of the committee members. Most were new to Shanghai and had few connections to Shanghai's local elite.

The other new members of the Winter Relief Committee were almost all businessmen. While this was an obvious continuity with past practices, the postwar committee did not include all or most of the city's most prominent businessmen and philanthropists, but only those who had proved their loyalty to the regime during the war. The inclusion of a few journalists and one woman also shows some continuity with the inclusive 1937 refugee relief committees—but again these members were chosen more for their connections to the KMT than their leadership in Shanghai's voluntary sector.

Polarizing politics did not come to an end with the Japanese defeat in 1945. Instead, the Chinese Civil War created new political divisions in Shanghai's elite, as some people rallied to the Nationalist side while others joined the peace movement. Municipal officials used their power of appointment to the Winter Relief Committee to exclude philanthropists who criticized the Nationalist war effort, further fragmenting the social networks binding committee members to one another. Kui Yanfang, for example, was a businessman who had been active in the 1937 refugee relief effort and was one of the few longtime Shanghai philanthropists reappointed to the postwar Winter Relief Committee in 1945.[67]

In 1946, however, Kui Yanfang became an activist within the peace movement and helped lead a delegation to Nanjing to petition the central government to end the Civil War. The petitioners never reached their destination—instead, they were met at the train station by a gang of plainclothes KMT agents who attacked and robbed them.[68] After that confrontation and the public controversy that ensued, Kui Yanfang was dropped from the 1946–47 Winter Relief Committee. Even people like Zhao Puchu, who were not involved in any anti-war protests but were sympathetic to the cause, were excluded from the 1946–47 Winter Relief Committee. Zhao turned his energy toward purely private endeavors and began preparations to establish a large orphanage modeled on the American organization, Boy's Town.[69] The effort to purge opponents of the Civil War posed a strong contrast with the more politically diverse refugee relief committees of the 1930s.

The end result of all these changes is that the Winter Relief Committee no longer encapsulated a preexisting, tight social network that included the leading philanthropists and businessmen in the city. The postwar committee brought together a group of people with much looser connections to one another than had been the case before the war. In addition, it was a group of people defined first and foremost by their relationship to the KMT rather than by their leadership in Shanghai's voluntary sector. As a result, the postwar relief committee did not have the same kinds of connections to Shanghai's private sector that facilitated the achievements of the 1930s.

The shifts in the membership of the Winter Relief Committee were accompanied by an even more significant change in its role in refugee relief. The postwar winter relief committees were no longer a coordinating mechanism for a broad-based public/private relief campaign. The private sector members of the winter relief committees played little or no role in setting policy or providing services after 1945. The men who ran the large wartime refugee shelter system, Huang Hanzhi and Zhao Puchu, were appointed to the Winter Relief Committee, but they played no role in managing the new refugee camps. Although private charities and other voluntary associations continued to provide services such as food pantries, soup kitchens, and health clinics to the homeless, there was little effort to coordinate these private initiatives, much less mobilize larger ones.

The new role of the Winter Relief Committee was limited to fund-raising for an essentially state-run program. Since the Shanghai municipal government did not have the resources to match the ambitions laid out in its wartime legislation, this limited role was vital, and its importance only increased over time. Du Yuesheng's Fund-raising Subcommittee provided the majority of the funding for the Committee. Similar to past fund-raising campaigns, he employed a wide variety of fund-raising techniques, ranging from radio fund-raisers to charity dances. But the majority of the funding came from trade associations and district representatives in the Shanghai Municipal Advisory Council (*Shanghai shi canyi hui*), who were given quotas to fill by soliciting from their members and residents.[70]

In 1946, private donations provided 56 percent of the funding for winter relief, while local and central governments contributed 44 percent. This funding only covered shelter and administrative costs, as most of the food and clothing were donated by the United Nations Relief and Rehabilitation Administration (UNRRA).[71] After UNRRA donations ran out in 1947, private donations comprised 88 percent of the total funding and the government's contribution fell to only 12 percent.[72] The fledgling new relief bureaucracy was thus extremely dependent on popular support.

Despite this vulnerability, the KMT sought to control and limit private fund-raising efforts, rather than encourage wider participation. To give one example, a Christian student group at Tongji University started a collection drive to provide winter clothing to the poor in December 1947. The drive soon developed into a university-wide effort, as hundreds of students volunteered to form collection teams to solicit donations of cash and clothing outside the university. Student activists also sought to spread their campaign to other universities in Shanghai. This activism came on the heels of Tongji students' active participation in the peace movement against the Civil War, which had been banned by the KMT earlier in the summer of 1947.[73]

Shanghai Mayor Wu Guozhen responded to the Tongji fund-raising efforts by issuing a directive prohibiting the students' collection drive and designating the Winter Relief Commission as the only authorized fund-raising organization for winter relief. Issuing orders proved to be much easier than gaining compliance. Rather than accede to the mayor's directive, the students managed to slip into a press conference and present the mayor with a cake from their charity bake sale, asking him to purchase it on behalf of the poor. Cornered in front of the press, Mayor Wu Guozhen was too embarrassed to refuse this plea for charity. He bought the cake. After the cake incident was widely reported, the prohibition on outside fund-raising proved to be unenforceable and the collection drive spread to more than 80 universities and high schools across the city. In all, the students collected almost 150,000 sets of winter clothes and billions of yuan in cash. In the wake of this failure, the KMT cancelled the Tongji University student council elections, precipitating a student strike in January 1948 that spread to 16 other universities and high schools. The strike was only broken after the KMT used force to gain control over the university.[74]

These clumsy efforts to contain and control charitable fund-raising left the Winter Relief Committee that much more dependent on its private sector committee members, especially Green Gang leader Du Yuesheng. Du was the one major figure in the philanthropic networks of the 1930s who survived all of the changes wrought by the Japanese invasion and the Civil War and who continued to play a central role in the Winter Relief program of the 1940s. Du's extensive personal networks and the fund-raising prowess of the Green Gang's enforcers made him an invaluable ally for the state's refugee relief efforts. As the KMT's popularity sank further and further, Du Yuesheng's role in refugee relief grew correspondingly more important.

Both popular support and Du Yuesheng's personal support for the KMT reached their nadir in August 1948, when the Nationalist government imposed a new currency and other economic controls to bring hyperinflation under control.[75] The KMT had so much difficulty securing compliance with the new regulations that it had to implement them by force. Chiang Kai-shek sent his son to Shanghai to organize large-scale investigations and arrests. The open confrontations that ensued made even loyal allies like Du Yuesheng question his ties to the Nationalist regime. One of his sons, Du Weiping, was among the thousands of businessmen arrested on vague charges by the KMT's "tiger-beating" teams enforcing the new economic regulations. The father was so angry by the humiliation that he retreated to his house and refused to see to anyone for over a month.[76]

This political crisis exposed the Winter Relief program's vulnerability. Not only was mobilizing voluntary donations extremely difficult in this environment, but the routinized collections from trade and industrial associations depended on Du Yuesheng's active cooperation. As a result, the Shanghai Relief Commission's Fund-raising Subcommittee did not meet or operate while its chairman's son was under arrest. All the municipal government could do was issue ever higher fund-raising targets that it had no means of reaching on its own.[77] Du's one-man strike vividly illustrated the risks of expanding the state bureaucracy and services without first doing the hard work of expanding the tax revenues to sustain it. In the end, Shanghai's fledgling refugee relief bureaucracy was still dependent on informal elite networks to function.

After the new Nationalist economic controls failed to slow hyperinflation, the tiger-beating teams were disbanded and the Shanghainese under arrest were released. Du Yuesheng resumed his cooperation with the KMT, but he also began making contingency plans to escape to Hong Kong rather than follow the KMT to Taiwan if the Nationalists lost the Civil War. Indeed, these kinds of small recoveries in Shanghai were overshadowed by the accelerating Communist victories on the battlefields of North China. By the spring of 1949, the collapse of the Nationalist regime itself was imminent. In preparation, the Winter Relief Committee was reconstituted as a private organization. As KMT officials and allies like Du Yuesheng evacuated Shanghai, Huang Hanzhi, Kui Yanfang, and others returned to the organization and took over its leadership. They moved the Relief Committee's offices from the Bureau of Social Affairs building to the Renji Benevolent Hall, where the main refugee relief operations of the 1930s had been housed.[78] The return of Shanghai's postwar refugee relief program to private hands illustrates the hollowness of postwar Nationalist state-building efforts.

Conclusion

While at first glance the Nationalist government's domination of refugee relief services after 1945 seems to fit the general model of state-building at the expense of civil society, closer examination reveals a much more complicated picture. In Republican Shanghai, there was no sharp divide between the public and private sector and the relationship between them cannot accurately be described as a competitive, zero-sum game. Shanghai's state and civil society both strengthened in the 1930s, and in different ways they both declined in the 1940s. Shanghai's local state was small and its authority limited before the war, but it was connected to local elites in ways that facilitated rapid expansion of both state and societal capacities. Although both the state and the voluntary sector grew in the postwar period, their efforts in the realm of refugee relief did not add up to the same kind of services and programs that they had achieved before. The key difference lay in the nature of the links that held state and society together.

Shanghai's decentralized refugee relief campaigns of the 1930s grew out of the city's unusual conditions rather than any intentional design. A politically divided city, extremely wealthy local elite, and vibrant voluntary sector set the stage for the public/private cooperation that emerged in the 1930s. During the relative stability of the early Republican period (stable within Shanghai, if not the rest of the country), a dense, multilayered social network developed among elite philanthropists. In the 1930s, this network effectively linked state and society to quickly and drastically increase their capacity to house, feed, and clothe hundreds of thousands of refugees. The achievements of this decentralized relief campaign in 1937 belie the widely held assumption that centralized states are inherently superior in mounting collective action in the midst of crisis.

This powerful model for effective public/private cooperation was not replicated after the Sino-Japanese War. Over the course of the war, Shanghai's elite networks grew increasingly fragmented, while at the same time the Nationalist regime became more interested in statist solutions to social problems and more bureaucratic in its relationship to local elites. Rather than trying to repair Shanghai's weakened social networks, the Nationalists, out of political interests, sought to divide or sidestep them as much as possible. Although the postwar refugee relief program was another hybrid public/private institution, the similarities with the prewar model in terms of formal institutions were contradicted by the differences in the informal social networks that underpinned them. The dense, multilayered networks among leaders in Shanghai's voluntary sector had been replaced by much more fragmented networks among leading KMT supporters. The postwar state refugee relief program continued to be dependent on elite support but could no longer leverage that support as effectively as it had in the past.

Although the KMT's postwar effort to routinize and institutionalize the fund-raising campaigns of the 1930s seemed more in keeping with past practices, the spirit of the earlier efforts was lost in the process. The political context for mobilizing resources had changed entirely. The common threat from Japan that helped bind people together in the National Salvation Movement was replaced by doubts and divisions over the Chinese Civil War. Furthermore, the KMT's concern with controlling political participation ran counter to the goal of maximizing contributions. Where the prewar refugee relief efforts had been expansive, with the independent contributions of thousands of individuals and hundreds of organizations adding up to a massive campaign, the postwar program was exclusive, seeking to control who could participate and in what manner.

Although Shanghai was clearly an outlier within the context of China as a whole, the changing relationship between Shanghai's elites and the state can lend some insight into the contradictions of Nationalist state-building efforts at the national level. The Nationalist state expanded quickly in Shanghai in the 1940s, but it was a hollow form of state-building that produced a large but weak state. Ambitious state officials took a shortcut by trying to leverage resources for new state agencies with voluntary fund-raising campaigns, rather than by imposing new taxes. But the effort to avoid political conflict over taxes was not accompanied by any kind of proactive effort to mobilize political support for a fund-raising campaign. Instead, the Nationalists put themselves in the politically untenable position of denying private charity to the poor even as state services failed to address the clear and growing problem. An ambitious agenda to expand the reach of state power was not matched by sufficient attention to the social roots of that power.

CHAPTER 10

Cosmopolitan Connections and Transnational Networks

JEFFREY N. WASSERSTROM

AS WE HAVE SEEN throughout this volume, the social, cultural, and political landscape of Republican Shanghai was a highly fragmented one. Throughout most of the period in question, the metropolis lacked a single political center, due to its division into three separate administrative districts; among the Shanghainese (a term used loosely here to refer to all Chinese denizens of the metropolis), factors such as class, dialect, and ideology were important sources of division; and within the foreign community, there were also internal divisions, some rooted again in class, others in language, religion, or nationality (separating, for example, White Russians from Japanese, to name just the two largest foreign groups).[1] In addition, many local Britons and Americans (whom I will refer to collectively as "Shanghailanders") viewed "their" Shanghai as a completely different one from that of the Shanghainese (whom they often called "native residents" and with whom some of them had only the most superficial of contacts).[2] Republican Shanghai was thus, in more than simply administrative terms, less a single unified entity than a constellation of separate cities-within-the-city—something captured very effectively in important work by Robert Bickers and Christian Henriot, among others.[3]

And yet, as the authors of this volume stress, the metropolis still managed to function during an often chaotic era, thanks in large part to two things: the viability of networks, often rooted in associations such as *tongxianghui* (native place associations) and philanthropic societies, linking those on different sides of social and political chasms; and the actions of linchpin individuals, such as Wang Yiting, who moved easily between the varied smaller Shanghais that together comprised China's largest treaty port. The chapters preceding this one have provided ample evidence to support the concept that different Chinese associations and Shanghainese served as key nodes in a vast collection of networks that helped Shanghai "go on" and hold together. The goal of this final chapter is to add to the picture by drawing attention to organizations that, unlike most discussed so far, crossed over or blurred the Chinese/foreign divide. I will alternate between focusing on Shanghainese linchpin individuals, as others in this volume have done, *and* on some of their Shanghailander counterparts.

Concentrating on associations and people who helped link together the often quite separate Shanghais-within-Shanghai of Chinese and foreign residents does not constitute a complete departure from preceding chapters by any means. After all, many groups and individuals discussed thus far held connections to both the Chinese and foreign social and political worlds. As Brian Martin stresses in Chapter 4, Du Yuesheng's Green Gang had ties to Western officials of the French Concession. Wang Yiting, as Kuiyi Shen notes in Chapter 3, was a comprador who cultivated business and other ties with Western and Japanese residents. Nara Dillon shows in Chapter 9 that philanthropic drives could link Shanghainese and Shanghailander elites. And so the examples continue.

In this chapter we will focus on associations with both Chinese and foreign members. Whereas previous chapters concentrated mostly on individual Shanghainese who moved between the social worlds of Chinese and foreign Shanghai, here we will concern ourselves equally with Shanghailanders who did the same—bringing into the picture some of the Britons and Americans who were equivalents of Wang Yiting, at least in the sense of serving as nodes in robustly transnational networks.

This chapter is designed to suggest directions for future investigation more than to present conclusive findings. As a first foray into largely uncharted terrain, it depends heavily at times on work that other scholars have done, including essays by James Huskey and Nicholas Clifford that highlight the close links that could and did exist between the most "cosmopolitan" of Shanghailanders and Shanghainese—individuals who served as "border-crossers" as we shall see next.[4] This last point deserves a bit of explanation before turning to the linchpin individuals and associations (which, following Clifford, I dub "Sino-Foreign" ones) that will be of main concern.[5]

A key reason behind the perhaps preliminary nature of any discussion of these individuals and organizations, and of the transnational webs of affiliations they helped create and extend, is the nature of the existing literature on social life in Republican Shanghai. For the most part, it consists of works that stay completely or nearly completely on just one side of the Chinese/foreign divide—generally the Chinese one. Most authors concerned with associational life have focused exclusively on the social scene within the Chinese community, a natural choice given that Shanghainese made up the great majority of the population within each of the treaty port's three administrative districts.[6] Other writers have focused primarily on organizations that linked together members of the foreign community, or rather that, in most cases, drew together foreign residents who already had something important in common, such as country of origin or, in the case of Jewish refugees, for example, religion.[7]

This bifurcation of the literature on associational life was most marked before the current international boom in Shanghai historical studies began in the 1980s. Prior to that point, relatively few detailed discussions of any treaty-port era associations existed. Virtually the only treatments of the social scene to go beyond the impressionistic views found in novels were provided in two types of texts. On the one hand, there were potted histories of the city, guidebooks and the like written by and mainly for Shanghailanders, which included sections with titles such as "Clubs and Associations" or "Clubland" that surveyed organizations with purely foreign memberships.[8] On the other hand, there were scattered studies, mostly in Chinese but occasionally in other languages, of groups to which only Chinese belonged, such as local labor unions, Communist Party cells, and the Chinese native place societies.[9] Given the concern with only one side of the Chinese/foreign divide, *tongxianghui* such as that for sojourners with ties to Ningbo, though definitely "clubs," would not earn a mention in the "Shanghai Clubland" sections of Shanghailander works (though they might be mentioned in a different section on native "guilds" and other exotic topics located elsewhere in the text).[10] And though there were local organizations designed to pull together Westerners who had strong ties to a given region, such as the St. David's Society (described in a famous Shanghailander guidebook as an entity intended to "unite the Welsh people of the community"), these were not discussed in surveys of "native place" societies by authors focusing on the city's Chinese residents.[11] And it was a very rare writer indeed who would refer at all to a Sino-Foreign association such as the Union Club, which was originally called the "ABC Club" to flag its goal of bringing together local Americans, Britons, and Chinese.[12]

Since the ongoing boom in Shanghai studies began, the situation has changed a good deal—at least when it comes to the *amount* of attention lavished on associations and the *range* of organizations that have been studied. Now one can find detailed investigations by Shanghai specialists of not just Chinese labor unions and *tongxianghui* but also Chinese professional associations, Chinese literary societies, Chinese campus clubs, and the sorts of multiclass protest leagues discussed by Coble in Chapter 6.[13] And yet, with some notable exceptions, scholars working on associations have still tended to stay on just one side of the Chinese/foreign divide, mirroring a larger tendency for many Shanghai specialists to focus mostly on either Chinese or foreign individuals and groups—even when they are interested in the types of people (cosmopolitan-minded Chinese modernist writers, to cite just one example) known for moving between the worlds of Chinese and foreign Shanghai.[14]

This tendency to stay on just one side or the other of one of the most basic of Republican Shanghai's many divides (that separating rich and poor being another such divide) is certainly understandable in the case of associations: most local clubs and societies had only Chinese members, while those created by Westerners and Japanese tended to have only foreign members of one or more nationalities. Still, one consequence is that any discussion that stresses the importance of those admittedly quite rare organizations that both Shanghainese and Shanghailanders could and did join is bound to have a tentative feel to it.

I should further note that for the purposes of this chapter, I will not provide either detailed biographies of border-crossers or sophisticated treatments of the Sino-Foreign associations they created or joined. Instead, the first part of the chapter covers briefly the activities of several local residents of different nationalities who moved between the world of the Shanghainese and that of the Shanghailanders, along with several local organizations that linked the two.

One border-crossing individual new to most readers is William Yinsom Lee (Li Yuanxin), a golf enthusiast and banker who was born in Australia, spent time in Europe, and after coming to Shanghai played leading roles in both the YMCA and the Guangzhou native place society.[15] Another is Norwood Allman, an American-born lawyer who learned Chinese, liked to start his day by exercising race horses, and helped found an Amity Masonic Lodge that, in contrast to nearly all other local fraternal societies, had both Asian and Western members.[16]

In addition to these individuals, we will discuss such associations as the aforementioned Union Club and the Shanghai Rotary Club, both of which had Chinese, Japanese, and Western members and leaders and in which both Lee and Allman were active. Some associations that fall outside of our Sino-Foreign category in terms of membership will also be mentioned. These were "returned students" societies open only to Chinese who had studied in foreign countries (in many cases, after having been born abroad). These societies, though of solely Chinese membership, deserve discussion in this chapter, given its central concern with transnational networks and groups that blurred the Chinese/foreign divide.

After giving a sense of the kinds of people and organizations that helped create robustly transnational networks drawing together individuals from varied points of origin and opposite sides of the Chinese/foreign divide, the final part of the chapter reflects on the significance of these admittedly unusual individuals and organizations. How, you may ask, can paying more attention to these individuals help us think more clearly about the tension between what Huskey and Clifford refer to as "cosmopolitan" (inclusive and outward looking) and "parochial" (exclusionary and inward looking) segments of the Shanghai population? What relevance does this exercise have for adding a new perspective to the ongoing debate over whether treaty-port society should be thought of as a "melting pot," one marked above all by a spirit of inclusiveness and equal opportunity for all, or as a warped creation of imperialism in which segregation and prejudice were crucial factors? Most important for the purposes of this volume, how can paying attention to border-crossers and Sino-Foreign organizations help us to better understand the city's ability to hold together in chaotic times?

In addressing these questions, one thing to be emphasized is change over time. Segregation, for example, while always a factor, had more blatant, more wide-ranging effects in some periods. And in the International Settlement, as Bickers has shown in his pioneering studies of its Britons (a group that was small in number but remained the enclave's most powerful until the Japanese military take-over), the Chinese/foreign divide was always important but not always the same. This is symbolized by the fact that toward the end of the treaty-port era, formerly foreign-only bodies (from the local governing council to the local municipal orchestra) began to include Shanghainese members.[17]

Compradors of Sociability

To get a fuller picture of the ways that unusually cosmopolitan individuals and organizations bridged the chasm that so often separated the worlds of Chinese and foreign residents, let us begin by looking a bit more closely at the contributions of William Yinsom Lee and Norwood Allman. Both of these individuals belonged to particularistic societies that catered to people with ties to a particular place (for Lee, a *tongxianghui* for Chinese with family ties to Guangzhou, for Allman, various organizations that served as hubs for the local American community), yet both belonged as well to organizations that brought together people of varied nationalities. More than that, each played leadership roles in Sino-Foreign associations.

In thinking about these two bilingual and bicultural individuals, it is helpful to keep in mind the degree to which (as Yeh shows in Chapter 2) Republican Shanghai was a setting where the comprador was an important figure. Neither Lee nor Allman was literally a comprador, but it is fair to say that each performed noneconomic intermediary functions reminiscent of those that actual compradors performed in the world of business. For example, Allman and Lee not only moved regularly between the Chinese and non-Chinese communities but also tried to articulate for people on both sides of the divide what those on the other thought and felt. Allman served this role in his law practice and then later in a fascinating book, *Shanghai Lawyer.* Lee performed this function by, among other things, submitting letters to the editors of local English-language publications, explaining the way he and other native residents felt slighted by those clubs founded by Shanghailanders (such as the prestigious Shanghai Club) that claimed to be "international," yet did not include Chinese members. These kinds of activities make Allman and Lee good candidates for being dubbed, to use a term coined by Nicholas Clifford, *compradors of rhetoric.*[18]

In fact, given how active each was in organizations that strove to increase social ties between Chinese and non-Chinese residents, we might equally call them *compradors of sociability.* This is a term that might also be used to describe several much more famous local figures, such as Carl Crow, a journalist and author of popular books about China, and Tong Shao-yi (Tang Shaoyi), a political leader and one of the first Chinese to study in America. Crow earns the title by being the first person to successfully nominate a Chinese national, Tong, for membership in the American Club. Up until then, it had been largely a gathering place for citizens of the United States but had welcomed into its ranks local foreigners from various other countries as well.[19] Tong, meanwhile, deserves to be thought of as a comprador of sociability because he made his home available to varied enterprises that included native residents and foreigners. The same was true of Sir Victor Sassoon, owner of the famous Cathay Hotel, head of a leading Baghdadi Jewish merchant family, and someone who prided himself in bringing together Chinese and non-Chinese residents of the city at the parties he threw.[20] And yet a still more famous comprador of sociability was Song Meiling (Soong Mei-ling), who moved easily between the social worlds of the Shanghainese and Shanghailanders and whose wedding ceremony brought together members of both the Chinese and foreign communities.

What sorts of transnational networks were created by or came to include figures such as Allman and Lee, and how were these extended and sustained? Formal organizations of what I have dubbed the joint Sino-Foreign variety provide a window to the answers. It is worth stressing, though, that a comprehensive answer would also require discussion of informal circles, institutions, and workplaces. Certainly, the autobiographical writings of Emily Hahn—another border-crossing American who, like Allman, formed close working relationships and friendships with foreigners and Chinese alike while in Shanghai—show how important informal circles could be in shaping transnational networks. Hahn notes that she first met many of the Chinese she got to know best (including the writer Shao Xunmei with whom she scandalously cohabitated and coedited a short-lived bilingual magazine) via her inclusion in informal gatherings hosted by Sassoon—a border-crosser himself who had served in the British Air Force and was known locally for his extravagant lifestyle, his womanizing, and his cultivation of personal ties to everyone from bohemians to Song Meiling.[21]

The importance of institutions and workplaces in shaping border-blurring networks, meanwhile, is brought home by the case of the University of Missouri's flagship Columbia campus and the *China Weekly Review,* a Shanghai periodical edited by John B. Powell, who had formerly taught in that American school's famed journalism program. One of Powell's former students was Hollington Tong, who served for a time as assistant editor of *China Weekly Review* and also coedited the reference work *Who's Who in China* with his one-time teacher. And Powell and Tong were far from the only journalists to live, or at least spend a period of time, in the treaty port (Edgar Snow being another) who had links to that American school and published in that Shanghai magazine, which Powell claims was eventually read by far more bilingual Chinese than foreign residents of the city.

The prevalence in local journalism circles of both graduates and former teachers from that Columbia-based institution has even led some to refer to a "Missouri Mafia" as something (a network perhaps?) that should not be ignored when trying to reconstruct the history of English-language reporting in and on China.[22] And the impact of this "mafia" was not restricted to English-language journalism. At least one graduate of the University of Missouri, after a stint at *China Weekly Review,* went on to work for *Shen Bao,* a leading local Chinese-language newspaper—itself, as Rudolf Wagner and other scholars have stressed, a fascinating example of a Sino-Foreign creation due to the central role that a Briton, Ernest Major, played in its origin and early development.[23]

Transnational networks were likewise created or sustained by many other institutions and workplaces. On the institutional front, one thinks of local schools, such as St. Johns University, that had Chinese students but teachers of varied nationalities, and local churches that had Chinese and non-Chinese pastors.[24] In terms of workplaces, there were local law firms that, like Allman's, had both Chinese and non-Chinese lawyers, as well as architectural firms and newspapers with both Chinese and non-Chinese employees.[25] There was also the local headquarters of the Chinese Maritime Customs Service, an organization with a multinational staff.[26]

Still, since the traces of formal organizations tend to be easier to find in standard historical sources than those of informal circles, and since a discussion of transnational institutions and workplaces could be the subject of an entire chapter, a focus here on associations such as clubs will suffice to give a sense of the way that networks that crossed the Chinese/foreign divide were created and extended. And in the particular cases of Lee and Allman (a foreigner who, like Sassoon, counted Song Meiling among his friends), we can get a lot of the information about their associational activities from just two publications: the former's *Shanghai Lawyer* and the latter's entry in the 1931 edition of Powell and Tong's *Who's Who in China* (Biographies of Chinese).[27]

We learn from *Shanghai Lawyer,* for example, that Allman played an "instrumental" role in the 1919 founding of the Union Club.[28] This organization held regular meetings for its members. It also sponsored special events, such as dances and speeches by visiting notables, the goals of which always included the organization's overarching purpose: to increase contact between Chinese and non-Chinese elite residents of the treaty port.[29] *Shanghai Lawyer* also mentions Allman's involvement in the Shanghai Rotary Club, noting that he was given his nickname, "Judge," by fellow Rotarians. And it may well have been at a Rotary function that Allman and Lee first met, for one of the many roles that the latter played in local society, according to *Who's Who in China*, was to serve as head of that club from 1926 until 1928.[30]

Neither of the two sources at hand tells us the extent to which Allman and Lee got to know one another, but *Shanghai Lawyer* suggests they did become well acquainted. It describes them as making up half of the quartet of people responsible for starting the Amity Masonic Lodge, the other two members of the team being C. T. Wang (a participant in the Versailles Peace Conference of 1919) and George Fitch (an American born in Suzhou to missionary parents).[31] Allman and Fitch would doubtless have crossed paths many times in Shanghai given the relatively small size of the local American community, a group of people tightly linked via a variety of special social organizations, including the American Club, the Columbia Country Club with its mostly American membership, and a local branch of the American Association of China to which only U.S. citizens could belong.[32] In addition, Allman and Fitch were, like Crow and Powell, part of a small subgroup within the American community; namely, they could speak and read Chinese.[33]

It would be too simple, though, to think of Fitch and Allman as one pair and Lee and Wang as another, for the links between all four criss-crossed and ran in varied directions. For example, Fitch and Lee would have had a good deal of contact with one another because each played a leadership role in the YMCA. It is true that the Ys were segregated within Shanghai, meaning that Chinese and non-Chinese members did not share facilities. Nevertheless, when it came to issues such as the management of the organizations and fund-raising drives, Western and Chinese activists and leaders often worked together.[34]

Fitch and Wang, meanwhile, were also connected to one another via Y leadership activities. Both were also involved in a civic organization known as the Pan-Pacific Association, or Pan-Pacific Union, the leading lights of which included Tong Shao-yi and other notable local border-crossers, such as T. H. Lee (Li Denghui). Lee was born in Java, educated in Singapore and the United States (graduating from Yale), and after coming to Shanghai, helped found Fudan University.[35] Fitch was for a time the Pan-Pacific Association's secretary and a member of its publicity committee; Wang chaired its committee on roads, was a vice president, and in that capacity presided over at least one meeting in the absence of its president, Tong Shao-yi.[36]

The preceding examples point to some of the varied webs of affiliation that could tie together elite members of the city's foreign and Chinese communities. Lee, Allman, Fitch, and Wang were all the kinds of men who helped "spin" these webs. Several others about whom the same could be said have also been touched on, from Crow and Tong Shaoyi, to Powell and Hollington Tong, to Sassoon and T. H. Lee. And there were as well men who made their living as compradors, in the standard sense of that term, who could be added to this list of compradors of sociability and key players in Sino-Foreign associations. Zhu Baosan, for example, was a leading figure in both the Ningbo *tongxianghui* and the Union Club.[37]

Women Who Crossed Borders

The men discussed thus far had their female counterparts. Easily the best known was Song Meiling. By virtue of being a Wellesley graduate, she was among the relatively few native residents who took part in the activities of a local club created to bring together women who had attended American colleges or universities. Both before and after she became linked to the Generalissimo, Song moved in social circles that included Westerners as well as Chinese.[38] Her sister, Song Qingling, was another female border-crosser who helped connect members of the Chinese and non-Chinese communities; while her husband Sun Yat-sen was alive, they sometimes cohosted dinner parties with multinational guest lists. And among border-crossing foreign women, Emily Hahn, who is perhaps best remembered as the author of *The Soong Sisters,* a group biography of Meiling, Qingling, and their sibling, Song Ailing, is among those worthy of a mention.[39]

Another female border-crosser, who was well-known in Shanghai social circles at the time but is now a more obscure figure than those just listed, was Mrs. Mei Hua-chuan (nee Anna Fo Jin Kong).[40] Who exactly was Mrs. Mei? According to the 1931 edition of Powell and Tong's *Who's Who in China* (my sole source at present for information on her, including the romanization of her maiden name), she was a graduate of Barnard College who was born in Hong Kong, raised in Hawaii, and married a lawyer named H. C. Mei (Mei Huaquan). Her entry in *Who's Who in China* begins by noting that she was a "clubwoman and social worker," then goes on to list her roles in a wide range of organizations, some with mixed Chinese and non-Chinese and some purely Chinese memberships. As if the foregoing did not suggest a sufficiently cosmopolitan existence, it is worth noting that one of the main organizations with an exclusively Chinese membership in which she was active had a decidedly transnational aspect to it, being open only to Chinese women who, like Mrs. Mei, had studied abroad: the Womens Returned Students' Club. This was a female-only counterpart to an influential all-male organization, the Returned Students' Club, in which many border-crossing Shanghainese men played leading roles. T. H. Lee, for example, chaired it for a time.[41]

Parochial Participants in Cosmopolitan Networks[42]

The people mentioned so far led unusually cosmopolitan lives, but it is worth stressing that there were Shanghailanders who knew only Western languages and Chinese who had never been abroad who became drawn into multinational webs of affiliation. These more parochial Shanghai residents typically did less to extend robustly transnational networks than did compradors of sociability such as Allman, Lee, or Song Meiling. Nevertheless, it is interesting to note how easily certain members of the Shanghailander and Shanghainese elites could be drawn into such networks, even if they were Western businessmen who moved mostly in Anglophone circles or Chinese businessman whose social lives tended to stay on the Chinese side of the Chinese/foreign divide. Often, no doubt, the process of entanglement in a broader web of affiliation began simply with an invitation to attend an event that a border-crossing individual had arranged or perhaps through sponsorship of a joint venture association made possible by personal ties (such as marriage to a border-crosser).

One network-expanding gathering of the sort I have in mind was a November 1920 reception that took place at the Union Club. It was held when a group of Britons based in different parts of China were in Shanghai for a conference of British chambers of commerce. Ostensibly, the main goal of the conference, according to the local press, was to offer attendees a chance to "meet the principle Chinese businessmen of Shanghai." But the reception also afforded opportunities for elite Shanghailanders and their Shanghainese counterparts to meet each other, since "the Shanghai British Chamber of Commerce" is listed as having hosted the event and guests are said to have included "the committeemen of the Chinese Chamber of Commerce and various of the guilds."[43]

Other events of this sort included banquets honoring Chinese or foreign business leaders that were attended by a mixture of Shanghailanders and Shanghainese. In 1926, for example, Westerners threw a banquet at which the powerful comprador and Ningbo *tongxianghui* leader Yu Xiaqing was among the honorees.[44] And in this same period, Chinese businessmen played key roles in a goodbye party for a departing Shanghailander, A. Brooke-Smith, who had been a leading figure in the Union Club.[45]

Turning now to the role that family ties could play in bringing additional people into networks that connected people on opposite sides of the Chinese/foreign divide, Chiang Kai-shek's marriage to Song Meiling is the most famous case in point. There are, however, other examples: the Western and Chinese wives of Union Club members who attended that organization's dances;[46] and the families who attended Rotary club parties such as the one immortalized in a group photograph (reprinted in *Fortune* magazine) depicting Shanghai residents of varied nationalities and ages gathered together in a seemingly very companionable way.[47]

Will the Real Shanghai Please Stand Up?

It is worth pausing here to consider briefly the tension between two competing visions of treaty port social life, one of which presents the border separating the social worlds of the Shanghainese and Shanghailanders as very porous, the other of which presents that same border as rock solid. The Rotary picnic photograph is a perfect symbol for the former view, conjuring up as it does the image of a city in which segregation was not a central issue and people of all nationalities and races worked together harmoniously.[48]

The *Who's Who in China* entries for many of the border-crossers mentioned earlier certainly suggest that there are many tales to tell that would support this vision of Shanghai as a place where opportunities were wide open to any person of talent. So, too, do the entries for many other figures, such as H. C. Mei (husband of the aforementioned Mrs. Mei) and Pei Tsu-yi (Bei Zuyi), father of the famed cosmopolitan architect I. M. Pei.[49] H. C. Mei was born in San Francisco, graduated from Columbia Law School, and once in Shanghai became a member of the city's Bar Association and was active in the local American University Club, American Returned Students' Club, and Rotary Club. In addition, *Who's Who* tells us he was "one of the organizers and directors of the International Anti-Opium Association, 1919–1922" (a group to which at least one of our Shanghailander border-crossers, George Fitch, also belonged).[50] Pei, meanwhile, was a banker; belonged to at least two local Sino-Foreign associations, the Pan-Pacific Association and the Union Club; and was elected in 1928 to the Shanghai Municipal Council (SMC), the main governing body of the International Settlement.[51]

There are, however, compelling photographs and various texts from the era that support a contrasting view of Shanghai as a place where discrimination against Chinese residents was a central fact of life in the foreign-run districts. One of the best known photographs of this ilk is an oft-reproduced image of a notice board containing a list of the rules for the International Settlement's nicest park, the Public Garden—a list that specified that the grounds were off-limits to all Chinese other than those who were the servants of foreigners.[52] As for texts from the era that highlight the limits to interchange between Chinese and foreigners, it will suffice here to mention a famous speech that the famous resident of the French Concession, Sun Yat-sen, gave in 1924. In it, he drew attention to the failure of the city's most prestigious club to admit Chinese members, a point also taken up by William Yinsom Lee in the letters to the editors of many local journals for which he is known.[53]

Sun also, quite understandably, viewed as discriminatory the SMC's all-foreign composition—a fact that did not change until 1928, the year that several slots were finally set aside for representatives of local Chinese taxpayers—as well as the SMC's failure even to consult with Shanghainese leaders, and the rules restricting admittance to the Public Garden. These features of the International Settlement, he insisted, supported his general claim that it was worse to be part of a subjugated nationality in a partially colonized setting than in a fully colonized one. After all, he asserted, Chinese were not banned from any Hong Kong parks or clubs and the local authorities there regularly consulted with members of its colonized Chinese population.[54]

So, which view represents the real Shanghai? The answer is, both. Exclusionary practices linked to nationality and invidious forms of segregation routinely influenced local social and political life, even within the very institutions (the Customs Service, for instance) sometimes lauded as representative of an ideal blending of Chinese and foreign influences and egalitarianism between Shanghainese and Shanghailanders.[55] Patterns of discrimination were particularly important during the final stages of the Qing period and the first years of the Republican era, when the local Shanghailander elite consistently rebuffed the attempts by well-to-do Shanghainese to be treated, due to their class and respectability, as exceptions to exclusionary practices. These practices not only kept all Chinese other than servants out of the Public Garden, they kept all Chinese off of decision-making bodies of any sort. (Despite the public addresses by French Concession standout Sun Yat-sen discussed earlier, the SMC had begun to periodically *consult* with Shanghainese businesses well before 1924.) Even after that point, however, when efforts by elite Shanghainese to have their class trump their nationality began to prove more successful (as the SMC structural changes of 1928 illustrate) and a new country club open to well-to-do Chinese and foreigners was established, some forms of discrimination lingered.[56]

In addition, we should remember that, when they did finally come, moves away from old patterns of exclusion and segregation tended to affect only the upper strata of local society. The case of the Public Garden is illustrative: when nationality ceased to be a criterion for access in 1928, it was replaced by the ability to pay an entrance fee. Thus, its gates were opened to monied Chinese at precisely the moment when it became difficult for the poorer members of any nationality to make use of the grounds.

It becomes clear from the writings left to us by border-crossing Shanghai residents of all nationalities that, even within the upper tiers of Shanghai society, the lifestyles of border-crossers always remained exceptional. Those who regularly socialized with people on the other side of the Chinese/foreign divide always saw themselves as doing something a bit unusual. And associations such as the Union Club did not emerge naturally out of the cosmopolitan flow of Shanghai sociability but were, rather, quite self-conscious efforts to overcome entrenched patterns of fragmentation.

Moreover, if the opening of the Public Garden symbolized the ability of class to trump nationality late in the treaty-port era, then the continued exclusivity of the Shanghai Club symbolized the degree to which national or racial categories could continue at times to trump everything else. Border-crossing Chinese, such as Tong Shao-yi and Wang Yiting, could be part of many webs of affiliation that drew together people of diverse nationalities, but even these highly respected native residents could not be part of the drinking and networking that took place at one of the city's most famous locations, the "longest bar in the world" that was the Shanghai Club's best known landmark.[57]

And yet, even if there were always significant limits to the inclusiveness of Shanghai treaty-port society, zones of cosmopolitan interaction such as that symbolized by the Rotary Club photograph did exist and the border-crossers and Sino-Foreign organizations discussed here should not be dismissed as of only marginal significance. Atypical though the lifestyles of the former and actions of the latter may have been, especially early in the Republican period, they constituted an important feature of the local milieu. They were exceptions, but exceptionally important ones, since the city could not function smoothly without the networks they helped to create and sustain. And, I am convinced, border-crossers and their associations played not only very significant but, over time, increasingly central roles in helping Shanghai "go on" in chaotic times.

Why Border-Crossers Matter So Much

One factor that makes the Sino-Foreign associations and informal circles that brought together Shanghailanders and Shanghainese worthy of attention in a book such as this is that, while their members may have been unusually cosmopolitan, they were in many cases unusually influential as well. It is striking, for example, how many of the people mentioned thus far earned entries in Powell and Tong's *Who's Who in China* or in an equivalent reference work edited by Carroll Lunt devoted to foreign residents of Chinese treaty ports. Further, several of these same people received mention or earned whole profiles as leading figures within Shanghai society in the January 1935 *Fortune* magazine cover story on the city.[58] Even the small amount of information readily available from newspapers and like publications on gathering places such as the Union Club illustrates the particular role these organizations—formal and informal—played in bringing together some of the most successful of all Shanghailander and Shanghainese businessmen, with Briton A. Brooke-Smith, American F. J. Raven, and Zhu Baosan, three of its early leaders, being cases in point.[59]

In addition, admittedly exceptional figures such as George Fitch, Norwood Allen, William Yinsom Lee, and Song Meiling are worthy of attention here because they were not connected merely to one another through participation in various Sino-Foreign organizations and cosmopolitan social circles but were active participants in associations and social circles that had only foreign or only Chinese memberships. This meant they were involved in and helped enlarge webs of affiliation that not only linked exceptionally cosmopolitan figures to one another but linked them to more parochial influential figures on both sides of the Chinese/foreign divide.

One thing that doubtless made it easier for business to get done in Shanghai—political business as well as the economic kind—was that so many individual members of the local Chinese and foreign elites were either part of the same social circles or part of overlapping ones. How many prominent local businessmen with ties to Canton did George Fitch know? We cannot say, but via his ties to William Yinsom Lee, a leader of the Cantonese *tongxianghui,* this American had a contact who could provide him with an introduction to any of that organization's members. Similarly, though Du Yuesheng was a less cosmopolitan figure than the people discussed here, Allen was not far removed from him socially, given the close link between the Green Gang leader and Chiang Kai-shek and the close link between the American lawyer and Song Meiling. In other words, even before Du began to be part of international philanthropic organizations, which made him part of groups including influential Shanghailanders, French Concession officials were not the only foreigners to whom he was linked directly or at one remove. In the mid-1920s, for example, he was already attending meetings with Yu Xiaqing, who was closely linked to Union Club figures such as Zhu Baosan and the like.

Allowing the Shanghais within Shanghai to Go On

This chapter has been, as stressed from the start, a preliminary foray into new terrain. If it has been at all successful, it will perhaps encourage other scholars to take a closer look at some of the associations introduced, to unravel in a much more systematic way (than is possible in the scope of this volume) webs of affiliation that linked border-crossing Shanghainese and Shanghailanders to one another and to powerful parochial figures based on opposite sides of the Chinese/foreign divide, and to add to the mix groups that I have passed over here (such as border-crossing Japanese residents of the treaty port). In closing, I want to make a brief effort to connect the story of changes over time in patterns of Shanghai society to changes in the political arrangements within the International Settlement, a particularly important part of the city.

It is no accident that the Union Club was founded in the wake of an upsurge of patriotic activity, the May Fourth Movement of 1919, and that the aforementioned banquet thrown by Shanghailander businessmen to honor Yu Xiaqing and other members of the local Shanghainese elite came just as the first anniversary of the May Thirtieth Movement of 1925 was drawing near (along with the fear of renewed popular agitation). Nor is it coincidental that the Shanghainese who served on the SMC in the late 1920s and 1930s, after that body began to include Chinese members—a group that included longtime YMCA stalwart and cotton magnate C. C. Nieh (Nie Qijie), one-time Union Club president J. H. Lee, and border-crossers such as Pei Tsu-yi and Yu Xiaqing—were typically people who were both highly regarded among the Shanghainese and already well known to the foreign Council members.[60] It surely made a difference that when the SMC became a Sino-Foreign *political institution*, many of its Chinese and non-Chinese members alike brought to the table experiences and contacts made at Sino-Foreign *social events*, such as Union Club and Rotary meetings and banquets honoring prominent Shanghainese or Shanghailanders.[61]

What we see emerging as a general pattern, which affected first social life and political institutions shortly thereafter, is a trend toward class interest being allowed to trump nationality or race in more and more settings—lessening patterns of segregation at the elite level without displacing them completely. Shanghai remained, until the end of the treaty-port era, a place marked socially and politically by imperialism, to be sure, but the nature of this marking changed with time. It remains an open question whether Sun Yat-sen was right to claim that the sort of *cizhimin* (hypo-colonial or subcolonial) status of the Shanghainese circa 1924 made them even worse off than their colonized counterparts in Hong Kong, but it is clear that the precise workings of nationality-based discrimination and racism within the treaty port, though still present, was quite different a decade after the speech quoted from earlier—even if Chinese still couldn't join the Shanghai Club.[62]

There were always Shanghailanders who insisted that the majority local Chinese population were in the Settlement on sufferance and had no rights to expect a say in local governance or equal access to public space. By the mid-to-late 1920s and even more so after the Japanese threat grew in the 1930s, however, this position became less and less tenable, and making common cause with the Shanghainese elite against radical forces calling for an end to the treaty-port system and for workers to rise up against foreign and Chinese bosses began to seem necessary—even to the most "parochial" Shanghailanders.

It would be too simplistic to say that the forming of the Union Club laid the groundwork for the transformation of the SMC into a body that included Chinese representatives, but these and other related developments were carried forward by similar currents—and the existence of Sino-Foreign associations made it easier for the Council to function as a body with a hybrid membership. What we see, on the whole, from around 1920 to 1937 is the Shanghailander elite searching for creative ways to ensure that their institutions and way of life would be able to "go on," albeit in a modified fashion, in a rapidly changing and increasingly uncertain political environment. We see at the same time the Shanghainese elite finding the crises of the day helpful in facilitating their longstanding claims that their class should trump their nationality and race in social and political affairs alike.[63]

Conclusion

The story of the social and political changes that allowed the always protean city of Shanghai to remake itself yet again during that part of the Republican era is a complex one. To do it justice, and to figure out how it managed to remain relatively intact and go on, rather than be pulled apart by the centrifugal forces of the time, many things must be taken into account that have not been touched on here, such as the chains of affiliations that linked elites within the International Settlement to those in control of the French Concession and the Chinese Municipality.[64] The tale will remain incomplete, however, until we know a good deal more about how border-crossers and Sino-Foreign associations—and the transnational networks they were part of and helped to extend—influenced the transformation of the treaty port's most economically significant and robustly cosmopolitan sectors.

Notes

1. Dillon and Oi: Middlemen, Social Networks, and State-Building

1. For some examples from just the English-language literature, see Bergère, *Golden Age of the Chinese Bourgeoisie*; Clifford, *Spoilt Children of Empire*; Clifford, *Shanghai, 1925*; Coble, *Shanghai Capitalists*; Cochran, *Inventing Nanjing Road*; Elvin and Skinner, *Chinese City between Two Worlds*; Fewsmith, *Party, State, and Local Elites*; Fu, *Passivity, Resistance, and Collaboration*; Goodman, *Native Place, City, and Nation*; Henriot, *Shanghai, 1927–1937*; Henriot and Wen-hsin Yeh, *In the Shadow of the Rising Sun*; Hershatter, *Dangerous Pleasures*; Honig, *Creating Chinese Ethnicity*; Honig, *Sisters and Strangers*; Howe, *Shanghai: Revolution and Development*; Lee, *Shanghai Modern*; Han-chao Lu, "Becoming Urban"; Han-chao Lu, *Beyond the Neon Lights*; Martin, *Shanghai Green Gang*; Perry, *Shanghai on Strike*; Perry, *Patrolling the Chinese Revolution*; Reed, *Gutenberg in Shanghai*; Smith, *Like Cattle and Horses*; Smith, *The Road Is Made*; Stranahan, *Underground*; Wakeman, *Policing Shanghai*; Wakeman and Yeh, *Shanghai Sojourners*; Wasserstrom, *Student Protests in Twentieth-Century China*; Xiaoqun Xu, *Chinese Professionals and the State*; Yeh, *Alienated Academy*; Yeh, *Wartime Shanghai*.

2. The exception is Sei Jong Chin, whose contribution ultimately became Chapter 7 of this volume.

3. For more on the civil society debate, see Rowe, "Public Sphere in Modern China"; Strand, *Rickshaw Beijing*; Bergère, "Shanghai Bankers' Association"; Goodman, "New Culture, Old Habits".

4. For example, see Bianco, *Origins of the Chinese Revolution*; Chesneaux, *Chinese Labor Movement*; Moore, *Social Origins of Dictatorship and Democracy*; Bergère, *Golden Age of the Chinese Bourgeoisie*, although this last work is transitional and also adopts a state–society framework.

5. Bergère, *Golden Age of the Chinese Bourgeoisie*; Hershatter, *Workers of Tianjin*; Honig, *Sisters and Strangers*.

6. Bergère, *Golden Age of the Chinese Bourgeoisie*; Coble, *Shanghai Capitalists*; Henriot, *Shanghai, 1927–1937*; Fewsmith, *Party, State, and Local Elites*; Martin, *Shanghai Green Gang*; Perry, *Shanghai on Strike*; Wakeman, *Policing Shanghai*; Xu Xiaoqun, *Chinese Professionals and the Republican State*.

7. Coble argued that the Nationalist regime was autonomous from social forces. See Coble, *Shanghai Capitalists*. Fewsmith argued that the Nationalists incorporated merchants into the regime, while Martin countered that it was organized crime, not merchants, that were incorporated. See Fewsmith, *Party, State, and Local Elites*; Martin, *Shanghai Green Gang*.

8. Bergère, *Golden Age of the Chinese Bourgeoisie*, 8; Esherick and Rankin, *Chinese Local Elites*, 341.

9. Bergère, *Golden Age of the Chinese Bourgeoisie*, 277.

10. Fewsmith, *Party, State, and Local Elites*, 119–20.

11. For some examples of social network analysis for the Republican period, see Cochran, *Encountering Chinese Networks*; Fried, *Fabric of Chinese Society*; Esherick and Rankin, *Chinese Local Elites*; Goodman, *Native Place, City, and Nation*; Schoppa, *Blood Road*; Yeh, *Provincial Passages*. For more contemporary examples, see: Gold, Guthrie, and Wank, *Social Connections in China*; Oi, *State and Peasant*; Mayfair Yang, *Gifts, Favors and Banquets*; Yunxiang Yan, *Flow of Gifts*.

12. Roger Gould, "Uses of Network Tools in Comparative Historical Research"; Scott, *Social Network Analysis*; Mizruchi, "Social Network Analysis"; Fischer et al., *Networks and Places*.

13. Putnam, *Bowling Alone*; Edwards, Foley, and Diani, *Beyond Tocqueville*.

14. Putnam et al., *Making Democracy Work*.

15. Ibid., 146–7.

16. Other research has also yielded evidence that the relationship between trust and collective action is not as direct as many social capital theorists have assumed. See, for example, Stolle and Rochon, "Are All Associations Alike?"

17. Foley, Edwards, and Diani, "Social Capital Reconsidered."

18. Some other efforts to tease out these relationships include Roger Gould, *Insurgent Identities*; Evans, *Embedded Autonomy*; Kohli, *State-Directed Development*.

2. Wen-hsin Yeh: Huang Yanpei and the CSVE

The author wishes to thank Jean Oi for her superb editorial guidance and exemplary collegiality.

1. Wakeman and Yeh, *Shanghai Sojourners*, intro.
2. Yen-ping Hao, *Comprador in Nineteenth-Century China*, 180–6.

3. Yeh, *Shanghai Splendor*, ch. 1.
4. Martin, *Shanghai Green Gang*; Wakeman, *Policing Shanghai*.
5. See, for example, Chow, *May Fourth Movement*; Joseph Chen, *May Fourth Movement in Shanghai*; Clifford, *Shanghai, 1925*.
6. For a fine explication on the concept of *lu lu tong*, see Sherman Cochran's depiction of Liu Hongsheng in Cochran, "Marketing Medicine and Advertising Dreams in China."
7. Perry, *Shanghai on Strike*.
8. Goodman, *Native Place, City, and Nation*.
9. Wen-hsin Yeh, *Provincial Passages*.
10. Guangjing Liu, *Jingshi Sixiang Yu Xinxing Qiye* (Statecraft Thought and Emerging Enterprises), 420; Yen-ping Hao, *Comprador in Nineteenth-Century China*, 205. After the Boxers fiasco and with the launching of the New Policies, political dynamics changed dramatically at the center. Negotiations over the Boxers indemnities clause, which led to a scrutiny of state finance, coincided with the application of the American Chinese Exclusion Act to the Philippines, which severely curtailed Chinese rights and activities on these islands. Merchant groups in coastal Chinese cities rallied to launch anti-American protests and boycotts. These developments powerfully shaped Chinese views of the role of the state in commerce.
11. Ermin Wang, *Wan Qing Zhengzhi Sixiang Shilun* (Historical Treatises on Late Qing Political Thought), 240–61.
12. Ibid., 326–31.
13. Ibid., 331.
14. These include purchasing, sales, renting, manufacturing, warehousing, reprocessing, public utilities (electricity, gas, or water), publishing, printing, banking, money exchange, lending, insurance, advancement of credit or credit-related services, operation of public gathering places, delivery and delivery-related services, service as a broker, middleman, or agency.
15. Wen-hsin Yeh, *Shanghai Splendor*, ch. 1.
16. Zhishi Min, "Kexue de Guanli" (Scientific Management).
17. Mingqi Jiang, "Jingshang Shibai de Yuanyin" (Causes for Business Failure).
18. These were Ji'nan, Fudan, Shanghai Baptist, Datong, Daxia, and Guanghua, each containing multiple departments of study and a constituent part of a larger university. In addition, there were two public institutions: the Shanghai College of Commerce, funded by the Ministry of Economics, and the Institute of Tax Revenue, funded by the Ministry of Finance.
19. See also Schwintzer, "Education to Save the Nation."
20. Xingtao Cai, *Kangzhan Qian de Zhonghua Zhiye Jiaoyu She* (Chinese Society of Vocational Education in the Years Prior to the War of Resistance).
21. Hansan Xu, *Huang Yanpei Nianpu* (Chronological Biography of Huang Yanpei), 10.
22. Ibid., 10–17.

23. Ibid., 31–2.

24. Xingtao Cai, *Kangzhan Qian*, 105–13.

25. The figure, coming in the depth of a recession, compared favorably with the employment rate of many colleges and universities. Some of the Society's graduates worked in teaching positions in county schools. Others (about 56 percent) became administrators in the agricultural bureaus of county governments. The best jobs went to those who claimed knowledge in fields such as civil engineering, road construction, electrical engineering, and mechanical engineering. The graduates of Vocational Education took in salaries that surpassed those with degrees in general education. See Qingru He, "Zhiye Xuexiao Xuesheng Chulu Diaocha" (Job Placement of Vocational School Students: An Investigation).

26. Hansan Xu, *Huang Yanpei Nianpu*, 50.

27. Sun Jianqiu, "Tongchang Chehang Shixi Baogao" (Internship at the Tongchang Bicycle Shop: A Report).

28. Zhonghua Zhiye Jiaoyu She, *Quanguo Zhiye Xuexiao Gaikuang* (A National General Survey of Vocational Schools), 4, 260.

29. Ibid., 68.

30. Hansan Xu, *Huang Yanpei Nianpu*, 40–8.

31. A Ministry of Education report, produced in 1934, showed that there were a total of 330 vocational schools in 24 provinces outside Jiangsu, Sichuan, Guangxi, and Xinjiang. Another report showed about 710 vocational schools all across the country. See Daozan Zhong, "Zhiye Xuexiao Xiaozhang Zhi Xueli Yu Jingyan" (Educational Background and Work Experience of Principals of Vocational Schools). A majority of the principals of vocational schools had started their careers as high school teachers or college lecturers. A large number of Jiangsu vocational school principals had been trained in industry or agricultural economy in Japan. A majority of commerce department heads in Shanghai, by contrast, had been trained in the United States. Ibid., 68.

32. Xingtao Cai, *Kangzhan Qian*, 15–16, 32–3.

33. Ibid., 40–4.

34. Duara, *Rescuing History*.

35. Gerth, *China Made*.

36. Guoshi Guan, Ministry of Education files, "*Zhonghua Zhiye Jiaoyu Hui*."

37. Yeh, "Progressive Journalism."

38. Zou Taofen's articulation of the "voice of the people" drew the ire of the Nationalist authorities. In 1936, Zou was put on trial and imprisoned, along with six other public figures, as a leader of the National Salvation Movement in Shanghai. Throughout the 1930s, Huang Yanpei offered Zou Taofen his staunch support. *Shenghuo* and its visceral patriotic message elicited strong responses from Shanghai's petty urbanites.

39. Guoshi Guan, Ministry of Education files, "*Zhonghua Zhiye Jiaoyu Hui*."

3. Kuiyi Shen: Wang Yiting in 1910s–1930s Shanghai

1. Entry under Wang Zheng in *Who's Who in China*, 4th ed., 415–16.

2. Tsao Hsing-Yuan, "A Forgotten Celebrity: Wang Zhen (1867–1938), Businessman, Philanthropist, and Artist."

3. Scholars have different opinions about when Wang Yiting went to Shanghai to work at Yichuntang. See Yang Longsheng, "Wang Yiting Shuhua Nianbiao" (Chronology of Paintings and Calligraphy of Wang Yiting); and Cai Chennan, "Wang Yiting Nianpu Jianbiao" (Biographical Chronology of Wang Yiting). Both Yang and Cai claimed Wang went to Shanghai in 1880. However, Wang Zhongrong, the grandson of Wang Yiting, believed that Wang Yiting entered Yichuntang to be an apprentice in 1881 (according to the interview with Wang Zhongrong conducted by Xiao Fenqi). See Xiao, *Wang Yiting*, 29–30. He Xinchang also raised questions about the date but did not provide evidence to support his doubt. See He, "Haishang Wenren Wang Yiting" (Shanghai Celebrity Wang Yiting), 55.

4. Li Weizhuang (1873–1913) was a well-known businessman in Shanghai. He joined Sun Yat-sen's Revolutionary Alliance in the late Qing period and was once the head of the Civil Affairs Bureau of Zhabei District, Shanghai, at the beginning of Republican period. His daughter, Li Qiujun (1899–1971), was a well-known painter in the 1920s and 1930s. She was one of the organizers of the Chinese Women's Painting Society, established in 1934.

5. Shengyu qianzhuang, a famous traditional Chinese bank in Shanghai, was established by Li Yeting (1807–1868), who was from Ningbo. Li Weizhuang (1873–1913) and Li Yunshu (1867–1935) were his descendants. In several sources the founder of Shengyu qianzhuang was mistakenly considered to be Li Pingshu. See Wang Renzi, "Wang Yiting," in *Minguo Renwu Zhuan* (Biographies of Republican Figures); and Cai Chennan, "Wang Yiting Nianpu Jianbiao." In Yang Longsheng's "Wang Yiting Chuanlüe" (Concise Biography of Wang Yiting), Shengyu qianzhuang was mistaken as Hengtai qianzhuang. Wang Yiting actually worked in Shengyu qianzhuang first, then entered Hengtai qianzhuang. Xiao Fenqi in *Wang Yiting* also pointed out this error.

6. Guangfangyanguan, a foreign language school, was established by Li Hongzhang in 1863 in Shanghai following the system of Tongwenguan, which had been established by the Qing court a year earlier in Beijing. There are several different stories about Wang Yiting studying at Guangfangyanguan. He Xinchang in "Haishang Wenren Wang Yiting" claimed that Wang studied English there (see He Xinchang, "Haishang," 56–57). Lao Shan, however, wrote that Wang was studying Japanese at the time (see Lao Shan, "Bailong Shanren Wang Yiting" (White Dragon Mountainman Wang Yiting), 180). According to Wang Zhongrong, Wang Yiting's grandson, Wang Yiting might have studied English at Guangfangyanguan, although he spoke neither Japanese nor English fluently. Later when

he worked in a Japanese company, he still relied on two secretaries as interpreters. See Xiao Fengqi, *Wang Yiting*, 30.

7. According to Hori Keijiro, the president of the Osaka Shipping Company, Wang was introduced to him by a Shanghai merchant, Yuan Zizhuang. Actually, Yuan recommended two people at the same time. The other one was Yu Xiaqing, who later also became one of the most important industrialists in Shanghai. But Hori Keijiro chose Wang Yiting because he looked very modest. See He, "Haishang Wenren Wang Yiting," 57.

8. Sawamura, "Wang Yiting," 1:18–22. Sawamura Sachio was the director of the Shanghai office of the Japanese newspaper *Mainichi Shinbun* (Mainichi Daily News) at the time.

9. Wang Renzi, "Wang Yiting," 225.

10. The reason for establishing this new federation was because the Shanghai General Chamber of Commerce during the 1927 incident was not willing to lend money to Chang Kai-shek, so after the Nationalist Party controlled Shanghai, they fired its staff, appointed some officials to take over the organization, and founded a new federation to support the new municipal government. See *Yishi Bao* (Yishi News), May 1, 1927.

11. Rankin, *Elite Activism and Political Transformation*; and Schoppa, *Chinese Elite and Political Change*.

12. This institutional structure was commonly called by its abbreviated name, *Zong gongchengju*, which yielded the English name, General Works Board. See Elvin, "The Gentry Democracy in Chinese Shanghai, 1905–1914"; and Henriot, *Shanghai, 1927–1937*, 10–11.

13. Zhang Zhongli, *Jindai Shanghai Chengshi Yanjiu* (Studies on Modern Shanghai), 13; and Elvin, "The Administration of Shanghai."

14. Yang Yi et al., eds., *Shanghai Zizhi Zhi* (History of Autonomous Shanghai), unpaginated chart.

15. See "Yubei Lixian Gonghui Bao" (Bulletin of the Constitution Preparation Committee), vol. 20.

16. *Shuntian Shibao* (Shuntian Times), December 17, 1909, the first year of the Xuantong reign.

17. Chen Qimei (1878–1916) was a native of Wuxing, Zhejiang. He went to Japan in 1906, participated in the anti-Qing movement, and joined the Revolutionary Alliance there. In 1908, he returned to Shanghai. In the Revolution of 1911, he founded the Central China Branch of the Revolutionary Alliance with Song Jiaoren and Tan Renfeng and organized the Shanghai Uprising in response to the Wuchang Uprising. In 1912, after the Qing regime collapsed, Chen was appointed as the head of the Shanghai municipal government, *Hujun dudufu*. In order to expand the revolutionary organization, he consolidated the Green Gang and Red Gang to form the China Mutual Progress Association (see Wakeman, *Policing Shanghai*, 28). After the New Republican government's expedition against Yuan Shikai failed in 1913, he fled to Japan. In 1914, he joined the Chinese Revolutionary Party in Japan and was assassinated in Shanghai on Yuan Shikai's instructions in 1916.

18. Li Pingshu, *Qiewan Laoren Qishi Zixu* (Li Pingshu on Himself at Age Seventy).

19. Wu Tegong, *Shanghai Shangtuan Kefu Shanghai Jilue* (Records of Shanghai Merchants Militia Recovering Shanghai City). Wang Zhongrong, a grandson of Wang Yiting and son of Wang Mengnan, said that Chiang Kai-shek studied in Japan with Wang Mengnan and received financial support from the Wang family. Chen Yi also wrote: "When Chiang Kai-shek studied in Japan, he had two closest friends. One was Dai Jitao, also called Dai Chuanxian, who later became the director of the supervisory committee; the other was the son of Wang Yiting, who is very rich because Wang Yiting was a very powerful person in Shanghai and was comprador of the Japanese shipping and transportation company. Wang Yiting was also well known as a painter and calligrapher. Wang's son, therefore, took care of Chiang and Dai's living expenses." See "Jiang Zi Dai Sheng," *Xin Bao* (Xin News), August 30, 1996; see also Xiao Fenqi, *Wang Yiting*, 33.

20. Among accounts of this are Henriot, *Shanghai*, 15–16; and Wakeman, *Policing Shanghai*, 23.

21. Wang Zhongrong recalled that Chen Qimei's tomb in Huzhou and the tomb of another revolutionary, Song Jiaoren (1882–1913), in Shanghai were all built by the Wang family. See Xiao Fenqi, *Wang Yiting*, 33.

22. *Minli Bao* (Minli News), December 20, 1912.

23. Barkan, "Patterns of Power," 192–93.

24. Kōhama Masako, *Kindai Shanhai no Kōkyōsei to Kokai* (The "Public" and the State of Modern Shanghai), 65–150.

25. Thanks to Kōhama Masako for this data (see Kōhama, *Kindai Shanhai*, 77–81). Her book provides a chart listing philanthropic societies of the late 1920s and early 1930s based on material from several sources: *Shanghai Tebieshi Shehuiju Yewu Baogao* (Shanghai City Social Affairs Bureau Work Report), 1928 and 1929; *Shanghai Xianzhi* (Gazetteer of Shanghai County), vol. 10, 1936; Xu Wancheng, ed., *Shanghai Cishan Jiguan Gaikuang* (General Situation of Shanghai Philanthropic Institutions), 1941; *Shanghai Shi Nianjian* (Yearbook of Shanghai City), T-Shehui Shiye, 1936; Ruan Renze and Zhennong Gao, eds., *Shanghai Zongjiaoshi* (History of Religion in Shanghai), 1992; *Shanghai Xian Xuzhi* (Gazetteer of Shanghai County Supplement), vol. 2, 1918; and reports of these societies.

26. Ruan Renze and Gao Zhennong, eds. *Shanghai Zongjiao Shi*, 869–74.

27. Xiao Fengqi, *Wang Yiting*, 204.

28. This painting is now in a collection in Berlin.

29. Kōhama, *Kindai Shanghai*, 120–23.

30. *Shen Bao*, August 2, 18, 19, 24, and 27, 1931.

31. Ibid., August 8, 12, and 26, 1931.

32. Ibid., September 13 and 17, November 1 and 2, 1931.

33. Ibid., September 1 and 7, 1931.

34. Ibid., September 3, 1931.

35. *Shanghai Minzhenzhi* (History of Shanghai Civil Affairs), "Dashiji" (Record of Important Events), 24.

36. *Shen Bao*, September 5, 1923.
37. Ibid., September 7, 1923.
38. Gao Zhennong, "Buddhism in Republican Shanghai," 12.
39. Xi Nan, "Wang Yiting in My Memory," *Shen Bao* (November 15, 1938), 18. Here I cite the translation by Tsao, "A Forgotten Celebrity," 97–8.
40. Shen, "Entering a New Era," 103–4.
41. See Wu Dongmai, *Wu Changshi Tanyilu* (Wu Changshi's Comments on Art), 249; and Wang Senran, *Jindai Ershi Jia Pingzhuan* (On Twenty Modern Artists), 16. Here I cite the translation of the preface from Davis, "For Fate, Faith, and Charity," 16.
42. Shen, "Traditional Chinese Painting," 82–3.
43. The album is now in the China National Museum of Art, Beijing.
44. Among the board members were Cai Yuanpei, Ye Gongchuo, Du Yuesheng, Wu Tiecheng, and others. See *Shanghai Art College Archive* in the Shanghai Municipal Archive.
45. *Xiaopenglai shuhuahui* (Xiaopenglai Calligraphy and Painting Society) might be the earliest one with a record. It was established by Jiang Baoling (1781–1841) in the old town of Shanghai in 1839 and attracted many artists who were active in the city, including Li Yunjia, Fei Danxu (1801–50), and Yao Xie (1805–64). See Yang Yi, *Haishang Molin* (Biographies of Artists in Shanghai), on Jiang Baoling, 5b; Xu Zhihao, *Zhongguo Meishu Shetuan Manlu* (List of Chinese Art Societies), 3–4. In 1851, the Pinghuashe (Duckweed Flower Club), was established in the Temple of the Lord Guan in the western part of the city by Wu Zonglin. The activities of the society were documented in a colophon written by Wu Zonglin in 1864 on a now lost painting, *The Elegant Gathering of the Pinghuashe*, which was painted by members Qian Huian (1833–1911), Wang Li (1813–1879), and Bao Dong (active 1849–1866). See Yang Yi, *Haishang Molin*, 61–2 for more on Wu Zonglin.
46. For example, Feidange shuhuahui (Feidan Pavilion Painting and Calligraphy Society) was active in the old town of Shanghai during the Tongzhi and Guangxu reigns (1862–1908). It was located at the original site of the Deyuelou fan shop in the Yu Garden. The owner of the Deyuelou was also one of the founders of the society. The members of the society included almost all famous Shanghai painters of the time, such as Gai Qi, Hu Yuan, Yang Borun, Ren Xiong, Ren Xun, Ren Yi, Zhang Xiong, Pu Hua, Wu Changshi, and Wu Jiayou. Yin Baohe, the son of the fan shop owner, who was also a member of the group, turned over the Deyuelou building to the club, which used it as a place to meet and to sell their paintings. It also provided lodgings to painters from other places who wished to temporarily stay in Shanghai. Ren Yi is believed to have stayed there frequently even before he permanently settled in Shanghai in 1868. The inscriptions on many of Ren Yi's paintings indicated that Ren Yi painted at Feidange. See Xu Zhihao, *Zhongguo Meishu Shetuan Manlu*, 7.
47. Wang Xun, *zi* Ziyuan, *hao* Yuanruo, was a native of Changzhou, Jiangsu. He received the *jinshi* degree by passing the national level of the

civil service examination in 1892 and was appointed as *bianxu* (senior editor at the *Hanlin yuan*, or Hanlin Academy). He excelled at calligraphy and seal carving. Then he moved to Shanghai where he lived as a professional artist for 20 years. See Yang Yi, *Haishang Molin*, 87.

48. See Yang Yi, *Haishang Molin*, 72–4 for more on Qian Huian.

49. Ibid.

50. Unpublished correspondence between Wang Yiting and Ha Shaofu, collection of the Shanghai Library.

51. Unpublished correspondence between Zeng Xi and Wang Yiting, collection of the Shanghai Library.

52. It was established in 1922 by Wang Yiting, Chen Shizeng, Huang Binghong, Wu Daiqiu, Gu Qingyao, and others with more than three hundred members. It published a monthly journal *Guocui Yuekan* (National Essence Monthly) in 1929.

53. This society was founded on November 28, 1925, in Shanghai. The director of the society was Cha Yiangu. Its major members included Wang Yiting, Yu Youren, Wu Changshi, Liu Haisu, Huang Binghong, and Qian Huafo. It began publishing the monthly journal *Mohaicao* (Ink Wave) in 1930.

54. It was established in 1929 by Zheng Wuchang, Sun Xueni, Zhang Shanzi, Qian Shoutie, He Tianjian, Li Zhuhan, and others. It published the journal *Mifeng* (Bee) in 1930.

55. With Ye Gongchuo's suggestion, it was formed in 1931 based on Mifeng Huahui and soon became the largest painting society in China. Its journal, *Guohua Yuekan* (Chinese Painting Monthly), was published in 1934 and 1935.

56. It was founded in 1925 by Yang Yi and others. Wang Yiting was the honorary director.

57. For example, the Yiyuan huihua yanjiusuo held an exhibition for charitable purposes at *Ningbo Tongxianghui* (Ningbo Native Place Association) in Shanghai in 1929. The four-day exhibition received donations of painting and calligraphy from more than 60 artists. Participants included not only ink painters, such as Chen Shuren, He Xiangning, Chen Xiaodie, Hu Shi, Zhang Daqian, Zhang Shanzhi, Zheng Wuchang, and Pan Tianshou, but also oil painters Pan Yuliang, Ding Song, Wang Yachen, Wang Jiyuan, Tang Yunyu, and Zhang Yuguang.

58. A photo entitled "The Celebration Party for the Establishment of Sino-Japanese Art Colleagues Association," published in *Liangyou Huabao* (Young Companion), no. 44 (2, 1933), shows Wang Yiting, Ye Gongchuo, and Di Chuqing with the Japanese Consul in Shanghai, Mr. Tanaka, Sawamura Sachio, the Japanese painter Yokoyama Taikan and his wife, and other Japanese.

59. For example, in 1931, Wang Yiting led a group of Shanghai painters, including Qian Shoutie, Wu Hufan, Sun Xueni, Li Qiujun, Zheng Wuchang, Zhang Shanzi, and Zhang Daqian, to participate in the Fourth Sino-Japanese Art Exhibition in Tokyo.

60. Interview with Wu Changye, grandson of Wu Changshi, with the author in August 1994 and October 1995 in Shanghai; see also Zhu Guantian, "Wu Changshi Yu Riben Youren Zhi Jiaoyou" (The Friendship between Wu Changshi and his Japanese Friends), 73–5.

61. *Hu She Yuekan* (Lake Society Monthly), no. 66 (January 1, 1933), 14.

62. Chen Dingshan, "Wang Yiting Wanjie Mijian" (Wang Yiting Upholds his Integrity in his Later Years), 24–6.

63. Photograph of Wang Yiting's funeral from Shanghai Municipal Archive.

64. For an early account of Dong's multifaceted career, see Nelson Wu, "Tung Ch'i-Chang (1555–1636): Apathy in Government and Fervor in Art."

4. Brian G. Martin: Du Yuesheng, the French Concession, and Social Networks

1. On the history of the Green Gang in early twentieth-century China, see Martin, *Shanghai Green Gang*, passim.

2. Martin, *Shanghai Green Gang*, 13, 17; Adshead, *Chinese Salt Administration*, 11–12.

3. On these activities of the Shanghai Green Gang in this early period, see Qian Shengke, *Qing Hong Bang zhi Heimu* (The Inside Story of the Green and Red Gangs).

4. Liu Nianzhi, *Shiye Liu Hongsheng Zhuanlue* (A Biographical Sketch of the Industrialist Liu Hongsheng), 54.

5. On the Mutual Progress Association and Chen Qimei's relations with the Green Gang, see Martin, *Shanghai Green Gang*, 80.

6. British Foreign Office, FO F3570/184/87 (Brenan to Legation, May 29, 1930).

7. On Huang Jinrong's career, see Martin, *Shanghai Green Gang*; and Su Zhiliang and Chen Lifei, *Haishang Xiaoxiong* (An Ambitious Shanghai Worthy).

8. On Lu Liankui, see Zhang Jungu, *Du Yuesheng Zhuan* (The Biography of Du Yuesheng), 1:124; Martin, "Shield of Collaboration," 95; Shanghai Municipal Police, Special Branch Files (August 1938) D8676 (hereafter, SMP); *Shanghai Mainichi*, August 20, 1938; Jiang Hao, "Qing Bang de Yuanliu Ji Qi Yanbian" (The Origins and Evolution of the Green Gang), 61, 66; Pal, *Shanghai Saga*, 186–188.

9. Pal, *Shanghai Saga*, 19; Peters, *Shanghai Policeman*, 113–14. Evidence of connections between gangsters and police can be found in other British colonial jurisdictions in East Asia. In Hong Kong, for example, there existed during the 1960s and early 1970s an accommodation between some members of the Hong Kong police and local Triads, especially the 14K Triad. The key element in this arrangement was the Chinese station sergeants who were either Triad members themselves or closely associated with Triads

and who enrolled their subordinate police constables into Triad cells controlled by the local station sergeants. The British police officers appear to have been largely oblivious to the extent of these connections, and where they were aware of them either turned a blind eye to the system or, in a few cases, cooperated with it. This corrupt compact was not finally addressed by the colonial authorities until the early 1970s with the setting up of the Blair-Kerr Commission of Enquiry that recommended the establishment of the Independent Commission Against Corruption (ICAC) in February 1974. (Source: Interview with Huang Shiu-Cheang, former Chief Investigator, Operations Department, Independent Commission Against Corruption, 26 July 1993.)

10. On the Green Gang's opium operations in the 1920s and its links with the French Concession authorities, see Martin, *Shanghai Green Gang*, 48–78.

11. The Green Gang system was not a single, integrated organization subject to the authority of one paramount leader. Rather, it was a loose structure of interlocking webs of influence and authority, allowing for the coexistence of different and competing groups. In the 30 years from 1919 to 1949, there was a total of 48 prominent Green Gang leaders in Shanghai. All of these leaders exercised real, if unequal, power in their own right, and their relations with one another swung from guarded cooperation to outright conflict. There were, in other words, different centers of power at any given moment, and these shifted and changed over time. The French Concession Green Gang was only one of these centers, though by the 1930s it had become the most powerful. See Martin, *Shanghai Green Gang*, 35.

12. Shanghai Tongshe. *Shanghai Yanjiu Ziliao* (Research Materials on Shanghai), 504. On the history of the Chenghuang Miao, see Tian Ren, "Qingdai Shanghai de Chenghuang Miao" (Shanghai's City God Temple in the Qing Period), 52–63.

13. Martin, *Shanghai Green Gang*, 67–8; Wan Molin, "Shanghai Wenren Huang Jinrong Zhiba" (Shanghai Notable Huang Jinrong, Part Eight), 173–5.

14. Henriot, *Prostitution and Sexuality in Shanghai*, 346.

15. Martin, *Shanghai Green Gang*, 55–6, 153–7; Zhang Jungu, *Du Yuesheng Zhuan*, 2:187.

16. Preface by Lu Jingshi in Zhang Jungu, *Du Yuesheng Zhuan*, 1:4.

17. *The North China Herald*, December 22, 1928, 496.

18. Martin, *Shanghai Green Gang*, 174.

19. On Du's involvement in the anticommunist coup of April 1927 and his relations with the Guomindang authorities, see Martin, *Shanghai Green Gang*, 79–112, 141–4, 163–8.

20. Martin, "Tu Yueh-sheng and Labour Control in Shanghai" 99–137; Martin, *Shanghai Green Gang*, 121–6, 168–72. On the politics of Shanghai labour in general, see Perry, *Shanghai on Strike*, passim.

21. Martin, *Shanghai Green Gang*, 135–41, 178–80; Slack, *Opium, State, and Society*, 104–14.

22. *Heng She Yuekan* (The Perseverance Society Monthly), nos. 10–11, November 22, 1936, 11–12.

23. Martin, *Shanghai Green Gang*, 177; Sha Qianli, *Manhua Jiuguohui* (A Casual Discussion of the National Salvation Association), 68; Zhou Tiandu, ed., *Jiuguohui* (The National Salvation Association), 238–470.

24. Martin, *Shanghai Green Gang*, 177.

25. Ibid., 190–4.

26. SMP (February 6, 1940) D9319.

27. Martin, *Shanghai Green Gang*, 197–9. On the politics of the Guomindang banking coup, see Coble, *Shanghai Capitalists*, 172–92.

28. Martin, *Shanghai Green Gang*, 117–21.

29. Ibid., 192, 201–6.

30. Goodman, *Native Place, City, and Nation*, 278–81; SMP, Special Branch Files (March 27, 1933) D4683; SMP (December 27, 1935) D4683; SMP (October 8, 1938) D4683.

31. Shanghai Shehui Kexue Yuan Zhengzhi FaluYanjiusuo Shehui Wenti Zu (The Social Issues Section of the Institute of Politics and Law of the Shanghai Academy of Social Sciences), ed. *Da Liumang Du Yuesheng* (Big Gangster Du Yuesheng), 55; Guo Lanxin, "Du Yuesheng yu Heng She" (Du Yuesheng and the Perseverance Society), 300. Another source who was a middle-ranking member of the Shanghai Guomindang Party Office, as well as a member of Du's Green Gang group in the 1930s, asserts that the decision to register the Perseverance Society as a social organization was to circumvent the Guomindang Government's formal proscription of secret societies and so gain legal standing. See Jiang Hao, "Hongmen Lishi Chutan" (Introduction to the History of the Triads), 80.

32. Shanghai Shehui Kexue Yuan Zhengzhi FaluYanjiusuo Shehui Wenti Zu, *Da Liumang Du Yuesheng*, 57.

33. Martin, *Shanghai Green Gang*, 181.

34. This formed Article 1 of the original regulations and Article 2 of the revised 1937 regulations. *Jiu Shanghai de Banghui*, Annex 1: *Heng She Shezhang* (Regulations of the Perseverance Society), 367; *Heng She Yuekan*, nos. 16–17, May 1937, 107.

35. Zhang Kechang, "Benshe Di'er Zhu Lishihui Yinianlai Gongzuo Gaikuang" (An Outline of the Work of our Society's Second Executive Committee over the Past Year). *Heng She Yuekan*, nos. 10–11, November 22, 1936, 18–19.

36. Martin, *Shanghai Green Gang*, 181; *Heng She Yuekan*, nos. 16–17, May 1937, 106.

37. Martin, *Shanghai Green Gang*, 181.

38. Zhang Jungu, *Du Yuesheng Zhuan*, 3:61–2.

39. Zhang Kechang, "Benshe Di'er Zhu Lishihui Yinianlai Gongzuo Gaikuang," 19–20; *Heng She Yuekan*, nos. 16–17, May 1937, 126.

40. Guo Lanxin, "Du Yuesheng," 308; *Heng She Yuekan*, passim.

41. Zhang Kechang, "Benshe Di'er Zhu Lishihui Yinianlai Gongzuo Gaikuang," 13–15; *Heng She Yuekan*, nos. 16–17, May 1937, 123–6.

42. Martin, *Shanghai Green Gang*, 181–2; Shanghai Shehui Kexue Yuan Zhengzhi FaluYanjiusuo Shehui Wenti Zu, *Da Liumang Du Yuesheng*, 59–60; *Heng She Yuekan*, nos. 16–17, May 1937, 107–11.

43. Martin, *Shanghai Green Gang*, 182.

44. Zhu Xuefan, "Shanghai Gongren Yundong yu Banghui Ersanshi" (One or Two Things About the Shanghai Labour Movement and the Secret Societies), 6.

45. *Heng She Yuekan*, nos. 10–11, November 22, 1936, 7.

46. Ibid., No.12, December 1936, 43.

47. Martin, *Shanghai Green Gang*, 36; Guo Lanxin, "Du Yuesheng," 301, 319; *Da Liumang Du Yuesheng*, 57; Wang Yangqing and Yinghu Xu, "Shanghai Qinghong Bang Gaishu" (A General Account of the Green and Red Gangs in Shanghai), 64; Fan Shaozeng, "Guanyu Du Yuesheng" (Concerning Du Yuesheng), 221.

48. Martin, "Resistance and Cooperation," 190, 193, and 199.

49. Shanghai Shehui Kexue Yuan Zhengzhi FaluYanjiusuo Shehui Wenti Zu, *Da Liumang Du Yuesheng*, 98.

50. Ibid.

51. Personal communication, August 1987.

52. Martin, *Shanghai Green Gang*, 196–7.

53. On the end of the foreign settlements in Shanghai, see Bickers, "Settlers and Diplomats," 229–56; and Cornet, "The Bumpy End of the French Concession and French Influence in Shanghai, 1937–1946," 257–76.

54. On Du's attempts to regain his prewar ascendancy in Shanghai after 1945, see Martin, "Eating Bitterness."

5. Elizabeth J. Perry: Popular Protest

1. Gould, "Collective Action," 182–196; Porta and Diani, *Social Movements*, ch. 5; Diani and McAdam, eds., *Social Movements and Networks.*

2. Gould, *Insurgent Identities*, 18.

3. Ibid., 18.

4. Wasserman and Faust, *Social Network Analysis.*

5. Unlike Paris, the Shanghai population seems to have become more centrally located in the period under consideration. In 1915, the Shanghai population totaled 2,006,573; by 1927, it had grown to 2,641,220. The biggest proportional increases, however, occurred not in the outlying Chinese districts (which grew from 1,173,653 to 1,503,922) but in the International Settlement (whose population increased from 683,920 to 840,226) and the French Concession (which saw a leap from 149,000 to 297,072). See Zou Yiren, *Jiu Shanghai*, 90.

6. Chen, Joseph, *May Fourth Movement in Shanghai*, 23.

7. Elvin, "Gentry Democracy," 41–3.

8. Ibid., 52–4; Elvin, "Administration of Shanghai."

9. Elvin, "Gentry Democracy," 45, 58; Elvin, "Administration of Shanghai," 255.
10. Ibid.
11. Fewsmith, *Party, State, and Local Elites*, 44.
12. Qiu Qianmu, *Zhongguo Zhengdangshi* (History of Chinese Political Parties), 197–354.
13. Fan Songfu, "Shanghai Banghui Neimu" (Inside Story of the Shanghai Gangs), 150–9; Bergère, *Chinese Bourgeoisie*, 195.
14. Jones, "Ningpo *Pang* and Financial Power"; Perry, *Shanghai on Strike*, 22–4; Goodman, *Native Place, City, and Nation*, 158–69.
15. Goodman, *Native Place, City, and Nation*, 270–1.
16. Ibid., 261.
17. Ibid., 272.
18. Martin, *Shanghai Green Gang*, 81.
19. Thompson, *China's Local Councils*.
20. Bergère, *Chinese Bourgeoisie*, 203–7.
21. Ibid., 213.
22. Ibid., 214; Fewsmith, *Party, State, and Local Elites*, 52.
23. Bergère, *Chinese Bourgeoisie*, 215.
24. Chen, *May Fourth Movement in Shanghai*, 115.
25. Ibid., 111.
26. Goodman, *Native Place, City, and Nation*, 265–6.
27. Perry, *Shanghai on Strike*, 70–1.
28. Wasserstrom, *Student Protests in Twentieth-Century China*, 58.
29. Ibid., 59.
30. Ibid., 60.
31. Ibid., 66. The proclivity of Chinese protesters to organize in decimal units both predated and postdated the May Fourth Movement, and was perhaps an imitation of the *baojia* system of mutual surveillance and responsibility put in place during the late Imperial period.
32. Ibid., 60.
33. Quoted in Chen, *May Fourth Movement in Shanghai*, 145.
34. Ibid., 112.
35. Ibid., 29.
36. Feng Xiaomin, *Zhongguo Gongchandang Zai Shanghai* (The Chinese Communist Party in Shanghai), 6.
37. Chen, *May Fourth Movement in Shanghai*, 188.
38. Ibid., 189–91.
39. Ibid., 195.
40. Perry, *Shanghai on Strike*.
41. Clifford, *Shanghai, 1925*, 23.
42. Tang Chunliang, *Li Lisan Quanzhuan* (Comprehensive Biography of Li Lisan), 75–87.
43. Clifford, *Shanghai, 1925*, 23.

44. Wasserstrom, *Student Protests in Twentieth-Century China*, 119.

45. Jiang Yi, *Zhongguo Gongchandang zai Shanghai* (The Chinese Communist Party in Shanghai), 65.

46. Qiu Qianmu, *Zhongguo Zhengdangshi* (History of Chinese Political Parties), 485.

47. Guo Xuyin, *Guomindang Paixi Douzheng Shi* (History of Factional Struggle in the Guomindang), 2–10; Tatsuo, *Chugoku Kokuminto Saha No Kenkyu* (Study of the Left-wing Guomindang), 71–131.

48. Rigby, *The May 30 Movement*, 31.

49. Ibid., 31.

50. Qiu Qianmu, *Zhongguo Zhengdangshi*, 475.

51. Jiang Yi, *Zhongguo Gongchandang zai Shanghai*, 41.

52. Wang Jiagui and Cao Xiyao, eds., *Shanghai Daxue* (Shanghai University), 1–22; Yeh, *Alienated Academy*, ch. 4.

53. Clifford, *Shanghai, 1925*, xiii.

54. Front organizations were of greater importance to the CCP than to the KMT, since during the 1920s the former could not operate openly in the foreign concessions of Shanghai.

55. Gould, *Insurgent Identities*, 21–2.

56. The Federation raised 17 formal demands, ranging from the withdrawal of warlord troops to the abolition of extraterritoriality. Feng Xiaomin, *Zhongguo Gongchandang Zai Shanghai*, 65–7.

57. Martin, *Shanghai Green Gang*, 81.

58. Perry, *Shanghai on Strike*, 74. See also Frazier, Martin, "Mobilizing a Movement" for a discussion of the pivotal position of factory foremen and forewomen, many of whom were gang members who also developed connections with CCP and KMT labor organizers, in mobilizing their workers during the May Thirtieth period.

59. Tang, *Li Lisan Quanzhuan*, 82–3.

60. Martin, *Shanghai Green Gang*, 81, 86.

61. Rigby, *May 30 Movement*, 36–7.

62. Fewsmith, *Party, State, and Local Elites*, 67.

63. Jones, "The Ningpo *Pang*," 86–7. For a fictionalized account of Yu's life, see Nan Boyong, *Shanghai Daheng Yu Xiaqing* (Shanghai Bigwig, Yu Xiaqing).

64. Clifford, *Spoilt Children of Empire*, 135.

65. Rigby, *May 30 Movement*, 52–3.

66. Martin, *Shanghai Green Gang*, 86; Tang, *Li Lisan Quanzhuan*, 81–3.

67. Xu Xiaoqun, *Chinese Professionals and the Republican State*, 95.

68. Zhou Shangwen and He Shiyou, *Shanghai Gongren Sanci Wuzhuangqiyi Shi* (History of the Shanghai Workers' Three Armed Uprisings), 204–5.

69. In the spring of 1926, the Organization Department of the KMT calculated that party's membership at 250,000, of whom some 70,000 were soldiers. Of the remaining 180,000 members, fully 150,000 were said to be

leftists and Communists, leaving fewer than 30,000 right-wingers and centrists. Qiu Qianmu, *Zhongguo Zhengdangshi*, 485. The overwhelmingly pro-Communist composition of the KMT renders Chiang Kai-shek's stunning anti-Communist coup the following year particularly impressive.

70. On the role of the Comintern, see *Liangong (Bu), Gongchan Guoji yu Zhongguo Guomin Geming Yundong* (The Soviet Communists (Bolsheviks), Comintern, and the Chinese National Revolutionary Movement), vol. 4.

71. Zhou Shangwen and He Shiyou, *Shanghai Gongren*, 77–92.

72. Martin, *Shanghai Green Gang*, 88; Clifford, *Spoilt Children of Empire*, 212–13.

73. Clifford, *Spoilt Children of Empire*, 213.

74. Martin, *Shanghai Green Gang*, 88–9.

75. Fewsmith, *Party, State, and Local Elites*, 115–16.

76. Martin, *Shanghai Green Gang*, 87–93.

77. Shanghai Municipal Archives, ed., *Shanghai Gongren Sanci Wuzhuang Qiyi* (Shanghai Workers' Three Armed Uprisings), 220–21, 262, 273.

78. Fewsmith, *Party, State, and Local Elites*, 117.

79. Bergère, *Chinese Bourgeoisie*, 238.

80. Goldman and Perry, eds., *Changing Meanings of Citizenship*, intro.

81. Xu Xiaoqun, *Chinese Professionals*, 88–89, 91; Shanghai Academy of Social Sciences, ed., *Xinhai Geming Zai Shanghai Shiliao Xuanji* (Compilation of Historical Materials on the 1911 Revolution in Shanghai), 853.

82. Thompson, *China's Local Councils*, 9–10.

83. Wakeman, *History and Will*, 140.

84. Shanghai Academy of Social Sciences, ed., *Wusi Yundong zai Shanghai Shiliao Xuanji* (Compilation of Historical Materials on the May Fourth Movement in Shanghai). The term *guomin* was already in evidence during the 1911 Revolution, but at that time it seems to have been much less popular than *gongmin* as a word for indicating the new political identity of citizenship. See Shanghai Academy of Social Sciences, ed., 1981, *Xinhai Geming Zai Shanghai*, 812, 859, 887.

85. Chen, *May Fourth Movement*, 77.

86. Shanghai Academy of Social Sciences, ed., *Wusa Yundong Shiliao* (Historical Materials on the May Thirtieth Movement), 314, 317.

87. Shanghai Municipal Archives, ed., *Shanghai Gongren*, 4.

88. Perry, *Shanghai on Strike*.

89. Shanghai Municipal Archives, ed., *Shanghai Gongren*, 6–7.

90. See especially Fried, *Fabric of Chinese Society*.

91. Yang, *Gifts, Favors and Banquets*, 1–2.

92. Ibid., 6.

93. Pye, "Factions and the Politics of *Guanxi*," 47.

94. Granovetter, "Strength of Weak Ties."

95. Bian Yanjie, "Bringing Strong Ties Back In," 366–85.

96. Hanser, "Youth Job Searches in Urban China," 142.

6. Parks M. Coble: The National Salvation Movement

1. Coble, *Facing Japan*, 292–94; on Ma Zhanshan, see Mitter, *Manchurian Myth*, passim.

2. Wasserstrom, *Student Protests in Twentieth-Century China*, 173–93; Israel, *Student Nationalism*, 75–78; Tadashi, *Chugoku Kakumei No Chishikijin* (Intellectuals in the Chinese Revolution), 19–21; *Shenghuo* (Life), no. 43 (October 17, 1931), 963–64.

3. Coble, *Facing Japan*, 35.

4. The best treatment of the January 28 Incident is Jordan, *China's Trial by Fire*.

5. Xu Xiaoqun, *Chinese Professionals and the Republican State*, 255; Coble, *Facing Japan*, 46.

6. Coble, *Facing Japan*, 76–89; Yeh, "Progressive Journalism and Shanghai's Petty Urbanites," 186–238; Ishijima, "Konichi Minzoku Toitsu Sensen to Chishiki Jin" (Anti-Japanese United Front and the Intellectuals); *Rekishi Hyoron* (Historical Criticism), 24–26; Mu Xin, ed., *Zou Taofen*, 88–93; Zou Taofen, *Huannan Yusheng Ji* (Record of an Old Age of Troubles and Tribulations), 3; on the assassinations, see Wakeman, *Spymaster*, 175–82.

7. This summary of events is taken from Coble, *Facing Japan*, passim.

8. Israel, *Student Nationalism*, 129; Israel and Klein, *Rebels and Bureaucrats*, passim; Ting, *Government Control of the Press*, 108–9.

9. Coble, *Facing Japan*, 289–91; Yeh, "Progressive Journalism and Petty Urbanites," passim. Readership for these journals was usually much larger than sales because copies were passed around or actually rented out at makeshift book stalls.

10. *Tazhong [Dazhong] Shenghuo* (Life of the Masses), vol. 1, no. 6 (December 21, 1935), 158.

11. Coble, *Facing Japan*, 289–91.

12. Translation in Rossinger, *China's Wartime Politics*, 86–93.

13. Linebarger, *China of Chiang Kai-Shek*, 175–76.

14. For discussions of these groups, see Goodman, *Native Place, City, and Nation*; McElderry, *Shanghai Old-Style Banks*; Linsun Cheng, *Banking in Modern China*; Martin, *Shanghai Green Gang*.

15. Xu Xiaoqun, *Chinese Professionals and the Republican State*, 255–6.

16. Ibid., 255.

17. Goodman, *Native Place, City, and Nation*, 290.

18. Ibid., 288–91.

19. Martin, *Shanghai Green Gang*, 30, 154, 196–7.

20. Yeh, "Progressive Journalism and Shanghai's Petty Urbanites," 193–8; Zou Taofen, *Jingli* (Experiences), 49–50; Zhang Naiqi, "Zhang Naiqi Qishi Zishu (Zhang Naiqi, A Self-Narration at 70)", 39; Rong Zhai, et al., *Jinling Jiumeng* (Dream of Old Nanjing), 58–6; Li Jin, "Cong Suowei 'Qi Junzi' Tandao 'Jiuguo'" (From the Seven Gentlemen Issue, Speaking of National

Salvation), 6; Zhou Tiandu, ed., *Qijunzi Zhuan* (Biography of the Seven Gentlemen), passim.

21. Wakeman, *Spymaster*, 175–7; Ting, *Government Control of the Press*, 96–7; Zheng Renjia, "Hu Yuzhi Qiren Qishi" (Hu Yuzhi, The Person and His Life), 123–4; He Yuwen, "Shen Junru de Sixiang yu Shenghuo" (Shen Junru's Thought and Life), 9–10.

22. "Shanghai Jiuguo Hui Dashiji" (Record of the Major Affairs of the Shanghai National Salvation Association); Dashiji (Record of Important Events), 87.

23. See Nankai Daxue Ma Lie Zhuyi Jiaoyan Shi (Teaching and Research Department of Marxism-Leninism at Nankai University) and Zhonggong Dangshi Jianyan Zu (Teaching and Research Group on the History of the Chinese Communist Party), eds., *Huabei Shibian Ziliao Xuanbian* (Selections of Historical Materials on the North China Incident), 420–53.

24. Israel makes the argument that the demonstrations strengthened Song's hand in *Student Nationalism*, 128. See also Dryburgh, *North China and Japanese Expansion*, 87–9; Qin Dechun, *Qin Dechun Huiyi Lu* (Memoirs of Qin Dechun), 41–6; Sun Dunheng, "Yi-Er-Jiu Yongdong Zai Qinghua" (The December Ninth Movement at Qinghua University); 28–30; Matsumoto Shigeharu, *Shanhai Jidai* (My Shanghai Years), 2:316–7.

25. Material in this section is based on Coble, *Facing Japan*, 334–42; see also Chongqing Shi Dang'an Guan (Chongqing City Archives), eds., "'Qi Junzi' Anjian Dang'an Xuan" (Selection of Archival Materials on the Seven Gentlemen Case); Lishi dang'an (Historical Archives), 3: 69–79.

26. Zhou Tiandu, *Jiuguohui* (The National Salvation Association), 180–3; *Gendaishi Shiryo* (Source Materials on Contemporary History), 13:3–14.

27. Sha Qianli, *Qiren Zhiyu* (Seven People go to Prison), 3–17; Shidai Wenxian She (Contemporary Literary Society), eds., *Jiuguo Wuzui Qijunzi Shijian* (The Seven Gentlemen Who are Innocent and Tried to Save the Nation), passim.

28. Quoted in *China Weekly Review*, December 5, 1936, 22; "He Xiangning Wei Yingqiu Qijunzi zhi Song Ziwen Sun Ke Han" (He Xiangning Writes T. V. Soong and Sun Fo to Aid the Seven Gentlemen); *Lishi dang'an*, no. 3, 1982, 58–9; Zou Taofen, *Jingli*, 169–80.

29. Ch'ien Tuan-sheng, *The Government and Politics of China*, 357; see also Shidai Wenxian She, *Jiuguo Wuzui*, 135–63.

30. Xu Xiaoqun, *Chinese Professionals and the Republican State*, 264–5.

31. Coble, *Facing Japan*, 342.

32. Zhou Tiandu, *Jiuguohui*, 223–4; Yang Mingyuan, "Tao Xingzhi Ershiliu Guoxing" (Tao Xingzhi's Overseas Trip in 1937); *Shanghai Wenshi Ziliao Xuanji* (Selection of Literary and Historical Materials from Shanghai), 91.

33. Zhonggong Shanghai Shi Weidang Shi Ziliao Zhengji Weiyuanhui (Commission to Compile Historical Materials on the History of the Party of Shanghai), eds., *Yi-Er-Jiu Yihou Shanghai Jiuguohui Shiliao Xuanji* (Selection of Historical Materials on the Shanghai National Salvation Association after the December Ninth Movement), 402, 464; Shi Liang, "Wodi Shenghuo

Daolu" (Path of My Life), 31–2; Zheng Renjia, "Hu Yuzhi," 125. For coverage of the trial itself, see Ao Song, "Hongdong Quanguo de Shen Junru Deng Qiren An" (Case of Shen Runru and Others, the Seven, Which Has Caused a Great Uproar in the Entire Nation), part 1, July 1, 1937, 267–81 and part 2, July 16, 1937, 90–5.

34. Wang Yunsheng, column dated July 12, 1937, from Shanghai, published in *Guowen Zhoubao* (National News Weekly), July 19, 1937, 9–11.

35. Zhonggong Shanghai Shi Weidang Shi Ziliao Zhengji Weiyuanhui, ed., *Zhonggong Shanghai Dangshi Dashi Ji* (Record of Major Events of the Shanghai Communist Party), 437, 443–7.

36. Feng Shaoting, "Shanghai Shi Gejie Kangdi Hou Yuanhui Shuping" (Commentary on the Association of Various Shanghai Circles to Aid in Resisting the Enemy), 217–27.

37. *Yinhang Zhoubao* (Bankers' Weekly), vol. 21, no. 30 (August 3, 1937), 6; Jin Gonghui, "Kangzhan Chuqi Quanguo Gejie Juanzi Jiuguo Gaishu" (Summary of Donations for National Salvation from Various Circles in the Nation in the Early Part of the War of Resistance), 66.

38. *Zhonggong Shanghai Dangshi Dashi Ji*, 433–8; Tang Zhenchang et al., eds. *Shanghai Shi* (History of Shanghai), 781–2; Chen Hui, *Taofen Zhuan* (Biography of Zou Taofen), 239–50.

39. Ba Jin, "Suowei Riben Kongjun de Weili" (The So-called Might of the Japanese Air Force), *Fenghuo* (Beacon Fire), 5.

40. Hu Yuzhi, "Zhunbei Xin Xingshi de Daolai" (Preparing for the New Situation Which Has Arrived); *Dikang Sanri Kan* (War of Resistance, Published Every Three Days), 3.

41. The French Concession authorities in Shanghai, subject to the pro-Axis Vichy regime, returned the French Concession to the Wang Jingwei government in Nanjing on July 30, 1943. See Cornet, "The Bumpy End of the French Concession," 257–76.

42. Fu, *Passivity, Resistance, and Collaboration*.

43. Chen Hui, *Taofen Zhuan*, 355–66; Yeh, "Progressive Journalism and Shanghai's Petty Urbanites," 224–5.

7. Sei Jeong Chin: Politics of Trial, the News Media, and Social Networks

1. Ma Changlin, "Xinsheng An" (The New Life Case), 46–8; Jin Chongji, "Du Zhongyuan yu Xinsheng Zhoukan" (Du Zhongyuan and the New Life Weekly), 111–21.

2. Alford, "Of Arsenic and Old Laws," 1180–256.

3. Lean, "Politics of Passion."

4. Ting, *Government Control of the Press*; L. Sophia Wang, "The Independence Press and Authoritarian Regimes"; Fitzgerald, "The Origins of the Illiberal Party Newspaper"; Narramore, "The Nationalists and the Daily Press"; Eastman, *Abortive Revolution*.

5. *Shanghai Shi Nianjian* (Shanghai Yearbook), T60.

6. As MacKinnon has pointed out, the 1930s are an important period for the study of Chinese journalism. See MacKinnon, "Toward a History of the Chinese Press," 7.

7. Concerning press control in Republican China, see Ting, *Government Control of the Press.*

8. *Shanghai Shi Nianjian*, T47. After the establishment of the Nanjing government, the Shanghai News Censorship Committee (*Shanghai xinwen jiancha weiyuan hui*) was established in August 1927. In June 1932, the Shanghai Newspaper and Periodical Censorship Committee (*Shanghai xinwen zazhi shencha weiyuan hui*) was established by the Shanghai municipal government. In March 1933, the Shanghai News Censorship Office (*Shanghai xinwen jianchan suo*) was established. This office was composed of personnel from the Shanghai municipal government, municipal party bureau, and military command (*jingbei siling bu*). It was subordinate to the Central Propaganda Committee (*Zhongyang xuanchuan weiyuan hui*). In August 1934, it became subordinate to the Central Censorship Newspaper Office (*Zhongyang jiancha xinwen chu*).

9. Zhongyang Xuanchuan Bu (Central Propaganda Department), "Ge xinwen jianchasuo" (News Censorship Offices), May 18, 1934, 718–129.

10. Shanghai Tebie Shi Dangbu Gongzuo Baogao (Shanghai Branch of the KMT Work Reports), *Te* 006–1.

11. Pan Gongzhan (1895–1975), a native of Wuxing in Zhejiang province, studied foreign languages at St. John's University and joined the Southern Society (Nan she). In 1918, he was a special contributor for the supplement, *Xuedeng* (The Academic Lantern) of *Shishi Xinbao.* In 1919, he became a special contributor for the supplement, *Juewu (The Awakening),* of Shanghai *Guomin Ribao.* In 1921, he was telegram news editor for Shanghai *Shangbao.* In 1926, he replaced Chen Bulei as an editor-in-chief of *Shangbao* and was transferred to *Shenbao* as an editor. After 1927, he was appointed as a member of the temporary Shanghai branch of the Central Political Council. In July 1927, he became head of the Bureau of Agriculture, Industry, and Commerce, which was reorganized into the Social Bureau in July 1928. In May 1932, he published *Chenbao* and *Xinyebao.* In October 1932, he was appointed head of the Education Bureau.

12. Chen Dezheng (1893–?) was a native of Pujiang, Zhejiang. He studied at Hangzhou Zhijiang University. He was appointed a member of the Central Publicity Bureau and later worked for *Minguo Ribao,* becoming an editor-in-chief for the newspaper in 1926. He also became head of the Propaganda Bureau of the Shanghai KMT Party branch. In 1929, he was appointed head of the Educational Bureau of the Shanghai Municipal Government and organized the Anti-Japanese Committee. In the summer of 1930, he was imprisoned in Nanjing.

13. Lin Bosheng (1902–1946) was a native of Xinyi, Guangdong. In 1920, he entered Linnan University in Guangzhou. In July 1925, he became secre-

tary to Wang Jingwei. In September, he went to the Soviet Union for study. In the winter of 1929, he established Nanhua News Agency in Hong Kong, and in February 1930 he also established *Huanan Ribao.* In January 1932, he established *Zhonghua Ribao.* In 1933, he became a member of the Legislative Yuan.

14. Guo Xiufeng, "Wangwei Shiqi de *Zhonghua Ribao*" (*Zhonghua Ribao* during the Wang Jingwei Period), 149–50.

15. Jia Shumei, ed., *Shanghai Xinwen Zhi* (Shanghai News Gazetteer).

16. Guoshi Guan (Academia Historica), December 1947, 200000000A, 1401/4461.01–01.

17. Guoshi Guan (Academia Historica), 1935–7, 200000000A, 0543/2700.01–02.

18. Henriot, *Shanghai, 1927–1937,* 102.

19. Martin, *Shanghai Green Gang,* 151; the Shanghai Citizen's Maintenance Association (*Shanghai Shimin Difang Weichihui*), which was organized on January 31, 1932, was reorganized into the Shanghai Civic Association.

20. Gerth, *China Made.*

21. Xu Xiaoqun, *Chinese Professionals and the Republican State.*

22. Martin, *Shanghai Green Gang,* 172–3; concerning Shi Liangcai's assassination, see Wakeman, *Spymaster,* 179–80.

23. *China Weekly Review,* July 13, 1935, 214.

24. Coble, *Facing Japan,* 204.

25. Du Zhongyuan was a native of Huaide County, then located in Fengtian (present-day Jilin). He was from a poor family, but local elites helped to pay for his education at the Fengtian Provincial Teacher Training College, where he studied science and foreign languages, including English and Japanese. In 1915, he returned to Huaide, where he became an English teacher. At that time, he developed an interest in the porcelain industry. Noting that the Japanese dominated the industry in the Northeast, he decided to start a Chinese firm to break into the market. To train for this enterprise, he attended the Tokyo Industrial College from 1917 to 1923, after which he returned to the Northeast and set up a porcelain manufacturing firm in Shenyang with the help of loans from friends.

26. *Xinsheng Zhoukan* (New Life Weekly), November 24, 1934, 867.

27. Ibid., March 1934 and April 14, 1934.

28. Bi Yuncheng, "Taofen He Shenghuo Shudian" (Zou Taofen and the Shenghuo Bookstore), 275.

29. They wanted to name the journal *Xin Shenghuo* (New Life) as a sequel to *Shenghuo* (Life Weekly), but they named it *Xinsheng* instead because they did not want it to sound too related to the New Life Movement that was going on at the time. See Bi Yuncheng, "Taofen He Shenghuo Shudian," 275.

30. Ai Hansong was born in 1905. He graduated from Fudan University in political science. He began working for Zou Taofen in 1931. See Liu Hongyuan, "Ai Hansong Zhuan" (Biography of Ai Hansong), 199–200.

31. Bi Yuncheng, "Taofen He Shenghuo Shudian," 275.

32. Du Zhongyuan's relationship with Zhang Xueliang goes back to Du's activities in Manchuria. Du Zhongyuan had originally opened a porcelain manufacturing firm in Shenyang, and later the Manchurian warlord Zhang Xueliang authorized a loan of 120,000 yuan from the Border Industrial Bank to support the factory. Du was closely associated with Zhang Xueliang and later Du even played a role in the Xi'an incident. The name of the firm was *Zhaoxin Yaoye Gongsi* (Zhaoxin Ceramic Company). Du became a prominent local figure while in Manchuria and was elected deputy chairman of the Liaoning Chamber of Commerce in 1927 and chairman in 1929. See Shenyang Shimin Jian (Shenyang Democratic Nation-building Association) and Shenyang Gongshang Lian (Shenyang Federation of Industry and Commerce), "Du Zhongyuan Zhuanlue" (Brief Biography of Du Zhongyuan), 305; Mitter, *Manchurian Myth*, 27.

33. *Shanghai Difang Xiehui Yuebao* (Shanghai Civic Association Monthly), vol. 2, August 1932, 10; vol. 4, October 1932, 18.

34. *Zhonghua Guohuo Chanxiao Hezuo Xiehui Meizhou Huibao* (Chinese National Products Production and Marketing Cooperative Association Weekly Report), Vol. 1–5, July 5, 1933, 21–23; *Shanghai Difang Xiehui Yuebao*, December 1933.

35. Wang Huaiyi, Gao Chongmin, Yan Baohang, Chen Xianzhou, and other northeastern nationalist activists announced the formation of the NNSS on September 16, 1931. During the 1920s, Du became friends with Yan Baohang, Lu Guangji, and the other nationalists who formed a circle around Zhang Xueliang. See Mitter, *Manchurian Myth*, 33, 133.

36. Li Ying, "Du Zhongyuan Shilue" (Brief Biography of Du Zhongyuan), 129.

37. Shi Kuiji, "Du Zhongyuan Yu Jing Dezhen" (Du Zhongyuan and Jing Dezhen), 28.

38. *Zhonghua Guohuo Chanxiao Hezuo Xiehui Meizhou Huibao*, vol. 1–6, July 12, 1933.

39. *Shanghai Difang Xiehui Yuebao*, October 1932, 16–7.

40. Martin, *Shanghai Green Gang*, 177–8.

41. Du Yi, "Wo Bi Kaixuan Gui: Ji Baba Du Zhongyuan Zai 'Ba Yisan Kangzhan Shi de Huodong" ('I Will Definitely Return in Triumph': Commemorating Father, Du Zhouyuan's Resistance Activities in the Marco Polo Incident), 98.

42. *Shanghai Shi Nianjian*, T51.

43. *China Weekly Review*, July 6, 1935, 205.

44. Wang Huabin and Wang Yanzi, *Huang Yanpei*, 133–4.

45. Martin, *Shanghai Green Gang*, 158–89.

46. *Xinsheng Zhoukan*, May 4, 1935.

47. Matsumoto Shigeharu, *Shanhai Jidai* (My Shanghai Years), 22–3.

48. In response to demands of the Japanese consular-general, Wu Tiecheng sent an apologetic letter on the 25th and promised the following: (1) suspension of the publication of the *New Life Weekly*, (2) legal action

against the publisher of the *New Life Weekly*, (3) confiscation of the assets of the *New Life Weekly*, and (4) prohibition of the article's re-publication in the Chinese press.

49. *Shen Bao*, July 1, 1935; "Local Japanese Agitated: Blaming Kuomintang for New Life Magazine Case," *North China Daily News*, July 3, 1935; Yan Changyan, "Xinsheng Zhoukan Shijian" (The New Life Weekly Incident), *Shanghai Wenshi Ziliao*, 87.

50. Coble, *Facing Japan*, 219; *Shi Bao*, July 8, 1935; *Shishi Xinbao*, July 10, 1935; *Shenbao Nianjian (Shen Bao Yearbook)*, 365.

51. This form of censorship did not come about until April 1934. With the proclamation of "The Method for Censoring Books and Magazines," the KMT Central Propaganda Committee's Shanghai Books and Magazine Censorship Committee (*Shanghai tushu zazhi shencha weiyuan hui*) was established in Shanghai in April 1934. The members of the committee were mostly members of the CC Clique in the Shanghai party branch, including Pan Gongzhan and Wu Kaixian. The committee also included the following individuals: (i) Fang Zhi, the head (*zhuren*) of the committee (Fang Zhi was deputy chief of the Central Propaganda Department of the KMT in 1933); (ii) Jiang Huaisu, vice-head of the committee (*fu zhuren*), also secretary-general of the Shanghai branch of the KMT; (iii) Pan Gongzhan, Li Songfeng, and Fang Zhi, standing committee members (*changwu weiyuan*); (iv) Pan Gongzhan, Li Songfeng, Fang Zhi, Wu Kaixian, Ding Mocun, Sun Dezhong, Hu Tiance, and Xiang Deyan, committee members (*weiyuan*). See Ma Guangren, *Shanghai Xinwen Shi* (History of News in Shanghai), 719.

52. Second Branch of the Jiangsu High Court, Court Records on the *New Life Weekly* Case, Shanghai Municipal Archives, Q181-0-570, 4–14.

53. Sima Zu, "Xinsheng Shijian Gaishu" (General Account of the New Life Case), 4: 147–8.

54. Ai Hansong, a graduate of the political science department of Fudan University, had written for *Shenghuo Zhoukan* and *Xinsheng Zhoukan*. See Coble, *Facing Japan*, 219.

55. Sima Zu, "Xinsheng Shijian Gaishu," 148–9.

56. Second Branch of the Jiangsu High Court, Court Records of the *New Life Weekly* Case, Shanghai Municipal Archives, Q 181-0-570, 1–2.

57. Second Branch of the Jiangsu High Court, Court Records of the *New Life Weekly* Case, Shanghai Municipal Archives, Q181-1-6, 16–19.

58. The Minister of Judicial Administration was Wang Yongbin (1881–1944), who was appointed with the support of the CC Clique. See Jin Peiren, "Luetan Xie Kuansheng Yu Guomindang Sifajie" (Brief Discussion on Xie Kuansheng and the Guomindang Judiciary), 70–1.

59. Shanghai Municipal Archives, Q181-1-6: 16–19.

60. Ibid.

61. On July 2, Du Zhongyuan was summoned before the Second Branch of the Jiangsu High Court in Shanghai for the preliminary inquiry by the procurator. Du testified that he had been in Jiangxi for several weeks and

claimed that the article in question was published while he was away from Shanghai (Shanghai Municipal Archives, Q181-0-570, 15). The procurator said that he would have the publisher indicted and ordered him to furnish 500 *yuan* in cash as security in addition to a guarantee that he would appear before the Court whenever required. See *North China Daily News*, July 2, 1935.

62. Ting, *Government Control of the Press*, 107.

63. *China Weekly Review*, July 13, 1935, 215.

64. Shanghai Municipal Archives, Q181-0-570, 12–15.

65. Shanghai Municipal Archives, Q181-0-570, 27.

66. Ibid.; *North China Daily News*, July 10, 1935.

67. *Daguang Bao*, July 12, 1935. *Daguang Bao* was founded by Zhang Zhuping and Jiang Guangtang on October 1, 1934. See "Jizhe Zuotan" (Journalists' Symposium), *Damei Wanbao*, August 1, 1934.

68. Mu Ouchu (1876–1943) was a native of Pudong, Shanghai. In 1909 he went abroad to study agriculture at the University of Wisconsin and received his doctoral degree in 1914. After returning to China, he established the Housheng cotton mill in Shanghai in 1916. In 1921, he established the Chinese Cotton Goods Exchange and was elected president of the board of directors. Mu Ouchu was president of the Chinese Cotton Goods Exchange (*Shanghai huashang shabu jiaoyisuo*), and a member of the Shanghai Civic Association. Du Zhongyuan had personal connections with Mu Ouchu, as Du Zhongyuan joined the Shanghai Civic Association in August 1932. As discussed above, Du Zhongyuan had been deeply involved with Shanghai local notables since 1931, when he arrived in Shanghai after the Manchurian Incident. Furthermore, Mu Ouchu had strong personal connections with Zou Taofen and Bi Yuncheng, as Mu Ouchu was one of the founders of the Chinese Society of Vocational Education (*Zhonghua zhiye jiaoyu she*) in 1913. The main organ of this society was *Shenghuo Zhoukan*, published by Zou Taofen. Mu Ouchu was also intimately connected with Shenghuo shudian. Mu Ouchu was an influential local elite and was appointed Standing Vice Minister of Industry in 1929. Mu thus had a connection with the Nationalist government.

69. Mu Ouchu had a good strategy for publicity, since journalists were usually stationed at the Shanghai Chamber of Commerce to gather news sources. Thus, a letter sent to the Shanghai Chamber of Commerce was more likely to be published.

70. Gao Jun, "Lun Mu Ouchu de Shiye Zhenxing Sixiang" (Discussion on Mu Ouchu's Thoughts on Industrial Development).

71. According to Article 22 of the Organic Law of Court, criminal cases in which the ruling of the Higher Court was disputed after the first trial came under the jurisdiction of the Supreme Court. However, Article 36 of the Criminal Procedure Law stipulated that appeals could be made to the Supreme Court if the accused was not content with the judgment by a

Higher Court and that procedure in the third trial was open to an appeal against the judgment by a High Court in the first trial. Article 368 of the same law ruled that after judgment was passed in the first trial by a High Court on a case involving any of the offenses punishable under Article 61 of the new Criminal Code appeal to a third court was not permitted. See *North China Daily News*, July 20, 1935.

72. *Shen Bao, Xinwen Bao*, and *Min Bao*, July 21, 1935.

73. Zhao Chen (1899–1969) was a native of Dongyang, Zhejiang. He went to Japan to study in the Department of Law at Meiji University. He came back in 1924 and became a professor at Anhui University, Shanghai Fudan University, Fazheng University, Fake University, and Zhengzhi University. In 1925, he joined the KMT. In 1928, he started his practice as a lawyer in Shanghai. In January 1933, he was appointed a member of the Legislative Yuan.

74. *Damei Wanbao*, July 21, 1935.

75. *Dagong Bao*, July 27, 1935; *Damei Wanbao*, July 25, 1935.

76. *Shishi Xinbao*, July 25, 1935.

77. Zheng Luosheng (1870–1939) was a native of Tong'an, Fujian. He joined the Zhongguo Tongmenghui (Revolutionary Alliance) in 1907. In the 1920s, he was in charge of raising funds for the Northern Expedition. In February 1931, he was appointed a member of the Control Yuan and was a member of the Committee for Affairs of Overseas Chinese.

78. Zuigao fayuan (The Supreme Court), "Letter from Jiancha Yuan (the Control Yuan) to Zuigao Fayuan (The Supreme Court)," 16-7078; Yu Youren (1879–1964) was a native of Sanyuan, Shaanxi. In 1903, he became a *juren* (provincial degree holder), but he was punished when he criticized the Qing government. The following year, he went to Shanghai to study at Zhendan University and helped Ma Xiangbo establish Fudan Gongxue (Fudan Public School). In 1906, he went to Japan and joined the Zhongguo Tongmenghui. In 1907, after he returned to China, he published *Shenzhou Ribao* and became its president. In 1909, he continued to publish *Minhu Ribao, Minyu Ribao*, and *Minli Bao*. After 1912, he was appointed vice-minister of the Ministry of Communication. In 1922, he went to Shanghai and helped Ye Chucang to establish Shanghai University. In October, he became president of Shanghai University. In 1926, he was elected a member of the Second Central Executive Committee of the KMT. In June 1931, he was appointed president of the Control Yuan.

79. Shanghai Municipal Archives, Q180-0-570, 3: 15–17.

80. Shanghai Municipal Archives, Shanghai Police Intelligence Report, U1-1-1221, July 30, 1935.

81. Shanghai Bar Association, *New Life Weekly* Case File, Shanghai Municipal Archives, Q190-1-535.

82. Shanghai Municipal Archives, Shanghai Police Intelligence Report, U1-1-1221, July 29, 1935.

83. Du Zhongyuan, *Yuzhong Zagan*, 5. This article was published in *Dazhong Shenghuo* (The Mass Life) while he was in jail.

84. Lu Guangji, "Huiyi Du Zhongyuan Tongzhi" (Recollection of the Comrade Du Zhongyuan), 15.

85. *China Weekly Review*, August 31, 1935, 460.

86. Coble, "Chiang Kai-shek and the Anti-Japanese Movement," 301.

87. *China Weekly Review* was first published by Thomas Millard in 1917.

88. He was also Shanghai correspondent for the *Chicago Tribune* and *Manchester Guardian*.

89. Ma Guangren, *Shanghai Xinwen Shi*, 788.

90. *China Weekly Review*, August 31, 1935, 460.

91. Ibid., August 24, 1935.

92. Ibid., October 19, 1935, 217.

93. Ibid.

94. Lu Xun, "Qiejieting Zawen Erji" (Miscellaneous Essay of Qiejie Studio, Part 2), 460–463.

95. Wales, "Notes on the Chinese Student Movement," 14.

96. *Dagong Bao*, July 16, 1935.

97. *Dagong bao*, July 15, 1935; *China Weekly Review*, September 7, 1935.

8. Bryna Goodman: What Is In a Network?

1. *Huiguan* (meeting hall) and *gongsuo* (public office, or public place) were the names of formal associations of sojourning fellow provincials that emerged in late imperial cities and persisted in urban society throughout the Republican era. As early as the late Ming, *huiguan* were established in Beijing by sojourning scholars and officials. Outside of the capital, sojourner associations were more commonly formed by merchants. Although some scholars have attempted to distinguish *huiguan*, as sojourner associations, from *gongsuo*, as trade associations, in Shanghai the two terms were used interchangeably, because of the overlap of trade organization with native place ties. The term *tongxianghui* emerged in the early Republican period to denote a more modern-style sojourner association that rejected the oligarchic and ritualistic practices of the older *huiguan* and *gongsuo* and emphasized instead new republican styles of governance. See Goodman, *Native Place, City, and Nation*, 38–9, 230.

2. Ibid. Indeed, it was not necessarily the case that being from one ancestral place presented an absolute obstacle to membership in another native place network.

3. Ibid., 13–14.

4. See Fogel and Zarrow, *Imagining the People*.

5. Goodman, "Being Public," 45–88.

6. On this "small circle of notables," see Henriot, *Shanghai*, 52–6.

7. Goodman, *Native Place, City, and Nation*, ch. 7.

8. Rankin, *Elite Activism and Political Transformation*; Rowe, *Hankow*; Liang Qizi (Angela Leung), *Shishan Yu Jiaohua* (Charity and Moral Transformation); Goodman, *Native Place, City, and Nation*, ch. 4.

9. On the development of *tongxianghui* as modern forms of native place organization, see Goodman, *Native Place, City, and Nation*, 217–31.

10. "Chaozhou Huiguan Yi'an Bu" (Meeting Record of the Chaozhou Huiguan); Ningbo Tongxianghui, *Ningbo Lü Hu Tongxianghui Yuebao* (Ningbo Sojourners' Association Monthly); Goodman, *Native Place, City, and Nation*, 244–7.

11. Hokari, "Kindai Shanhai Ni Okeru Itai Shori Mondai to Shimei Kōsho—dōkyō Girudo to Chūgoku no Toshika" (The Management of Human Remains in Modern Shanghai and the Siming Gongsuo—Native-Place Guilds and China's Urbanization); Goodman, *Native Place, City, and Nation*, 252–3; Hu She, *Hu She Di Shisan Jie Sheyuan Da Hui Tekan* (Special Issue for the Thirteenth Annual Membership Meeting of the Hu She), 1: 68–72; *Shanghai Zhinan* (Guide to Shanghai) and *Shanghai Shangye Minglu* (Shanghai Commercial Directory). These figures probably underestimate the actual numbers, omitting smaller concerns.

12. Liang Qizi, *Shishan Yu Jiaohua*.

13. Wu Mianbo, "Guang-Zhao Gongsuo Fengchao Shimo Ji" (Record of the Guang-Zhao Gongsuo Controversy), 126. I am grateful to Song Zuanyou for providing me with a copy of this document. See Goodman, "Being Public."

14. Wu Mianbo, 112–13; *Minguo Ribao*, December 16, 1918.

15. By 1927, for example, the Ningbo Tongxianghui managed seven elementary and middle schools and offered adult lecture series.

16. Goodman, "Democratic Calisthenics," 71.

17. Ningbo Tongxianghui, *Ningbo Lü Hu Tongxianghui Yuebao*; Chen Lizhi, *Hu She Cangsang Lu* (Vicissitudes of the Hu She); Shaoxing Qixian Lü Hu Tongxianghui (Association of Sojourners from the Seven Counties of Shandong), *Shaoxing Qixian Lü Hu Tongxianghui Ge Gong Zhangcheng* (Regulations of the Association of Sojourners from the Seven Counties of Shaoxing).

18. Such new developments do not reflect the diminishing salience of native place ties so much as they reflect developing ideals of the public that facilitated the linkage or identification of the *gong* of the native place community with the new *gong* of the state and a citizenry awakened to national consciousness. Goodman, "Locality as Microcosm of the State?"

19. Chen Lizhi, *Hu She Cangsang Lu*; Hu She, *Hu She Di Shisan Jie*.

20. Kōhama, "Hoshōin to Shōkaijō No Tsunagu Kyūsai" (Guarantors and Introduction Connections in Charity), 197–218.

21. Kōhama "Hoshōin to Shōkaijō," 205–7, notes that whereas in the majority of cases, individual names are listed under "name of guarantor," organization names were often listed under "address of guarantor," conveying the impression that many of the individuals listed were indeed

representatives of associations. Similarly, guarantors listed as individuals often wrote on association stationery.

22. Kōhama, "Hoshōin to Shōkaijō," 206–8.

23. On the CSRWC, see Henriot, *Prostitution and Sexuality in Shanghai*, 194–8, 346–51, and Iwama, "Yūkai to Kyūsai no Toshikan Nettowāku: Nijū Sēki Zenhan Shanhai no Shiten Kara" (Urban Kidnapping and Rescue Networks from the Perspective of 1920s Shanghai), 241–3.

24. Wang Yiting, for example, was general manager for the Riching Steamboat Company and Yu Xiaqing operated the Sanbei Shipping Company. Fu Xiaoan (from Zhenhai, another prominent member of the Shanghai Ningbo native place association) was accountant for the China Merchants' Steam Shipping Company. Iwama suggests that these men were able to mobilize native place networks that organized the steamboat staffs, which were commonly recruited along native place lines. Iwama, "Yūkai to Kyūsai," 241–3.

25. Hu She, *Hu She Di Shisan Jie*.

26. Ibid.; *Ningbo Lü Hu Tongxianghui Dibajie Zhengqiu Huiyuan Dahui Jiniankan* (Commemorative Publication of the Eighth Membership Drive of the Ningbo Tongxianghui); *Chaozhou Huiguan Yishibu* (Meeting notes of the Chaozhou Huiguan); *Pudong Tongxianghui Nianbao* (Yearly Report of the Pudong Tongxianghui); *Jiangning Liuxian Lü Hu Tongxianghui Huikan* (Journal of the Association of Sojourners from Six Counties of Jiangning in Shanghai).

27. Henriot, *Prostitution and Sexuality in Shanghai*, 349.

28. Iwama, "Yūkai to Kyūsai, 246.

29. See, for example, *Hu She Di Shisan Jie*, 1: 64.

30. *Chaozhou Huiguan Yishibu*, August 1914 and March 1917; Goodman, *Native Place, City, and Nation*, 255. Although the CSRWC established branches in numerous northern cities, cities with sojourning Jiangsu and Zhejiang communities, it did not establish a branch in Guangdong. Iwama recounts unsuccessful initiatives to create branches and connections in Hong Kong and Guangzhou. Iwama, "Yūkai to Kyūsai," 244.

31. *Pudong Tongxianghui Nianbao*. The Pudong Tongxianghui also temporarily housed rescued children. It may have occasionally assisted in the recovery of children of other native place origins because of the Pudong association's particular efficacy with local authorities, given the powerful social influence of the Pudong Tongxianghui leader, Du Yuesheng. Du became a member of the CSRWC board of directors in 1935. Henriot, *Prostitution and Sexuality in Shanghai*, 346.

32. To a more limited extent, this was also the case in the late Qing, when native place association leaders were commonly major figures in a range of commercial, political, and philanthropic causes, emerging together as leaders of new urban quasi-representative associations: the Shanghai General Chamber of Commerce and the consultative guilds assembled by the Shanghai Municipal Council. See Goodman, *Native Place, City, and Nation*, ch. 4.

33. Martin, *Shanghai Green Gang*, 159–63.

34. Police Daily Report, May 29, 1919, Shanghai Municipal Archives 1-1-1122; Shanghai Municipal Police Files, July 23, 1919, IO-2882; Shanghai Shehui Kexueyuan Lishi Yanjiusuo (Institute of History, Shanghai Academy of Social Sciences), ed., *Wusi Yundong Zai Shanghai Shiliao Xuanji* (Compilation of Historical Materials Concerning the May Fourth Movement in Shanghai), 300, 304, 654.

35. Barely known today, Tang appeared so frequently in the news in the years 1919–1922 that the "mosquito" paper, *Jingbao* (Crystal), listed him in its chart of Shanghai celebrities, which included the most well-known businessmen, cultural figures, social leaders, military men, and courtesans of the city. "Shanghai Zuijin Yi Bai Ming Ren Biao" (Chart of One Hundred Current Famous People in Shanghai), *Jingbao*, March 30, 1922.

36. Goodman, "New Woman Commits Suicide."

37. *Minguo Ribao*, September 15, 1922, September 16, 1922, September 17, 1922; *Shenbao*, September 15, 1922, September 16, 1922; *Xinwenbao*, September 18, 1922.

38. *Minguo Ribao*, September 17, 1922.

39. See, for example, *Minguo Ribao*, "Ge Tuanti Dui Tang An Zhi Ji'ang" (The Indignation of Each Organization in Regard to Tang's Case), December 11, 1922; *Shenbao*, "Ge Tuan Daibiao Wei Xi An Ye Tingzhang Ji" (Each Association Representative Visits the Judge in Regard to the Xi Case), December 12, 1922.

40. *Minguo Ribao*, December 11, 1922.

41. The Chamber of Commerce directors held several meetings to discuss the case, during which Feng Shaoshan made a passionate appeal for Chamber intervention on Tang's behalf. Other directors were more reticent, noting that Dongting bankers were also important in the Chamber and adamantly opposed Tang. (Tang's secretary Xi Shangzhen was also from the Dongting area.) Chamber of Commerce minutes for December 1922, Gong-Shang-Lian Archives.

42. *Minguo Ribao*, December 12, 1922. These included the abolition of the procuratorial system (which combined investigation, prosecution, and administration of the law); the establishment of a jury system; the creation of a separate Commercial Affairs Court; the supervision of lower courts by higher courts; and the establishment of a system of compensation for victims of improper arrest and detention. These proposals were consistent with the contemporaneous national conference on Chinese judicial process and a contemporary movement to abolish the procuratorial system. Chen Zemin, "Fei Jiancha Zhidu Zhi Yundong" (Movement to Abolish the Procuratorial System).

43. *Shishi Xinbao* (China Times), "Si Yi Bu Shi Gonglun" (Private Friendships Are Not Public Opinion), "Qingguang" suppl., December 15, 1922.

44. Goodman, *Native Place, City, and Nation*, ch. 3.

45. Gu Bingquan and Zhang Yingen, "Pudong Tongxianghui Ji Qi Dui Pudong de Xianqi Kaifa" (The Pudong Tongxianghui and Early Development of Pudong).

46. Pudong Tongxianghui, *Pudong Lü Hu Tongxianghui Zhengqiu Huiyuan Ce* (Record of the Pudong Tongxianghui Membership Drive).

47. *Shenbao*, September 2, 1931.

48. Pudong Tongxianghui, *Pudong Tongxianghui Huisuo Luocheng Jinian Tekan* (Special Commemorative Publication for the Inauguration of the Pudong Tongxianghui Building).

49. Ibid.

50. In the May Fourth era, the associational politics of the time clearly emphasized the strength of the group and the public nature of groups. Native place association publications featured groups of leaders rather than a preeminent leader; public statements of native place and other associations emphasized the names of the group rather than the names of the leaders. See, for example, the many notices preserved in Shanghai Shehui Kexueyuan Lishi Yanjiusuo, ed., *Wusi Yundong Zai Shanghai*; Shanghai Shehui Kexueyuan, Lishi Yanjiusuo, ed., *Wusa Yundong Shiliao* (Historical Materials on the May Thirtieth Movement).

51. Pudong Tongxianghui, *Pudong Tongxianghui Zhenmi Handu Jiyao* (Collection of Correspondence Concerning Pudong Tongxianghui Rice Collection).

52. Gu Bingquan and Zhang Yingen, "Pudong Tongxianghui," 81.

53. Shanghai Municipal Police Files, October 20, 1937, D-8133.

54. Goodman, "Creating Civic Ground," 164–77.

55. Fang Yinchao, "Guangdong Lü Hu Tongxianghui Gongzuo Zhuiji" (Remembrance of Guangdong Sojourners' Association Work in Shanghai); Guangdong Tongxianghui, *Guangdong Lü Hu Tongxianghui Jiuji Nanmin Weiyuanhui Baogaoshu* (Report of the Refugee Relief Committee of the Guangdong Tongxianghui); Ningbo Tongxianghui, *Ningbo Lü Hu Tongxianghui Jiuji Beinan Tongxiang Zhengxinlu* (Record-book of Ningbo Tongxianghui aid to Fellow-provincial Refugees), 1–36. For an overview of the wartime refugee work, see Feng Yi, "Le Problème des Réfugiés à Shanghai" and Goodman, *Native Place, City and Nation*, 287–91.

56. For a summary of the vital role of native place associations in the May Fourth and May Thirtieth Movements, see Goodman, *Native Place, City, and Nation*, ch. 6. Similarly, native place associations played important supporting roles in the National Salvation Movement. See, for example, Chaozhou Tongxianghui, *Chaozhou Lü Hu Tongxianghui Tekan* (Special Publication of the Chaozhou Sojourners' Association in Shanghai); *Quan Zhe Gonghui Huiwu Baogao* (Report of the Work of the All-Zhejiang Association). The Pudong Tongxianghui was especially notable in this regard, in 1937 housing eight anti-Japanese associations on its premises. See Shanghai Municipal Police Report, November 15, 1937, D-8141.

57. Goodman, *Native Place, City, and Nation*, 314.

58. Henriot, *Shanghai*, 107–10.

59. This was the Yueqiao Shangye Lianhehui (Guangdong Sojourners Commercial Federation).

9. Nara Dillon: The Politics of Philanthropy

1. In this paper I use the term *philanthropist* to refer to all of the people who donated to charity, regardless of their motives. The term *refugee* is used to translate the Chinese word *nanmin*. The Chinese term refers to homeless people as well as to the victims of war or natural disasters. I want to thank Jean Oi, Patricia Stranahan, Edward Rhodes, Robert Culp, Jeffrey Wasserstrom, and one anonymous reviewer for their comments and suggestions for revisions.

2. Elvin, "The Administration of Shanghai, 1905–1914."

3. Henriot, *Shanghai, 1927–1937*, 222–5.

4. For the clearest statement of this argument, see Swaan, *In the Care of the State*. Many other welfare state theorists build this assumption into their models. For a few examples, see Flora and Heidenheimer, eds. *Development of Welfare States in Europe and America*; Esping-Andersen, *Three Worlds of Welfare Capitalism*; Hicks, *Social Democracy and Welfare Capitalism*.

5. On state-building during the Nanjing decade, see Bedeski, *State-building in Modern China*; Henriot, *Shanghai*; Kirby, "Engineering China"; Wakeman, *Policing Shanghai*; Xu, *Chinese Professionals*. For state-building during and after the war, see Frazier, *Making of the Chinese Industrial Workplace*; Kirby, "Chinese War Economy"; Perry, *Patrolling the Revolution*; Strauss, *Strong Institutions in Weak Polities*.

6. Shanghai Tebie Shi, *Linshi Bihansuo Baogao Ce* (Report on Temporary Cold Weather Shelters).

7. Henriot, *Shanghai*, 89.

8. Ibid., *Shanghai*, 88; Wakeman, *Policing Shanghai*, 190–1; Jordan, *China's Trial by Fire*, 20–1.

9. Xu Shiying, *Shanghai Zhanqu Nanmin Linshi Jiuji Hui Gongzuo Baogao Shu* (Work Report of the Shanghai War Zone Refugee Provisional Relief Association), 79–143; Jordan, *China's Trial by Fire*, 70.

10. Xu Shiying, *Shanghai Zhanqu Nanmin Linshi Jiuji Hui*, 96–7.

11. Henriot, *Shanghai*, 60.

12. Xu Shiying, *Shanghai Zhanqu Nanmin Linshi Jiuji Hui*, 100.

13. Jordan, *China's Trial by Fire*, 118.

14. Wakeman, *Policing Shanghai*, 191; Xu Shiying, *Shanghai Zhanqu Nanmin Linshi Jiuji Hui*, 69; Jordan, *China's Trial by Fire*, 117.

15. Xu Shiying, *Shanghai Zhanqu Nanmin Linshi Jiuji Hui*, 1; Xiong Yuezhi et al. *Lao Shanghai* (Old Shanghai); Henriot, *Shanghai*, passim.

16. Wang Renzi, "Wang Yiting"; Elvin, "Administration of Shanghai," 250; Xu Wancheng, *Shanghai Cishan Jiguan Gaikuang* (Survey of Shanghai's Charitable Organizations); Lu Lishi, ed., *Shanghai Tebie Shi Jiuji Shiye Gaikuang* (Survey of the Shanghai Municipal Relief Services); Kōhama, "The

Urban Society and Social Welfare in Republican China"; Shanghai Municipal Archives (SMA) File #Q114-1-1.

17. Xiong Yuezhi et al., *Lao Shanghai*, 324–325; SMA Q115-16-4.

18. This group included Huang Hanzhi, Qu Wenliu, Guang Jiongzhi, and Wen Lanting. Like Wang Yiting, all of these men were active in a number of other charities as well. Gao Zhennong, "Shanghai Fojiao Gaikuang" (Survey of Buddhism in Shanghai), 12–13; Goodman, *Native Place*, 302; Xiong Yuezhi, et al., *Lao Shanghai*, 8.

19. Xiong Yuezhi et al., *Lao Shanghai*, 8, 166. Henriot, *Shanghai*, 53.

20. Xu Shiying, *Shanghai Zhanqu Nanmin Linshi Jiuji Hui*, 1–3; Martin, *Shanghai Green Gang*, 99–112, 164–5.

21. Xiong Yuezhi et al., *Lao Shanghai*, 172–3.

22. Henriot, *Shanghai*, 41.

23. Xu Shiying, *Shanghai Zhanqu Nanmin Linshi Jiuji Hui.*

24. Liu Yanru, "Kangzhan Chuqi Shanghai Nanmin Gongzuo" (Refugee Work in Shanghai at the Beginning of the War of Resistance), 47; Stranahan, "Radicalization of Refugees," 169.

25. Zhao Puchu, "Kangzhan Chuqi de Shanghai Nanmin Gongzuo" (Refugee Work in Shanghai at the Beginning of the War of Resistance), 27.

26. Goodman, *Native Place*, 287–8; Shanghai International Relief Committee [SIRC], *Six-Month Report*, IV.

27. Liu Yanru, "Kangzhan Chuqi Shanghai Nanmin Gongzuo," 53; Xu Wancheng, *Shanghai Cishan Jiguan Gaikuang*, 36; Chinese Child Welfare Association, *1934 Annual Report*, 3–4. *Chinese Recorder*, vol. 69, no. 3, March 1938, 155. Chen Shanxiang, "Shanghai Jidujiao Nuqingnianhui Bashi Nian" (Eighty Years of the Shanghai YWCA), 279–280; Honig, *Sisters and Strangers*, 233.

28. Shanghai International Relief Committee, *Six-Month Report*, X.

29. Henriot, *Shanghai*, 59–60.

30. Martin, *Shanghai Green Gang*, 151, 173; Jordan, *China's Trial by Fire*, 70.

31. Tang Guoliang, *Bainian Pudong Tongxianghuai* (One Hundred Years of the Pudong Native Place Association), 305.

32. Goodman, *Native Place*, 278.

33. *Shen Bao*, September 16, 1937, 5; Liu Yanru, "Kangzhan Chuqi Shanghai Nanmin Gongzuo," 48–53; Shanghai International Relief Committee, *Six Month Report*, n.p.

34. Zhao Puchu, "Kangzhan Chuqi de Shanghai Nanmin Gongzuo," 25–7; Shanghai International Relief Committee, *Six-Month Report*, n.p.

35. Liu Yanru, "Kangzhan Chuqi Shanghai Nanmin Gongzuo," 48.

36. Shanghai International Relief Committee, *Shanghai International Relief Committee Annual Report*, 93–4.

37. Liu Yanru, "Kangzhan Chuqi Shanghai Nanmin Gongzuo," 52–3; Shanghai International Red Cross, *News Bulletin*, vol.1, no.1, June 1938, 1–2.

38. *Shen Bao*, November 6, 1937, 8; Liu Yanru, "Kangzhan Chuqi Shanghai Nanmin Gongzuo," 48.

39. Liu Yanru, "Kangzhan Chuqi Shanghai Nanmin Gongzuo," 62–3.

40. Ibid., 61.
41. Henriot, *Shanghai*, 145.
42. Coble, *Facing Japan*, 293, 296.
43. Pan Dacheng, "Huiyi Shanghai Guoji Jiuji Hui Diyi Nanmin Shourongsuo" (Remembering the Shanghai International Reief Committee's First Refugee Shelter), 89–90; Li Jiaji, ed., *Shanghai Gongyun Zhi* (Shanghai Labor Movement Gazetteer), 31.
44. Li Jiaji, ed., *Shanghai Gongyun Zhi*, 27; Lu Zhiren, "Nanmin Gongzuo" (Refugee Work), 7; Pan Dacheng, "Huiyi Shanghai," 89–90.
45. Lu Zhiren, "Nanmin Gongzuo," 7; Stranahan, "Radicalization of Refugees," 176.
46. Zhao Puchu, "Kangzhan Chuqi," 26–27. 5; Stranahan, "Radicalization of Refugees," 180.
47. Shanghai International Relief Committee, *Annual Report*, 68; Liu Yanru, "Kangzhan Chuqi," 61.
48. Stranahan, "Strange Bedfellows," 42.
49. Yeh, "The Republican Origins of the Danwei," 72.
50. Wu Wenzhong, "Ben Ju Yinian Lai Shi Zheng Gaikuang" (Survey of Municipal Administration: This Department's Last Year), 30–31.
51. Hinder, *Social and Industrial Problems of Shanghai*, 67; Xu Wancheng, *Shanghai Cishan Jiguan Gaikuang*, 3–4.
52. Liu Yanru, "Kangzhan Chuqi Shanghai Nanmin Gongzuo," 61–2; Xu Shiying (Hsu Shih-ying) "Problem of War Refugees Relief," 498.
53. Xiong Yuezhi et al., *Lao Shanghai*, 79; Shanghai International Relief Committee, *Annual Report*, 69.
54. Zhao Puchu, "Kangzhan Chuqi de Shanghai Nanmin Gongzuo," 28; Shanghai shi, Zhabei Qu Zhibian Weiyuanhui, *Zhabei Qu Zhi* (Gazetteer for Zhabei District), 1175; SMA Q114-1-1; Liu Yanru, "Kangzhan Chuqi Shanghai Nanmin Gongzuo," 62–3; Xu Wancheng, *Shanghai Cishan Jiguan Gaikuang*, passim.
55. Xiong Yuezhi et al., *Lao Shanghai*, 8, 13, 40, 49.
56. Xu Wancheng, *Shanghai Cishan Jiguan Gaikuang*, 19; Hinder, *Social and Industrial Problems of Shanghai*, 67.
57. Zhao Puchu, "Kangzhan Chuqi de Shanghai Nanmin Gongzuo," 28; Shanghai shi, Zhabei Qu Zhibian Weiyuanhui, *Zhabei Qu Zhi*, 1175.
58. Xiong Yuezhi et al., *Lao Shanghai*, 96, 122, 128; Xu Wancheng, *Shanghai Cishan Jiguan Gaikuang*, passim; Lu Lishi, *Shanghai Tebie Shi*, passim.
59. Xiong Yuezhi et al., *Lao Shanghai*, 96, 122, 128.
60. Eastman, *Seeds of Destruction*.
61. Shehui Bu, *Shehui Fagui Huibian* (Collection of Social Legislation and Regulations).
62. Shanghai Shi, *1946 Niandu Dongling Jiuji Gongzuo Baogao* (1946 Work Report on Winter Relief), 6.
63. The organization was renamed the Shanghai Municipal Relief Committee (*Shanghai shi jiuji weiyuanhui*), but for the sake of simplicity I will refer to all three postwar relief committees as winter relief programs.

64. Shanghai Shi, *1946 Niandu*, 1, 5.

65. These included Du Yuesheng, Huang Hanzhi, Kui Yanfang, Li Guiyong, Liu Hongsheng, Pan Gongzhan, and Wang Xiaolai.

66. Shanghai Shi, *1946 Niandu*, 1, 5.

67. Ibid., 5–6.

68. Zhu Hua et al., *Shanghai Yibai Nian* (One Hundred Years in Shanghai), 270; Xiong Yuezhi et al., *Lao Shanghai*, 443–4.

69. Shanghai Shi, *1947 Niandu Dongling Jiuji Gongzuo Baogao* (1947 Work Report on Winter Relief), 1–4; Shanghai Shi Jiuji Weiyuanhui, *Choumu Weiyuanhui Gongzuo Baogao* (Fundraising Committee Work Report), 2; Shanghai Ertong Fuli Zujin Hui, *Shanghai Shehui Fuli Jiguan Yao Lan* (Guide to Shanghai's Social Welfare Organizations).

70. Shanghai Shi, *1946 Niandu*, 10–11.

71. Ibid., 23, 207.

72. Shanghai Shi, *1947 Niandu*, 11.

73. Xiong Yuezhi et al., *Shanghai Tongshi* (General History of Shanghai), 7: 461; Xiong Yuezhi et al., *Lao Shanghai*, 219.

74. Xiong Yuezhi et al., *Lao Shanghai*, 219.

75. Pepper, *Civil War in China*, 121–5; Xiong Yuezhi et al., *Shanghai Tongshi* 470–5.

76. Mei Zhen and Pu Shao, *Haishang Wenren Du Yuesheng* (Du Yuesheng: Famous in Shanghai), 266.

77. Shanghai Shi Jiuji Weiyuanhui, *Choumu Weiyuanhui Gongzuo Baogao*, 2.

78. SMA Q6-9-535.

10. Jeffrey N. Wasserstrom: Cosmopolitan Connections and Transnational Networks

I am grateful to Lynn Pan and Barbara Mittler for helpful suggestions; Sherman Cochran and Jean Oi for their close readings of an earlier draft of this chapter; and Robert Bickers and Nicholas Clifford, both of whom have done work on relevant issues that I draw upon here (as later notes indicate) and have been generous over the years in sharing sources, unpublished papers, and ideas with me.

1. The term *Shanghainese* is defined in varied ways in differing settings, sometimes referring only to those Chinese with longtime ties to the city, but I am using it here in a much more capacious sense, preferring it to alternatives such as "native residents" (the phrase often used in English language works of the treaty-port era) and bulky phrases such as Shanghai's Chinese residents. For the diversity within Shanghai's Chinese population, see Wakeman and Yeh, eds., *Shanghai Sojourners*; Lu Han-chao, *Beyond the Neon Lights*. For the diversity of and fissures within the local foreign

community, see Bickers and Henriot, eds., *New Frontiers*; Xiong Yuezhi et al., eds., *Shanghai de Waiguo Ren* (Foreigners in Shanghai); Ristaino, *Port of Last Resort*. On the size of different foreign populations, see Zou Yiren, *Jiu Shanghai Renkou Bianqian de Yanjiu* (A Study of the Evolution of the Population of Old Shanghai), 145 and passim.

2. The term *Shanghailander* is, like *Shanghainese*, open to varied interpretations (e.g., it has sometimes been employed to refer only to Britons and sometimes only to those who had clearly decided to make their lives, not just live for a time, in the treaty port), but it is used here in one of its most common senses, which is to refer to local Britons and Americans. For the attitudes of local Britons toward the Shanghainese, see Bickers, *Britain in China*; idem., *Empire Made Me*; Clifford, *Spoilt Children of Empire*.

3. See Christian Henriot and Zu'an Zheng, *Atlas de Shanghai* (Atlas of Shanghai); and Bickers and Henriot, *New Frontiers*.

4. Clifford, "A Revolution Is Not a Tea Party"; and Huskey, "Cosmopolitan Connection".

5. Clifford, *Spoilt Children*, 71, refers to the local Rotary Club as a "Sino-foreign social organization."

6. See, for example, various contributions to Wakeman and Yeh's *Shanghai Sojourners*.

7. On Jewish refugees, see Ristaino, *Port of Last Resort*; on associations that brought together members of other foreign groups, see various contributions to Bickers and Henriot, *New Frontiers*.

8. See, for example, the "Clubland" section of *The Jubilee of Shanghai*, 14–17, and the "Clubs and Associations" section of the Darwent, *Shanghai: A Handbook for Travellers and Residents*, 141–71.

9. Chinese labor unions and CCP organizations, for example, are the main associations discussed in Chang Hui and Bao Cun et al., *Shanghai Jinbainian Geming Shihua* (History of Shanghai During a Century of Revolution). One of the most important pre-1949 works to look at Chinese workers' associations is Zhu Bangxing et al., eds., *Shanghai Chanye Yu Shanghai Zhigong* (Shanghai Industry and Workers). Notable works on Shanghai *tongxianghui* and related organizations that predate the 1980s include Tadashi, *Shanhai no Girudo* (Guilds of Shanghai); Susan Mann Jones (Susan Mann), "The Ningbo *Pang* and Financial Power at Shanghai"; and Elvin, "The Administration of Shanghai, 1905–1914." See also the comments on Shanghai in pre-1980s works on *tongxianghui* with a national focus, such as Ho Ping-ti, *Zhongguo Huiguan Shilun* (Historical Study of Chinese Native-Place Societies).

10. See, for example, *All About Shanghai: A Standard Guidebook*, which lists information about a variety of foreign associations, under the subheading "clubs" within ch. 8, titled "Entertainment," but discusses organizations such as the Ningbo *tongxianghui* and other "guilds" in ch. 15, titled "Miscellenea" (the book's third from last chapter).

11. Darwent, *Shanghai*, 142. See also, within that same chapter subsection on "National and Local Associations," other organizations that have

tongxianghui-like qualities, such as (on the same page), the "Association of Lancastarians in Shanghai," which is described as having been open only to those who were "born in Lancashire, or who have, in the opinion of the committee, sufficiently identified themselves with the county by residence or otherwise." The first work that I know of to draw parallels between associations for foreigners such as these and Chinese *tongxianghui* is Clifford, *Spoilt Children of Empire*, 72.

12. F. L. Hawks Pott mentions the Union Club in *A Short History of Shanghai*, 238; on the "ABC" name, see Allman, *Shanghai Lawyer*, 147.

13. Limiting myself here to works in English (the footnotes and bibliographies to which will lead the interested reader to relevant works in other languages, especially the enormous number that are in Chinese), notable post-1980 publications on Shanghai organizations to which only Chinese belonged include the following: Bergère, *Golden Age of the Chinese Bourgeoisie*, which discusses various associations for Shanghainese businessmen; Honig, *Sisters and Strangers*, on unions; Leo Ou-fan Lee, *Shanghai Modern*, on literary societies; Xu Xiaoqun, *Chinese Professionals and the Republican State*, on organizations for Shanghainese lawyers and journalists, etc.; and Wasserstrom, *Student Protests in Twentieth-Century China*, on campus clubs. For citations to the Chinese literature on the subject, see also the bibliographies that accompany Chapters 5, 6, and 8 of this volume.

14. In Leo Ou-fan Lee, *Shanghai Modern*, for example, while there is a wonderfully detailed account of the foreign *books* with which Chinese modernist writers came into contact, only occasionally (as in the discussion of Emily Hahn, about whom more follows herein, on pp. 242–43) does the reader learn much about the foreign *indviduals* with whom these literary figures interacted. Sample works that, contrary to the norm, pay roughly equal attention to Chinese and foreign actors include Wagner, "The Role of the Foreign Community"; Cochran, *Encountering Chinese Networks*; Clifford, "A Revolution Is Not a Tea Party"; and Bickers, "'The Greatest Cultural Asset East of Suez,'" 2: 835–75.

15. Romanization is a tricky issue with cosmopolitan figures such as Lee, given not just the usual issues (the different spelling systems used at varied times for Mandarin pronunciations, plus the use of Cantonese and Mandarin pronunciations, etc.) but also sometimes an English first name as well. My choice here will be to refer to them by the main name used in their entry in *Who's Who in China*, which seems likely to have reflected (as it definitely did in this case, since he published letters to the editor of local newspapers as "William Yinsom Lee") the way the individuals were known in the largely Anglophone Sino-Foreign organizations and circles of interest here. When known, Pinyin spellings for their names will be placed in parentheses. My information on Lee comes from *Who's Who in China*, 252. No credit for editing this particular edition, on which I rely heavily, is given in the copy I have used (though one Ho Chieh-hsiang is mentioned as its editor in the University of California's online catalogue). But the bulk of

the biographies are adapted from those that appeared in earlier editions edited by John B. Powell and Hollington Tong, created when the former was the editor and the latter the associate editor of the magazine that was first known as *Millard's Review of the Far East* and then as the *China Weekly Review*. I will therefore refer to the book here as Powell and Tong's work. Powell played a greater roll than Tong in updating it (assisted by Ho and other *China Weekly Review* employees); the second edition (1920) has a "Preface" signed by Powell and Tong; that to the third edition (1925) is signed just by Powell; and that to the fourth edition, simply by "The Publishers."

16. For Allman, see his memoir, *Shanghai Lawyer*, and Huskey, "Cosmopolitan Connection."

17. On this point in particular, in addition to previously cited works by Bickers, see his "Settlers and Diplomats."

18. Clifford, "A Revolution is Not a Tea Party."

19. Crow, *Foreign Devils in the Flowery Kingdom*, 206–7; on Tong Shao-yi, see Powell and Tong, *Who's Who in China*, 369–70. For additional information on Crow, see French, *Carl Crow: A Tough Old China Hand—The Life, Times, and Adventures of an American in Shanghai*, a biography that appeared too late for me to make use of it in writing this chapter, but which contains references to many of the aspects of the subject's life to which I refer.

20. On the Sassoon family and Baghdadi Jewish community of which they were part, see Betta, "Marginal Westerners in Shanghai"; on Sir Victor himself, see Hahn, *China to Me*.

21. On both Emily Hahn and Victor Sassoon and citations to relevant sources that have more to say about both, see Hutt, "*La Maison D'Or*—The Sumptuous World of Shao Xunmei."

22. On the "Missouri Mafia," see MacKinnon and Friesen, eds., *China Reporting*; see also Powell, *My Twenty-Five Years in China*. Powell was also involved in Sino-Foreign associations, such as the local Advertising Club, which had both Chinese and non-Chinese in leadership roles; see the report on one of the group's meetings that ran in *Millard's Review*, November 13, 1920, 598–9.

23. The Missiouri graduate in question was Pei-yu Chien (Qian Peiyou); see his entry in Powell and Tong, *Who's Who in China*, 86. On *Shen Bao*, in addition to Wagner, "Foreign Community," see Mittler's important book, *A Newspaper for China?*

24. On ties across national lines established via religious activities, see for example, Fitch, *My Eighty Years in China*, 26 and passim.

25. On the cosmopolitan nature of some Shanghai newspapers and magazines, see the works on *Shen Bao* cited in the preceding notes; Gould, Randall, *China in the Sun*, 318 and passim; and the following articles with a Shanghai focus in the special issue of *The China Review* (guest edited by Bryna Goodman) on "Transnationalism in the Chinese Press"—Vittinghoff, "'British Barbarians' and 'Chinese Pigtails'?"; and Goodman, "Semi-Colonialism, Transnational Networks and News Flows."

26. Brunero, *Britain's Imperial Cornerstone in China.*

27. Allman, *Shanghai Lawyer*; Powell and Tong, *Who's Who in China*, 252.

28. Allman, *Shanghai Lawyer*, 147.

29. For a sense of the kinds of activities the Union Club sponsored and in some cases also details about its membership and internal organization, see "Reception at Union Club," *North China Herald*, November 13, 1920, 476; "Says Britain Seeks only Peace in China," *New York Times*, December 4, 1926, 6 (accessed via ProQuest Historical Newspapers, July 5, 2006), which describes a speech that British diplomat Miles Lampton gave at the club; and "The Union Club of China," *North China Herald*, March 31, 1928, 534. By the late 1920s, the Club was open to members of all nationalities, but its governing structure reflected its origin as an organization designed to increase contact between local Americans, Britons, and Chinese, as each of these three constituencies elected a representative and the presidency rotated from nationality to nationality (with the representatives of the other two national groups serving as vice presidents for that year). In 1928, according to "The Union Club of China," for example, Norwood Allman was elected to serve as the American vice president, while one G. L. Wilson served as the British vice president, and it being the turn of the Chinese members to select the president, J. H. Lee (Li Luxiong) took on that role. On J. H. (James Haiong) Lee, a businessman of many talents and interests, see Powell and Tong, *Who's Who in China*, 235–6. Two events held at the Union Club are also mentioned in Clifford, *Spoilt Children*, 71, 174 and 204.

30. See Allman, *Shanghai Lawyer*, 70; and *Who's Who in China*, 252.

31. On the Amity Mason Lodge, see Allman, *Shanghai Lawyer*, 143; on previously established local Mason groups without Chinese members, see Bickers, *Empire Made Me*, 135–6; and *North China Herald*, compilers, *The Jubilee of Shanghai*, 115.

32. On American clubs, see Wilkinson, "The Shanghai American Community, 1937–1949."

33. Fitch, *My Eighty Years in China*. Fitch was also a member of the Shanghai Rotary Club and he describes a joint effort that the Western, Japanese, and Chinese members of that club made in the early 1930s to work for peace in ibid., 419; for more on the Rotary Club's involvement in Sino-Japanese disputes, see "Anti-Japanese Meeting: Attitude of Local Civic Bodies: Rotary Club Resolution," *North China Herald*, September 29, 1931, 444.

34. On the Y in general, see Garrett, "The Chambers of Commerce and the YMCA." For joint efforts by Chinese and Western leaders and activists within the local YMCA and YWCA, see "Summer Camp for Y.W.C.A. Works"; *Millard's Review of the Far East*, October 2, 1920, 232; the comments on a YWCA fund-raising drive involving "four Chinese and two foreign teams" (the heads of which presumably were in close contact and together coordinated the drive) in "$14,000 Netter in Y.W.C.A. Campaign," *Millard's Review of the Far East*, Nov. 20, 1920, 647; and Fitch, *My Eighty Years in China*,

51–2 and passim. There is a good deal of evidence, though in widely scattered places, for other kinds of fund-raising drives of the 1920s, besides those sponsored by the Y, that were led by committees made up of Chinese and non-Chinese members; for one example, see "Famine Relief Work Progressing," *Millard's Review of the Far East*, October 23, 1920, 408.

35. Powell and Tong, *Who's Who in China*, 246–7.

36. "A Pan-Pacific Association," *North China Herald*, June 19, 1920, 727; and "The Pan-Pacific Association: Inaugural Dinner," *North China Herald*, October 2, 1920, 96–7. Fitch also presided over at least one meeting (at which Sun Yat-sen spoke); see Fitch, *My Eighty Years in China*, 31.

37. On Zhu as a comprador and *tongxianghui* leader, see Jones, "The Ningbo *Pang*," 89 and passim; Zhu's leading role in the Union Club is mentioned in "Union Club Proprietary, LD: Statutory Meeting," *North China Herald*, November 22, 1919, 512; two other heads of the Club mentioned in that article are A. Brooke-Smith and F. J. Raven, a Briton and American, respectively (see more in following notes).

38. On Soong Mei-ling's social and civic activities before her marriage, see for example the comments in Allman, *Shanghai Lawyer*, 147, and the reference in "College Club May Affiliate with U.S. Collegiate Alumnae," *Millard's Review*, Nov. 27, 1920, 716, on her stepping down as "acting president" of the American College Club.

39. Hahn, *The Soong Sisters*.

40. Bergère, *Sun Yat-sen*, 277.

41. My information on Mrs. Mei comes from her entry in Powell and Tong, *Who's Who in China*, 315 (and the one on her husband on the preceding page that refers to his similar mix of activities, including membership in the Rotary Club). See also the description of Mrs. Mei's participation in an American Woman's Club event in "With the American Woman's Club," *Millard's Review*, November 20, 1920, 644–5. On the political roles that returned students' associations played, see Wasserstrom, *Student Protests*, 42–3.

42. My division of local residents along a continuum running from "parochial" to "cosmopolitan" is borrowed from Huskey, "Cosmopolitan Connection," but there is one limitation to his approach worth noting. Huskey gives the impression that all of the "cosmopolitan" Westerners were Americans, whereas there were some local Britons who demonstrated the traits he describes, as Clifford points out in "A Revolution Is Not a Tea Party." Thus, for example, while Huskey is right that more American than British Shanghailanders called for Chinese to have political representation on the International Settlement's main governing board, E. S. Little, a Briton, pushed for this quite early in the Republican period, as noted in Wasserstrom, "Questioning the Modernity of a Model Settlement." In addition, the Union Club had, as mentioned, a significant British membership, and one of its leading lights early on was A. Brooke-Smith, a prominent local Briton; see *North China Herald*, November 22, 1919.

43. "Reception at Union Club," *North China Herald*, November 13, 1920, 476.

44. The banquet honoring Yu and other Chinese business leaders is mentioned in Rigby, *May Thirtieth Movement*, 166.

45. "Farewell Dinner to Mr. Brooke Smith," *North China Herald*, April 10, 1926, 35; the main host was Pan Ching-poo, described as "chief compradore of the Ewo house and director of the Chinese General Chamber of Commerce," the Chinese guests included Tong Shao-yi and Yu Xiaqing, and the event, fittingly enough, was held at the Union Club.

46. One such dance is mentioned in *China Weekly Review*, March 21, 1925, 82.

47. This photograph is reproduced, courtesy of "The Rotarian," in *Fortune*, January 1935, 38.

48. For a particularly flamboyant presentation of this position by a former Shanghailander, looking back nostalgically at the treaty-port era, see Pal, *Shanghai Saga*, 227, which presents the city as a "warm-hearted" place, a wondrous "melting pot" where people of "all nations could live in harmony"; for more restrained academic versions, see Fairbank, *Trade and Diplomacy on the China Coast*; and Pye, "How China's Nationalism Was Shanghaied."

49. On these two figures, see Powell and Tong, *Who's Who in China*, 314–15 and 332.

50. For Fitch's involvement in the anti-opium committee, see Lunt, ed., *The China Who's Who* (Foreign), 88.

51. On Chinese representation on the Council, see Wasserstrom, "Questioning the Modernity of a Model Settlement"; as well as Li Tiangang, "1927: Shanghai Shimin Zizhi Yundong de Zongjie" (1927, the culmination of the self-government movement by Shanghai citizenry); and Goodman, "Democratic Calisthenics."

52. On this image and the claims that prominently placed park notice boards had rules that were not just rooted in prejudice (they were) but added insult to injury by explicitly likening Chinese to dogs (this was and still is widely believed but was not the case), see Bickers and Wasserstrom, "Shanghai's 'No Dogs or Chinese Allowed' Sign as History, Legend, and Contemporary Symbol."

53. I have not found the original letter Lee sent to local newspapers, in which he lamented the unfairness of being unable to join or enter as someone's guest the kinds of clubs in Shanghai that he routinely frequented while abroad, but it is referred to in several places. His original letter and the correspondence it inspired provided the inspiration, for example, for a long editorial in Shanghai's leading American weekly, "Chinese Membership in the Foreign Clubs," *China Weekly Review*, August 15, 1925, 209–10. See also the letter of rebuttal that ran in the August 8, 1925, edition of the *North China Herald* (titled "Chinese Membership in Foreign Clubs" and signed "Westminster Bridge") and Lee's untitled response to that letter (both on

p. 90). The author of the letter of rebuttal claimed that Englishmen had the right to organize their affairs within Shanghai just as they did at home when it came to social life and also pointed out that the membership of clubs was often limited by profession or political persuasion, so exclusion need not be seen as offensive or as a sign of racial or national prejudice by those left out. Lee disputed this by pointing out that he had himself been allowed at least to accompany friends to very exclusive clubs in London and that the Shanghai Club was not one whose membership was limited to people who shared ideological positions and so forth. His main point was simple: "Organizations holding functions at the Shanghai Club (such as the annual dinner of the Oxford and Cambridge Club) of course occasionally include some Chinese, but apart from these I have yet to hear of a single Chinese gentleman who has been invited to visit the Shanghai Club as a guest of a member. The policy is obviously race discrimination as if it meant loss of prestige for a Britisher to associate with Chinese." He went on to note that, while in England, he socialized with "members of the British nobility and of the distinguished orders, merchant princes and captains of industry" so it was particularly galling, while in Shanghai, to be "considered not good enough to converse with junior clerks of British nationality if they happen to be members of the Shanghai Club."

54. Sun Yat-sen, "Zhongguo Neiluan Zhi Yuanyin" (Causes of China's Domestic Turmoil), speech given November 25, 1924, reprinted in *Sun Zhongshan Quanji* (Collected Writings of Sun Yat-sen), 2: 899–911, see especially 908–909.

55. On inequality between and social segregation of Chinese and foreign workers in the Customs Service, see Brunero, *Britain's Imperial Cornerstone*, 16–17, 26–7, and passim; for a rosier view of the same institution, see various writings by Fairbank, including *Trade and Diplomacy on the China Coast*.

56. The "Husi Country Club" (founded to promote relations between foreign and native taipans) is mentioned in *Fortune*, vol. 11, no. 1 (January 1935), 104. In that same extended *Fortune* cover story on Shanghai, reference is made to the general increase in recent interactions, formal and informal, between Chinese and Western elites in the metropolis. But the story also stresses the degree of prejudice that continued to exist among Shanghailanders, claiming that it was not uncommon for members of this group to "despise" the Chinese and view them as "Baghdadi Jews," no matter how rich and assimilated their speech and manners, and therefore beneath them.

57. Here and elsewhere I use the phrase "national or racial," as in cases such as this, neither term on its own seems to quite do the trick. On the one hand, many Shanghailanders thought of Chinese and Japanese as members of the same "race," and yet the latter could join some of the most elite foreign clubs from which the former were banned. And yet, to describe it as a difference based in "nationality" seems too weak to describe what was, in large part, a form of racism. This is illustrated by the fact that ethnic

Chinese who had been born and lived most of their lives outside of China were kept out of certain public spaces. The racist aspect of International Settlement park and club rules was something that cosmopolitan-minded, liberal American Shanghailanders wrestled with in different ways in their writings. Compare, for example, Crow's rather tortured effort to differentiate the situation from that which characterized the Jim Crow South (*Foreign Devils in the Flowery Kingdom*, 199) and Randall Gould's two references to the ridiculousness of Japanese but not Chinese being allowed to join the Shanghai Club (*China in the Sun*, 149 and 314). For more on this and related issues, see Bickers and Wasserstrom, "Shanghai's 'No Dogs and Chinese Admitted' Sign."

58. See the pages already cited in Powell and Tong, *Who's Who in China*, as well as Lunt, *The China Who's Who*. See also "Appendix I: Men of Shanghai," *Fortune*, vol. 11, no. 1 (January 1935), 115–16, which devotes two paragraphs to Union Club leader Frank Jay Raven and three to Yu Xiaqing, who attended at least one event held at that Sino-Foreign institution (the goodbye party for Brooke-Smith) and had a long track record of border-crossing activities, and earlier pages of that same cover story that refer to other famous border-crosses such as Victor Sassoon.

59. *North China Herald*, November 22, 1919, 512. Similarly, while only a fraction of local Chinese residents had studied abroad and hence qualified for membership in a society for returned students, those who did were often among the most prominent Shanghainese.

60. For information on Nieh, see Powell and Tong, *Who's Who in China*, 320–1.

61. As for how involved foreigners on the Council were in Sino-Foreign associations, the case of F. J. Raven is illustrative. In addition to his aforementioned tie to the Union Club, the short biography of him given in "Appendix I: Men of Shanghai" (see note 58) says that along with liking to play tennis at two country clubs (both with only foreign members), he was a "fervid Rotarian," meaning that his social activities took place in a mixture of foreign-only and Sino-Foreign settings.

62. For an insightful critical discussion of Sun's vision of the status of treaty-port Chinese, see Rogaski, "Hygienic Modernity in Tianjin."

63. Bickers, "Settlers and Diplomats," contains an excellent discussion of the changing political strategies and viewpoints of Shanghailanders in this period.

64. It would take another chapter to trace these linkages, but some potentially fruitful lines of investigation to follow have been hinted at earlier. For example, the ties between Yu Xiaqing and Du Yuesheng lead us from the Settlement to the French Concession, while Song Meiling's connection to various American Shanghailanders leads us from the Settlement to the Chinese Municipality under Nationalist rule.

Bibliography

Periodicals and Newspapers

China Weekly Review
Chinese Recorder
Chunqiu
Dagong Bao
Daguang Bao
Damei Wanbao
Dazhong Shenghuo
Dikang Sanri Kan
Dongfang Zazhi
Fenghuo
Fortune
Guowen Zhoubao
Heng She Yuekan
Hu She Yuekan
Jingbao
Liangyou Huabao
Millard's Review of the Far East
Min Bao
Minguo Ribao
Minli Bao
The New York Times
News Bulletin of the Shanghai International Red Cross
North China Daily News
North China Herald
Rekishi Hyoron
Renwu

Shanghai Difang Xiehui Yuebao
Shanhai Mainichi
Shehui Kexue
Shen Bao
Shenghuo
Shishi Xinbao
Shuntian Shibao
The North China Herald
Xin Bao
Xinsheng Zhoukan
Xinwen Bao
Yinhang Zhoubao
Yishi Bao
Zhonghua Guohuo Chanxiao Hezuo Xiehui Meizhou Huibao
Zhuanji Wenxue

Archives

British Foreign Office. "Command Paper." FO F3570/184/87, May 29, 1930.

Gong-Shang-Lian Archives. Shanghai General Chamber of Commerce, Meeting Minutes. 200-1-008, 1922.

Guoshi Guan (Academia Historica). Ministry of Education Archives, Folder on *Zhonghua Zhiye Jiaoyu Hui*.

———. *Guomin Zhengfu* (The National Government). 200000000A: Guomin Zhengfu 0543/2700.01-02, 1935–7.

———. *Guomin Zhengfu* (The National Government). 200000000A: Guomin Zhengfu 1401/4461.01-01, December 1947.

Lishi Dang'an (Historical Archives).

Mingguo Dang'an (Republican Archives).

Shanghai Library. Unpublished correspondence between Wang Yiting and Ha Shaofu.

———. Unpublished correspondence between Zeng Xi and Wang Yiting.

Shanghai Municipal Archives. Police Daily Report, 1-1-1122, May 29, 1919.

———. File Q115-16-4, 1927–49.

———. File Q114-1-1, 1936.

———. File Q6-9-535, 1949.

———. Shanghai Bar Association, New Life Weekly Case File, Q190-1-535, 1935.

———. Second Branch of the Jiangsu High Court, Court Records on the New Life Weekly Case, Q181-0-570, 1935.

———. Q181-1-6, 1935.

———. Q180-0-570, 1935.

———. Chaozhou Huiguan Yi'an Bu (Meeting Record of the Chaozhou Huiguan). Unpublished manuscript series, August 1922.

———. Chaozhou Huiguan Yishibu (Meeting Notes of the Chaozhou Huiguan). Unpublished manuscript series, 1914, 1917, 1934.
———. Shanghai Art College Archive.
———. Shanghai Police Intelligence Report. U1-1-1221, 1935.
Shanghai Municipal Police Files. IO-2882, July 23, 1919.
Shanghai Municipal Police Files, Special Branch Files. D8676, August 1938.
———. D4683, December 27, 1935.
———. D4683, March 27, 1933.
———. D4683, October 8, 1938.
———. D9319, February 6, 1940.
Shanghai Tebie Shi Dangbu Gongzuo Baogao (Shanghai Branch of the KMT Work Reports). Guomindang Dangshi Hui (KMT Party Historical Archives). Taiwan, October 1935.
Zhongyang Xuanchuan Bu (Central Propaganda Department). "Ge Xinwen Jianchasuo" (News Censorship Offices), 718–129. Number Two Archives. Nanjing: Central Propaganda Department Archives, May 18, 1934.
Zuigao Fayuan (the Supreme Court). "Letter from the Jianchayuan (the Control Yuan) to Zuigao Fayuan (the Supreme Court)." 16-7078. Number Two Archives. Nanjing: Supreme Court Archives, August 14, 1935.

Books and Other Publications Cited

Adshead, S. A. M. *The Modernization of the Chinese Salt Administration, 1900–1920*. Cambridge: Harvard University Press, 1970.
Alford, William. "Of Arsenic and Old Laws: Looking Anew at Criminal Justice in Late Imperial China." *California Law Review* 72, no. 6 (1984): 1180–256.
All About Shanghai: A Standard Guidebook. Oxford: Oxford University Press, 1983. Reprint, a work originally issued in Shanghai by the University Press in 1934–5.
Allman, Norwood. *Shanghai Lawyer*. New York: McGraw-Hill, 1943.
Ba, Jin. "Suowei Riben Kongjun de Weili" (The So-Called Might of the Japanese Air Force). *Fenghuo*, no. 1 (September 5, 1937): 5.
Barkan, Lenore. "Patterns of Power: Forty Years of Elite Politics in a Chinese County." In *Chinese Local Elites and Patterns of Dominance*, edited by Joseph W. Esherick and Mary Backus Rankin, 191–215. Berkeley: University of California Press, 1990.
Bedeski, Robert E. *State-Building in Modern China: The KMT in the Prewar Period*. Berkeley: Institute of East Asian Studies, 1981.
Bergère, Marie-Claire. *The Golden Age of the Chinese Bourgeoisie, 1911–1937*. Translated by Janet Lloyd from the 1986 original French. New York: Cambridge University Press, 1989.
———. *L'Age d'Or de la Bourgeoisie Chinoise, 1911–1937* (The Golden Age of the Chinese Bourgeoisie, 1911–1937). Paris: Flammarion, 1986.

———. "The Shanghai Bankers' Association, 1915–1927: Modernization and the Institutionalization of Local Solidarities." In *Shanghai Sojourners*, edited by Frederic E. Wakeman Jr., and Wen-hsin Yeh, 1–14. Berkeley: Institute of East Asian Studies, 1992.

———. *Sun Yat-Sen*. Translated by Janet Lloyd. Stanford: Stanford University Press, 1998.

Betta, Chiara. "Marginal Westerners in Shanghai: The Baghdadi Jewish Community, 1845–1931." In *New Frontiers: Imperialism's New Communities in East Asia, 1842–1953*, edited by Robert Bickers and Christian Henriot, 38–54. Manchester: Manchester University Press, 2000.

Bi, Yuncheng. "Taofen He Shenghuo Shudian" (Zou Taofen and the Shenghuo Bookstore). *Ershi Shiji Shanghai Wenshi Ziliao Xuanji* 6 (1999): 274–80.

Bian, Yanjie. "Bringing Strong Ties Back In: Indirect Ties, Network Bridges and Job Searches in China." *American Sociological Review*, no. 62 (1997): 366–85.

Bianco, Lucien. *Origins of the Chinese Revolution, 1915–1949*. Translated by Muriel Bell. Stanford: Stanford University Press, 1971.

Bickers, Robert. *Britain in China: Community, Culture and Colonialism, 1900–1949*. Manchester: Manchester University Press, 1999.

———. *Empire Made Me: An Englishman Adrift in Shanghai*. New York: Columbia University Press, 2003.

———. "'The Greatest Cultural Asset East of Suez': The History and Politics of the Shanghai Municipal Orchestra and Public Band, 1881–1946." In *Ershi Shiji de Zhongguo Yu Shijie* (China and the World in the Twentieth Century), edited by Chi-hsiung Chang. Taipei: Institute of History, Academia Sinica, 2001.

———. "Settlers and Diplomats: The End of British Hegemony in the International Settlement, 1937–1945." In *In the Shadow of the Rising Sun: Shanghai Under Japanese Occupation*, edited by Christian Henriot and Wen-hsin Yeh, 229–56. Cambridge: Cambridge University Press, 2004.

Bickers, Robert, and Christian Henriot, eds. *New Frontiers: Imperialism's New Communities in East Asia, 184\2-1953*. Manchester: Manchester University Press, 2000.

Bickers, Robert, and Jeffrey N. Wasserstrom. "Shanghai's 'No Dogs or Chinese Allowed' Sign as History, Legend and Contemporary Symbol." *China Quarterly*, no. 142 (1995): 444–66.

Brunero, Donna. *Britain's Imperial Cornerstone in China: The Chinese Maritime Customs Service, 1854–1949*. London: Routledge, 2006.

Cai, Chennan. *Bailongshanren Wang Zhen Shuhua Daguan* (Great Survey of Paintings and Calligraphy of White Dragon Mountainman Wang Zhen). Taipei: Guotai Meishuguan, 1982.

———. "Wang Yiting Nianpu Jianbiao" (Biographical Chronology of Wang Yiting). In *Bailongshanren Wang Zhen Shuhua Daguan* (Great Survey of Paintings and Calligraphy of White Dragon Mountainman Wang Zhen), edited by Cai Chennan. Taipei: Guotai Meishuguan, 1982.

Cai, Xingtao. *Kangzhan Qian de Zhonghua Zhiye Jiaoyu She, 1917–1937* (Chinese Society of Vocational Education in the Years Prior to the War of Resistance, 1917–1937). Taipei: Dongda Tushu Gongsi, 1988.

Ch'ien, Tuan-sheng. *The Government and Politics of China, 1912–1949*. Stanford: Stanford University Press, 1950.

Chang, Hui, and Cun Bao et al. *Shanghai Jinbainian Geming Shihua* (History of Shanghai During a Century of Revolution). Shanghai: Shanghai Renmin Chubanshe, 1963.

Chaozhou Tongxianghui. *Chaozhou Lü Hu Tongxianghui Tekan* (Special Publication of the Chaozhou Sojourners' Association in Shanghai). Shanghai, 1932.

Chen, Dingshan. "Wang Yiting Wanjie Mijian" (Wang Yiting Upholds His Integrity in His Later Years). In *Chunshen Jiuwen*, Dingshan Chen, 24–6. Taipei: Shejie Wenwu Chubanshe, 1971.

Chen, Hui. *Taofen Zhuan* (Biography of Zou Taofen). Nanchang: Jiangxi Renmin Chubanshe, 2001.

Chen, Joseph T. *The May Fourth Movement in Shanghai: The Making of a Social Movement in Modern China*. Leiden: Brill, 1971.

Chen, Lizhi. *Hu She Cangsang Lu* (Vicissitudes of the Hu She). Taipei, 1969.

Chen, Shanxiang. "Shanghai Jidujiao Nuqingnianhui Bashi Nian" (Eighty Years of the Shanghai YWCA). *Shanghai Wenshi Ziliao* (Shanghai Cultural and Historical Sources), no. 81 (1996): 276–94.

Chen, Zemin. "Fei Jiancha Zhidu Zhi Yundong" (Movement to Abolish the Procuratorial System). Pamphlet. Shanghai, 1922 (Beijing Library Collection).

Cheng, Linsun. *Banking in Modern China: Entrepreneurs, Professional Managers, and the Development of Chinese Banks, 1897–1937*. Cambridge: Cambridge University Press, 2003.

Chesneaux, Jean. *The Chinese Labor Movement, 1919–1927*. Translated by H. M. Wright. Stanford: Stanford University Press, 1968.

Chinese Child Welfare Association. *1934 Annual Report*. Shanghai: Chinese Child Welfare Association, ca. 1935.

Chongqing Shi Dang'an Guan (Chongqing City Archives), eds. " 'Qi Junzi' Anjian Dang'an Xuan" (Selection of Archival Materials on the Seven Gentlemen Case). *Lishi Dang'an*, no. 3 (1985): 69–79.

Chow, Tse-Tsung. *The May Fourth Movement: Intellectual Revolution in Modern China*. Stanford: Stanford University Press, 1967.

Clifford, Nicholas R. "A Revolution Is Not a Tea Party: The 'Shanghai Mind(s)' Reconsidered." *Pacific Historical Review* 59 (November 1990): 501–26.

———. *Shanghai, 1925: Urban Nationalism and the Defense of Foreign Privilege*. Ann Arbor: University of Michigan Center for Chinese Studies, 1979.

———. *Spoilt Children of Empire: Westerners in Shanghai and the Chinese Revolution of the 1920s*. Hanover: University Press of New England, 1991.

Coble, Parks M. "Chiang Kai-Shek and the Anti-Japanese Movement in China: Zou Taofen and the National Salvation Association, 1931–1937." *Journal of Asian Studies* 44, no. 2 (February 1985): 293–310.

———. *Facing Japan: Chinese Politics and Japanese Imperialism, 1931–1937, Harvard East Asian Monograph Series*. Cambridge: Harvard University Press, 1991.

Coble, Parks M. Jr. *The Shanghai Capitalists and the Nationalist Government, 1927–1937*. Cambridge: Harvard University Press, 1980.

Cochran, Sherman. *Encountering Chinese Networks: Western, Japanese and Chinese Corporations in China, 1880–1937*. Berkeley: University of California Press, 2000.

———. *Encountering Chinese Networks: Western, Japanese, and Chinese Corporations in China, 1880–1937*. Berkeley: University of California Press, 2000.

———. *Inventing Nanjing Road: Commercial Culture in Shanghai, 1900–1945*. Ithaca, NY: East Asia Program, Cornell University, 1999.

———. "Marketing Medicine and Advertising Dreams in China, 1900–1950." In *Becoming Chinese: Passages to Modernity and Beyond*, edited by Wen-hsin Yeh, 62–97. Berkeley: University of California Press, 2000.

Cornet, Christine. "The Bumpy End of the French Concession and French Influence in Shanghai, 1937–1946." In *In the Shadow of the Rising Sun: Shanghai Under Japanese Occupation*, edited by Christian Henriot and Wen-hsin Yeh, 257–76. Cambridge: Cambridge University Press, 2004.

Crow, Carl. *Foreign Devils in the Flowery Kingdom*. New York: Harper and Brothers, 1940.

Darwent, Rev. C. E. *Shanghai: A Handbook for Travellers and Residents*. Taipei: Ch'eng Wen, 1970. Reprint, 1920 edition issued by Kelly and Walsh, Shanghai.

"Dashiji" (Record of Important Events). In *Shanghai Minzhenshi* (History of Shanghai Civil Affairs). Shanghai: Shanghai Shehui Kexueyuan Chubanshe, 2000.

Davis, Walter. "For Fate, Faith, and Charity: Wang Yiting's Paintings of Street People." In *The Challenge of Modernity: Chinese Painting in the Late Nineteenth and Early Twentieth Centuries*. Asian Cultural Council, in conjunction with the 1997 China On Site Graduate Seminar, New York, 1998.

Diani, Mario, and Doug McAdam, eds. *Social Movements and Networks: Relational Approaches to Collective Action*. New York: Oxford University Press, 2003.

Dryburgh, Marjorie. *North China and Japanese Expansion, 1933–1937: Regional Power and National Interest*. Richmond, Surrey: Curzon Press, 2000.

Du, Yi. "Wo Bi Kaixuan Gui: Ji Baba Du Zhongyuan Zai 'Ba Yisan Kangzhan Shi de Huodong" ("I Will Definitely Return in Triumph": Commemorating Father, Du Zhouyuan's Resistance Activities in the Marco Polo Incident). *Changning Wenshi Ziliao (Shanghai)* 3 (1987): 97–103.

Du, Zhongyuan. *Yuzhong Zagan*. Shanghai: Shenghuo Shudian, 1937.

Duara, Prasenjit. *Rescuing History from the Nation: Questioning Narratives of Modern China*. Chicago: University of Chicago Press, 1995.

Eastman, Lloyd. *The Abortive Revolution: China Under Nationalist Rule, 1927–1937*. Cambridge: Harvard University Press, 1974.

———. *Seeds of Destruction: Nationalist China in War and Revolution, 1937–1949*. Stanford: Stanford University Press, 1984.

Edwards, Bob, Michael W. Foley, and Mario Diani, eds. *Beyond Tocqueville: Civil Society and the Social Capital Debate in Comparative Perspective*. Hanover: University Press of New England, 2001.

Elvin, Mark. "The Administration of Shanghai, 1905–1914." In *The Chinese City Between Two Worlds*, edited by Mark Elvin and G. William Skinner, 239–62. Stanford: Stanford University Press, 1974.

———. "The Gentry Democracy in Chinese Shanghai, 1905–1914." In *Modern China's Search for a Political Form*, edited by Jack Gray, 41–65. Oxford: Oxford University Press, 1969.

Elvin, Mark, and G. William Skinner, eds. *The Chinese City Between Two Worlds*. Stanford: Stanford University Press, 1974.

Esherick, Joseph W., and Mary Backus Rankin, eds. *Chinese Local Elites and Patterns of Dominance*. Berkeley: University of California Press, 1990.

Esping-Andersen, Gosta. *The Three Worlds of Welfare Capitalism*. Princeton: Princeton University Press, 1990.

Evans, Peter. *Embedded Autonomy: State and Industrial Transformation*. Princeon: Princeton University Press, 1995.

Fairbank, John K. *Trade and Diplomacy on the China Coast: The Opening of the Treaty Ports, 1842–1854*. Cambridge: Harvard University Press, 1953.

Fan, Jingsi, ed. *Shanghai Minzhenzhi* (History of Shanghai Civil Affairs). Shanghai: Shanghai Shehui Kexue Chubanshe, 2000.

Fan, Shaozeng. "Guanyu Du Yuesheng" (Concerning Du Yuesheng). In *Jiu Shanghai de Banghui* (The Gangs of Old Shanghai), edited by Zhongguo Renmin Zhengzhi Xieshang Huiyi Shanghai Shi Weiyuanhui Wenshi Ziliao Gongzuo Weiyuanhui (Work Committee on Literary and Historical Materials of the Chinese People's Political Consultative Council's Shanghai Municipal Committee), 195–247. Shanghai: Shanghai Renmin Chubanshe, 1986.

Fan, Songfu. "Shanghai Banghui Neimu" (The Inside Story of the Shanghai Gangs). *Wenshi Ziliao Xuanji* (1980): 150–9.

Fang, Yinchao. "Guangdong Lü Hu Tongxianghui Gongzuo Zhuiji" (Remembrance of Guangdong Sojourners' Association Work in Shanghai). *Dacheng*, no. 45 (August 1977): 26–27.

Feng, Shaoting. "Shanghai Shi Gejie Kangdi Hou Yuanhui Shuping" (Commentary on the Association of Various Shanghai Circles to Aid in Resisting the Enemy). In *Minguo Dang'an Yu Mingguo Shixue Taolun Hui* (Collection of Articles from an Academic Conference on Republican Archives and Republican History), edited by Xianwen Zhang et al., 217–27. Beijing: Dang'an Chubanshe, 1988.

Feng, Xiaomin. *Zhongguo Gongchandang Zai Shanghai Bashinian* (Eighty Years of the Chinese Communist Party in Shanghai). Shanghai: Shanghai Renmin Chubanshe, 2001.

Feng, Yi. "Le Problème des Réfugiés à Shanghai, 1937–40." *Memoire de DEA, Université Lumière-Lyon 2* (September 1993).

Fewsmith, Joseph. *Party, State, and Local Elites in Republican China: Merchant Organizations and Politics in Shanghai, 1890–1930*. Honolulu: University of Hawaii Press, 1985.

Fischer, Claude S., et al. *Networks and Places: Social Relations in an Urban Setting*. New York: Free Press, 1977.

Fitch, George A. *My Eighty Years in China*. Taipei: Mei Ya, 1967.

Fitzgerald, John. "The Origins of the Illiberal Party Newspaper: Print Journalism in China's Nationalist Revolution." *Republican China* 21, no. 2 (April 1996): 1–22.

Flora, Peter, and Arnold J. Heidenheimer, eds. *The Development of Welfare States in Europe and America*. New Brunswick, NJ: Transaction Publishers, 1982.

Fogel, Joshua, and Peter Zarrow. *Imagining the People: Chinese Intellectuals and the Concept of Citizenship, 1890–1920*. Armonk, NY: M. E. Sharpe, 1997.

Foley, Michael W., Bob Edwards, and Mario Diani. "Social Capital Reconsidered." In *Beyond Tocqueville: Civil Society and the Social Capital Debate in Comparative Perspective*, edited by Bob Edwards, Michael W. Foley, and Mario Diani, 266–79. Hanover: University Press of New England, 2001.

Frazier, Mark W. *The Making of the Chinese Industrial Workplace: State, Revolution, and Labor Management*. Cambridge: Cambridge University Press, 2002.

Frazier, Martin W. "Mobilizing a Movement: Cotton Mill Foremen in the Shanghai Strikes of 1925." *Republican China* 19 (1993): 1–45.

French, Paul. *Carl Crow: A Tough Old China Hand—the Life, Times, and Adventures of an American in Shanghai*. Hong Kong: Hong Kong University Press, 2006.

Fried, Morton H. *The Fabric of Chinese Society*. New York: Praeger, 1953.

Fu, Po-shek. *Passivity, Resistance, and Collaboration: Intellectual Choices in Occupied China, 1937–1945*. Stanford: Stanford University Press, 1993.

Gao, Jun. "Lun Mu Ouchu de Shiye Zhenxing Sixiang" (Discussion on Mu Ouchu's Throughts on Industrial Development). Shanghai: Fudan University, 2006.

Gao, Zhennong. "Buddhism in Republican Shanghai." Unpublished paper presented at the conference, "Social Networks in Republican Shanghai." Stanford: Stanford University, Center for East Asian Studies, 2003.

———. "Shanghai Fojiao Gaikuang" (Survey of Buddhism in Shanghai). *Shanghai Wenshi Ziliao* (Shanghai Cultural and Historical Sources) 81 (November 1996): 1–14.

Garrett, Shirley S. "The Chambers of Commerce and the YMCA." In *The Chinese City Between Two Worlds*, edited by Mark Elvin and G. William Skinner, 213–38. Stanford: Stanford University Press, 1974.

Gendaishi Shiryo (Source Materials on Contemporary History), vol. 13. Tokyo: Misuzu Shobo, 1962–1967.

Gerth, Karl. *China Made: Consumer Culture and the Creation of the Nation*. Cambridge: Harvard University Asia Center, 2003.

Gold, Thomas, Doug Guthrie, and David Wank. *Social Connections in China: Institutions, Culture, and the Changing Nature of Guanxi*. New York: Cambridge University Press, 2002.

Goldman, Merle, and Elizabeth J. Perry, eds. *Changing Meanings of Citizenship in Modern China*. Cambridge: Harvard University Press, 2002.

Goodman, Bryna. "Being Public: The Politics of Representation in 1918 Shanghai." *Harvard Journal of Asiatic Studies* 60, no. 1 (June 2000): 45–88.

———. "Creating Civic Ground: Public Maneuverings and the State in the Nanjing Decade." In *Remapping China: Fissures in Historical Terrain*, edited by Gail Hershatter, Emily Honig, Jonathan Lipman, and Randall Stross, 164–77. Stanford: Stanford University Press, 1996.

———. "Democratic Calisthenics: The Culture of Urban Associations in the New Republic." In *Changing Meanings of Citizenship in Modern China*, edited by Merle Goldman and Elizabeth Perry, 70–109. Cambridge: Harvard University Press, 2002.

———. "The Locality as Microcosm of the State? Native Place Networks and Urban Nationalism in China, 1874–1937." *Modern China* (October 1995): 387–419.

———. *Native Place, City, and Nation: Regional Networks and Identities in Shanghai, 1853–1937*. Berkeley: University of California Press, 1995.

———. "New Culture, Old Habits: Native Place Organization and the May Fourth Movement." In *Shanghai Sojourners*, edited by Frederic Wakeman Jr., and Wen-hsin Yeh, 76–107. Berkeley: University of California, Institute of East Asian Studies, 1992.

———. "The New Woman Commits Suicide: The Press, Cultural Memory, and the New Republic." *Journal of Asian Studies* 64, no. 1 (February 2005): 67–101.

———. "Semi-Colonialism, Transnational Networks and News Flows in Early Republican Shanghai." *The China Review* 4, no. 1 (Spring 2004): 55–88.

Gould, Randall. *China in the Sun*. New York: Doubleday, 1946.

Gould, Roger V. "Collective Action and Network Structure." *American Sociological Review* 59 (1993): 182–96.

———. *Insurgent Identities: Class, Community and Protest in Paris from 1848 to the Commune*. Chicago: University of Chicago Press, 1995.

———. "Uses of Network Tools in Comparative Historical Research." In *Comparative Historical Analysis in the Social Sciences*, edited by James

Mahoney and Dietrich Rueschemeyer, 241–69. New York: Cambridge University Press, 2003.

Granovetter, Mark. "The Strength of Weak Ties: A Network Theory Revisited." In *Social Structure and Network Analysis*, edited by Peter N. Marsden and Nan Lin. Beverly Hills: Sage, 1982.

Gu, Bingquan, and Yingen Zhang. "Pudong Tongxianghui Ji Qi Dui Pudong de Xianqi Kaifa" (The Pudong Tongxianghui and Early Development of Pudong). *Chuansha Wenshi Ziliao* (Chuansha Historical Materials), no. 2 (1990): 73–87.

Guangdong Tongxianghui. *Guangdong Lü Hu Tongxianghui Jiuji Nanmin Weiyuanhui Baogaoshu* (Report of the Refugee Relief Committee of the Guangdong Tongxianghui). Shanghai, 1938.

Guo, Lanxin. "Du Yuesheng Yu Heng She" (Du Yuesheng and the Perseverance Society). In *Jiu Shanghai de Banghui* (The Gangs of Old Shanghai), edited by Zhongguo Renmin Zhengzhi Xieshang Huiyi Shanghai Shi Weiyuanhui Wenshi Ziliao Gongzuo Weiyuanhui (Work Committee on Literary and Historical Materials of the Chinese People's Political Consultative Council's Shanghai Municipal Committee), 300–20. Shanghai: Shanghai Renmin Chubanshe, 1986.

Guo, Xiufeng. "Wangwei Shiqi de *Zhonghua Ribao*" (*Zhonghua Ribao* During the Wang Jingwei Period). In *Ershi Shiji Shanghai Wenshi Ziliao Wenku*, 149–59, 1999.

Guo, Xuyin. *Guomindang Paixi Douzheng Shi* (History of Factional Struggle in the Guomindang). Shanghai: Shanghai Renmin Chubanshe, 1992.

Hahn, Emily. *China to Me: A Partial Autobiography*. New York: Doubleday, 1945.

———. *The Soong Sisters*. Garden City, NJ: Doubleday, 1942.

Hanser, Amy. "Youth Job Searches in Urban China: The Use of Social Connections in a Changing Labor Market." In *Social Connections in China: Institutions, Culture and the Changing Nature of Guanxi*, edited by Thomas Gold, Doug Guthrie, and David Wank. New York: Cambridge University Press, 2002.

Hao, Yen-ping. *The Comprador in Nineteenth-Century China: Bridge Between East and West*. Cambridge: Harvard University, Council on East Asian Studies, 1970.

He, Qingru. "Zhiye Xuexiao Xuesheng Chulu Diaocha" (Job Placement of Vocational School Students: An Investigation). *Jiaoyu yu Zhiye*, no. 168 (October 1935): 535–54.

He, Xinchang. "Haishang Wenren Wang Yiting" (Shanghai Celebrity Wang Yiting). *Dang'an yu Shixue* (Archives and Historical Studies) no. 6 (1996): 54–59.

He, Yuwen. "Shen Junru de Sixiang Yu Shenghuo" (Shen Junru's Thought and Life). *Chunqiu* 2, no. 10 (December 1, 1957): 9–10.

Heng She Shezhang (Regulations of the Perseverance Society). Annex 1 in Jiu Shanghai de Banghui (1986): 367–8.

Henriot, Christian. *Prostitution and Sexuality in Shanghai: A Social History, 1849–1949*. Cambridge: Cambridge University Press, 2001.

———. *Shanghai, 1927–1937: Municipal Power, Locality, and Modernization*. Translated by Noël Castelino. Berkeley: University of California Press, 1993.

Henriot, Christian, and Wen-hsin Yeh, eds. *In the Shadow of the Rising Sun: Shanghai Under Japanese Occupation*. Cambridge: Cambridge University Press, 2004.

Henriot, Christian, and Zu'an Zheng. *Atlas de Shanghai: Espace et Représentation de 1849 à nos Jours* (Atlas of Shanghai: Space and Representation from 1849 to the Present). Paris: CNRS-éditions, 1999.

Hershatter, Gail. *Dangerous Pleasures: Prostitution and Modernity in Twentieth Century China*. Berkeley: University of California Press, 1997.

———. *The Workers of Tianjin, 1900–1949*. Stanford: Stanford University Press, 1986.

Hicks, Alexander. *Social Democracy and Welfare Capitalism: A Century of Income Security Politics*. Ithaca, NY: Cornell University Press, 1999.

Hinder, Eleanor M. *Social and Industrial Problems of Shanghai*. New York: Institute of Pacific Relations, 1942.

Ho, Ping-ti. *Zhongguo Huiguan Shilun* (Historical Study of Chinese Native-Place Societies). Taipei: Xuesheng Shuju, 1966.

Hokari, Hiroyuki. "Kindai Shanhai Ni Okeru Itai Shori Mondai to Shimei Kōsho—Dōkyō Girudo to Chūgoku no Toshika" (The Management of Human Remains in Modern Shanghai and the Siming Gongsuo—Native-Place Guilds and China's Urbanization). *Shigaku Zasshi* (History Journal), no. 103 (February 1994): 67–93.

Honig, Emily. *Creating Chinese Ethnicity: Subei People in Shanghai, 1850–1980*. New Haven: Yale University Press, 1992.

———. *Sisters and Strangers: Women in the Shanghai Cotton Mills, 1919–1949*. Stanford: Stanford University Press, 1986.

Howe, Christopher. *Shanghai: Revolution and Development in an Asian Metropolis*. Cambridge: Cambridge University Press, 1981.

Hu She. *Hu She Di Shisan Jie Sheyuan Da Hui Tekan* (Special Issue for the Thirteenth Annual Membership Meeting of the Hu She). Shanghai, 1937.

Hu, Yuzhi. "Zhunbei Xin Xingshi de Daolai" (Preparing for the New Situation Which Has Arrived). *Dikang Sanri Kan* 25 (November 9, 1937): 125.

Huskey, James. "The Cosmopolitan Connection: Americans and Chinese in Shanghai During the Interwar Years." *Diplomatic History* 11, no. 3 (Summer 1987): 227–42.

Hutt, Jonathan. "*La Maison d'Or*—the Sumptuous World of Shao Xunmei." *East Asian History*, no. 21 (June 2001): 111–42.

Ishijima, Noriyuki. "Konichi Minzoku Toitsu Sensen to Chishiki Jin" (The Anti-Japanese United Front and the Intellectuals). *Rekishi Hyoron* 1, no. 256 (1971): 22–50.

Israel, John. *Student Nationalism in China, 1927–1937.* Stanford: Stanford University Press, 1966.

Israel, John, and Donald W. Klein. *Rebels and Bureaucrats: China's December 9ers.* Berkeley: University of California Press, 1976.

Iwama, Kazuhiro. "Yūkai to Kyūsai no Toshikan Nettowāku: Nijū Sēki Zenhan Shanhai no Shiten Kara" (Urban Kidnapping and Rescue Networks from the Perspective of 1920s Shanghai). In *Shanhai—Chōsōsuru Nettowāku,* edited by Shanhai shi kenkyū kai Nihon. Tokyo: Kyūko Shoin, 2000.

Jia, Shumei. *Shanghai Xinwen Zhi* (Shanghai News Gazetteer). Shanghai: Shanghai Sheke Xueyuan Chubanshe, 2000.

Jiang, Hao. "Hongmen Lishi Chutan" (An Introduction to the History of the Triads). In *Jiu Shanghai de Banghui* (The Gangs of Old Shanghai), edited by Zhongguo Renmin Zhengzhi Xieshang Huiyi Shanghai Shi Weiyuanhui Wenshi Ziliao Gongzuo Weiyuanhui (Work Committee on Literary and Historical Materials of the Chinese People's Political Consultative Council's Shanghai Municipal Committee), 68–86. Shanghai: Shanghai Renmin Chubanshe, 1986.

———. "Qing Bang de Yuanliu Ji Qi Yanbian" (The Origins and Evolution of the Green Gang). In *Jiu Shanghai de Banghui* (The Gangs of Old Shanghai), edited by Zhongguo Renmin Zhengzhi Xieshang Huiyi Shanghai Shi Weiyuanhui Wenshi Ziliao Gongzuo Weiyuanhui (Work Committee on Literary and Historical Materials of the Chinese People's Political Consultative Council's Shanghai Municipal Committee), 51–67. Shanghai: Shanghai Renmin Chubanshe, 1986.

Jiang, Mingqi. "Jingshang Shibai de Yuanyin" (Causes for Business Failure). *Shanghai Zong Shanghui Yuebao* 6, no. 1 (January 1926): 1–2.

Jiang, Yi. *Zhongguo Gongchandang Zai Shanghai* (The Chinese Communist Party in Shanghai). Shanghai: Shanghai Renmin Chubanshe, 1991.

Jiangning Tongxianghui. *Jiangning Liuxian Lü Hu Tongxianghui Huikan* (Journal of the Association of Sojourners from Six Counties of Jiangning in Shanghai). Shanghai, 1935.

Jin, Chongji. "Du Zhongyuan Yu Xinsheng Zhoukan" (Du Zhongyuan and the New Life Weekly). *Lishi Yanjiu* 5 (2000): 111–21.

Jin, Gonghui. "Kangzhan Chuqi Quanguo Gejie Juanzi Jiuguo Gaishu" (Summary of Donations for National Salvation from Various Circles in the Nation in the Early Part of the War of Resistance). *Mingguo Dang'an,* no. 3 (2002): 66–72.

Jin, Peiren. "Luetan Xie Kuansheng Yu Guomindang Sifajie" (Brief Discussion on Xie Kuansheng and the Guomindang Judiciary). *Wenshi Ziliao Xuanji* 78 (1982): 70–86.

Jones, Susan Mann. "The Ningpo *Pang* and Financial Power at Shanghai." In *The Chinese City Between Two Worlds,* edited by Mark Elvin and G. William Skinner, 73–96. Stanford: Stanford University Press, 1974.

Jordan, Donald A. *China's Trial by Fire: The Shanghai War of 1932*. Ann Arbor: University of Michigan Press, 2001.
The Jubilee of Shanghai, 1843–1893. Shanghai: North China Daily News, 1893.
Kirby, William C. "The Chinese War Economy." In *China's Bitter Victory: The War with Japan, 1937–1945*, edited by James C. Hsiung and Steven I. Levine, 185–212. Armonk, NY: M. E. Sharpe, 1992.
———. "Engineering China: The Birth of the Developmental State, 1928–1937." In *Becoming Chinese: Passages to Modernity and Beyond*, edited by Wen-hsin Yeh, 137–60. Berkeley: University of California Press, 2000.
Kōhama, Masako. *Kindai Shanhai no Kōkyōsei to Kokai* (The "Public" and the State of Modern Shanghai). Tokyo: Keibun Shuban, 2000.
———. "The Urban Society and Social Welfare in Republican China." *Shigaku-Zasshi* 103, no. 9 (1994): 60–64.
———. "Hoshōin to Shōkaijō no Tsunagu Kyūsai" (Guarantors and Introduction Connections in Charity). In *Shanhai—Chōōsuru Nettowāku*, edited by Shanhai shi kenkyū kai Nihon, 197–218. Tokyo: Kyūko Shoin, 2000.
Kohli, Atul. *State-Directed Development: Political Power and Industrialization in the Global Periphery*. Cambridge: Cambridge University Press, 2004.
Lao, Shan. "Bailong Shanren Wang Yiting" (White Dragon Mountainman Wang Yiting). In *Haishang Mingrenlu* (Shanghai Celebrities). Shanghai: Shanghai Huabao Chubanshe, 1991.
Lean, Eugenia. "Politics of Passion: The Trial of Shi Jianqiao and the Rise of Public Sympathy in Nineteen-Thirties China." University of California, Los Angeles, 2001.
Lee, Leo Ou-fan. *Shanghai Modern: The Flowering of a New Urban Culture in China, 1930–1945*. Cambridge: Harvard University Press, 1999.
Li, Jiaji, ed. *Shanghai Gongyun Zhi* (Shanghai Labor Movement Gazetteer). Shanghai: Shanghai Shehui Kexueyuan Chubanshe, 1997.
Li, Jin. "Cong Suowei 'Qi Junzi' Tandao 'Jiuguo'" (From the Seven Gentlemen Issue, Speaking of National Salvation). *Chunqiu*, no. 144 (July 1, 1963): 5–6.
Li, Pingshu. *Qiewan Laoren Qishi Zixu* (Li Pingshu on Himself at Age Seventy). Shanghai: Shanghai Guji Chubanshe, 1989.
Li, Tiangang. "1927: Shanghai Shimin Zizhi Yundong de Zongjie" (1927: The Culmination of the Self-Government Movement by Shanghai Citizenry). In *Shanghai: Chengshi, Shehui Yu Wenhua* (Shanghai: City, Society, and Culture), edited by Hui Wang and Kwok-leung Yu, 57–72. Hong Kong: Hong Kong University Press, 1998.
Li, Ying. "Du Zhongyuan Shilue" (Brief Biography of Du Zhongyuan). *Jilin Wenshi Ziliao* 16 (1987): 128–31.
Liang, Qizi, (Angela Leung). *Shishan Yu Jiaohua: Ming-Qing Di Cishan Zuzhi* (Charity and Moral Transformation: Philanthropic Organizations of the Ming and Qing Periods). Taipei: Linking Publishers, 1997.

Liangong (Bu). Gongchan Guoji Yu Zhongguo Guomin Geming Yundong, 1926–1927 (Soviet Communists (Bolsheviks), Comintern, and the Chinese National Revolutionary Movement, 1926–1927). Translated (from Russian) by the Chinese Communist Party Central Party History Research Office. Beijing: Beijing Tushuguan Chubanshe, 1998.

Linebarger, Paul M. A. *The China of Chiang Kai-Shek: A Political Study*. Boston: World Peace Foundation, 1943.

Liu, Guangjing. *Jingshi Sixiang Yu Xinxing Qiye* (Statecraft Thought and Emerging Enterprises). Taipei: Lianjing Chuban Shiye Gongsi, 1990.

Liu, Hongyuan. "Ai Hansong Zhuan" (Biography of Ai Hansong). *Gao'an Shizhi Ziliao (Jiangxi)* 1 (1986): 199–202.

Liu, Nianzhi. *Shiye Liu Hongsheng Zhuanlue: Huiyi Wode Fuqin* (A Biographical Sketch of the Industrialist Liu Hongsheng: Memories of My Father). Beijing: Wenshi Ziliao, 1982.

Liu, Yanru. "Kangzhan Chuqi Shanghai Nanmin Gongzuo" (Refugee Work in Shanghai at the Beginning of the War of Resistance). In *Kangzhan Chuqide Nanmin Gongzuo* (Refugee Work at the Beginning of the War of Resistance), edited by Zhonggang Shanghai Dangshi Ziliao Zhengji Weiyuanhui, 48–87. Shanghai: Shanghai Xinwen Chubanju, 1993.

Lu, Guangji. "Huiyi Du Zhongyuan Tongzhi" (Recollection of the Comrade Du Zhongyuan). *Shenyang Wenshi Ziliao* 5 (1984): 7–20.

Lu, Han-chao. "Becoming Urban: Mendicancy and Vagrants in Modern Shanghai." *Journal of Social History* 33, no. 1 (Fall 1999): 7–36.

———. *Beyond the Neon Lights: Everyday Shanghai in the Twentieth Century*. Berkeley: University of California Press, 1999.

Lu, Lishi, ed. *Shanghai Tebie Shi Jiuji Shiye Gaikuang* (Survey of the Shanghai Municipal Relief Services). Shanghai: Shanghai Tebie Shi, Shehui Ju Jiuji Yuan, 1942.

Lu, Xun. "Qiejiating Zawen Erji" (Miscellaneous Essay of Qiejie Studio, Part 2). In *Lu Xun Quanji*, 460–63. Beijing: Renmin Wenxue Chubanshe, 1981.

Lu, Zhiren. "Nanmin Gongzuo" (Refugee Work). In *Kangzhan Chuqide Nanmin Gongzuo* (Refugee Work at the Beginning of the War of Resistance), edited by Zhonggang Shanghai Dangshi Ziliao Zhengji Weiyuanhui, 7–11. Shanghai: Shanghai Xinwen Chubanju, 1993.

Lunt, Carroll, ed. *The China Who's Who (Foreign): A Biographical Dictionary*. Shanghai: Kelly and Walsh, 1924.

Ma, Changlin. "Xinsheng an" (The New Life Case). *Shanghai Dang'an* 33 (1990): 46–48.

Ma, Guangren. *Shanghai Xinwen Shi* (History of News in Shanghai). Shanghai: Fudan Daxue Chubanshe, 1996.

MacKinnon, Stephen R. "Toward a History of the Chinese Press in the Republican Period." *Modern China* 23, no. 1 (January 1997): 3–32.

MacKinnon, Stephen R., and Oris Friesen, eds. *China Reporting: An Oral History of American Journalism in the 1930s and 1940s*. Berkeley: University of California Press, 1987.

Martin, Brian G. "Eating Bitterness: Du Yuesheng and Guomindang Politics in Shanghai, 1945–1949." *East Asian History*, no. 29 (June 2005): 129–52.

———. "Resistance and Cooperation: Du Yuesheng and the Politics of the Shanghai United Committee, 1940–1945." In *In the Shadow of the Rising Sun: Shanghai Under Japanese Occupation*, edited by Christian Henriot and Wen-hsin Yeh. Cambridge: Cambridge University Press, 2004.

———. *The Shanghai Green Gang: Politics and Organized Crime, 1919–1937*. Berkeley: University of California Press, 1996.

———. "Shield of Collaboration: The Wang Jingwei Regime's Security Service." *Intelligence and National Security* 16, no. 4 (2001): 89–148.

———. "Tu Yueh-Sheng and Labour Control in Shanghai: The Case of the French Tramways Union, 1928–1932." *Papers on Far Eastern History* 32 (1985): 99–137.

Matsumoto, Shigeharu. *Shanhai Jidai* (My Shanghai Years), vol. 2. Tokyo: Chuokoronsha, 1974.

McElderry, Andrea L. *Shanghai Old-Style Banks (Ch'ien-Chuang), 1800–1935: A Traditional Institution in a Changing Society*. Ann Arbor: Center for Chinese Studies, University of Michigan, 1976.

Mei, Zhen, and Pu Shao. *Haishang Wenren Du Yuesheng* (Du Yuesheng: Famous in Shanghai). Zhengzhou: Henan Renmin Chubanshe, 1987.

"Memories of Hori Keijiro." In *Dang'an Yu Shixue* (Archives and Historical Studies), 1996.

Min, Zhishi. "Kexue de Guanli" (Scientific Management). *Shanghai Zong Shanghui Yuebao* 5, no. 3 (March 1925): 1–3.

Mitter, Rana. *The Manchurian Myth: Nationalism, Resistance, and Collaboration in Modern China*. Berkeley: University of California Press, 2000.

Mittler, Barbara. *A Newspaper for China? Power, Identity, and Change in Shanghai's News Media, 1872–1912*. Cambridge: Harvard University Asia Center, 2004.

Mizruchi, Mark S. "Social Network Analysis: Recent Achievements and Current Controversies." *Acta Sociologica* 37 (1994): 329–43.

Moore, Barrington Jr. *Social Origins of Dictatorship and Democracy: Lord and Peasant in the Making of the Modern World*. Boston: Beacon, 1967.

Mu, Xin, ed. *Zou Taofen*. Hong Kong: Sanlian Shudian, 1959.

Nan, Boyong. *Shanghai Daheng Yu Xiaqing* (Shanghai Bigwig, Yu Xiaqing). Haikou: Hainan Chubanshe, 1996.

Nankai Daxue Ma Lie Zhuyi Jiaoyan Shi (Teaching and Research Department of Marxism-Leninism at Nankai University), and Zhonggong Dangshi Jiaoyan Zu (Teaching and Research Group on the History of the Chinese Communist Party), eds. *Huabei Shibian Ziliao Xuanbian* (Selections of Historical Materials on the North China Incident). Zhengzhou: Henan Renmin Chubanshe, 1983.

Narramore, Terry. "The Nationalists and the Daily Press: The Case of the Shen Bao, 1927–1934." In *The Nationalists and Chinese Society, 1923–1937,* edited by John Fitzgerald, 106–32. Melbourne: University of Melbourne Press, 1989.

Ningbo Tongxianghui. *Ningbo Lü Hu Tongxianghui Dibajie Zhengqiu Huiyuan Dahui Jiniankan* (Commemorative Publication of the Eighth Membership Drive of the Ningbo Tongxianghui). Shanghai, 1939.

———. *Ningbo Lü Hu Tongxianghui Jiuji Beinan Tongxiang Zhengxinglu* (Record-Book of Ningbo Tongxianghui Aid to Fellow-Provincial Refugees). Shanghai, 1939.

———. *Ningbo Lü Hu Tongxianghui Yuebao* (Ningbo Sojourners' Association Monthly). Shanghai, 1921.

North China Herald, compilers, *The Jubilee of Shanghai*. Shanghai: North China Herald, 1893.

Oi, Jean C. *State and Peasant in Contemporary China: The Political Economy of Village Government*. Berkeley: University of California Press, 1989.

Pal, John. *Shanghai Saga*. London: Jarrolds, 1963.

Pan, Dacheng. "Huiyi Shanghai Guoji Jiuji Hui Diyi Nanmin Shourongsuo" (Remembering the Shanghai International Reief Committee's First Refugee Shelter). In *Kangzhan Chuqide Nanmin Gongzuo* (Refugee Work at the Beginning of the War of Resistance), edited by Zhonggang Shanghai Dangshi Ziliao Zhengji Weiyuanhui, 89–92. Shanghai: Shanghai Xinwen Chubanju, 1993.

Pepper, Suzanne. *The Civil War in China: The Political Struggle, 1945–1949*. Berkeley: University of California Press, 1978.

Perry, Elizabeth. *Patrolling the Chinese Revolution: Worker Militias, Citizenship, and the Modern Chinese State*. Lanham, MD: Rowman and Littlefield, 2006.

Perry, Elizabeth J. *Shanghai on Strike: The Politics of Chinese Labor*. Stanford: Stanford University Press, 1993.

Peters, E. W. *Shanghai Policeman*. London: Rich and Cowan, 1937.

Porta, Donatella Della, and Mario Diani. *Social Movements: An Introduction*. Malden, MA: Blackwell Publishing, 1999.

Pott, F. L. Hawks. *A Short History of Shanghai*. Shanghai: Kelly and Walsh, 1928.

Powell, John B. *My Twenty-Five Years in China*. New York: MacMillan, 1945.

Pudong Tongxianghui. *Pudong Lü Hu Tongxianghui Zhengqiu Huiyuan Ce* (Record of the Pudong Tongxianghui Membership Drive). Shanghai, 1931.

———. *Pudong Tongxianghui Huisuo Luocheng Jinian Tekan (Special Commemorative Publication for the Inauguration of the Pudong Tongxianghui Building)*. Shanghai, 1937.

———. *Pudong Tongxianghui Nianbao* (Yearly Report of the Pudong Tongxianghui). Shanghai, 1933, 1934, 1935, 1936, 1937, 1938.

———. *Pudong Tongxianghui Zhenmi Handu Jiyao* (Collection of Correspondence Concerning Pudong Tongxianghui Rice Collection). Shanghai, 1932.

Putnam, Robert D. *Bowling Alone: The Collapse and Revival of American Community*. New York: Simon and Schuster, 2000.
Putnam, Robert D., et al. *Making Democracy Work: Civic Traditions in Modern Italy*. Princeton: Princeton University Press, 1993.
Pye, Lucian W. "Factions and the Politics of *Guanxi*: Paradoxes in Chinese Administrative and Political Behaviour." In *The Nature of Chinese Politics: From Mao to Jiang*, edited by Jonathan Unger, 38–57. Armonk, NY: M. E. Sharpe, 2002.
———. "How China's Nationalism Was Shanghaied." In *Chinese Nationalism*, edited by Jonathan Unger, 86–112. Armonk, NY: M. E. Sharpe, 1996.
Qian, Shengke. *Qing Hong Bang Zhi Heimu* (The inside Story of the Green and Red Gangs). Shanghai: Qian Shengke Heimu Faxingsuo, 1919.
Qin, Dechun. *Qin Dechun Huiyi Lu* (Memoirs of Qin Dechun). *Zhuanji Wenxue* (1967): 41–46.
Qin, Xitian, et al., eds. *Shanghai Xianzhi* (Gazeteer of Shanghai County). Shanghai, 1936.
Qiu, Qianmu. *Zhongguo Zhengdangshi* (History of Chinese Political Parties). Taiyuan: Shanxi Renmin Chubanshe, 1991.
Quan Zhe Gonghui. *Quan Zhe Gonghui Huiwu Baogao* (Report of the Work of the All-Zhejiang Association). Shanghai, 1931–2.
Rankin, Mary Backus. *Elite Activism and Political Transformation in China: Zhejiang Province, 1865-1911*. Stanford: Stanford University Press, 1986.
Reed, Christopher A. *Gutenberg in Shanghai: Chinese Print Capitalism, 1876–1937*. Honolulu: University of Hawaii Press, 2004.
Rigby, Richard W. *The May 30th Movement: Events and Themes*. Canberra: Australian National University Press, 1980.
Ristaino, Marcia Reynders. *Port of Last Resort: The Diaspora Communities of Shanghai*. Stanford: Stanford University Press, 2001.
Rogaski, Ruth. "Hygienic Modernity in Tianjin." In *Remaking the Chinese City: Modernity and National Identity, 1900–1950*, edited by Joseph W. Esherick, 30–46. Honolulu: University of Hawaii Press, 1999.
Rong, Zhai, et al. *Jinling Jiumeng* (Dream of Old Nanjing). Hong Kong: Zhicheng Chubanshe, 1963.
Rossinger, Lawrence. *China's Wartime Politics, 1939–1944*. Princeton: Princeton University Press, 1944.
Rowe, William T. *Hankow: Commerce and Society in a Chinese City, 1786–1889*. Stanford: Stanford University Press, 1984.
———. "The Public Sphere in Modern China." *Modern China* 16, no. 3 (1990): 309–29.
Ruan, Renze, and Zhennong Gao, eds. *Shanghai Zongjiao Shi* (History of Religions in Shanghai). Shanghai: Shanghai Renmin Chubanshe, 1992.
Sawamura, Sachio. "Wang Yiting." In *Shanhai Jinbutsu Yinshoki* (Impression of Shanghai Figures), 18–22. Tokyo: Toyo Kenkyukai, 1930.
Schoppa, R. Keith. *Blood Road: The Mystery of Shen Dingyi in Revolutionary China*. Berkeley: University of California Press, 1995.

———. *Chinese Elite and Political Change: Zhejiang Province in the Early Twentieth Century*. Cambridge: Harvard University Press, 1982.

Schwintzer, Ernest P. "Education to Save the Nation: Huang Yanpei and the Educational Reform Movement in Early 20th-Century China." Seattle: University of Washington, 1992.

Scott, John. *Social Network Analysis: A Handbook*. London: Russell Sage Foundation, 2000.

Sha, Qianli. *Manhua Jiuguohui* (A Casual Discussion of the National Salvation Association). Beijing: Wenshi Ziliao Chubanshe, 1983.

———. *Qiren Zhiyu* (Seven People Go to Prison). Shanghai: Shenghuo Shudian, 1938.

Shanghai Academy of Social Sciences, eds. *Wusa Yundong Shiliao* (Historical Materials on the May Thirtieth Movement). Shanghai: Shanghai Renmin Chubanshe, 1981.

———, eds. *Wusi Yundong Zai Shanghai Shiliao Xuanji* (Compilation of Historical Materials on the May Fourth Movement in Shanghai). Shanghai: Shanghai Shehuikexueyuan Chubanshe, 1980.

———, eds. *Xinhai Geming Zai Shanghai Shiliao Xuanji* (Compilation of Historical Materials on the 1911 Revolution in Shanghai). Shanghai: Shanghai Shehuikexueyuan Chubanshe, 1981.

Shanghai Ertong Fuli Zujin Hui. *Shanghai Shehui Fuli Jiguan Yao Lan* (Guide to Shanghai's Social Welfare Organizations). Shanghai: Shanghai Ertong Fuli Zujin Hui, 1948.

Shanghai International Relief Committee. *Shanghai International Relief Committee Annual Report*. Shanghai: Shanghai International Relief Committee, 1938.

———. *Six-Month Report*. Shanghai: Shanghai International Relief Committee, 1938.

"Shanghai Jiuguo Hui Dashiji" (Record of the Major Affairs of the Shanghai National Salvation Association). *Shehui Kexue*, no. 4 (1984): 87–90.

Shanghai Municipal Archives, eds. *Shanghai Gongren Sanci Wuzhuang Qiyi* (Shanghai Workers' Three Armed Uprisings). Shanghai: Shanghaishi Dang'anguan Chubanshe, 1983.

Shanghai Shangye Minglu (Shanghai Commercial Directory). Shanghai, 1931.

Shanghai Shehui Kexue Yuan Zhengzhi FaluYanjiusuo Shehui Wenti Zu (The Social Issues Section of the Institute of Politics and Law of the Shanghai Academy of Social Sciences), eds. *Da Liumang Du Yuesheng* (Big Gangster Du Yuesheng). Beijing: Chunchong Chubanshe, 1965.

Shanghai Shi. *1946 Niandu Dongling Jiuji Gongzuo Baogao* (1946 Work Report on Winter Relief). Shanghai, 1946.

———. *1947 Niandu Dongling Jiuji Gongzuo Baogao* (1946 Work Report on Winter Relief). Shanghai, 1947.

Shanghai Shi Jiuji Weiyuanhui. *Choumu Weiyuanhui Gongzuo Baogao* (Fundraising Committee Work Report) Shanghai, 1949.

Shanghai Shi Nianjian (Shanghai Yearbook). Shanghai: Zhonghua, 1936.
Shanghai Shi, Zhabei Qu Zhibian Weiyuanhui. *Zhabei Qu Zhi* (Gazetteer for Zhabei District). Shanghai: Shanghai Shehui Kexueyuan Chubanshe, 1998.
Shanghai Zhinan (Guide to Shanghai). Shanghai, 1914, 1919.
Shanghai Tebie Shi. *Linshi Bihansuo Baogao Ce* (Report on Temporary Cold Weather Shelters). Shanghai: Shanghai Tebieshi, 1929.
Shanghai Tongshe, ed. *Shanghai Yanjiu Ziliao* (Research Materials on Shanghai). Shanghai: Shanghai Shudian, 1936.
Shaoxing Qixian Lü Hu Tongxianghui. *Shaoxing Qixian Lü Hu Tongxianghui Ge Gong Zhangcheng* (Regulations of the Association of Sojourners from the Seven Counties of Shaoxing). Shanghai, 1920.
Shehui Bu. *Shehui Fagui Huibian* (Collection of Social Legislation and Regulations). Shanghai: Shehui Bu Jing-Hu Qu Tepai Yuan Banshichu, 1945.
Shen, Kuiyi. "Entering a New Era: Transformation and Innovation in Chinese Painting, 1895–1930." In *Between the Thunder and the Rain: Chinese Paintings from the Opium War through the Cultural Revolution, 1840–1979*, Julia Andrews, Claudia Brown, David E. Fraser, and Kuiyi Shen, 97–117. San Francisco: Asian Art Museum of San Francisco, 2000.
———. "Traditional Chinese Painting in a Transitional Era, 1900–1950." In *A Century in Crisis: Modernity and Tradition in the Art of Twentieth Century China*, Julia Andrews and Kuiyi Shen, 80–95. New York: Guggenheim Museum, 1998.
Shenbao Nianjian (Shen Bao Yearbook). Shanghai, 1936.
Shenyang Shimin Jian (Shenyang Democratic Nation-building Association) and Shenyang Gongshang Lian (Shenyang Federation of Industry and Commerce). "Du Zhongyuan Zhuanlue" (Brief Biography of Du Zhongyuan). *Liaoning Wenshi Ziliao* 26 (1989): 304–7.
Shi, Kuiji. "Du Zhongyuan Yu Jing Dezhen" (Du Zhongyuan and Jing Dezhen). *Jilin Wenshi Ziliao* 22 (1987): 25–59.
Shi, Liang. "Wodi Shenghuo Daolu" (Path of My Life). *Renwu* 1, no. 5 (1983): 125.
Shidai Wenxian She (Contemporary Literary Society), eds. *Jiuguo Wuzui Qijunzi Shijian* (The Seven Gentlemen Who Are Innocent and Tried to Save the Nation), n.p., 1937.
Siu, Funkee. "Wang Zhen, a Master of the Shanghai Painting School." *Besides—a Journal of Art History and Criticism* (Hong Kong), vol. 2 (1999): 79–102.
Slack, Edward R. Jr. *Opium, State, and Society: China's Narco-Economy and the Guomindang, 1924–1937*. Honolulu: University of Hawaii Press, 2001.
Smith, S. A. *Like Cattle and Horses: Nationalism and Labor in Shanghai, 1895–1927*. Durham, NC: Duke University Press, 2002.
———. *The Road Is Made: Communism in Shanghai 1920–1927*. Richmond, VA: Curzon, 2000.

Song, Ao. "Hongdong Quanguo de Shen Junru Deng Qiren an" (Case of Shen Runru and Others, the Seven, Which Has Caused a Great Uproar in the Entire Nation). *Dongfang Zazhi* 34, no. 13 (part 1, July 1, 1937): 267–81.

———. "Hongdong Quanguo de Shen Junru Deng Qiren an" (Case of Shen Runru and Others, the Seven, Which Has Caused a Great Uproar in the Entire Nation). *Dongfang Zazhi* 34, no. 14 (part 2, July 16, 1937): 90–5.

Stolle, Dietland, and Thomas R. Rochon. "Are All Associations Alike? Member Diversity, Associational Type, and the Creation of Social Capital." In *Beyond Tocqueville: Civil Society and the Social Capital Debate in Comparative Perspective,* edited by Bob Edwards, Michael W. Foley, and Mario Diani, 143–56. Hanover: University Press of New England, 2001.

Stranahan, Patricia. "Radicalization of Refugees: Communist Party Activity in Wartime Shanghai's Displaced Person's Camps." *Modern China* 26, no. 2 (2000): 166–93.

———. "Strange Bedfellows: The Communist Party and Shanghai's Elite in the National Salvation Movement." *China Quarterly* 129 (March 1992): 26–51.

———. *Underground: The Shanghai Communist Party and the Politics of Survival, 1927–1937.* Lanham, MD: Rowman and Littlefield, 1998.

Strand, David. *Rickshaw Beijing: City People and Politics in the 1920s.* Berkeley: University of California Press, 1989.

Strauss, Julia C. *Strong Institutions in Weak Polities: Statebuilding in Republican China, 1927–1940.* Oxford: Oxford University Press, 1998.

Su, Zhiliang, and Lifei Chen. *Haishang Xiaoxiong: Huang Jinrong Yu Shanghai Shehui* (An Ambitious Shanghai Worthy: Huang Jinrong and Shanghai Society). Nanjing: Jiangsu Renmin Chubanshe, 2000.

Sun, Dunheng. "Yi-Er-Jiu Yongdong Zai Qinghua" (The December Ninth Movement at Qinghua University). *Wenshi Ziliao Xuanbian* (Selection of Literary and Historical Materials), no. 8 (1980): 14–34.

Sun, Jianqiu. "Tongchang Chehang Shixi Baogao" (Internship at the Tongchang Bicycle Shop: A Report). *Zhiye Shi Shikan,* no. 1 (November 1934): 54–61.

Sun, Yat-sen. *Zhongguo Neiluan Zhi Yuanyin* (The Causes of China's Domestic Turmoil), speech given November 25, 1924. Reprint, Sun Zhongshan Quanji (Collected Writings of Sun Yat-sen), Beijing: Zhonghua Shuju, 1956.

Swaan, Abram de. *In the Care of the State: Health Care, Education, and Welfare in Europe and the USA in the Modern Era.* Cambridge: Polity Press, 1988.

Tadashi, Hirano. *Chugoku Kakumei no Chishikijin* (Intellectuals in the Chinese Revolution). Tokyo: Kaizo, 1977.

Tadashi, Negishi. *Shanhai no Girudo* (The Guilds of Shanghai). Tokyo: Nippon Hyoronsha, 1951.

Tang, Chunliang. *Li Lisan Quanzhuan* (Comprehensive Biography of Li Lisan). Hefei: Anhui Renmin Chubanshe, 1999.

Tang, Guoliang. *Bainian Pudong Tongxianghuai* (One Hundred Years of the Pudong Native Place Association). Shanghai: Shanghai Shehui Kexue Chubanshe, 2005.

Tang, Zhenchang, et al., eds. *Shanghai Shi* (History of Shanghai). Shanghai: Shanghai Renmin Chubanshe, 1989.
Tatsuo, Yamada. *Chugoku Kokuminto Saha no Kenkyu* (Study of the Left-Wing Guomindang). Tokyo: Keio Tsushin, 1980.
Thompson, Roger R. *China's Local Councils in the Age of Constitutional Reform*. Cambridge: Harvard University Press, 1995.
Tian, Ren. "Qingdai Shanghai de Chenghuang Miao" (Shanghai's City God Temple in the Qing Period). In *Shanghai Zhanggu* (Anecdotes of Shanghai), 52–63. Shanghai: Shanghai Wenhua Chubanshe, 1982.
Ting, Lee-hsia Hsu. *Government Control of the Press in Modern China, 1900–1949*. Cambridge: Harvard University, Council on East Asian Studies, 1974.
Tsao, Hsing-Yuan. "A Forgotten Celebrity, Wang Zhen (1867–1938), Businessman, Philanthropist, and Artist." In *Art at the Close of China's Empire*, edited by Ju-Hsi Choi, 94–109. Phoenix: Arizona State University, Herberger College of the Arts: *Phoebus, Occasional Papers in Art History*, 1998.
Vittinghoff, Natascha. "'British Barbarians' and 'Chinese Pigtails'? Translingual Practice in a Transnational Environment in Nineteenth Century Hong Kong and Shanghai." *The China Review* 4, no. 1 (Spring 2004): 27–54.
Wagner, Rudolf. "The Role of the Foreign Community in the Chinese Public Sphere." *China Quarterly*, no. 142 (June 1995): 423–43.
Wakeman, Frederic E. Jr. *History and Will*. Berkeley: University of California Press, 1973.
———. *Policing Shanghai, 1927–1937*. Berkeley: University of California Press, 1995.
———. *Spymaster: Dai Li and the Chinese Secret Service*. Berkeley: University of California Press, 2003.
Wakeman, Frederic E. Jr., and Wen-hsin Yeh. "Introduction." In *Shanghai Sojourners*, edited by Frederic Wakeman Jr., and Wen-hsin Yeh, 1–14. Berkeley: University of California, Institute of East Asian Studies, 1992.
———, eds. *Shanghai Sojourners*. Berkeley: University of California, Institute of East Asian Studies, 1992.
Wales, Nym. "Notes on the Chinese Student Movement, 1935–36." In *Guidance Notes Prepared for the Nym Wales Collection on the Far East*. Stanford: Stanford University, Hoover Institution on War, Revolution, and Peace, 1959.
Wan, Molin. "Shanghai Wenren Huang Jinrong Zhiba: Cong Tiaojie Lincheng Jieche'an Dao Shemo Bingshi" (Shanghai Notable Huang Jinrong, Part Eight: From Mediation of the Lincheng Incident to His Death). *Shidai Wenzhe* (Current Digest) 4, no. 5 (1982): 173–75.
Wang, Ermin. *Wan Qing Zhengzhi Sixiang Shilun* (Historical Treatises on Late Qing Political Thought). Taipei: Shangwu Yingshu Guan, 1995.
Wang, Huabin, and Yanzi Wang. *Huang Yanpei*. Shijiazhuang: Huashan Wenyi Chubanshe, 1997.
Wang, Jiagui, and Xiyao Cao, eds. *Shanghai Daxue* (Shanghai University). Shanghai: Shanghai Shehuikexueyuan Chubanshe, 1986.

Wang, L. Sophia. "The Independence Press and Authoritarian Regimes: The Case of the Dagong Bao in Republican China." *Pacific Affairs* 67, no. 2 (Summer 1994): 216–42.

Wang, Renzi. "Wang Yiting." In *Minguo Renwu Zhuan* (Biographies of Public Figures in the Republican Period), vol. 4, 255–60. Beijing: Zhonghua Shudian, 1984.

Wang, Senran. *Jindai Ershi Jia Pingzhuan* (On Twenty Modern Artists). Beijing: Shumu Wenxian Chubanshe, 1987.

Wang, Yunsheng. *Guowen Zhoubao* 14, no. 28 (July 19, 1937): 9–11.

Wang, Yangqing, and Yinghu Xu. "Shanghai Qinghong Bang Gaishu" (A General Account of the Green and Red Gangs in Shanghai). *Shehui Kexue* (Social Sciences), no. 5 (1982): 63–5.

Wasserman, Stanley, and Katherine Faust. *Social Network Analysis: Methods and Applications.* Cambridge: Cambridge University Press, 1994.

Wasserstrom, Jeffrey N. "Questioning the Modernity of a Model Settlement: Struggles for Political Representation in Old Shanghai." In *Changing Concepts of Citizenship in Contemporary China*, edited by Elizabeth J. Perry and Merle Goldman, 110–32. Cambridge: Harvard University Press, 2002.

———. *Student Protests in Twentieth-Century China: The View from Shanghai.* Stanford: Stanford University Press, 1991.

Who's Who in China, Containing the Pictures and Biographies of China's Best Known Political, Financial, Business and Professional Leaders, 4th ed. Shanghai: *China Weekly Review*, 1931.

Who's Who in China. 4th ed. Shanghai: *China Weekly Review*, 1931.

Wilkinson, Mark. F. "The Shanghai American Community, 1937–1949." In *New Frontiers: Imperialism's New Communities in East Asia, 1842–1953*, edited by Robert Bickers and Christian Henriot, 231–49. Manchester: Manchester University Press, 2000.

Wu, Dongmai. *Wu Changshi Tanyilu* (Wu Changshi's Comments on Art). Beijing: Renmin Meishu Chubanshe, 1993.

Wu, Mianbo. "Guang-Zhao Gongsuo Fengchao Shimo Ji" (Record of the Guang-Zhao Gongsuo Controversy). Unpublished manuscript, Shanghai Historical Museum, 1919.

Wu, Nelson. "Tung Ch'i-Chang (1555–1636): Apathy in Government and Fervor in Art." In *The Confucian Personalities*, edited by Arthur F. Wright and Denis Twitchett, 260–93. Stanford: Stanford University Press, 1962.

Wu, Tegong. *Shanghai Shangtuan Kefu Shanghai Jilue* (Records of Shanghai Merchants Militia Recovering Shanghai City). Manuscript collected from the Shanghai Academy of Social Science, n.d.

Wu, Wenzhong. "Ben Ju Yinian Lai Shi Zheng Gaikuang" (Survey of Municipal Administration: This Department's Last Year). *Shehui Yuekan* (Social Affairs Journal) 2, no. 4 (October 1939): 28–33.

Xiao, Fenqi. *Wang Yiting*. Shijiazhuang: Hebei Jiayou Chubanshe, 2002.

Xiong, Yuezhi, et al. *Lao Shanghai: Mingren Mingshi Mingwu Daguan* (Old Shanghai: Famous People, Events, and Things). Shanghai: Shanghai Renmin Chubanshe, 1997.

Xiong, Yuezhi, et al., eds. *Shanghai de Waiguo Ren (1842–1949)* (Foreigners in Shanghai, 1842–1949). Shanghai: Shanghai Guji Chubanshe, 2003.

Xiong, Yuezhi, et al. *Shanghai Tongshi: Minguo Zhengzhi* (General History of Shanghai: Republican Politics), vol. 7. Shanghai: Shanghai Renmin Chubanshe, 1999.

Xu, Hansan, ed. *Huang Yanpei Nianpu* (Chronological Biography of Huang Yanpei). Beijing: Wenshi Ziliao Chubanshe, 1985.

Xu, Shiying. "The Problem of War Refugees Relief." *China Quarterly* 4, no. 3 (Summer 1939): 497–506.

———. *Shanghai Zhanqu Nanmin Linshi Jiuji Hui Gongzuo Baogao Shu* (Work Report of the Shanghai War Zone Refugee Provisional Relief Association). Shanghai: Shanghai Nanmin Linshi Jiujihui, 1933.

Xu, Wancheng. *Shanghai Cishan Jiguan Gaikuang* (Survey of Shanghai's Charitable Organizations). Shanghai: Longwen Shudian, 1941.

Xu, Xiaoqun. *Chinese Professionals and the Republican State: The Rise of Professional Associations in Shanghai, 1912–1937*. Cambridge: Cambridge University Press, 2001.

Xu, Zhihao. *Zhongguo Meishu Shetuan Manlu* (List of Chinese Art Societies). Shanghai: Shanghai Shuhua Chubanshe, 1994.

Yan, Changyan. "Xinsheng Zhoukan Shijian" (the New Life Weekly Incident). *Shanghai Wenshi Ziliao* 32 (1980): 83–91.

Yan, Yunxiang. *The Flow of Gifts: Reciprocity and Social Networks in a Chinese Village*. Stanford: Stanford University Press, 1996.

Yang, Longsheng. "Wang Yiting Shuhua Nianbiao" (Chronology of Paintings and Calligraphy of Wang Yiting). In *Wang Yiting Xiansheng Shuhuaji* (Calligraphy and Paintings of Mr. Wang Yiting), edited by Longsheng Yang. Taipei: Zhongguo Meishu Chubanshe, 1979.

———. "Wang Yiting Chuanlüe" (Concise Biography of Wang Yiting). In *Wang Yiting Xiansheng Shuhuaji* (Calligraphy abd Paintings of Mr. Wang Yiting), edited by Longsheng Yang. Taipei: Zhongguo Meishu Chubanshe, 1979.

———. *Wang Yiting Xiansheng Shuhuaji* (Calligraphy and Paintings of Mr. Wang Yiting). Taipei: Zhongguo Meishu Chubanshe, 1979.

Yang, Mayfair. *Gifts, Favors and Banquets: The Art of Social Relationships in China*. Ithaca, NY: Cornell University Press, 1994.

Yang, Mingyuan. "Tao Xingzhi Ershiliu Guoxing" (Tao Xingzhi's Overseas Trip in 1937). *Shanghai Wenshi Ziliao Xuanji* (Selection of Literary and Historical Materials from Shanghai), no. 45 (1984): 84–97.

Yang, Yi. *Haishang Molin* (Biographies of Artists in Shanghai), 2nd ed., vol. 3. Shanghai: Yuyuan Shuhua Shanhui, 1919. Reprint, 1921.

Yang, Yi, et al., eds. *Shanghai Zizhi Zhi* (History of Autonomous Shanghai). Shanghai: 1915.

Yeh, Wen-hsin. *The Alienated Academy: Culture and Politics in Republican China, 1919–1937.* Cambridge: Harvard University Press, 1990.

———. "Progressive Journalism and Shanghai's Petty Urbanites: Zou Taofen and the Shenghuo Weekly, 1926–1945." In *Shanghai Sojourners*, edited by Frederick Wakeman Jr., and Wen-hsin Yeh, 186–238. Berkeley: University of California, Institute of East Asian Studies, 1992.

———. *Provincial Passages: Culture, Space and the Origins of Chinese Communism*. Berkeley: University of California Press, 1996.

———. "The Republican Origins of the Danwei: The Case of Shanghai's Bank of China." In *Danwei: The Changing Chinese Workplace in Historical and Comparative Perspective*, edited by Xiaobo Lu and Elizabeth Perry, 60–88. Armonk, NY: M. E. Sharpe, 1997.

———. *Shanghai Splendor: Economic Sentiments and the Making of Modern China*. Berkeley: University of California Press, 2007.

———. *Wartime Shanghai*. New York: Routledge, 1998.

"Yubei Lixian Gonghui Bao" (Bulletin of the Constitution Preparation Committee). Shanghai. Thirty-fourth year of the Guangxu reign (1908).

Zhang, Jungu. *Du Yuesheng Zhuan* (The Biography of Du Yuesheng). 4 vols. Taipei: Zhuanji Wenxue, 1980.

Zhang, Naiqi. "Zhang Naiqi Qishi Zishu" (Zhang Naiqi, a Self-Narration at 70). *Zhuanji Wenxue* 39, no. 3 (September 1984): 38–42.

Zhang, Zhongli, ed. *Jindai Shanghai Chengshi Yanjiu* (Studies on Modern Shanghai). Shanghai: Shanghai Renmin Chubanshe, 1990.

Zhao, Puchu. "Kangzhan Chuqi de Shanghai Nanmin Gongzuo" (Refugee Work in Shanghai at the Beginning of the War of Resistance). In *Kangzhan Chuqide Nanmin Gongzuo* (Refugee Work at the Beginning of the War of Resistance), edited by Zhonggang Shanghai Dangshi Ziliao Zhengji Weiyuanhui, 25–33. Shanghai: Shanghai Xinwen Chubanju, 1993.

Zheng, Renjia. "Hu Yuzhi Qiren Qishi" (Hu Yuzhi, the Person and His Life). *Zhuanji Wenxue* 48, no. 5 (May 1986): 123–28.

Zhong, Daozan. "Zhiye Xuexiao Xiaozhang Zhi Xueli Yu Jingyan" (Educational Background and Work Experience of Principals of Vocational Schools). *Jiaoyu yu Zhiye*, no. 169 (November 1, 1935): 639–43.

Zhonggong Shanghai Shi Weidang Shi Ziliao Zhengji Weiyuanhui (Commission to Compile Historical Materials on the History of the Party of Shanghai), eds. *Yi-Er-Jiu Yihou Shanghai Jiuguohui Shiliao Xuanji* (Selection of Historical Materials on the Shanghai National Salvation Association after the December Ninth Movement). Shanghai: Shanghai Shehui Kexue Yuan Chubanshe, 1987.

———. *Zhonggong Shanghai Dangshi Dashi Ji, 1919.5 1949.5* (Record of Major Events of the Shanghai Communist Party, May 1919 May 1949). Shanghai: Zhishi Chubanshe, 1988.

Zhongguo Renmin Zhengzhi Xieshang Huiyi Shanghai Shi Weiyuanhui Wenshi Ziliao Gongzuo Weiyuanhui (Work Committee on Literary and Historical Materials of the Chinese People's Political Consultative

Council's Shanghai Municipal Committee), eds. *Jiu Shanghai de Banghui* (The Gangs of Old Shanghai). Shanghai: Shanghai Renmin Chubanshe, 1986.

Zhonghua Zhiye Jiaoyu She, ed. *Quanguo Zhiye Xuexiao Gaikuang* (A National General Survey of Vocational Schools). Shanghai: Commercial Press, 1934.

Zhou, Shangwen, and Shiyou He. *Shanghai Gongren Sanci Wuzhuangqiyi Shi* (History of the Shanghai Workers' Three Armed Uprisings). Shanghai: Shanghai Renmin Chubanshe, 1987.

Zhou, Tiandu, ed. *Jiuguohui* (The National Salvation Association). Beijing: Zhongguo Shehui Kexue Chubanshe, 1981.

———, ed. *Qijunzi Zhuan* (Biography of the Seven Gentlemen). Beijing: Zhongguo Shehui Kexue Chubanshe, 1989.

Zhu, Bangxing et al., eds. *Shanghai Chanye Yu Shanghai Zhigong* (Shanghai Industry and Workers). Shanghai: Shanghai Renmin Chubanshe, 1984. Reprint, 1939 publication.

Zhu, Guantian. "Wu Changshi Yu Riben Youren Zhi Jiaoyou" (The Friendship Between Wu Changshi and His Japanese Friends). In *Huiyi Wu Changshi* (Memories of Wu Changshi), 66–75. Shanghai: Shanghai Renmin Meishu Chubanshe, 1986.

Zhu, Hua, et al. *Shanghai Yibai Nian* (One Hundred Years in Shanghai). Shanghai: Shanghai Renmin Chubanshe, 1999.

Zhu, Xuefan. "Shanghai Gongren Yundong Yu Banghui Ersanshi" (One or Two Things About the Shanghai Labour Movement and the Secret Societies) In *Jiu Shanghai de Banghui* (The Gangs of Old Shanghai), edited by Zhongguo Renmin Zhengzhi Xieshang Huiyi Shanghai Shi Weiyuanhui Wenshi Ziliao Gongzuo Weiyuanhui (Work Committee on Literary and Historical Materials of the Chinese People's Political Consultative Council's Shanghai Municipal Committee), 1–20. Shanghai: Shanghai Renmin Chubanshe, 1986.

Zou, Taofen. *Huannan Yusheng Ji* (Record of an Old Age of Troubles and Tribulations). Yan'an: Taofen Shudian, 1946.

———. *Jingli* (Experiences). Shanghai: Taofen Chubanshe, 1937.

Zou, Yiren. *Jiu Shanghai Renkou Bianqian de Yanjiu* (A Study of the Evolution of the Population of Old Shanghai). Shanghai: Shanghai Renmin Chubanshe, 1980.

Zu, Sima. "Xinsheng Shijian Gaishu" (General Account of the New Life Case). In *Zhongguo Xiandai Chuban Sheliao, Xiandai Yibian* (Sources on the Modern Printing of China), edited by Jinglu Zhang. Beijing: Zhonghua Shuju, 1955–59.

Index